CRAIG BROWN

THE GAME OF MY LIFE

JB

JOHN BLAKE

Published by Blake Publishing Ltd,
3 Bramber Court, 2 Bramber Road, London W14 9PB,
England

First published in Great Britain in 2003

ISBN 1 904034 13 6

British Library Cataloguing-in-Publication Data:
A catalogue record for this book is available from
the British Library.

Typeset by Jon Davies

Printed and bound in Great Britain by
Bookmarque Ltd, Croydon, Surrey

1 3 5 7 9 10 8 6 4 2

CRAIG BROWN

Contents

1

Why Me?

ONE HOT NIGHT in Rome I faced the crushing responsibility of life as manager of Scotland and I began to wonder, Why me? What on earth was I doing there at all? I was not the only one asking that question. The regulars in the press box had already posed the same query.

Nevertheless, there I was, head in hands as Italy threatened to take apart the Scotland team that I was leading – a Scotland team that was playing for pride. Much has happened since that warm night in Rome in October 1993 but much had happened before it too.

I was born just as the Second World War was getting into its stride. At the time, my father was in the RAF and I saw very little of him. My earliest recollection of the place I called home was of a house in Corkerhill, Glasgow – a railway village where nearly all the men, my mother's father included, worked in the manufacture and maintenance of railway locomotives and rolling stock. My grandfather was an engine-driver, a job which, to me, was something very special indeed. He was one of my very first heroes, and I could think of nothing finer than becoming an engine-driver myself. Yes, I was one of those typical wee boys whose dreams never went far beyond becoming a train-driver – or perhaps a footballer!

My grandfather's home was supplied by the railway and it was small, but cosy. A staircase ran up the outside of the building and provided us children with a play area – which frequently caused my mother's heart to leap into her mouth. Corkerhill, in those days, was a happy village full of hard-working men. Full employment, of course, meant that nobody starved but while there were no paupers, there were no stray princes either. There was an air of equality and a common cause.

As I said, my father, Hugh, was in the RAF, having volunteered to engage the Luftwaffe in battle. However, just before the war, he had bought a house in Larbert, where Stenhousemuir play. My parents had lived there for a time before he went off to war. My formative years, however, were spent in Corkerhill, and I have vivid memories of the air-raids. As a railway repair area, we were among the Luftwaffe's prime targets. Hitler thought that it would be a good idea to paralyse the transport system of Great Britain, and his idea caused me to have many a sleepless night. I remember well the wailing siren which demanded an instant response to its warning of an impending raid. Nobody ever hesitated for a moment – adults running everywhere, it seemed, and children being hoisted up with their legs dangling and hurriedly carried to a safer place.

I, of course, was one of those children usually carried along by my mother, Margaret. My grandmother had died before the war and I had an Aunt Jess – my mother's elder sister – who seemed to fulfil the role of the family's female guide. My mother was one of eight children and, with my father away, my grandfather had been left with quite a large brood to care for. My Aunt Jess became his chief assistant.

As the raids got under way, we would be transported to the air-raid shelter – a damp, dingy place, brightened only by the flickering candles we took along and a singsong. I'm told that, as a two-year-old, I could sing 'Onward Christian Soldiers' perfectly because I had heard the adults singing it so often in the air-raid shelter. Our faith in God was naturally encouraged, and I believe that it has stayed with me to this day. I'm not, perhaps, as devout as I should be, but I was certainly brought up with a strong Christian belief, and it should come as no surprise to know that I have a brother in the ministry.

On some occasions there just wasn't enough time to get to the shelter and, when that happened, my mother used to push me under the living-room table and then lie on top of me until the sound of the bombers had gone away and the 'all-clear' sounded. We would listen to the thuds and explosions as the German bombs rained down. When I think about it, my mother must have been very frightened, and yet she always seemed to remain so calm and therefore always gave me a great feeling of confidence.

Another feature of life in Corkerhill was the baths. No, I'm not talking about swimming baths, but a series of large individual baths. I was often taken across to the baths by my mother – to where the hot water gushed and bubbled from a pipe and all the people had the chance to clean off the grime from much of their bodies with the strong smelling carbolic soap. The private bits were taken care of at home in a tin bath on the living-room floor! Going to the baths in Corkerhill became quite an outing for me.

You can imagine from what I've said that life in Corkerhill was not exactly living in the lap of luxury – and yet this is not any sort of hard-luck story. There were many in those days who were a lot worse off than we were. We had a roof over our heads and shoes on our feet – there were many, many more people in Britain who were not so well taken care of. I must say that I do like to remember how things were then, because it means that I never lose my appreciation for what has been achieved over the last fifty years and, more to the point, how things are for me today.

We were a very close family in those days, as I believe most families were at that time. All the privations brought on by the war drew people so much closer together. Family life in Scotland has always been an important thing – it is still important today, but in those turbulent years of the war it seemed to be even more so.

Whenever my father came home on leave during the 1940s, I was always overjoyed to see him – even though there were always those awkward moments when he had to take in how much I was growing and I had to learn just a little more about him. Prior to going into the RAF, he had played football professionally for King's Park – now known as Stirling Albion. He was a hard, tough-tackling midfielder or full-back who never shirked it when the going got rough and would fight to get a result for the full ninety minutes. He also played for Hamilton Academicals and even guested for Wolves when he was stationed nearby during the war. He became very friendly with a famous Wolverhampton Wanderers manager, Ted Vizard, and I well remember him visiting our home in later years when he came to Scotland in search of players. They stayed at our home and it was a great honour for us to have the manager of the great Wolves team under our roof.

Needless to say, my first encounter with the game of football was through my father. He always spared a few treasured minutes of his precious time during his visits home to introduce me to this wonderful game that was to play such a major role in my life. Almost as soon as I could stand, my father had introduced a ball to my feet.

Another aspect of the railway village life of the 1940s was getting dressed up every Sunday to go to church. The service was always held in the local village hall. I used to stand on a chair and could just about see what was going on over the heads and between the shoulders of the rest of the congregation. I can remember just how hot it used to get with my woolly hat and gloves on. There was no air-conditioning in our village hall in those days – unless someone broke a window, that is!

So, my abiding memories of Corkerhill are of cleanliness, togetherness, family, and air-raids – plus, of course, those very special times when my father came home on leave and we were all united for a short while.

My father did well in the RAF. Having started as a PE teacher, he eventually reached the status of squadron leader and was in charge of the RAF School of Physical Education at Cosford near Wolverhampton, where he specialised in parachuting skills. I think his wartime job certainly helped his postwar career, as his CV from the RAF was very impressive.

Meanwhile, my mother had four brothers taking part in the war. The eldest Robert was in the Education Corps in the army, John was an RAF mechanic, and Willie volunteered for the RAF whilst still at school and trained as a pilot. During his war years he was awarded the DFM, AM and DSO. The youngest, Jimmy, who after the war took me to watch Queen's Park, trained as an air gunner and was kitted out for Japan when the war finally finished. So there was much anxiety in my family during those turbulent war years.

When the war ended my father became head of physical education at Marr College in Troon. There was a tied house that went with the job, and so we all moved there and lived on that beautiful part of the Ayrshire coast. The house in Larbert was sold, meaning that we were not too badly off. Before my father taught at Marr College it was a rugby-playing school – but it wasn't too long before the goalposts came out and the school found itself specialising in football and golf.

After moving to Troon, I started at the local primary school. I had two brothers by this time – Bob, who was born in Glasgow when I was about two, and then Jock, who arrived in Kilmarnock about three years after Bob. When I started going to school I was the big lad of the family and began to feel quite grown up – not that I was in any hurry to do that. Going out early every day and leaving my little brothers to enjoy their time with my mother was not my idea of a good deal, but I got used to it in time.

My father's big interests outside his PE teaching were football and golf. My brothers and I were encouraged to take part in both sports as early as possible. The back gate of our house opened on to the school playing field, a vast area which was just like an enormous back garden to us.

I liked Troon and I still do, but we were not there for very long because my father was offered an even better job as Physical Education Adviser for the whole of Lanarkshire. It was quite a job because the county was the biggest in Scotland and therefore had a large number of schools and colleges.

For his new appointment, my father had to be based in Glasgow, and so we were soon all on the move to take up residence in Rutherglen. I moved to another primary school and began to play competitive football in Stonelaw Park. I had got used to kicking a ball about on the lush grass of the college playing field, so it came as quite a culture shock when I discovered that my new 'home ground' was an ash pitch!

I had been accustomed to playing with the older boys at school, who didn't seem to mind me taking part in their games, so it was natural that I should join them in their games in the park. The only problem was that to get to the park you had to cross a very busy cobbled road which had trams running back and forth every few minutes. You had to take your life in your hands every time you crossed the road, and I knew that there was a danger that I would be banned from going altogether unless my mother was able to see me safely across.

With all due respect, and with all the love in the world for my mother, no lad wants to be seen turning up for a game of football with the bigger lads having been escorted by the hand across the road by his mother. It can make your aggressive tackles seem just a little less formidable. I hate to admit it, but I resorted to sneaking off and, if I was asked where I was going, I would say that I was going to play football with the other lads but didn't know exactly where. Luckily, it seemed to work.

A neighbour of ours in Rutherglen was one of the most famous – if not the most famous – referees in Scottish football, Jack Mowat. He used to stop at the gate, or sometimes come in for a coffee, and he and my father would talk about football for hours. He was another man of powerful character, whose love of the game served to fuel further my burgeoning enthusiasm for all things to do with football.

My father always wanted the best for his three sons and he decided that we would get a better education if we lived in Hamilton, where he thought the standard might be higher. He was opposed to private education and, despite him having such a good job, I doubt if he could have afforded the fees for all of us – anyway, he decided that Hamilton schooling would be better for all three of us. Coincidentally, the Lanarkshire office in which he was based also decided to move to Hamilton, so it all worked out rather well in the end.

I was still at primary stage when we moved, being aged about ten, and so I went to St John's Primary School. Fortunately, the people of Hamilton were very keen on football and so there was no shortage of the game that I had come to love. My father bought a house that was only three minutes' walk away from the famous Hamilton Academy. Right next to our house was an area of waste ground, covered in a base of red ash, which proved to be such a good training ground that I often wondered whether my father had bought the house because he liked it – or because he could see the potential of that area of waste ground at the side.

That ground was in the shape of a triangle – which meant that you could only put a goal at one end. However, you could get crosses in and there was the added advantage of the wall of our house which ran alongside our improvised pitch, providing a great place for target practice, wall passes and various other soccer-skill games. I played for countless hours on that ground. As long as we had a ball, my pals and I never once complained about being bored, and we would play football on that red-ash pitch as often as we could. The good thing about our love of the game was that our parents always knew exactly what we were doing and where we could be found. My father made us a wooden set of goalposts and even put a net on it.

If there was any drawback at all to our 'ground', it was the fact that the mainline railway ran alongside it. The Hamilton–Glasgow train regularly thundered past, separated from us by a tall metal fence. The trouble was that, although we were kept out by the metal fence, the ball wasn't. If we became a little careless it could become quite a costly business in stray footballs. But as it happened, we discovered a saviour.

There was a professional footballer with Hamilton who was also a train-driver – he used to take small cargo trains up and down the line on a fairly regular basis. His name was Stan Anderson, and he became quite famous with Hamilton, and later with Clyde and Rangers. Later in his career he became manager of Clyde. Every time Stan saw one of our footballs on the line he would stop his train, climb down and then kick the ball back over to us. In fact there were even times when he would abandon his train altogether, climb over the fence and give us a few tips. I often saw Stan in later life and have always remained grateful to him for the kindness and patience he showed to us as teenagers in those days. Sadly, in November 1997, after bravely enduring a long illness, Stan passed away, aged 58.

Sometimes, of course, a ball would be irretrievably lost or else become worn out. When that happened, my father, or one of the other boys' parents, would invariably come up with a replacement. Remember, these were the heavy leather footballs of yesteryear and the very fact that we were able to wear them out gives you some idea of how much work we gave them. The red ash, the rough-cast house wall and the incessant booting by us boys meant that the lifespan of our footballs was well below the average.

My father was eventually promoted again, this time to become the director of the Scottish School of Physical

Education establishment at Jordanhill, which trained all the male PE teachers in Scotland. Naturally, he was an extremely busy man and became quite preoccupied by his work. I did occasionally go with him to see Hamilton play, but these were invariably mid-week matches because on Saturdays he was fully occupied by the Jordanhill football set-up. They ran five teams at the time and all the organisation was down to him and his superb colleague, Roy Small.

I was really interested in my father's work, and it certainly foreshadowed the job I would be doing in later life. It often amuses me to listen to people talking about my job now. Many people think that all I had to do was pick a Scotland team, spend a few days with them, play the game and then go on holiday, watching football matches in other parts of the world. Oh, how I wish! Let me assure anyone who thinks that the job is a bed of roses of one thing, that even the most beautiful petals are surrounded by many painful thorns!

Because my father's work kept him so busy, I was dependent on my Uncle Jimmy Caldow, my mother's youngest brother, to take me to senior games at weekends. His was a famous footballing name because of Eric Caldow, Rangers captain and Scotland international. He was a Queen's Park fan and so we used to travel to Hampden to see them. They had a good team at the time. I seem to remember that their regular side was Weir, Harnett, Hastie, Cromar, Valentine, Robb, Reid, McCann, Church, Dalziel and Omand. I learned a great deal from those trips to Hampden to see Queen's Park with my uncle.

During holiday times my father was able to take me to see Hamilton Accies. The manager, Jackie Cox, was a good pal of my father and was an extremely well-known character in Scottish football. He had played at a good level himself and was a cousin of Sammy Cox a very popular Scottish international who played for Rangers.

Jackie had some wonderful phrases which I can still recall clearly even though I was just a lad on the fringes of the conversations at the time I first heard them. His team talks were littered with the most amazing expressions and were audible to anyone within a hundred yards. Just to give a couple of examples of his verbal skills, he once told his men, 'I could frighten 'im just by clearin' mah throat!' That was in reference to a winger whom Jackie thought to be cowardly. He used to totally destroy the opposition verbally. I heard it all because I was just down the passage giving all the boots a good clean – it's amazing what you'll do just to be involved!

One day, when Jackie Cox was playing for Hamilton against Rangers, he caused some consternation. Now Jackie used to love to mix it a bit and take the big scalps and, on this particular day, he had given most of the Rangers side a hard time. Then there came a very strong tackle on the talented inside forward Jimmy Caskie, which resulted in Caskie being stretchered off. As he was leaving the pitch, Jackie ran over to him and said, 'Jimmy, while you were in the jeelie-pieces, I was on the porridge and the breast of the pheasant!'

Hamilton's big rivals were Motherwell, who were just the other side of the bridge over the Clyde and they had a fine team managed by Bobby Ancell. Guys like Willie Hunter, Ian St John, Charlie Aitken, Andy Weir and Pat Quinn were playing for them in the 1950s, so we sometimes used to sneak over and take a look at them.

My boyhood hero was playing for Hearts so, whenever the opportunity showed itself, I never missed the chance to go and see him in action. He was the one and only Dave Mackay and, whenever he was playing in the Glasgow or Motherwell area, I would plead with my Uncle Jimmy, my father, or just about anyone else who might be persuaded, to take me to see the game. I idolised him, and if any one player could be said to have made a huge impression on me in the formative years of my life, it was Dave Mackay of Heart of Midlothian. Every time I saw him I knew that I wanted to be just like him. The course of my future career was clear to me, and I was beginning to burn with ambition. Would I be good enough?

It was a question that would have to remain unanswered for some time. My exploits on the pitch were, at that stage, limited to the kind of games I've already mentioned, and so there could be no knowing whether or not my brothers and I were destined for careers in the game. Nowadays, of course, it is all very different, with lads as young as eight being marked by clubs and then wooed for years until they are ready to become full-blown trainees.

My father took a strict view of the exposure of youngsters to too much sporting activity too early in their lives, and this applied as much to golf as it did to football. He was a very keen player, but even so he would not let me actually play until I was eleven years of age. I used to caddy for him, which meant that I did learn about the game and its etiquette – but not until I was eleven could I actually take part. I could hardly wait and often used to trudge around the Hamilton golf course yearning for the day when I would be allowed to tee off.

I was learning the game of football in a similar passive way from my trips to watch Hamilton, Motherwell, Queen's Park and Dave Mackay. I remember great games and great players at Hamilton, but I also remember a great groundsman, Bobby Shearer, father of another Bobby Shearer who played for Rangers. Shearer senior was known as 'Bush', but I never found out why, although I suspect his hair had something to do with it. I do know that he kept the Accies ground – Douglas Park – in absolutely immaculate condition. He took great pride in giving the players the best possible playing conditions, and he certainly succeeded.

The Hamilton side of those early 1950s contained a number of names probably well remembered by some of you – Jimmy Cron, Bobby Cunning (an outside left who went to Rangers), Jim McLean (who later became well known as manager and chairman of Dundee United and who Sir Alex Ferguson, in his autobiography says makes cussedness an art form!), Andy Paton, the centre-half, Pat Holton (who was later to join Chelsea) and Sam Hastings. They were all players whom I remember watching, enjoying their skill and determination.

That, then, was my football upbringing. I was a Hamilton supporter and a Queen's Park supporter with a long road ahead of me.

My childhood memories are of bombs, baths, boot rooms, a friendly train-driver, a close family, moving house, having two younger brothers, and watching Dave Mackay. I also remember the luxury of the occasional daydream that perhaps, one day, it would be possible that I could become a professional footballer myself. Being a train-driver could have been fine, and even joining the forces or following my father into physical education might have been acceptable – but the power and the sheer magic contained in the game of football had already begun to work its charm on me.

2

A Star in the Making?

MY FATHER HAD this strict policy that we should always support our local club. That was no problem to me because I never needed any encouragement at all to be an Accies supporter – I really liked the club and its ground. Of course, if everyone's father had taken the same view as mine, then clubs like Manchester United, Liverpool, Celtic and Rangers would never have had the widespread following that they all enjoy today. However, it was my father's policy and both my brothers and I stuck to it.

Throughout my life I had supposed that it was quite a well-known fact that we were Hamilton supporters and so, years later, it came as quite a surprise to receive a sharp letter as a result of a favourable comment I made in support of another club. It came in 1994, when Clyde moved to their new ground in Cumbernauld. I had previously been manager of Clyde for over nine years – although my good friend Alex Smith was currently in charge at this momentous time in the club's history. I was interviewed about the exciting new era in the story of Clyde and was asked what I thought would be the outcome of their first game in their new stadium. I replied that I hoped there would be a good crowd for such a gala occasion and that Clyde would win their match.

The chairman of Hamilton at that time was George Fulston – later the chairman of Falkirk. Apparently his wife had heard, or was told about, the radio interview, and she wrote to me – and I do believe that it was without George's knowledge. She stated that, in her opinion, what I had said was deplorable, and how could I expect the support of the Scottish people for the national team if I was showing favouritism to one team or another.

Needless to say, I quickly wrote back to Mrs Fulston – who, incidentally, is a very charming lady – and explained to her that I had been a Hamilton supporter for a long time and had remained so. Having worked at Clyde for so long, as both manager and a director, and with the club moving to a lovely new ground, it should be perfectly understandable to anyone that I would want them to win their opening match. I do hope that she thought my letter was a pleasant one – it was meant to be!

That incident demonstrated to me just how important it is to be careful about your comments to the press – especially when you are in charge of something as important as a national team. I always tried to make my comments constructive, unbiased and objective – but there is rarely any response when people are in agreement with you. It is only when you say something that strays beyond your own confines that people seem to take umbrage if your comments don't support their own particular viewpoint.

I must point out that I have remained on good terms with both Mr and Mrs Fulston – and I certainly have nothing but respect and admiration for George Fulston's tireless efforts for Hamilton and Falkirk.

I see that I have digressed yet again, but it seems that the present is always tied up with attitudes and events from the past.

As my years advanced into double figures, the two big loves of my life, namely football and golf, had grown even closer to my heart. When I was eleven years of age I was finally unleashed into the world of golf – and I really took to the game. I played at Hamilton Golf Club and steadily improved until I had a handicap of four – while I was still at school. I was runner-up in the Lanarkshire Boys' Championship and reached the last eight in the Scottish Boys' Championship, as well as playing for the West of Scotland boys' team.

There never seemed to be any question that I would pursue a career in golf, but I have to say that even though I was very enthusiastic, I was not quite good enough. However, my love of golf continued to develop and has endured to this day. In fact, golf proved to be a very useful tool to me on a number of occasions during my playing days. Although successive knee operations have taken their toll on the number of times I can play without the discomfort of fluid in my knees.

At around the same time, I played my earliest competitive games with St John's primary school, where one of my teachers was Curly Thompson. Naturally enough, he was called 'Curly' because he was completely bald. Another of my teachers was Bob Roan, who was in charge of the football team at St John's.

It was Bob Roan who also had the unenviable job of taking us for swimming. He had developed his own technique for teaching youngsters how to swim. Once you had learned how to 'sprachle' – a Scottish term for getting about in the water at the shallow end without drowning yourself or anyone near you – Bob would take you to the deep end and order you in, sometimes with the assistance of a discreet push. Naturally, you didn't argue, and the primitive urge to live took over. Your innate sense of survival helped you to sprachle your way from one side to the other – or even back to the shallow end. Either way, when you finally clung breathlessly to the side of the pool – after what seemed like a battle across the Bay of Biscay

– Bob would be there, smiling down at you. 'There you are, son, I told you that you could swim!' He was absolutely right, of course – you were still alive to prove his point! To be fair, I never heard of any fatalities as a result of his 'scientific' approach to the art of swimming, and we were all able to swim shortly after becoming his pupils.

Swimming was very popular in Hamilton because we had such good facilities. The town was also very proud of Eleanor Gordon, who had won countless national and international breaststroke championships. She was a very famous swimmer, and her exploits inspired many youngsters throughout Scotland, especially in her home town of Hamilton, where the baths were one of the most popular venues for young and old alike.

So you see I enjoyed my golf and I enjoyed my swimming, but it was football that was the most important to me. If ever I had to choose from among the sports, football would always be the winner.

As I grew up, I played in all the Hamilton Academy school football teams. We had a variety of coaches, who were also teachers. I recall Cliff Bruce, science teacher; Alf McCracken, our English teacher; Eddie Young, also an English teacher who was keener on rugby but was, nevertheless, a good football coach; and the principal teacher of PE, Willie Liddell. Mr Liddell encouraged all sports at the school and, certainly, football was no exception.

I played constantly throughout my school years and took part in trials for the Scottish Under-15 team, which was a great experience even though it was unsuccessful. Joe Baker was also around at the time and was centre-forward in the Under-15 team. It would have been great for me if I could have joined him, but it was not to be. I was disappointed, but I have always considered that disappointments only put you down for as long as you let them. If you use them as a springboard to better times ahead, then they become much more bearable.

A couple of years later I was offered a trial for the

Scotland Schools Under-18 team. There were some excellent players in the squad. The goalkeeper was Fred Renucci, who went to Partick Thistle. We had Phil Lynch, who went to Celtic, and Davie Hilley, who went to Third Lanark and then on to Newcastle. He still writes a column for the Sunday Post. We also had Sandy Turpie, who played for Queen's Park, Brian McIlroy, who went to Rangers and then Kilmarnock, and Hugh Brown, who also went to Kilmarnock. But probably the most famous of that particular squad was Billy McNeill, who went on to become the first British captain to hold aloft the European Cup when he led Celtic to their historic triumph in 1967.

To my immense delight I found myself selected to be among these guys, and I played for my country at the age of seventeen. We scored a memorable 3–0 victory over England at Celtic Park. It was a tremendous experience for me – quite awesome to be walking out at Celtic Park, and very emotional too to be wearing the shirt of my country. I think I must have had a reasonable game because I kept my place in the squad. As you might imagine, my family were nearly as thrilled as I was about the whole thing.

While I was at school I was also playing for one of the very best amateur teams in the country. Willie Waddell, the former Rangers player, was manager of Kilmarnock at the time, and he had a firm belief in youth development for football clubs. To this end Kilmarnock Amateurs were formed, and this was the team that I played for – one of the strongest sides in Scotland at that time. There was probably only one team to rival us at the time – and that was Drumchapel Amateurs. There were certainly some epic matches between us.

I used to go down to Kilmarnock for training. It was about an hour's journey from Hamilton and, of course, it was an invaluable experience to be training there. I was also invited to train at Celtic Park, and I went along with Billy McNeill. The coach of the Celtic youth players at that time was the late, great, legendary Jock Stein – who was then in the early stages of his management and coaching career. He was something of a father-figure even then, as he took a personal interest in each one of his charges and coached them as individuals. Jock also had an amazing memory and, from our very first meeting, he remembered everything about me. Even when I hadn't seen him for ages he still remembered that our first encounter had been when I was a young hopeful visiting Celtic Park for the first time.

The manager at Celtic Park in those days was Jimmy McGrory, but he didn't offer terms to either Billy or me – which turned out to be quite ironic, really, when you consider how great a name Billy was to become at Celtic. As it happened, they later had a change of heart and did offer to sign him. As for me – well, I was pretty confident in my ability and I lived in the expectation of some club offering me a career in the game. I was hopeful, and I was informed repeatedly that this or that club had phoned my father to establish my availability. However, my father liked to keep my feet on the ground and didn't tell me of the enquiries.

Not long after running into the Celtic cul-de-sac I was back in the Scotland Schools Under-18 side. One of my teammates was to go on and make himself very famous indeed. He was Alex Ferguson, who was then playing for Govan High School and was an extremely good attacking player. We were to play against England again, this time at Dulwich Hamlet, the home of one of England's most famous amateur clubs. Jim Cruikshank was our goalkeeper and he went on to play for Hearts and Scotland as a senior. We lost the game 4–3 as it happened, but it could have gone either way, and there was the special memory for me of scoring from the penalty spot.

To be really honest I was playing far too much football, what with school matches, Kilmarnock Amateurs, training with the big clubs and the internationals too. It was a lesson to me that you can have too much of a good thing. I don't think it was good for me to have so many physical demands placed on my body. I believe that the same thing applies today. A boy who is still developing physically should not have his body overtaxed by the rigours of too much competitive football. No, I'm not one of those people who say that the competition should be taken out of youth football – I think that competition is very necessary – but you should keep a balance. Sadly, I feel that little has changed over the years, and that many of today's youngsters are often overworked with competitive games.

I eventually joined Rangers at the age of seventeen. The newspaper headline at the time read 'Rangers sign the boy they all wanted'. It was a fact that there were quite a few clubs in the frame for me.

Rangers did not have a youth team as such, but would farm out youngsters to clubs in the Scottish junior leagues where they could gain some experience against semi-professionals. I was sent to Coltness United and was at the same level as Billy McNeill, who was playing for Blantyre Victoria. Our careers seemed to be moving in parallel – if anything I had the edge because I was also later picked for the Scottish Junior squad.

At this time, in 1958, I was concentrating on playing football and golf, and I didn't really know much about what else was going on. My father did all my talking for me, and he often neglected to tell me everything because he didn't want me distracted from developing my game. Had I known that there were clubs on both sides of the border chasing after me, it could well have gone to my head.

In the Daily Mirror of 15 July 1958, Jimmy Stevenson wrote:

'The future of a teenage Scot who has been the rage of soccer scouts for a year was settled yesterday. Craig Brown signed for Rangers.' He also quoted Bob Jackson, a top scout and former Portsmouth manager, as saying: 'Whoever gets the lad gets the best proposition I've seen in years.'

My father was well respected in the sports world because

of his rise through the academic world and because he talked a lot of sense. He had helped and guided me since childhood, and I had no reason to think that he would not be the best person to act as my personal guide through the rest of my career. I listened to what everyone had to say, but it was my father's words that really counted. As he told the Evening Citizen a month after I had joined Rangers, 'Craig has been brought up in an atmosphere of football. He has played in the garden with a ball at his feet since he could toddle.'

I continued to play in the garden with a ball at my feet – and on my head as well. I knew that there was always room for improvement and, even though I was training and playing matches all the time, I still wanted to put in extra work at home. One of my exercises was to take the dining-room chairs out into the garden and line them up as obstacles, then I would slalom my way through them with the ball at my feet and repeat the exercise whilst heading the ball.

I continued my studies at Hamilton Academy and quite fancied my chances of gaining a BSc degree in engineering when I left school. At 5 feet 7½ inches and 10 stone 2 pounds, I also wanted to build myself up a bit, and so I began to do some labouring work as a steel bender's labourer at Costain Concrete works in Newmains. I was probably burning the candle at both ends, but not in the same way that many youngsters do today. All my activities were to do with my career. My efforts finally gained me a ticking-off! The Rangers manager, Scot Symon, called me to one side and cautioned me against doing too much. I was playing three times a week and training at least once every day.

'You need to take it a little easier. There's such a thing as overdoing it – even in football,' said Mr Symon. He did have a twinkle in his eye as he said it and so I knew that I wasn't really being told off but was being offered some genuine advice. It was a valuable lesson – and it is one that I pass on to youngsters today if I feel that it is appropriate. When the newspapers heard of my 'ticking-off' they immediately began drawing parallels with Pelé, who had been told exactly the same thing by his national coach. Pelé was big news at the time because of the 1958 World Cup, and I was honoured to be considered worthy of being mentioned in the same breath. I didn't take the comparison too seriously, though – I was already learning that you should have a pinch of salt with your newspaper, even without the fish and chips inside!

As things progressed I was selected for the Scottish Junior squad to play against the Irish Junior side – which was quite an achievement for a youngster of my age. One of my proudest possessions is the cap I earned for that match. I keep it at my house and always get a thrill when I look at it.

When I went to Ibrox I found myself amongst players I had only ever heard of. They were big stars and I was quite overawed to be mixing with them – players like Eric Caldow, the late Alex Scott, Bobby Shearer, Ralph Brand, Jimmy Millar, Billy Stevenson, and the other heroes of Glasgow Rangers. These men were like gods to the fans, and to me. They were people whom I had read about and talked about – but never, ever contemplated as becoming my teammates.

After a year with Coltness I was called up to Ibrox as a full-timer. My studies for my BSc were shelved and I was ready to see what the journey on the magic carpet of football was going to be like. I was put into the reserve squad – and even there I was playing alongside great players like Sammy Baird, Johnny Hubbard, Ian McColl, Billy Ritchie, John Queen, John Currie, Max Murray and others. Most were in the twilight of their careers, but they were still great players and big stars nevertheless. The reserves had their own manager, Bob McPhail, who was legendary throughout Scotland as a pre-war international. Assisting Bob was Joe Craven and, between them, they kept a happy and successful squad going strong. It was a very happy time for me because I was wearing the shirt of one of the greatest clubs in the history of the game and learning something from my coaches every day. With all those great players around me I felt that everything was going brilliantly for me. I was playing football all the time and I couldn't have wished for life to be any better.

At a reserve game between Rangers and Celtic in 1997 there was a crowd of 33,000. In the back end of the 1950s we could expect crowds of 20,000-plus for reserves Old Firm clashes, and almost the same for all the other fixtures. As a result, there was never any disgrace in being listed among the reserves every week.

I was quick to learn that star footballers are only human after all. Sometimes the stars of stage, screen and sport can seem to be a race apart and nothing like the rest of us. However, as I became friendly with the internationals at Ibrox, I found them all easy to get on with. We talked about all the normal things of life – what sort of pet dog this one had, which horse to back at Newmarket, and so on. I was included in all these conversations about everyday matters and soon settled in.

There were, of course, little cliques at Ibrox – as there have always been at every club. Because I lived in Hamilton I fell into the clique of players who lived near me, among them Eric Caldow, Willie Telfer, Doug Baillie, Stan Anderson and Bobby Shearer, the captain. We also used to pick up Davy Wilson on the way in – he stayed in Cambuslang. We all travelled in from Hamilton to train at Ibrox, which brought us together in all sorts of ways.

These were happy days for me at Ibrox with the company I was keeping, my playing progress and my golf. I was also making progress on another front. I've already mentioned giving up on my engineering course, but I did switch to taking a PE course at Jordanhill, because it was more in keeping with my footballing career.

There was an odd atmosphere at Jordanhill in those days. There were strict doctrines like never showing that you were injured, never allowing an opponent to know that you were hurt. Trainers were never allowed on to the football pitch to attend the injured. There were no substitutes so you were expected to play on regardless. I'm sure that only broken legs, broken necks or death were regarded as acceptable reasons for not completing the full 90 minutes. That wasn't the end of the discipline – everything from your boots to the rest of your kit had to be kept scrupulously clean, and it was your responsibility. Everything took place with military precision.

Quite a few professional players were taking courses at Jordanhill at that time. Graham Leggat was one, and he was a fair influence on me. He played for Aberdeen and then Fulham. When I was in my final year at the Hamilton Academy he had arrived there as a student and, of all people, he influenced me the most and made me take a serious look at the possibilities of a PE teaching course. I suppose it was because he was such a wonderful sportsman, a great all-rounder and an excellent gymnast. He excelled at every sport he took part in. He was also in the spotlight because of playing for Aberdeen and Scotland at the time.

There were other professional players at Jordanhill, too. Bobby Clark, a top goalkeeper with Aberdeen and Scotland, Ian Riddell of St Mirren, Roger Hynd, a nephew of the Shanklys who played for Rangers, Doug Houston, who played for Dundee, Dave Hilley of Third Lanark, Frank Coulston and Dick Staite of Partick Thistle, Joe Gilroy of Dundee, Derek Whiteford of Airdrie, and many others, who I hope will forgive me for failing in my struggle to bring their names to mind.

We often had games between the professionals and the top amateur players and these were usually held on a Wednesday on one of those red-ash pitches that were prevalent in Scotland at the time. They were tough matches, and very often my direct opponent was a young man by the name of Archie MacPherson, who later became a top commentator with the BBC. I found him a difficult opponent. He was a very fast winger who was very clever with the ball and, quite unashamedly, I used to have a kick at him to try to slow him down a bit. I saved some of my hardest tackles for Archie.

My PE course was to last three years. It was very thorough and rigorous. For instance, three times a week we went to Cranstonhill baths and started our day with swimming instruction in cold water – and I do mean cold water! We went up and down that pool until we were too exhausted to notice just how cold it was. In those days my Ibrox training happened during the evenings and, even though I was working so hard at my PE course, I was still able to drag one leg after the other. When I think back, I must have been pretty fit in those days! The Ibrox training was hard enough in itself. Our fitness trainer was Davie Kinnear, a military-type gentleman who was very strict and had us running round the track wearing spikes to maximise our ability. He was quite a taskmaster but he did have a sense of humour. I remember once when Johnny Hubbard broke away and ran up into the terraces. 'What are you doing up there?' asked Davie Kinnear.

'I've come to collect some of Sammy Baird's long passes,' replied Johnny.

We all held our breath, waiting for the explosion we were sure would follow. It didn't come. The trainer just burst into laughter. So, we had some fun as well as our hard work. Ibrox then was a really happy environment.

Johnny Hubbard, or 'Hubby' as he was predictably called, still does a wonderful job coaching youngsters in Prestwick and Ayr and his acute sense of humour prevails. I recall when, yet again, he was accusing his inside forward, Sammy Baird, of being a selfish player. After a match against Aberdeen he said to Sammy in his distinctive South African accent: 'Sam, there were 58,742 spectators out there today!'

Sammy replied, 'How the hell do you know that, wee man?'

'Because I was counting them when you were on the ball, you greedy b…!'

However, I did have one problem at Ibrox. My best position was that of left half – or left midfield as it is now called. It was a position in which there were some very good players, and I always make a joke and say that I was third choice. The first choice was an amputee and the second one was a Catholic!

On that subject I have to say that I always found the religious differences that surrounded Rangers and Celtic to be despicable. It isn't so bad these days with both clubs playing down that factor in their Glasgow coexistence. In the past it was a different story, with the religious divide being quite a serious problem. Yet it never seemed to be a problem in the dressing room. The players of both clubs have always mixed well socially and, when called up for their country, the subject never seemed to be on the agenda. It appears to be something that has been carried through the generations by the supporters. I never heard anything about religious differences in the Rangers dressing room, and I'm sure it was the same in the Celtic camp.

The Old Firm games were a cauldron of hate – much more than I realised in the innocence of my teenage years. I used to have an umbrella that could have been mistaken for a white-and-blue design – although it wasn't. In fact it was a Bank of Scotland umbrella. I was a young player at Ibrox at the time and was using the umbrella in the rain when I was accosted by a couple of Celtic fans who told me what to do with my umbrella ... 'or else!' It came as quite a shock to me. I had always looked at the rivalry as a natural condition between two clubs in the same city. I had never realised that there were greater undercurrents than just seeing who was top dog in Glasgow football. I soon learned that it was better not to identify yourself with one club or the other when you were out and about in Glasgow – it was safer that way. As I've said, there was no such animosity between players and my friendship with Billy McNeill continued even though we were in opposing clubs. Our friendship prevailed and still does to this day.

As Scotland manager I was sometimes accused of favouritism towards one or other of the two Glasgow giants. It was a ridiculous charge, of course. In the summer of 1997, my brother Jock became general manager of Celtic, and that caused more than a little consternation because it was suggested that he was a Rangers fan. He has never been a Rangers fan. I can assure you that he, and the rest of the family, have always been Hamilton fans. There is hardly a day that goes by without some rumour or other getting started in the football world. Most of them are very wide of the mark.

Both my brothers are smashing guys, really decent chaps, and although both are well qualified academically this is never apparent in their attitude or speech in their dealings with other people.

My middle brother, Bob, is a Church of Scotland minister in Queen's Cross Church in Aberdeen. He has an MA degree from St Andrew's University which involved four years of study, a Bachelor of Divinity from Glasgow University which required three years of study, and a Master of Theology degree from Duke University in North Carolina. Bob was, in fact, a student for eight years, during which time he took various jobs to supplement his income. He was always committed to joining the ministry.

People who know that my brother is a minister often say to me that I must be a devout person also. However, if my brother were in Barlinnie Prison, that wouldn't make me a criminal. That is probably a very flippant remark because, while I don't consider myself to be a devout person in the extreme sense, I like to think that I have a degree of faith, although I can never aspire to the tremendously strong Christian beliefs that my brother Bob has.

My other brother, Jock, also has great academic qualifications, and he must be a really clever guy because I never ever saw him study. He left school in Hamilton and went straight to Cambridge University where he gained his MA degree in law. That, of course, was English law and, when he returned to Scotland, he had to sit the Law Society of Scotland exams to be qualified to practise law in Scotland. After gaining dual qualification he went on to embark on a very successful legal career. While at Cambridge he captained the university soccer team and, unlike me, he has played at Wembley three times in the annual varsity fixture against Oxford. He acquitted himself very well as a rugged, dirty centre-half playing in a high standard of game for Cambridge.

While he was general manager of Celtic, I hardly ever saw or heard from him. He spent much of his first period there travelling abroad to meet players and set up transfer arrangements recommended by the Celtic coach, Wim Jansen. So, although Jock and I get on very well, our contact was greatly reduced because of his all-embracing club commitments.

When the job was first mooted he asked for my opinion. I, rather selfishly, said: 'I don't think you should take that job because I get enough abuse when I go to Rangers as it is, and if my brother is at Celtic it is only going to get worse. No doubt the abuse I get at Celtic will increase as well if the team is not doing too well. Please stay out of it. Stick with your legal world and your role as BBC football commentator.' He was the top man for BBC Scotland, after all.

The next day I phoned him again and changed my tune.

'I've phoned because my reply to you yesterday was very selfish. I was thinking of how it would affect me, but I never gave a thought to how you felt about it. I should be strong enough to take whatever comes and I'm sure I can handle any comments that come my way. So, if the job appeals to you, go for it, don't worry about me.'

Jock admitted that I had put him off but then told me that he felt that at this stage in his career a new challenge would be rejuvenating for him. Not long after our phone conversation he contacted Celtic and accepted their offer. Although Jock is no longer in that post his regard for Celtic FC remains undiminished and he will not hear a word against his former employers.

I think the press and the public have grown to realise that there was no reciprocal influence whatsoever, any more than there was when he had to interview me for the BBC once in his capacity as a football commentator.

Those are my brothers and, of course, I'm very proud of both of them.

All this was still a long way off for a young Rangers player and third choice for the left half position at Ibrox. Billy Stevenson was first choice for my position and Stan Anderson, my old friend, was second. Then, after I had been at Ibrox for about eighteen months, Rangers signed another player with whom I had to compete for the No. 6 shirt. He was to become the most famous of them all, but he certainly didn't look like the part when he and I first shook hands. Anyone who remembers his first day at Ibrox will tell you that he was a very nervous young man. When he and I said hello, little did I know that I was meeting a legend in the making – the one and only Jim Baxter.

3

Hello, Jim!
Goodbye, Rangers!

JIM BAXTER who sadly died became one of Scotland's biggest ever stars, and by coincidence I was the first player he met when he arrived at Ibrox. I was getting treatment for the first of many knee injuries and that is why I was there when Jim arrived. It was during the summer of 1960, and I met him for the first time when the manager, Scot Symon, was showing him around the Glasgow Rangers' stadium.

Jim was noticeably nervous, and when Scot left him with me in the treatment room we had quite a long chat. He had just joined Rangers from Raith Rovers for £17,500, which was quite a lot of money in those days, especially for a club like Raith. They had paid £200 when he had first joined them a few years earlier, and he had certainly become something of a sensation. His displays included a great game against Rangers in 1958 which had resulted in a shock 3–1 win for Raith. Rangers began tracking him after that and eventually they got their man.

On the pitch, Jim Baxter was supremely confident, but that first day at Ibrox he showed me another side of his character, a side that very few people know. I remember him saying to someone else a bit later on that he had felt like a country yokel at the time of his arrival. He later offered this explanation: 'I know that I've been called arrogant and I can't help what people say. I know that's probably how I have looked. But when I was eighteen I was called up to play for the Scotland Under-23 side against Wales at Tynecastle. I was with Raith then and it was a big day for me. I travelled to Edinburgh to meet up with everyone else. I was feeling quite pleased with myself until I saw the other lads. They all looked really something, very sharp and exactly as professional footballers should look. I felt out of place ... a nobody.

'A couple of kids asked me for my autograph and then I saw them looking at their books to see who I was. That was the day when I decided that everyone would know who I was. I knew I could play, but I had to make sure that everyone else knew too. But I never tried anything that I didn't know I could achieve.'

The legend of Jim Baxter has been told many times. He was undoubtedly a brilliant player, and one of the greatest to wear the Rangers and Scotland shirts. When we reported for pre-season training it seemed natural that his peg should be next to mine – partly because the pegs were arranged in alphabetical order, but also because we already knew each other. As the season wore on, players changed their pegs to be near their best pals, but Baxter and Brown always remained together. We became good friends. I discovered that inside that flamboyant and brash exterior was a very warm human being.

Whenever we chance to meet, I always got the best of greetings and hospitality from Jim Baxter, and I always tried to reciprocate. I had the marvellous privilege of watching him play for Rangers and to see at close-hand the magnificent talent that he had. He made an instant impact in the first team. The Scottish League Championship was won for the 32nd time, the League Cup was also won, and the Scottish Cup was only just lost, thanks to a battling Motherwell side. Rangers also took part in the inaugural European Cup Winners' Cup competition, and reached the final in which they faced a cynical Fiorentina side. As it happened, Fiorentina did win by the odd goal, a wonder strike by Kurt Hamrin, a Swedish international. You can see from all this that Jim Baxter's first season at Ibrox was exciting to say the least.

While all this was going on I was becoming even more anonymous. My knee injury, which at first appeared to be just an annoyance, was beginning to look a little more serious. I kept on getting fluid on the joint. I was ordered to keep on working at strengthening the quadriceps, which I did, but I still continued to get the fluid problem. When I trained with Rangers it appeared, and when I was working on my PE course it appeared – and it was beginning to become a bit of a worry.

I was not a very important player at the time and so I did not receive the urgency of treatment that might have helped me to recover a lot more quickly – and possibly permanently. It is simply the way of things in football, not just then but now as well. If I had been a first-team player, I would have received the care and attention that was due to my status, but I was not and I understood my situation perfectly. Many a player has been told, 'Go on, lad, get yourself sorted!'

David Kinnear was an excellent remedial gymnast, but he was not a qualified physiotherapist and so it was not his fault. My knee problem refused to respond, and so my chances of first-team football became limited.

It didn't stop me playing, but I did have to live with this knee problem, which kept niggling at me incessantly. I was quickly beginning to realise that, unless something very dramatic happened, my career was going in one direction only – and it wasn't up. Everyone tried to be encouraging, but I had this awful feeling that my dreams of winning the championship and playing in Europe as a regular first-team player at Rangers were destined to end in tatters.

Before I signed for Rangers, one of the other teams that

tried to take me on board was Third Lanark – now defunct, but regarded then with great affection by everyone interested in Scottish football. Their manager at that time was Bob Shankly, brother of the great Bill Shankly. He was a fine man but, at the time, I was dazzled by the Ibrox marble staircase and the smooth, gentlemanly encouragement of Scot Symon – not to mention being well aware of the fact that wearing a Rangers shirt could earn me more status and a little more money.

However, Bob Shankly did not forget me and, when he left Third Lanark, he became manager of Dundee. He and his brother Bill were not only great managers but also took a very personal interest in just about everyone who was playing the game, no matter who they were playing for. It had not escaped Bob Shankly's notice that I was not getting first-team football for Rangers, and so he asked them if they would transfer me to Dundee.

I was extremely surprised when Bob Shankly was turned down by Rangers. My surprise was all the greater because Rangers at that time were certainly not short of players and I was not among the top ones. I felt that I did not figure very highly on their list of priorities, and so I fully expected them to be only too glad to unload me. I don't know who was the more surprised, Bob Shankly or myself, when they said they were going to keep me.

After his initial surprise, Bob asked if it would be possible for me to join his club on loan. This time Rangers were in agreement, and I didn't mind at all. I didn't really want to leave the Rangers set-up for one minute – but I was also eager to stop my career falling into stagnation. Since it was for a loan spell only, there was no danger that I couldn't return to Ibrox, and so, in October 1960, I became a temporary Dundee player.

I hadn't been at Dundee for very long – in fact I'd played just a few reserve games – when my knee began to be troublesome again. Lawrie Smith was the physiotherapist at Dundee, and he took a good, long look at the problem. He was a great guy and an outstanding physio as well, and after studying my knee for some time he told me quite simply that there was only one way it was going to get any better – and that was through surgery.

I was sent to see a world-renowned knee specialist, Mr Smillie, who had written a number of books on the subject. After examination, he confirmed what Lawrie Smith had said, adding that surgery was not simply an option – it was essential. I was packed off to a local nursing home for the first of what turned out to be five operations on my left knee.

Nowadays, I know, there are wonderful ways of performing operations with the minimum of fuss and disruption to everyday life. Keyhole surgery has taken away those big incisions and the necessity to be confined to bed, sometimes for weeks. It was not the same when I had my operations – it was necessary then to have several weeks of recuperation before there was any possibility of getting back to any serious work, and in my case that meant getting back to being considered for first-team football.

Dundee were very good to me and extremely patient. Rangers also kept a sharp eye on my progress and were very encouraging. Fortunately, I did recover before the end of the season and I played in the reserves at Dens Park to prove my match fitness. Whether or not I had done enough to secure a place in first-team football with Dundee remained to be seen.

Even though I was a Rangers player and knew that I would be returning to Ibrox once the loan period was over, I felt really at home at Dens Park. I was still finding it quite difficult to understand why the Ibrox club were so unwilling to sell me, and even began to think that it was possibly because I was so useful in the Rangers golf team. We had been very successful in various competitions. In fact, in the month before I joined Dundee on loan, Harold Davis, Bobby Shearer and I had won the Daily Record Footballers' Golf Team Trophy for Rangers with an eight-stroke win over second-placed Hibernian. Just for the record, Dundee had finished third in the competition.

I had never had any trouble in being accepted at Rangers –
and I am sure that my golfing ability went a long way towards
that acceptance. A lot of Rangers players were keen on the
game. When the team went out on golf outings, I usually
managed to play in the top four – which was pretty good really
because a lot of the team were class players, and the manager,
Scot Symon, was very good indeed, besides being very
enthusiastic. Bobby Shearer had a very low handicap, as did
Harold Davis. Max Murray was a scratch player and there
were several others who were a force to be reckoned with on
the golf course. I always seemed to do well and, even if my
soccer skills didn't earn many plaudits, my golf had certainly
raised my esteem among my Rangers colleagues.

We had a few interesting golf outings while I was at Ibrox,
many of which I can recall. I shall never forget one in
particular. Let's be absolutely frank – the etiquette of golf had
been quite lost on many of the players, who would do things
that would have golf officials holding their heads in despair and
disbelief. Players would share clubs and a caddy car, some
wouldn't have golf shoes and would wear trainers with
tracksuit bottoms tucked into their socks. Normally you
wouldn't get on too many courses dressed like that – maybe it
was because it was Rangers that many a blind eye would be
turned?

On this particular occasion we were playing at Erskine
Golf Club and the lads had been out on the course. The last four
to go out were Ralph Brand and Jimmy Miller against Willie
Henderson and Davie Provan. They were sharing one set of
clubs and you could hear them shouting during the round –
which means that they were shouting pretty loudly. So they
were coming up the fairway to the last hole, long after everyone
else. Their earlier shouting had mostly been about the score.

'Is that eleven?'

'No, it's twelve!'

'It never is.'

'Aye, it is!'

So it went on. I think it was Ralph who was pulling the caddy car and, as they went up to the last green, he was giving out the clubs. He took the caddy car right on to the green and up to the flag. It was a wet day and the scars from the wheels of the caddy car could clearly be seen on the green. Apparently they had been doing this all over the course but, since they were the last to go, nobody had noticed. When Scot Symon found out he was none too pleased – in fact he was furious. The club officials shared his views and, needless to say, we were not invited back to that particular golf club.

In the dressing room of a football club there is invariably plenty of what we call 'patter'. Ibrox was no exception. Friday morning was always full of anticipation because, in blue typewritten letters, the team names were pinned to the noticeboard.

On this particular Friday, the newspaper heading on the back page was 'Henderson To Get Contact Lenses'. It was well known that the outside left, deputising for the injured Davy Wilson, was Bobby Hume – one of the first professional players to use contact lenses. Our groundsman, Davie McLeod, on studying the Scot Symon selection and bearing in mind his reading of the Daily Record, was loud in his condemnation. He read the forward line and made his customary remark: 'I see it and I don't believe it. Henderson, McMillan, Millar, Brand and Hume. Two blind wingers! I don't know whether to line the park tomorrow or just put kerbstones along the sides!'

Anyway, back at Dundee, I was determined to make the best of my loan spell and, when I was back in full action in the reserve team, I set out to prove myself. I felt that by doing so I would be able to reciprocate for the interest that they had shown in me. I did not really expect to be given a first-team chance at this stage, although of course there was always the hope that in the latter games of the season there would be an opportunity.

The first team had not experienced the best of seasons. Their Scottish League Cup hopes had been dashed before I had arrived at the club. Rangers had been the team to put paid to their hopes over two legs of the quarterfinals in September 1960. In fairness, Dundee had succeeded in giving Rangers quite a scare. The first leg, played at Ibrox, had ended 1–0, but the return at Dens Park finished in a 3–3 draw as Dundee refused to capitulate. Rangers had learned a valuable lesson from that experience, however, and when the two teams met again at Dens Park – in the Scottish Cup second round – the Ibrox men were easy 5–1 winners. The League campaign was also a disappointing one for Dundee, even though they had put in some very good performances. Despite this, they still only managed to finish in the middle of the table, in tenth place out of eighteen clubs. Rangers had won the championship but perhaps the worst blow of all as far as Dundee was concerned was that our great rivals, Dundee United, finished one place above us – in ninth position with just one point more!

Despite my injuries I was continuing with my course at Jordanhill and I certainly enjoyed a wide range of sports there. The course meant that you had to be fairly proficient in just about every sport that it is possible for a human to play. I played football and golf, of course, but I also found myself taking part in swimming, rugby, rowing, cricket, hockey, basketball, skiing and mountaineering. I once had to set off after a Dundee evening match to go to Aviemore as part of my skiing and mountaineering education. You can just imagine how amusing many of my soccer colleagues found it. I came in for huge amounts of stick from these so-called pals, who even suggested that I might be a better footballer if I wore my ski boots on the pitch instead of the regulation ones!

I did enjoy keeping fit and having a go at all these different sports. My father had instilled in all of us the benefits of regular exercise and a healthy diet. It was rare for me to eat anything but fruit at lunch-time. I'm sure that it helped me, and I would recommend it to anyone who wants to give his body a fighting chance of enduring the rigours of life.

Another big interest of mine, of which not too many people were aware, was country dancing – in fact, I became quite good at it. I even reached the stage of being a member of a 'Jig-time' dance team which appeared regularly on Scottish Television. I still do like country dancing, but these days it is mostly for the music, as I don't have the knees for 'pas de bas'. When I'm at a wedding, or some similar social event, I'll still have a go, however – after all, those are the times when it's almost obligatory for you to make a fool of yourself, aren't they?

Anyway, we finally came to the end of the season, and I had really enjoyed my time at Dundee. I was impressed with the management style of Bob Shankly, who was quite different from Scot Symon. I would hate to have to say which of the two men was the better manager because, after all, they both had so many fine attributes. Suffice it to say that they were both good at their jobs. I prepared myself for a return to Ibrox and was determined that I would have another go at proving that I was worth a try in the first team.

As it turned out, I never did get to say goodbye to all my new friends at Dundee. Just before I was due to return to Ibrox, Bob Shankly made a final attempt to sign me on a regular basis – and this time Rangers agreed.

We called Bob Shankly 'The Wily Old Fox' – and with considerable justification. He used all his astute managerial skills to get me to Dundee for as small a fee as possible. Early on during my loan spell I had played well in a reserve game against Willie Henderson but, when Rangers were due to play us again in a second-eleven match at Dens Park towards the end of the season, our boss came to me and said, with a knowing look, 'Henderson can have a better game tonight, son!'

I had started that season as a reserve with the club that had finished as champions of Scotland, and now I had become a reserve with the club that had finished below the halfway line in the table. Certainly on paper it did not look to be the best thing that could have happened to me, but nevertheless I could not help feeling that there were going to be better days ahead. Bob Shankly really knew his business, and he was more than enthusiastic. It seemed to me that Dundee were experiencing the dawning of a very exciting time in the club's history.

My family were all very encouraging, as they always were, but ultimately the decision was mine. I was not being forced to join Dundee and I didn't have to go there if I didn't really want to, but at the time it seemed to be the right move to make and so I signed the necessary forms. In the end I was right to make the move when I did, but I have to admit that, when I said goodbye to Glasgow Rangers, I was not really filled with regret.

4

Champions!

I FELT THAT there was a much better opportunity for me at Dundee to play a part in a team that I considered to be destined for much greater things. I was delighted to sign for Dundee because I felt that here was a club that was going places. There was such a strong squad at Ibrox that I felt sure my chances would have become more and more limited as time went on. I had been very impressed with the drive and ambition of Bob Shankly, and I knew that he was not the man to settle for second best in anything. I wanted to be there when he guided the Dark Blues to success.

The excitement began almost as soon as we reported for pre-season training. A tour had been arranged for us in Iceland – a country that I had only read about and been fascinated by, never considering that I would actually be seeing it for real one day.

On the tour we played against the Reykjavik side and also against the Iceland national team, and I felt that I was settling in quite well. There had been a few changes to the playing staff as Adamson, Horsburgh, Jardine and May were released,

but the biggest surprise for the Dundee fans was when Doug
Cowie was placed on the transfer list. Doug, then 34, had been
at Dundee for sixteen years and had become one of the club's
all-time greats, having been capped for Scotland twenty times.
He had rarely turned in a bad performance, either for club or
country. I think he was very disappointed at being placed on
the transfer list, because he felt that he still had a lot to offer
Dundee. As it happened, he was not idle for long because
Morton quickly signed him as player-coach.

Coming into the club was another veteran player – and I
hope he doesn't mind me calling him that – Gordon Smith.
Twice before, Dundee had tried to sign him and now it was a
case of third time lucky. There was no doubting his talent. He
had played eighteen times for Scotland and had won the
Scottish Championship with both Hearts and Hibs. Some of
the Dundee fans were surprised at the signing, however,
because Gordon was 37 – and therefore older than Doug
Cowie, who was being transferred. They need not have
worried, as it happened. There was never any need to doubt a
Shankly signing, whether it was Bill or Bob that was involved.

I wanted to be considered as a first-team choice but
Dundee had a pretty settled side, despite all the comings and
goings. The team sheet was almost always the same during the
opening games of the season, and I remember it well – Liney,
Hamilton, Cox, Seith, Ure, Wishart, Smith, Penman, Cousin,
Gilzean and Robertson. No doubt you will remember some of
those famous names. I wasn't at all sure how I was going to
get my big chance, but I still felt a lot closer to it than I had at
Rangers, so I was not worrying unduly.

There was a mixed start to the season because Dundee fell
early in the Scottish League Cup competition, but put together
a few good opening League results – including a 4–1 win at
home to our local rivals, Dundee United. Kilmarnock and
Rangers led the table after a couple of games but we were soon
up with them. Alan Gilzean had been the club's top scorer the
previous season with 32 League and Cup goals, and he just

continued where he had left off. In the centre of our defence was the mighty Ian Ure – so there were giants of the game in both of the most important positions in the team.

I was continuing to play in the reserves but I was already in the reckoning for the first team. It was an amazing season, really, because in addition to those eleven players I have already mentioned, the club used only four others. If that was the first eleven, then I was hanging in at No. 12.

We were scoring plenty of goals – five against Kilmarnock, four against Motherwell – and Bob Shankly was enjoying himself. He was a very similar character to his brother Bill and rarely missed an opportunity to tell the world how wonderful his players were. It was all going very well for the club, but not quite so well for me because I had yet to play for the first team in a competitive game. Had substitutes been allowed in those days I reckon I would have created a record for the greatest number of appearances as a sub, because I was always with the squad both home and away.

At long last I got my chance when our skipper, Bobby Cox, was injured. I was not at all happy about his injury because I was a club man and wanted us to be at our strongest at all times, but I can't deny that I was excited when I was told that I would be playing. My only problem was that I would be out of position at left back. It was something that I was asked to do a number of times and it did prove to be a successful switch for me, even though I was more at home in the left half position.

The newspapers were very kind to me. I played in the return away game at Kilmarnock where we drew 1–1 One writer, Jimmy Stevenson, introduced his match report with the headline 'Stand-in Sets An Example'. Another writer said of Dundee: 'They got a point because of the rugged defence of Ian Ure and the speed and tackling of young Craig Brown, a big hit in his first top team game.

I was thrilled to read such things about myself and, if I look at those press cuttings now, I still get pleasure when I read about 'young' Craig Brown. There were other descriptions of me as 'the crew-cut Craig Brown'. Yes, I had a crew cut in those days, and I was young and, yes, we are talking about the same Craig Brown. It's not the years – it's the mileage!

Those were thrilling days at Dens Park. A 5–1 win over Rangers had demonstrated to everyone that Dundee meant business and, as the season wore on, it became more evident that our position at the top of the table was no mere flash in the pan. Even when we lost Alan Gilzean with a broken jaw, the goals continued to flow.

Alan was a big element of that early success. He was a tremendous goalscorer, a typical bustling centre-forward who was excellent with his head as well as his feet. He had all the courage that you expect from a top goalscorer whom every defender in the country was determined to stop. Even when he broke his jaw, he was not out for long.

Things were a little different in those days. Games were played in conditions that would have meant very definite postponements today. If there was snow on the ground, as long as the lines were visible and the snow didn't come up over your ankles, the game would still be on. I remember 'Gillie' once wearing sandshoes on a frozen pitch and scoring two goals while everyone else struggled to keep on his feet.

I don't really think that I was to blame – I hope not, anyway – but after I came into the side we seemed to go through a bit of a slump. We were beaten 3–0 at Partick and then had a stern test away to Celtic. We lost that one as well, 2–1, but I was pleased with my own performance, and one of the journalists at the game wrote: 'I was particularly impressed by young Craig Brown. The former Ranger showed something of the play which, as a youth internationalist, hinted at taking him right to the top.' Another newspaper made me Dundee's top player for that game and I, of course, took great encouragement from such things. It didn't go to my head, but it didn't do my confidence any harm either.

I might have guessed that it was all going too well for me by now. There had to be another blow just around the corner and, sure enough, it was waiting for me when we played away to Raith Rovers. My left knee let me down again and I had to go off. Another trip to hospital beckoned and, as you may imagine, I was pretty distraught. I desperately wanted to continue in the side as we entered the run-in to the season. It had developed into a two-horse race between ourselves and Rangers, and I wanted to do my bit to bring home the championship to Dens Park for the first time in the club's history.

There was nothing that I could do except enter Fernbrae Nursing Home and keep reading the newspapers, listening to the radio, and watching television. I was forced to sit in that Dundee nursing home, hungry for any news of what was happening to my team. Our rivals, Dundee United, actually did us a very big favour. Rangers seemed to have taken the initiative in the title chase even though we were still picking up points. Our standard of play seemed to have slipped a little, while theirs was gaining in momentum. Despite all that, Ibrox was stunned when Rangers came up against our rivals Dundee United and slipped up. On the day that we scraped a 1–0 win over Hibs, mighty Rangers went down 0–1 against United. I was overjoyed at the news but more than a little sad that I had not been able to play. It is very frustrating to be in a hospital bed while your teammates are playing their hearts out.

Dundee United might well have done us a favour with that spectacular victory away to Rangers, but they were no less determined to beat us in the return local derby game in April. A 20,000 all-ticket crowd witnessed a great game which Dundee won 2–1, with Alan Gilzean driving a sensational shot past Rolando Ugolini to get the winner with just four minutes left. With two games remaining, Rangers had to go to Aberdeen and Dundee were at St Mirren. When the news came through that Rangers were trailing 1–0 there was a buzz of excitement around the ground which reached the ears of the players. Pat Liney, in goal, must have been inspired by it because he saved a penalty with a spectacular leap which stopped St Mirren skipper Jim Clunie's shot going right into the top right-hand corner of the net. It was 1–0 at the time and touch and go. The relief of that penalty save encouraged Andy Penman to score our second goal, bringing the championship even closer to reality.

The last game of the season was absolute agony for me as so much was at stake. Everything hinged on getting at least a point from a visit to St Johnstone – who also needed points to save them from relegation. It is amazing how often history repeats itself. Just thirteen years earlier, Dundee had been in a similar position, needing to take points from the last game of the season or risk Rangers stealing the championship at the last gasp. On that day everything went wrong and a 4–1 defeat saw Dundee having to make do with the runners-up spot.

I have never been one to bite my nails but, if I had, I would have been down to my elbows before the final scores came through. Rangers had been held to a 1–1 draw by Kilmarnock, while Dundee had gone through a battle royal with St Johnstone, who included in their line-up the very same Alex Ferguson who has demonstrated so often since how much he hates the taste of defeat. St Johnstone gave Dundee a number of scares early in the game as the tension seemed to get to everybody but, in the 24th minute, there was a flood of relief when Alan Gilzean headed home. 'Gillie' scored again in the second half and then Andy Penman drove home via the crossbar to make it 3–0 and signal the start of the party.

The whole of Dundee celebrated that piece of football history while I was still in my hospital bed. It would have been very easy for everyone at the club to have forgotten all about me during those ecstatic celebrations, but the manager made sure that I was not neglected. We were all paid in cash in those days and on the first pay-day after that championship-winning game he came to see me personally with my brown envelope.

'I've brought you this, son,' he said as he put the envelope on my bed. I stared at it – it looked very much bigger than usual. I thought for a moment that he had brought me a letter telling me that my services would no longer be required by the club. Tentatively I opened the envelope while he watched me with a smile on his face. Inside was a big bundle of cash.

'That's your bonus for winning the championship, son!' said Bob Shankly. 'You played your part just the same as the others.'

I was amazed. It wasn't the money – it was the fact that I was being treated no differently to the other members of the side who had played in many more games. They were the big shots as I saw it, and yet here was the club treating me in just the same manner. I was one of the exclusive band of only fifteen players who were involved in Dundee's first-ever Scottish championship. I received the same bonus as everyone else and – more importantly – I also received my championship medal, something which I cherish to this day.

I also cherish the experience of having worked for such a great manager as Bob Shankly. He always expected the best from his players, but he invariably gave them the best too and I learned an enormous amount from him. He also got me into a habit that I have maintained to this day.

After winning the title, Dundee went on a summer tour to New York. The manager took the trouble to send me a postcard because I was still undergoing treatment for my knee injury. He wrote, 'Sorry you missed this trip Craig...' What a thoughtful gesture!

That card meant a lot to me. Bob Shankly was a busy man and I really appreciated the fact that he had taken time out to get in touch with me. It was also a thrill to get a card from someone whom I had grown to respect and admire so much.

Yes, but you were talking about a habit! I can almost hear you say it. Well, receiving that card meant so much to me that it taught me a lesson. It taught me that there are those left at home when you are away on your travels and they could well do with a card from you – even with the smallest of notes. I picked up the habit of sending cards to friends all over the world whenever I was on my travels. I have become quite famous for it among my circle of friends – and it all started with that postcard I received from Bob Shankly, one of the finest managers and men it has ever been my privilege to know.

I don't just stop at sending cards to friends either, because I also learned then what a morale-booster such a message can be. To give you an insight into how I ran the Scotland team – if I had to leave a player out of my plans because he was injured, or just not suitable for a particular game, I always tried to make sure that he didn't feel rejected. I arrange for him to be sent postcards, faxes and anything else that will help to make him feel that he is with us in spirit at least. I learned that from Bob Shankly, and I am sure that it has gone a long way to helping with the great team spirit we had in the Scotland camp.

I must tell you a little more about life at Dundee when I wasn't injured, because it was a great set-up. I had been among friends at Rangers, and that certainly didn't change when I joined Dundee. I stayed in digs run by a lady called Mrs Garvie, who had four other Dens Park players staying at her place. We quickly became known as the 'Garvie Five', and consisted of Ian Ure, George Ryden, Tommy Mackle, Hugh Robertson and Craig Brown.

We were notorious for being late for training because we all used to travel in the one wee car – which had a habit of refusing to start. We had all sorts of fun together while we were at Mrs Garvie's. My next digs were at Mrs Duncan's in Sagar Street, and then later Doug Houston and I moved to Mrs Clark's digs in Americanmuir Road in Downfield, Dundee. So you see, during my time with Dundee I was in three different lots of digs, but, I hasten to point out, I was never evicted from any of them!

Another thing that happened while I was at Dundee was that I completed my PE course at Jordanhill and also another one-year course which I looked upon as a kind of insurance.

The latter course qualified me to teach subjects at primary level in schools, and I considered that it would be useful to have that as well as my PE qualification. I did actually start to teach while I was at Dundee because we used to train only in the mornings for four days a week, which left me with the afternoons and the whole of Monday free. I was what was known as a peripatetic, or itinerant, PE teacher, because I went round various schools in the Dundee area. I thoroughly enjoyed myself in the teaching profession, even though I was still classed as a full-time professional footballer. It was not uncommon in those days, but today, with so many more fixtures and other commitments, players would find it virtually impossible to have such a part-time career – even if they wanted, or even needed it.

While all this was happening I was still very much a part of the Dundee first-team squad, which was not only trying to defend the championship in the new season, but was also making its debut in the European Cup. This meant that there were quite a few problems with my teaching work as I often had to change my appointments, and that, in turn, would throw out some of the timetables at the schools where I was working. The other problem was that the PE work also caused my knee to swell up once more. I discussed the problem with the education authority, and they suggested that it would probably be better, and more convenient all round, if I concentrated on my primary teaching instead of my PE teaching. I took their advice, and that really is how I got started in primary teaching.

Meanwhile, there was plenty happening on the football pitch. The New York visit that I mentioned earlier was planned to enable us to take part in a soccer tournament involving teams like Reutlingen of West Germany, Hadjduk Split of Yugoslavia, Guadalajara of Mexico, Palermo of Italy and America of Brazil.

It provided some valuable experience in playing against foreign sides. Doug Houston, whom I mentioned earlier, had joined Dundee from Queen's Park, and the well-known goalkeeper Bert Slater had also signed for us. Three players had left us and there was a cloud hanging over the club because six of the top Dundee players had not signed new contracts. The club had offered £25 a week but Hamilton, Penman, Robertson, Seith, Ure and Gilzean were not yet committed, and there was the obvious worry that they might go elsewhere. That £25-a-week offer was not bad in those days. The two Glasgow giants, Rangers and Celtic, would possibly have paid more, but nobody else in Scotland would have done at that time. As it happened it was all a storm in a teacup anyway, because all six of them eventually signed on the dotted line, meaning the team was intact when we opened our campaign against our arch-rivals Dundee United at Tannadice.

It was a League Cup game, and I'm pleased to say that I had recovered sufficiently from my knee problems to be picked for the team and receive a roasting from Dennis Gillespie who, sadly, died in June 2001. Unfortunately we lost 3–2, which was a blow – but we made up for it a few days later with a 1–0 win over Celtic.

I have to admit that we struggled during our remaining League Cup games, and not even a civic reception at Dundee's Chamber of Commerce, in honour of our championship success of the previous season, could rekindle the flame that had burned so brightly. A lot of our confidence did return, however, when we beat Dundee United 2–1 in the return League Cup game, and it was probably that victory that set us up for our very first European Cup game. We had been drawn against Cologne – one of the most daunting challenges any side could be asked to face on their European Cup debut. The manager decided that the best policy would be to go for experience rather than for enthusiasm, and therefore four other younger players and I found ourselves left out to make way for those with possibly cooler heads.

On the face of it we were in for a hiding by the Germans. There is no shame in the fact that we were pretty well written off, with questions being asked about how many Cologne would score rather than if they would score. Scottish football has always been a game full of surprises – not all of them pleasant ones. In recent times, Scottish clubs have struggled in European competitions. We cannot use the English excuse of being banned for so many years because we have never had a break in continuity but, somehow, these days it does not seem to pay off for us.

I thought that Celtic played very well before going out to Liverpool in the 1997/98 UEFA Cup and in the away match against Ajax in August 2001, but I could not honestly say that about others – Rangers included. They should have done much better. The clubs' management and coaches, along with their players, also seem to find it a mystery that no serious progress has been made in any of the European competitions for so long. We can only put it down to not being 'all right on the night', and hope that, soon, a psychological barrier can be broken down and that Scottish clubs will set the matter right by once again making their mark on the European football stage.

We have had our European triumphs, of course, and I'm sure that we will again – but we are certainly starved at the moment. Anyway, let us turn the clock back and follow the fortunes of Dundee in the 1962/63 European Cup competition, to a time when the first hurdle was looking more like one of those nightmare fences in the Grand National.

What was about to happen in that tie against Cologne nobody really knew – how could they? As I said, we had already been written off by many people. However, since the event, it has become one of the most talked-about clashes in European football history.

5

Marching on in Europe

NOBODY COULD POSSIBLY have written the script for Dundee's first European encounter. There had been a buzz of real excitement when we heard that we had been drawn out of the hat with FC Cologne. They were a well-known side and the tie was eagerly awaited. You can imagine that as the time approached for the first leg – which was at Dens Park in September 1962 – the newspapers were carrying daily bulletins on the build-up to the big day. They were given some real gems by a gentleman called Karl Frohlich, who was the advance guard for Cologne and had been sent ahead to take a look at the hotel and training facilities. During an interview he said one or two things that could hardly be thought of as flattering towards Dundee. The newspapers loved it and their banner headlines whipped up even more frenzy for the approaching clash.

Not only did Dundee fans feel insulted by Herr Frohlich's remarks – which he later denied making, by the way – but they also lulled Cologne into an air of complacency. He had insinuated that they only had to turn up to get through to the next round of the European Cup.

I was not playing in that game but I was in my customary place with the squad – not on the bench, of course, because substitutes were not allowed then. I did not make the eleven on the team sheet but I was involved in all the preparations as usual – just in case. The match began at a frenzied pace. Dundee, roared on by the fans, were determined to go for the jugular from the very start. The Germans were startled, so much so that after ten minutes their experienced defender, Matt Hammersbach, put the ball into his own net while under pressure.

About a minute later we scored again with one of the most incredible goals that I have ever seen. Bobby Wishart found himself in a position to have a go. He let fly but completely miskicked the ball, his foot ploughing into the turf. Instead of rocketing towards the goal, the ball merely trickled along – but Fritz Ewart, the German goalkeeper, dived in the opposite direction. Bobby had sent a large divot into the air and the goalkeeper had mistaken it for the ball. He flew in one direction and caught the turf as the ball gently rolled in at the other post. Long-term Dundee fans will remember that goal for as long as they live – as will I.

It didn't end there either, because Hugh Robertson took advantage of the Germans' dismay to put us 3–0 ahead with only thirteen minutes gone. Alan Gilzean and Gordon Smith both scored too, putting us 5–0 ahead when we went in for half-time. That scoreline must have sent shock waves all around Europe. Emotions were running very high indeed during the interval, and not just because of the goals. Alan Cousin and the German goalkeeper had both gone for a high ball and the Cologne man had ended up on the ground, rolling about as though he had been pole-axed. In fairness, he did go to the local hospital later for treatment to a head injury, but Alan denied that he had made any deliberate contact with Ewart. The German newspapers had other ideas, though, and a photo of Alan Cousin punching their goalie hero was splashed all over the media. It was not a fake photo but it was a misleading one. Photos taken from a different angle showed that there was no question of a punch being landed.

At the end of that first leg we had conceded a deflected goal but Andy Penman had got one for us and a brace from Alan Gilzean completed his European hat-trick. I think that we all had to rub our eyes to make sure that we hadn't been dreaming; the final score was Dundee 8, FC Cologne 1. The Germans returned home seething. Their supporters did not not blame them – they put it all on Dundee. Even one of their officials stated that if the goalkeeper happened to be injured early on in the second leg, a complete reversal might be on the cards. We shrugged that off, even though the newspapers made something of it. On reflection, I think that we were a little naive. Prior to that second meeting, we took it that the problems over our accommodation and training facilities were simply down to language differences and our own inexperience. We never even considered that there might be something more cynical behind it.

On the night of the match things had reached boiling point in Cologne. The Dundee directors and officials were virtually ignored by their German counterparts, even down to having to find their own seats as their hosts refused to have anything to do with them. At the very least it was extremely ill mannered but, once the game was underway, we quickly learned that there was a lot more to it than that. Once again I was not in the team, but even from the side of the pitch you could see that some of the German antics were far from gentlemanly. There was kicking, punching, spitting and even scratching going on – all with the total support of about 40,000 home fans.

Cologne took the lead after Ian Ure mistimed a tackle and had a penalty awarded against him. Habig scored from the spot. A few minutes later we were two goals down when Mueller scored what was, to be fair, an excellent goal. Then, with the game 27 minutes old, our goalkeeper, Bert Slater, dived to save a low ball and Mueller came in feet first with no hope of getting the ball. Sammy Kean, our trainer, rushed on to see blood running down Bert's face and he knew that it was serious. Andy Penman took over in goal as Bert was stretchered off, but then the real drama began as the German ambulance drivers attempted to get Bert into the ambulance – which had been parked behind the goal – and off to hospital. Bert jumped off the stretcher and went with Sammy Kean to the dressing room amid a lot of shouting and arm-waving. I like to think that this was all a coincidence, but many remembered what had been said after the first leg about the possibility of our goalkeeper being injured.

Andy Penman did his best in goal but by half-time the Cologne side were three goals ahead on the night and the overall scoreline was now 8–4. The Dundee players trooped off the pitch blazing with anger at the German team's conduct, and it was left to Bob Shankly – even though he was obviously angry himself – to calm the situation down. Meanwhile, Lawrie Smith had managed to patch up Bert Slater and had wrapped so much bandage around his head that he looked as if he were wearing a turban.

'I look like Lana Turner,' joked Bert, and that managed to take some of the heat out of the mood in the dressing room. The very fact that he was returning to action also gave everyone a lift. He played on the wing for a while, just to make sure that all was well, and then went back in goal – much to the relief of Andy Penman. Later, Bert claimed that he had been a better winger than Gordon Smith – another example of the famous Slater wit!

The second half was played in much the same style as the first, but the Dundee side had grown up a lot during the interval and refused to give in to the provocation. We mounted much more pressure on the Cologne goal and came close to scoring several times. Ian Ure unfortunately scored an own goal, but that was the end of the scoring and at the end Dundee had won the tie 8–5. It was not the end of the drama, however! As the final minutes ticked away there was a vast gathering of

German fans around the touchlines. Taking throw-ins was difficult to say the least, and yet the German officials assured everyone from Dundee that this was quite normal in Germany. We weren't convinced, and our worst fears were realised when the final whistle went and the pitch was invaded. The Dundee players were marooned together in the middle of the pitch as the home fans began to swamp them. Fists began to fly and it began to look very nasty indeed until the next part of the drama unfolded – as our skipper Bobby Cox explained, 'Above all the noise I suddenly heard a voice say: "Don't worry about this lot – the Jocks are here!" It was like the relief of Mafeking. It seemed that every British soldier stationed within a radius of a couple of hundred miles had come to the game and, at the end, they swept on to defend us. They were all in civvies but there was no mistaking them. They fearlessly wrapped themselves around us and practically carried us off the pitch to safety.'

It was quite a scene, I can assure you, and one never to be forgotten although it was later forgiven. Immediately after the game there should have been a banquet, but the Dundee party boycotted it. Years later the two sides met again in the UEFA Cup, and this time there was a much greater feeling of entente cordiale – and Dundee won again, 5–4 on aggregate.

Much of the ill feeling in that tie had been caused by the German press, and that was another lesson I learned. I try to be very careful in what I say and to whom I say it. One false move and you can have all sorts of problems on your hands. That doesn't mean to say that I blame the media for all the troubles of the world, but it does mean that certain members of the journalism profession could act a little more responsibly.

I suffered an example of this early in my career as Scotland manager when I left Davie McPherson out of the squad and called in Colin Hendry. When asked for the reason for Colin's selection, I included in a list of his attributes that he was slightly younger than Davie. Imagine my consternation the next day when, beside a large photograph of Davie

McPherson, was the heading – 'Too Old At 29!'

So, Dundee survived their first sortie into Europe with honours, and we were all looking forward to the next round. The League season wasn't going too badly – we had a good run which kept us within four points of the leaders, Hearts. It was a fairly confident Dundee side that went to Portugal to face Sporting Club of Lisbon in the next round of the European Cup. It was an exciting game, and we had gone into it to defend, which I felt we had done quite well. Two minutes from time, Sporting scored with a controversial goal. Everyone was sure that Bert Slater had punched the ball on to the crossbar and away, but the referee decided that it had crossed the line and he awarded the goal. We didn't protest too much because in reality the Portuguese side deserved their victory, even if it was only 1–0. We felt that the possibility of turning the game around in the second leg was well within our capabilities. As it turned out we were right. About 32,000 turned up to see the side beat Sporting 4–1, with Alan Gilzean scoring another hat-trick and Alan Cousin getting the other. The 4–2 aggregate scoreline meant that Dundee were in the quarterfinals, and suddenly everyone began to sit up and take notice.

On the League front our form had slipped a little – although a 10–2 win over Queen of the South in December helped a bit. Alan Gilzean's seven goals in that match equalled a club record.

Unfortunately, the gap between the leaders and ourselves was beginning to widen. Anderlecht were to be our next European Cup opponents. They had beaten Real Madrid in the previous round, so the Belgians had built quite a reputation – especially with nine internationals in their side, including Paul Van Himst. The first leg was at the Heysel Stadium in front of about 60,000. They were all set to cheer their team nearer to the European Cup final, but there was a stunned silence when Alan Gilzean met a Gordon Smith cross and put us ahead after only 60 seconds. Anderlecht were rocked for a moment but soon got their act together and played some great football. However, Alan Gilzean fired in another goal on twenty minutes and, even though Anderlecht pulled one back from the penalty spot before half-time, the dressing room was buzzing during the interval. Alan Cousin added to the Belgians' woes just after the interval but, to their credit, Anderlecht kept cool and continued to play some attractive football. The Dundee defenders held firm, with both Ian Ure and Bobby Cox clearing off the line on the rare occasions when Bert Slater was beaten. When Gordon Smith scored our fourth goal with only nineteen minutes left, the game was all but over. It is to the credit of the Belgian fans that when the final whistle went to end the game they gave the Dundee side a standing ovation.

The return match at Dens Park a fortnight later was also a classic, with almost 30,000 people packed into the ground. Anderlecht put on another great display of football and took the lead in the first half. However, after the break, it was the home side who dominated, and the pressure eventually told when Alan Cousin equalised with twelve minutes left. A few minutes later Gordon Smith hit the winner and the final scoreline was 6–2. Part of the reason why Anderlecht had conceded goals at Dens Park was because they had been following the wrong man. They knew that Alan Gilzean would be the danger and they put two men on him – which gave freedom to our other forwards. What the Belgians didn't know was that 'Gillie' had gashed his foot in the first leg and had only had the six stitches removed a few hours before the return game. He had been used as a decoy and it had worked handsomely.

At the start of the season, the thought that Dundee would make it to the semifinals of the European Cup would have produced smiles from even the staunchest of supporters – and yet here we were in the last four. I was in and out of the side for League matches and I was present as one of the fourteen-man squad at every European game, home and away. Never getting on the pitch for any of those special games is something that I really regret. I do take some consolation, though, from being a part of the squad, and therefore in the dressing room and alongside the pitch at every game. It is frustrating when you are not actually playing, but it would have been much worse to have been left behind in Scotland while the side was engaged in battle in Germany, Portugal and Belgium.

Our semifinal opponents were to be AC Milan, expected to be the toughest yet of our European opposition. The first leg was away, and 78,000 fans were there in the famous San Siro Stadium. Bobby Cox was injured, and it would have been the natural choice for me to stand in for him but, unfortunately, I was injured as well, and so it was decided not to take the risk.

Dundee were a goal down after three minutes of the game starting – but they kept their heads and Alan Cousin finished some great work by Andy Penman and grabbed us an equaliser. Spirits were high in the dressing room at half-time because we felt we could contain the Italians and set up a great second leg back at Dens Park. AC Milan had other ideas, however, and soon scored two hotly disputed goals to go into a comfortable 3–1 lead. I say that the goals were controversial because there were suggestions that the ball was out of play before being crossed to Bariston who made it 2–1. As for the third goal, there was a Milan player standing in an off-side position on our goal line. The referee had given off-side but then changed his mind and awarded the goal. Milan scored again later in the game and we were disappointed to leave the pitch at the end of a 4–1 defeat.

It always sounds like sour grapes and so I try to make a point of not criticising officials or even crying over spilt milk. What's done is done! Others, though, complained bitterly about the Spanish referee, and it does have to be said that the slightest hint of a tackle from a Dundee player did seem to bring forth an immediate whistle! Later, it was discovered that he had accepted gifts from AC Milan before the game, and he was eventually banned after some other charges of bribery, which were nothing to do with our game, had been revealed. At the end of that first leg, the Dundee players were dismayed and could not really understand how they had come to lose 4–1 to a team they considered to be inferior to the other three teams they had already encountered and beaten.

Milan were programmed to defend their lead when they came to Dens Park for the second leg, and they did it almost perfectly, although their tactics were rugged, to say the least. It was impossible to get any rhythm into the game because the Italian players continually broke it up with fouls and niggling incidents. As it was, Alan Gilzean scored just before half-time to reduce the aggregate deficit but, after having a later goal disallowed, a blatant penalty denied and a frustrated player sent off, we were forced to concede. It had been a great experience in the European Cup, and I think that Dundee had done Scotland – and indeed Britain – more than proud. I would not have missed it for the world.

Our League form suffered as a result of the pressure of the European games and in the end we finished at ninth place in the table, despite finishing quite strongly. Sadly, there would be no European football for us the following season.

Dundee Football Club was very good for me. I have already mentioned how much I admired our manager Bob Shankly, and that I learned so much from him. He was a very honest, straight Ayrshire man who had played for the famous Glenbuck Cherrypickers in the mining village of Glenbuck, where he and his brother Bill grew up with the rest of their football-mad family. Bob was also a close friend of Jock Stein, and they were all of the same mould. Bob Shankly was never one for giving out a lot of praise. He would sometimes put a hand on my shoulder before a game and say, 'Nothing clever from you today, son!' It might sound like a very negative way of motivating someone when all the psychologists say that positive affirmation is what is required, but we all knew what he meant and became accustomed to his special phrases. As an example, if someone said, 'I think I'll pass the ball inside the full-back for our winger to run on to', Bob would say, 'Christ, there's nae need to get complicated!'

The lads always joked because he never ever called me Craig. He always exalted me to a deity and called me 'Christ Craig'! Even on the rare occasions when I had a good game he would come to me after the match and say, 'Christ Craig, that wasnae bad today, son.' Also, if a player was being a bit bombastic in the bath, boasting about his prowess, Bob would come in and cut him dead by saying something like, 'Will you shut up, we've all seen you playing!' He had a perfect way of putting you down if you were getting too big for your boots, but he always had kind words when they were needed.

Another of Bob Shankly's favourite sayings would be heard when a pressman asked him the team selection for the next game. Bob's wife was named Greta, and he always gave the pressman the same answer – 'Oor Greta hasnae picked it yet!' It was just an amusing way of saying that he was keeping his cards close to his chest and would not reveal anything until the last possible moment before the game.

Sammy Kean was his right-hand man, coach and trainer. He was a former Hibs player and he knew his stuff all right. Between them they gave us training sessions that were long on hard work but probably a little short on imagination. There was little or no time spent on tactics. The players themselves worked those out, and some of us used to stay behind after official training to plan a few things. The senior players, particularly our right half, Bobby Seith, who had won the English League championship with Burnley, would evolve the set pieces from throw-ins and free kicks and we would practise these without supervision when the regular training had been completed. I would suggest that this was pretty unusual – not only then, but also now.

Of course, there were many light-hearted events too. One of the many other lessons I learned was never to take on a supporter in the crowd. I made that mistake playing against Celtic once. It was at Celtic Park, probably around January

1962, a cold, wet afternoon, but with the usual huge crowd. I was given the job of marking a young Celtic lad making his debut for the club. Bobby Lennox was his name, and he later went on to become one of the famous Lisbon Lions.

I was given the job of keeping him out of the game. Bob Shankly knew all about him and realised that he would be a threat. He had a saying which sounds quite chilling – 'One from eleven is ten'. As there were no substitutes in those days, if a player was ineffective you were stuck with it for the whole game. At least, that's what I like to think he meant! Being absolutely blunt, I had been given the job of kicking Bobby Lennox every time there was an opportunity – and to make sure that he made no real contribution to the game. You can just imagine how the Celtic supporters responded to that. I came in for a lot of stick from the home fans – and that is when I made my mistake. One fan in particular took tremendous exception to the way I was doing my job. He questioned my parentage and hurled all kinds of other abuse at me. I was aware of what he was saying about me, and so was the Dundee full-back, Alex Hamilton. He was quite a character, as well as being a great Scotland international. He came over to me and said, 'You see that guy in the crowd? If he shouts at you again, and you get a wee chance, tell him that he's a mug because he's paid to get in.' It would have been a stinging retort because Celtic were struggling against us at the time.

Sure enough, the moment came when the ball went out of play and landed in a big puddle in front of where this guy was. The ball-boy was a bit slow getting to the ball because it was in the puddle, so I just went in and retrieved it. As I did this the guy started up again, telling me what a terrible player I was, the worst he had ever seen, and this game was the worst he had ever seen. I took Alex's tip.

'Well, pal,' I said, 'you're the mug because you paid to get in!'

Quick as a flash, he replied, 'Aye! But you'll be paying next season!'

It was a great answer and I felt very small indeed because I had absolutely no reply. It taught me never to try to mix verbals with the crowd, and the Dundee lads kept telling me that the guy was likely to be a prophet! It also taught me never to listen to Alex Hamilton again!

Talking about Alex Hamilton, he was the player who originated the back-handed insult that players today are often heard to repeat in jest. For instance, he called Ian Ure over once and said, 'Well, Ian, you and I have got thirty-three Scotland caps between us – and I've got thirty-two of them!' It is a much-used leg-pull between players, but it was Alex who started it. He was always joking, and not just with his teammates either. He used to love winding up the opposition, and especially enjoyed tormenting the stars of Rangers and Celtic whenever he got the chance. One of his jokes was to take a complimentary ticket and put it in his shorts. He pulled this stunt on both John Hughes, the Celtic winger, and Davy Wilson, the Rangers outside left. He waited until there was a lull in the game and would then go up to his victim with the ticket in his hand, saying, 'Here, John, here's a ticket for you to get into the game.' He also used to joke with them that they ought to have paid to get in for the privilege of being a spectator watching him play!

There was quite a bit of humour at Dundee, with everyone getting his chance as well as being on the receiving end. During that 1962/63 season I was given my nickname of 'Bleep' or 'Bleeper'. It originated during a game against Partick Thistle. The Jags goalkeeper, John Freebairn, sent a long, long clearance way down the pitch over all our heads and I chased after it. Because I had my back to the rest of the pitch, I decided to try a fancy overhead scissor kick as I had seen the continentals do. I completely mistimed it and, instead of the ball going back up the field, it just went straight up into the air like a rocket. It seemed to hang way up there for some time over our penalty spot, almost as if it had gone beyond our sphere of gravity. While we were all waiting for it to come down it reminded Alex Hamilton of the sound of the Russian Sputnik that was in the news at the time, and he began shouting, 'Bleep bleep! Bleep bleep!' That's how I came to be given such a unique nickname.

We had another interesting excursion that season when we played against Arsenal in a testimonial match for Jack Kelsey. We played two games against them, both home and away, and I played in both matches. The Arsenal side had some very famous names – Geoff Strong, George Armstrong, Alan Skirton, George Eastham, John Barnwell and Eddie Clamp among them. We had two very good games, and it was a delight to play at a wonderful ground like Highbury. We drew there 2–2, with Alan Gilzean scoring both Dundee's goals which, I think, led to his eventual transfer to Tottenham where he – quite rightly – became a hero.

On the eve of the Highbury game we all went to Chelsea to see them play Blackpool. Tommy Docherty was manager of Chelsea at the time, and I remember the game well. We stayed at the Mount Royal Hotel, which was in a noisy part of town but very pleasant nonetheless. It was an especially enjoyable trip because we were not there for a cut-throat competition and were therefore able to relax and enjoy the visit to London and two of the most famous grounds in the game.

It was a great honour for us to be invited to play in such a high-profile testimonial, and it shows the esteem in which Dundee was held after their European Cup and Scottish championship exploits. In 1997, Nigel Winterburn's testimonial at Highbury produced a big crowd for the visit of Glasgow Rangers. It was a parallel with our 1962 visit. As many a Dundee fan has said in recent times: 'Those were the days!'

6

The End
of the Beginning

AFTER OUR VISIT to Highbury there was newspaper talk of
me signing for Arsenal. Ian Ure and myself were both in the
frame, it seemed. I felt that I had performed well against the
Gunners, but I could not imagine that they were seriously
interested in me, although I could clearly see why they would
be keen on big Ian. As it happened, I was officially told that
there had been some interest in me, but as I had no wish to
leave Dundee and the club were not particularly keen to
unload me, I stayed where I was.

Dundee, like most clubs at that time, were in good
financial shape. Players were earning nothing like the
astronomical figures of today, and I believe it was to use up
some surplus cash before the end of the financial year that the
club would take us away for training. We were told that we
would be staying at a pleasant hotel in Crieff or Pitlochry, and
we would look forward to going because we would train in the
mornings and then have the afternoons free for golf or some
fishing. It was no more exciting than that because we were
never taken to places famed for their nightlife.

On those trips, therefore, we had to amuse ourselves. Some players liked to play cards – but not as many as you might think, or even as many as nowadays. So we used to have a bit of a singsong in the evenings, and the old folk who would be staying in the same hotel as ourselves loved it. We would get round the piano and sing all their favourite songs. One or two of the guys were quite musical. Alex Hamilton played the piano, Hugh Robertson played the guitar, and a couple of the others could sing very well, and so we would stage an impromptu concert around that old piano, doing all the old-time songs as well as a few Beatles favourites.

As I said, the other people at the hotel would enjoy this immensely – and so did we. It was good fun and gave a great boost to our camaraderie and team spirit. I would like to think that it went a long way to helping Dundee to be successful on the pitch. After all, team harmony has often been the secret of many a club's successes. It is something that I have always tried to foster in my various roles as coach, club manager and national team manager. It has always been my objective to make sure that there is a good relationship amongst my players.

So, there we were singing our heads off each evening, until gradually it developed into six of us becoming a singing group. A local musician, a guy called Johnny Battersby – who had a sixteen-piece orchestra in the JM Ballroom in Dundee – asked us if we would go into the ballroom and sing as a special attraction. We thought it might be a bit of fun, and someone wrote a couple of songs for us. It was hardly the start of any threat to Frank Sinatra, but it was certainly the start of an interesting diversion.

Murdoch Wallace Junior was the local businessman who ran the JM Ballroom, and he was in the process of forming his very own recording company. The pop business was really booming at the time and Murdoch was keen to have his share. We were becoming quite well known for our singing group, led by Alex Hamilton, but, really, we only thought of it as another way of amusing ourselves. We had started by singing in the bath, then progressed to the hotel lounge, and now the JM Ballroom. We had no plans for going any further than that – but Murdoch Wallace had other ideas.

Alex involved Kenny Cameron, Alex Stuart, Andy Penman, Hugh Robertson and me. For engagements we wore the club blazer and a bow tie, but it was a bit of a mouthful to try to introduce us all individually and so we became known as Hammy and his Hamsters. The gigs came flooding in and we could probably have taken up many more offers but, after all, we were essentially professional footballers just out for a lark!

All this was developing in the 1963/64 season. By now we had lost Ian Ure, who had fallen out with the club. He had refused another contract and attempted to go on the dole, before being given a sales job by John Bloom, the famous washing-machine tycoon – who was a keen Arsenal fan – and eventually signing for the Gunners just after the start of the season for what was then a record Scottish fee of £62,500. We missed Ian on the pitch and also away from it because he was always a good leg-pull. In digs, we tormented him constantly.

He was a very clever guy with an excellent education record at Ayr Academy. He had a wealth of general knowledge and liked to tax his mind with crossword puzzles. Each night in digs we had a crossword competition. We would each get a copy of the Dundee Evening Telegraph and, starting the puzzle together before our evening meal, we would see who could complete it first – or who had filled in the most before our landlady called us down for the meal. Doug Houston, Tommy Mackle, George Ryden and I were the others involved, and of course Ian was always the best at it, so we hit on a scheme to wind him up a little bit. The four of us took to buying the early edition of the paper and getting the crossword mastered among ourselves – then we would go through the motions in the evening, taking it in turns to be the winner for the night. The big man, Ure, used to rage because we would keep an eye on him and, just as he was about to fill in the last answer, our 'winner' would say, 'Aye, that's me finished.'

Ian would jump up and shout, 'Och, ye so-and-so!' He got really mad about it. It was a long time before he realised the secret of our 'success'.

Another of our little games with Ian Ure was to tear a piece out of the sports pages of a newspaper that he didn't have and, when he asked us what it was, we would casually say, 'Oh, it was just a piece about you going to AC Milan or somewhere. We tore it out to give to you in case the paper was lost.' We would then discuss among ourselves what had been done with the cutting, each one saying that the other had put it for safe-keeping somewhere. Eventually one of us would go off to pretend to look for it, only to return with a shrug of the shoulders, apparently unable to find it. By this time the big man would be beside himself and would jump into his car and go off and tour the newsagents until he found a copy – only to discover that he had been conned again. He fell for that one only once. It is no reflection on his mentality that he did so – he was just far too trusting. We even used to get people to put on foreign accents and phone him, pretending to be from top foreign clubs like Juventus or Barcelona, and ask him if he would be interested in joining them. Yes, we certainly missed Ian Ure, who was a great guy and a wonderful defender for his clubs and his country.

Despite the loss of Ure and one or two other comings and goings, our season was going well. We recorded some very big scorelines and kept pace with the leaders, Kilmarnock and Rangers. Alan Gilzean was still finding the net regularly and, by the end of the season, he had broken Alan Stott's record League goals tally in a season, which had been standing for nearly twenty years. Gillie scored 52 in the League that season and we had some great results, including a 9–2 home win over St Mirren and a 6–1 victory over St Johnstone. We scored a total of 92 goals in 36 league matches and, had our defensive record been a little better, we would surely have finished higher than the sixth place we finally occupied at the end of the season.

The biggest excitement was probably in our Scottish Cup campaign. We began by knocking Forres Mechanics, a very good non-League side, out of the competition with a 6–3 away win. Next we were drawn to play Brechin City away and we beat them 9–2. Our third-round tie was against Falkirk, at home for once. We defeated them 6–1 and were thus in the quarterfinals, having scored 21 goals in three games. Motherwell were our opponents for the next round and they provided quite a test, holding us to a 1–1 draw at home. Four days later we played them again in the return match and beat them 4–1 at Fir Park.

The four semi finalists were Rangers, Kilmarnock (then managed by Willie Waddell), Dunfermline (who had Jock Stein in charge in those days) and us. Dundee were to play Kilmarnock on the neutral ground of Ibrox. A look at the scoreline now will tell you that Dundee won 4–0 – but that was not a true reflection of the game. The two sides were even in the first half and it was really only in the last quarter of the game that supremacy was gained by the Dark Blues.

April 25th was the Hampden date for Dundee to play Rangers in the final of the Scottish Cup, and the whole of Dundee was excited because it was the first final appearance for the club since 1952.

It was an exciting time for Hammy and his Hamsters too! Yes, while all that had been going on we were still making a name for ourselves. It was decided that we would record 'My Dream Came True' on the new JM Records label. The song was a romantic number and we were backed by the Johnny Battersby Showband, who provided a tasteful melody line. On the 'flip' side – you see I was even into the pop jargon – was a much more up-tempo number with a great beat. It was entitled 'She Was Mine'.

The recording session was held in a studio in Edinburgh and it took a lot of rehearsals and takes before we finally got it 'in the can'. Murdoch Wallace knew his way around the publicity machine and the record was given a lot of exposure –

especially since it was released just four days before the Scottish Cup Final. Although we were called Hammy and his Hamsters, everyone knew that we were Dundee players so, in a way, it was probably the start of the tradition of footballers recording songs before major events like cup finals, World Cups and so on.

It was a very busy time for us because there were the record promotional events as well as preparations for the Cup Final. Even on the day after the Cup Final – Sunday, 26 April – we were due to appear in a special show at Dundee's Green's Playhouse. Others in that show included Harry Douglas and the Deep River Boys, Stratford Johns, the actor, Eileen Keegan, compere Charlie Sim and the Johnny Battersby Showband. It was a great show and we enjoyed it – although we were not in the best mood for fun as Rangers had won the Scottish Cup by beating us 3–1. It was heartbreaking to see our opponents score twice in the last 90 seconds when it had looked as though a replay might be on the cards. The rain-soaked crowd of some 120,000 had enjoyed a thoroughly entertaining afternoon, and I don't think our side let their fans down in any way. A lapse of concentration at the very end proved to be fatal.

Some consolation was provided by the fact that our record sold well and, even though we were losers on the pitch and Rangers had completed a clean sweep of the championship and both major cups, we were not down-hearted, because Dundee was still there among the top clubs in the country. Besides, if all else failed, we knew we could earn a living busking on street corners!

Dundee was at that time a fine example of how a football club should be. I believe that it was the best footballing side I've ever known, and the harmony among the players was exactly how I like my teams to be. There were stars, but not one of them ever elevated himself above anyone else. Even those, like myself, almost permanently on the edge of the first-choice eleven were considered to be a part of the team. You expect that these days with substitutes and a squad mentality – but in those days it was much more rare, and a credit to the manager and his coaching team.

It would be remiss of me if I did not give a further mention to Gordon Smith, who was a hero of that side and a famous outside right who, as I said earlier, had already won the championship with both Hibs and Hearts before doing the same with Dundee. He was a terrific example of fitness, and of courtesy. Bearing in mind that he was the wrong side of his mid-thirties when he was performing for Dundee, he was truly outstanding in every respect.

Gordon was also very encouraging to the younger, less experienced players like me. When we were on that trip to Iceland he gave me a lot of tips to improve my game, but he also weighed in with one or two other items of advice. He once asked me what kind of shaver I used.

'I've got the very best kind of electric shaver,' he told me – and, indeed, he had a top-of-the-range Ronson which, I have to confess, I admired.

'Some day, when you've had a really good game, I'll buy you a Ronson like this,' he told me. I must admit that I didn't take him too seriously and soon forgot all about it. Some time later, we were playing alongside each other against Kilmarnock. He had the No. 7 shirt and I had the No. 6 – which meant that we were next to each other in the dressing room. It was quite a good game and I managed to give a reasonable account of myself. A few days later we were at home to Rangers. I arrived at the ground and went to my place in the dressing room. There at my seat was a box – and in it was a brand-new Ronson electric razor, together with a note that read simply, 'I thought you had an outstanding game last week.'

Gordon had not forgotten what he had promised, even though I had, and it was a magnificent gesture which was so typical of the man.

These were the halcyon years of Dundee and, in my

present job, the experience that I gained with that club at the time has proved to be invaluable. The European experience and the coaching, preparation and methods were an education to me that money would have been unable to buy. Yes, of course, I would have liked to have been one of the regular eleven who were constantly at the forefront of the manager's plans, but I was, after all, in the top fourteen, and therefore always involved in some way with everything – and I'm extremely grateful for that.

I was still teaching through those heady days as a Dundee 'star' and a 'pop icon', but I continued to have trouble with my knee. I decided, after I had been at the club for about six years, that I would pluck up the courage to ask the manager if I could go part-time officially. I explained that, with my knee still giving me problems, I was not expecting to have a very long playing span, and I wanted the insurance of my teaching career. He agreed with me and I was allowed to do my training with Hamilton Academicals. I continued to play for Dundee, but mostly as a reserve player with just the occasional first-team excursion. Meanwhile, I was gaining experience in my teaching work.

It was around 1965 when Falkirk, at the bottom of the First Division, made an approach for me. I talked to Bob Shankly, who was still Dundee manager, and asked for his advice, because I was due a benefit payment from the club. He looked me straight in the eye and said, 'Son, I'm getting the hell out of here – and I would advise you to do the same!'

I think he had fallen out with the chairman by this time, but I took his advice and agreed to join Falkirk. I had been the first signing that Bob Shankly had made when he joined Dundee, and I was his last transfer away from the club before he left. It was the end of a great time for the club and for me personally.

The deal went through and I did get my benefit payment, plus a little bit, which enabled me to buy a new car and still have some left over. I was also pleased to hear that Doug

Baillie, with whom I had been at Rangers, was also joining Falkirk from Third Lanark the same week.

As I said, Falkirk were bottom of the table when we joined, but we managed to get some good results in the last weeks of the season and successfully steered the club to the safety zone away from the threat of relegation. I had been nursing my knee and disguising the fact that I was really only performing on one leg. I had been playing as sweeper, and I enjoyed myself because I found it a simple position in which to play.

Our last home game of the season was particularly memorable because we were visited by Celtic, and we delighted the Brockville Park crowd by beating them 6–2. It was an important end to the season for us because the club wanted to show its supporters how much it appreciated their loyalty when relegation was looking to be a certainty. There is no better way to send a crowd home happy than to give one of the biggest clubs in the game a real thumping.

I had three managers while I was at Falkirk. The man who signed me was Alec McCrae, and then he was sacked and replaced by Sammy Kean. That was bad news for me because Sammy had been the trainer at Dundee and, while there was no problem between us on a personal basis, he knew all about my injury problems. I remember that when we turned up for pre-season training, our coach – the excellent Willie Ormond – brought him into the dressing room to introduce us. We were all sitting around in our brand-new tracksuits and I was the first person that he clapped his eyes on.

With no hesitation, Sammy borrowed Bob Shankly's name for me and said, 'Christ Craig, you're not a full-timer, are you?'

I replied, 'No, boss, I'm only here during my school holidays.'

He said, 'Thank Christ for that!'

The players all laughed, and they knew that I wasn't going to figure too prominently in the forthcoming team selections.

To be fair, Sammy was not an unreasonable man and I did get into the side. Unfortunately, he was later sacked and replaced by a well-known manager called John Prentice – one-time Scotland manager.

John Prentice had been an impressive manager in his day and was actually in the Falkirk side that won the Scottish Cup in 1957, so you can imagine that he was a very popular manager for the club. He had a tremendous knowledge of the game and the respect of everyone. By the time he arrived I was really struggling and spending nearly all my time with the second team. In fact, in the programme notes for first-team games, references to me usually said something like, 'Craig Brown, the "Auld Heid", is doing a great job in the reserves.'

I was still only in my mid-twenties but I was already classed as an 'Auld Heid'! I was captain of the reserves but I was still struggling, and it was quite good news for me that substitutes were to be allowed for the first time. I was now able to start a game and then, when I could not go on any longer, I would put up my hand and my replacement would be prepared to take over. Before the advent of substitutes I would either have not been able to play or been something of a lame duck during the latter part of the game. If substitutes had been allowed some years earlier, my playing career might have lasted much longer.

I had another knee operation when I was at Falkirk which slowed me down again – and then came the moment that every player dreads. I was told that I was being freed by the club. I was very disappointed that the news was given to me by Gibby Ormond, the reserves' coach and brother of Willie. He handed me an envelope. Inside was a letter that said that my services were no longer required.

It hurt that the manager had not told me face to face, and I learned another lesson. Having suffered the ignominy of being given a free transfer, I would never do the same to someone else without talking to him in a direct fashion, face to face, man to man! The letter I received was just a brief note thanking me for my services, which were no longer required. It went on to tell me to make sure that I only took one pair of boots with me! The letter came after a reserve game against Rangers at Ibrox, and I did feel that I had been treated rather badly. It wasn't the matter of being freed, but the manner in which it was done. I have never knowingly treated any player in my charge in such a fashion, and I never will.

So, Falkirk didn't want me any more. I thought long and hard about my situation and decided that my playing career was over. The knee was still playing me up and I felt that I was enjoying my teaching career enough to be able to turn my back on the game as a professional footballer. While at school I was coaching youngsters and so I was still involved in a very pleasant aspect of the game – giving tips to boys who might well turn out to be the stars of tomorrow.

It turned out that my playing days were not entirely over, however, when I had a surprise approach from Stranraer Football Club. They asked if I would be interested in trying to resurrect my career. I thought about it again and decided to have a go. I received a small signing fee and turned up for work. I started to train at Shawfield Stadium, the home of Clyde, where the physiotherapist was Lawrie Smith, who had been the first person to identify my knee problem when I was at Dundee. Lawrie was now at Clyde where the manager was Davie White, who later went on to manage Rangers.

So I trained at Clyde and began my Stranraer career with a friendly match against Larne, the Irish team. I was delighted, because I found that football at that level was very comfortable and I had high hopes of a good season with Stranraer. I should have known that it was all too good to be true. During training I received yet another knee injury, and I went to the Law Hospital in Carluke where I saw the surgeon, Mr Garden. He was a top man who knew his job, and he gave my knee a thorough examination, inside and out. Finally he came and talked to me with a very serious expression on his face. I could feel the tension rising within me as I waited to hear the result of the exploratory operation.

'I'm sorry, Craig, but your knee is a mess. It will not withstand any more wear and tear – and it is arthritic. I have cleaned it up the best I can but you have a condition known as exostosis, a bone problem. The truth is, you will have to give up playing.'

I swallowed hard. I had been expecting something like this but it was still painful to hear. Was that it? Never again to be able to kick a ball in anger? It was a bitter blow, but I knew that there was no point in arguing. The medical facts were evidence enough that my playing career was over – this time for good. I did not dwell on feeling sorry for myself. I felt bad for Stranraer. It was now August 1967 and the season was underway. They had paid me a signing-on fee and had started to pay wages. I felt that I had given nothing in return, and I well knew that for clubs like Stranraer there was a constant financial struggle. They had been good enough to offer me the chance of getting my career back together and it had not worked out. I knew they needed every bit of cash they could muster, and that was why I spontaneously paid back all they had given me. I felt that it was wrong for them to be out of pocket for something that was not their fault. For me, it was bad enough being told that I would never play again, but I would have found it very difficult to live with myself if I had gone out of football with the feeling that I had taken money under false pretences from such a friendly club as Stranraer.

Unlike many players, I had no need to worry about where the next penny was coming from or, indeed, what to do with my time. I would now have more time to devote to the teaching profession. While undergoing various courses during my Dundee days, I also attained my Scottish FA coaching certificates, my preliminary badge and my 'A' licence badge at Inverclyde, Largs, so I was already qualified enough for professional coaching had I chosen to pursue this option. If I might just give a bit of advice to today's players, it is a good idea to take your coaching certificates while you are still playing, because you have both the time and the money to invest in your future. In Scotland, the Professional Footballers' Association, whose dedicated secretary is Tony Higgins, is a big help, because it contributes two-thirds of the cost, which I believe is a very generous way of giving players extra options when they find it is time to be hanging up their boots.

I could name many among today's top football management and coaching staff who took the trouble to take their coaching courses quite early on in their playing careers. Men like Sir Alex Ferguson, Alex Miller, Walter Smith, Archie Knox, Jim McLean, Alex Smith, Jimmy Bone, Tommy McLean, Murdo MacLeod, Alex McLeish, Andy Watson, Tommy Burns, Paul Sturrock, Billy Davies, Sandy Clark, Billy Kirkwood, Jimmy Nichol, Donald Park, Tom Hendrie, Gordon Strachan, Willie Miller, Mark McGhee, Dave Moyes, Roy Aitken, Craig Levein John Blackley, Terry Christie, Jim Leishman, Bobby Williamson, Billy Stark, the Late and Alex Wright and Wilson Humphries. Some of today's younger managers have followed the same pattern, planning well ahead for a continuation of their football careers. We are very proud in Scotland that virtually all the managers in senior football have taken their coaching courses at Largs and hold the 'A' or 'B' badges of the SFA. We encourage that, and we are also moving on to the higher course for a European pro licence which is co-ordinated by UEFA. It is a very good course at Largs, and we continue to promote it, both for the good of Scottish football and for the good of those players and others who want to coach at the highest possible standard.

For me, the summer of 1967 proved to be the twilight of my playing career. I had my championship medal, my youth and school caps, and many adventures and experiences to treasure. Now, it seemed, I was destined to be a schoolteacher who used to play football.

7

What the Doctor Ordered

THERE IS NO prescription for football. It was 1969, my professional interest in football was over and I was happily continuing my role as primary and PE teacher when I was invited to join the coaching team at Largs by Roy Small, who was running the courses there. I was asked along with my present colleague, Frank Coulston, who was – and still is – an excellent coach. The staff at Largs included Eddie Turnbull, Aberdeen manager, Jimmy Bonthrone, who was then at East Fife, Wilson Humphries, then at St Mirren, Archie Robertson, the manager of Clyde, Willie Ormond, then in charge at St Johnstone, and Peter Rice, who was a former player with Hibs and became a lecturer at St Andrew's College.

All those men I have just mentioned have been fine coaches in their own right. Everyone has different ideas – which is why I maintain that there is no prescription for football. It is something that I have kept in mind since then. I have had it as a belief throughout my coaching career. You have a philosophy of football that suits you and you stick to it. It is totally wrong to criticise someone else's beliefs because what might work for one coach may not work for another – and vice versa! Flexibility has to be a highly important factor – you cannot be hide-bound to one system, one set of rules for set pieces in attack or defence.

All this was brought home to me once when I had a minor disagreement with the late Peter Rice, who was in charge of the course at this particular time. Peter had been No. 2 to Roy Small and, as Roy was away at this time, Peter was in charge. I was watching one of my coaches taking an excellent session. He was Eddie Thomson who later became coach of Australia after he had finished playing for Hearts and Aberdeen. Eddie was very successful with Australia and gave them a much higher profile on the international scene than they had previously had. When he left the job he became a coach in the J League. I have often wanted to be a fly on the wall at one of his sessions, just to see how the Japanese and other nationalities coped with his team talks. The last time I saw him they were still being delivered in one of the most pronounced Edinburgh accents you could ever wish to hear – I sometimes had difficulty in understanding him myself!

Eddie was coaching the use of a sweeper behind a back four. Peter came along and said, 'What's he doing, Craig?'

'Well, you can see what he's doing, Peter,' I replied.

'Surely he's not using a sweeper behind the back four?'

'He certainly is,' I responded.

'Well, you never do that!' Peter said.

I rose to defend Eddie's right to try his own methods. 'I think that's a bit of a sweeping statement, Peter.' One thing led to another and Peter and I disagreed over it. Eddie's idea was unusual but it was working for him – and it has since worked for Willie McLean and me when I was assistant manager at Motherwell. If we had a tricky away match we would use Eddie's system to good effect. Peter felt that Eddie should fail his exam because it was an unrealistic system – but I strongly disagreed.

In the end, Eddie completed an excellent session and I

passed him. Later, both Frank Coulston and I were dropped from the coaching staff at Largs. I think it was a direct result of my disagreeing with Peter, who said that he was going to use a pool of coaches instead of having the same people involved all the time. I don't think anyone has been dropped since then, so I think I am probably correct in my assertion that it was all down to my backing Eddie.

I am sure that Peter, fine coach though he was, felt that there was a prescription for football and that if you used a sweeper it had to be behind a two- or three-man defence, and adopting any other system was unthinkable. Since then I have always kept an open mind while doing my own coaching thing. I have my own thoughts and systems but I am always prepared to have any aspect of my knowledge of the game improved by sensible suggestions. There is no set formula for anything, whether you are scoring goals or stopping them, and I defy anyone to show me a long-term success story involving anybody who is not prepared to adapt, adopt and try to improve.

While I was adding to my coaching experience I was working tirelessly with school and youth teams as well. I was also working to further my teaching career. When I finished my professional playing, the Open University was starting up and so I took a degree through that medium. I had been taking course after course for some time in my thirst for knowledge and qualifications, but there always seems to be a stigma attached to the role of a PE teacher – everyone thinks that you are an ignorant acrobat! People don't seem to realise that the academic qualifications needed to get into a PE teaching course were a lot more stringent than those needed for a primary teaching course in those days. I knew from my father's experience that qualifications were of the utmost importance if you were going to have a good career in teaching and, as with everything else, I did not see the point in getting involved with anything unless it was with a full commitment.

I thought I'd better get some academic respectability, so I

took a BA degree through the Open University. I also did some additional courses that were relevant to my job – courses such as the development of reading, geography, and so on. Studying was becoming something of a hobby for me. I was really enjoying it and it provided me with something totally different from my PE and football coaching – which were taking up most of my time, of course.

As a result of all this – and possibly also because there was a shortage of teachers in Lanarkshire where I was working – I became deputy head teacher in Bellshill. Things seemed to move quite quickly because not long after that I became, for a short time, a head teacher in Uddingston, and then later applied for a post as lecturer at the Craigie College of Education in Ayr, now the Craigie Campus of Paisley University.

This prompted a move from my home in Hamilton where I had lived since I was married to Johan at the age of 24. So we moved to Prestwick and started a new kind of life in Ayrshire. My relationship with football was still continuing with me managing and coaching football teams. This early experience has proved invaluable to me in my current job as the Director of Football Development for the Scottish Football Association. For example, when I was at the Macalpine School in Dundee, while I was still playing, I ran three teams, which was quite an undertaking. I did get help from some of my Dundee playing colleagues, in particular from Terry Christie, who is now manager of Alloa Athletic Football Club and also rector of Musselburgh Grammar School. Doug Houston, my room-mate in digs, Ian Ure and Tommy Mackle all helped me with the school, so I had my own coaching team even in those days. I was determined to give as many youngsters as possible a taste of the enjoyment of playing football.

I often wish that I had known and realised the value then of the seven-a-side games and mini-festivals that we now encourage youngsters to play. In those days it was all eleven-a-side games. In the playground little has changed. The youngsters still like to be identified with their favourite teams and players, just as they did when I was a schoolboy myself. Lads love to get the chance to wear their team's shirt – and that means the school shirt as well as their favourite club's.

Today, we at the Scottish Football Association want everyone, girls as well as boys, to take part in small-sided football while they are still under twelve, as we feel that it is a much better introduction to the game during those developing years. We also promote mixed soccer because the game is such a good recreation for everyone. Women's football in Scotland, inspired by our Dutch national coach, Vera Pauw, who, as well as being an accomplished coach, played 87 times for her country, is really taking off, and we have no wish to do anything other than encourage it in Scotland. Just as in men's football, you cannot be too young to learn the basics of how to kick a ball and to get some healthy exercise from doing it at the same time.

During my teaching days in Dundee, the rivalry between the two local sides – Dundee and Dundee United – was as keen as ever and, in the classroom after a local derby, there was much banter between the supporters of the two sides. In those days Dundee was the stronger and more successful of the two sides but, in recent years, the pendulum has swung the other way – mostly because of the great effort put in by Jim McLean, and recently by Alex Smith.

I can remember walking along the corridor at the Macalpine School on one occasion. I was talking to another teacher, Bill Young, at the time, when a parent appeared at the end of the corridor. He looked at me and said, 'Are you Craig Brown?'

I thought that he was about to congratulate me on our team's performance the day before, so I smiled and said, 'Yes, that's me.' With that this huge guy hit me with a right uppercut and down I went. I was pretty fit and not short of aggression myself in those days, but he had taken me by surprise. I didn't leave it at that, though. I caught hold of him, wrestled him to the ground and started to repay the 'compliment' – which meant that quite a nasty fight ensued in the foyer of the school. By this time the head teacher had arrived on the scene along with all the cleaners and various other people.

The head teacher, Mr Baxter, told the man that if he wanted to interview any of his staff he should see him first. The man told the head teacher exactly what he thought of him and then threw him along the corridor. Once again chaos broke out until we were able to restrain the man. It transpired that he was the father of a boy to whom I had administered some corporal punishment earlier in the day. I had caught the boy hitting another lad across the face with the end of a climbing rope when they were supposed to be packing away the PE equipment, so I dealt him the appropriate punishment of the time – the belt!

It was a measure of my inexperience that I had punished the boy at the end of the day. It was the first time I had administered the belt, which was an acceptable part of school life in those days. The boy went home with his hand stinging. His father had been working in the fields collecting potatoes, casual work which was common in the area at the time. The workers were paid cash in hand at the end of the day and invariably spent it much more quickly than they had earned it, with the local hostelries proving to be the ultimate winners.

By the time this guy had met his son he was already half cut and, when he heard that it was Craig Brown who had punished his lad, it was like a red rag to a bull – because this guy was a Dundee United supporter and there was no way that he was going to let a Dundee player get away with such a thing. Along he came to remonstrate with me. Eventually he managed to struggle free and started to run away, all the time pointing at me and shouting, 'I've not finished with you.'

I had to report the matter to my manager, Bob Shankly. He listened patiently while I told him the story, then he took a long, hard look at the bruise under my eye.

'Is that what he did to you, son?'

'Yes, boss, I wasn't expecting it,' I replied.

'What did you do to him? I'll tell you this – nobody messes with any of my players like that!'

His concern was not for the ignominy that might be brought upon the club by the incident but the fact that one of his players at least gave as good as he got. That was the Shankly philosophy. The whole episode was soon forgotten and I heard no more about it until months later when I went into my digs one day and one of my teammates was reading the evening newspaper. The headlines read 'Dundee Player Assaulted'. It was Ian Ure, the avid newspaper reader, who was sitting with the paper, so I asked, 'Who's that, Ian?'

He laughed and replied, 'It's you!'

The story was all about the court case that had followed the incident. Because the guy had pleaded guilty I had not been called to give evidence – in fact, I didn't even know that there was to be court action. He was fined £10 – a significant figure because it comprised £6 for hitting Mr Baxter, the head teacher, and £4 for assaulting me. It wasn't the severity of the assault which counted, it was the rank of the person who had been attacked!

The following Saturday we were playing St Mirren and I was fouled by one of their players. As I was getting up from the ground I heard a voice in the enclosure shout, 'Go on, Brown, get your strap out!' The supporters never miss a trick!

It didn't do me any harm in the educational world because, in those days, corporal punishment was the accepted thing and, although I didn't condone it, I followed instructions and, on that particular occasion – as well as on very rare others – I used it, albeit very sparingly.

My time as a teacher, and in particular at the Macalpine School, taught me a lot about the great enthusiasm in Scotland for playing games and for football. When I moved to Lanarkshire I also ran the school teams. At Blantyre I had a very good football team, and also a very fine gymnastics display team of which I was very proud. Our main rivals were

envious of our facilities and the way we were turned out for all
our sporting activities – a reflection on our head teacher, who
was not only a great educationalist but also extremely keen on
the recreational aspects of school life. His name was Mr David
Crawford, a wonderful man who died early in 2001. With him
and our janitor, Mr John Baird, I had two very strong allies in
providing the best for the youngsters at the school. We tried to
encourage them in sport as well as in every aspect of
education.

I must have had a charmed life as a teacher because when
I went to Bellshill, to the Belvedere School, I had enthusiastic
support from the head teacher and the rest of the staff. We
excelled in football, swimming and gymnastics and had some
great individuals. One of my pupils at that primary school was
not only in my football team but also in the class of which I
was appointed teacher. He went on to become a top player and
in 1979 was named Scottish Footballer of the Year. You know
him as Andy Ritchie, and his career spanned Celtic, Greenock
Morton and eventually Motherwell. He was impressive even as
a boy – a very big lad who was obviously destined for an
exciting career in football.

Andy Ritchie was a prime example of the argument
against eleven-a-side football on big pitches for young kids.
All Andy had to do was to get into the opponent's half and
shoot. Because of his size, and the size of the goalmouth when
compared to the lack of size of the goalkeeper, he would grab
a handful of goals every time he played. You could get a
jumbo jet to fly under the crossbar and over the young
goalkeeper's head, and Andy soon learned where to place his
shot. He was a prized asset to us because he could score so
easily but, because his size and ability gave him such an
advantage over other boys of his own age, he effectively
ruined the game each time he played. It wasn't his fault, but it
did show how inappropriate it was to have eleven-a-side
matches in that primary age group. I tried to even the games a
little by making arbitrary rules such as that he could only score

with his head one day, or from outside the area on another. It succeeded in evening up the games and hopefully furthered his football education too.

While at Blantyre, I also ran the local Hamilton district schools side along with the local priest, Father Glachan. Between us we had the privilege of selecting the best boys from the local schools – and it would have been totally enjoyable but for the various parents who continually tried to influence our selection. The best example of this is provided in a series of award-winning short stories written by William McIlvanney. He wrote about the single parent watching her son playing football. Whereas the rest of the 21 players appear merely as a blur to that parent, her son remains in sharp focus throughout.

Because I was so busy with my school coaching, I gave up coaching seniors for a while, but I was still remembered in Dundee as being a player and a coach, and also as being semi-literate. As a result, DC Thomson, the well-known publishing company based in Dundee, got in touch with me with a view to my writing a column. They produced all manner of newspapers and magazines, ranging from the Sunday Post and other newspapers to the Weekly News, the Topical Times, the Beano and miscellaneous women's and children's publications and assorted journals.

I was asked if I would comment on one of the matches of the previous weekend every Monday in the Dundee Courier, and I was delighted to do so. Then I was asked if I would write actual match reports for the Sunday Post. I was no longer playing at this time, and I was thrilled to be involved in the game from a completely different angle. So, for the next eighteen months, I was a regular in the press box. It taught me a great deal. I was sometimes given one of the top games, but I was always getting First Division matches – remember that there was no Premier Division in those days.

Once again, I consider this period as part of my education. I was able to listen to the comments of the press men and join in with their discussions, which gave me a great insight into the way the press viewed things. As well as commenting on the match I used to write the introduction to the piece and learned that you have to make it brief, to the point, and interesting enough for the reader to continue through to the match report, rather than just flash-read the scorers. I quickly learned the value of those people who write the actual headlines in the newspapers.

Usually, your introduction is something that you think up during the second half of the game when you can see how the match is going. You may already have been given your introduction by goals, sendings-off or injuries. I was once at a game between Airdrie and Aberdeen and it was, arguably, the worst game of all time. It was 0–0 with a minute to go and I had been struggling to dream up my intro before finally settling on resorting to William Shakespeare and his famous work, Much Ado About Nothing. I had branded the game a bore with nothing to say for itself.

Not long before the final whistle, Drew Jarvie scored to break the deadlock – but my intro still held because the rest of the game was totally forgettable. I just added that Jarvie of Airdrie popped up to give us the only bright spot of the whole game. It was then that I realised the importance of those headline writers because, when the report appeared in the Sunday Post, the heading read 'Jarvie – Merchant of Menace' – totally in keeping with my Shakespearean intro.

I have often been amused by – or admired – newspaper headlines since then, although there have been times when I have been disgusted by the inaccuracies or innuendo contained in stories that are way off the mark – or headlines that are meant to sensationalise the unsensational.

Anyway, I learned the ways of the press box. I would hear the late John Begg, the famous freelance writer, say, 'Who scored? Left leg or right leg? Who passed it to him? What time was that?' It wasn't that he didn't watch the game, but he would be so busy telephoning constant reports to seven or eight newspapers that he didn't have time for the details. The other reporters would shout him the answers to his questions. When a goal is scored these questions are usually flying around the press box so that everyone is in agreement – even if they all have it wrong! Nowadays there is more factual reporting because of TV monitors at most big games. I found also that it was easy to influence the reports if you just made a chance remark to someone near the end of a game. As an example, I might say, 'Doug Houston is having some game for Dundee today. Some of his passes have been great.' If you say it at the right time, when the reporters are considering which players have done well, you will almost certainly read the next day that the player you were touting 'put on a great performance'.

Most managers co-operate with the press – but not all. I can remember being asked to get a statement on injuries from one manager who was fairly new to that particular job, and whose side was playing in Europe a few days later. I waited for an hour and ten minutes after the game only to be told to 'F*** off' by the manager when I asked him if he had any injury worries. He didn't know who I was, and really it would have made no difference if he had. There is no need for anyone to be uncivil – after all, we all have a job to do. I made up my mind, then and there, that if ever I was in a similar situation I would not speak in that manner to any journalist who was just trying to do his job. As far as I am aware, I never have.

To get back to my job at the college in Ayr, part of my role in lecturing on primary education was to watch students teaching in schools. It meant that I was out quite a bit, and when you add to that all the work I was doing with football teams, it doesn't take a genius to see that I was not at home very much. We had long holidays from the college, but I spent most of those involved in football coaching at some level or another. There was a lot of hard work done, but at various times of the year I would have a month off, which gave me the freedom to still be involved in football almost as a full-time occupation.

I have always liked to be busy all the time. I can't stand having nothing to do. It was no different in my teaching days – or even in my childhood. If I wasn't actively doing something, then I had to be thinking about things. During my time at Craigie College in Ayr, I would involve myself in football and golf – as well as catching up with all the latest paperwork and guidelines involved in my teaching profession. If there was an evening when I found that I was free I would have a game of golf – or dream up some new coaching idea to try out when next I got the chance.

The doctor had ordered me to stop playing football and I had done exactly as I had been told. I did not even take part in any of the training games I organised as part of the coaching work. If I kicked a ball at all, it was to demonstrate a point or just to pass it to someone who needed it for an exercise. I kept myself fit by taking part in the training and indulging myself in a bit of golf or swimming.

For all that, I could not stop thinking about the game. I was not bitter about the way my career had ended, and I was certainly grateful for the successes I had enjoyed during my all-too-short playing years, but it was frustrating not to be involved at the highest level of the game. I felt that I'd had something to offer and had been denied the chance of finding out whether or not I was right.

I had done what the doctor ordered and that was that. But then came the day when I was asked if I would like to become part-time assistant to Willie McLean, who was then manager of Motherwell, having taken over from Ian St John.

Would I?

Now, that really was just what the doctor ordered!

8

Back in the Game

I KNEW WILLIE McLean from the days before he took over at Motherwell. He was a very successful manager at Queen of the South in Dumfries where I also turned up as education lecturer to supervise overspill students in their training practice in Dumfries. Willie had collected some very good players at Queen of the South, talented and tough guys who gave him a well-balanced side. As an example he had Alan Ball in goal, Billy McLaren, Ian McChesney, John Murray and Rab Thorburn – who was later to become a player and my assistant at Clyde. Willie had a flat in Dumfries and I was staying in a hotel in the town, and we used to meet up and have long chats about football. I was delighted to discover that we were on the same wavelength, and I used to enjoy taking time out to go and watch his training sessions with Queen of the South, as well as seeing mid-week matches.

When Willie invited me to become his assistant, I didn't hesitate. He knew all about my commitment to my career in education but, as it happened, I was well able to fit in all that he required of me. The advantage of those long holidays was that I had plenty of time available during the period that was the all-important pre-season training time. From December to January I also had a full month off, and then again around Easter, which was the crucial run-in time to the football season, I had another full month in which to concentrate totally on my work with Motherwell.

Suddenly I had two full-time jobs again, and I was closely involved with one of the top teams in Scotland. It did not do a lot for my home life as I was always going out early in the morning and not returning until very late. My family knew where I was, but I don't suppose that was much consolation really.

On the plus side, I was able to work closely with Willie McLean and learn a great deal from him. We would sit and discuss training schedules, tactical techniques and all kinds of aspects of running a football team. There has never been a harder-working manager than Willie McLean, and his enthusiasm and drive were certainly an inspiration to anyone who came into contact with him – myself included. When I was not available he would take care of just about everything – including the reserves, who were my concern really.

With my education work and my football work, I found myself involved in three training sessions a day, morning, afternoon and evening – which, of course, is why I spent so much time away from home. I believe that it was the making of me as a potential manager because I had to follow Willie's example – there was no other way. We inherited a big squad of players, full-timers, of whom many were never seriously going to be first team-regulars – but everyone had to be treated the same. We had to spend a great deal of time looking at training and coaching innovations to keep so many players interested and motivated all the time.

You can imagine that the bulk of my reserve squad were disgruntled guys who were full-time on full-time pay, but with the knowledge that they would be unlikely to see any first-team action. They were experienced professionals and it would have been advantageous to have sold them – but they had to be seen to be sold, and that made it all something of a vicious circle. We could not afford to use the first team as a shop window, and reserve-team football is not exactly the most flattering scenario for a player that you are hoping to sell for a decent fee.

It was certainly a trying, and yet also an enlightening and instructive, time for me at Motherwell. Willie did very well for the club. He was a master of coaching, tactical awareness and man management – although I have to say that his man management skills did not extend to the directors of the club, the carpark attendants, the ball-boys, tea ladies or any of the other backroom people. Willie's efforts were focused exclusively on his players and immediate coaching staff. The players responded by always listening and exactly following the instructions given by Willie. Nobody ever formed the opinion that they knew better than he did.

I learned more from Willie McLean than I have ever learned from any other manager, either before or since.

We had a good, hard side at Motherwell in those days. When Willie took over the team they were not in a good situation. It was the very last season of the old two-division system and, if you did not finish among the top ten of the First Division, you would not be in the new-look Premier Division, which was due to commence in August 1976. I think we were around fifteenth when the new management regime took over. The emergence of Stewart MacLaren, Gregor Stevens and Willie Pettigrew from the reserves about halfway through the season transformed the side. Pettigrew ended the season as top scorer with 20 League goals in 28 games – seven of which were as substitute. We finished in tenth place and assured ourselves of Premier League football the following season.

That inaugural season of the Premier Division was an exciting one because there was the novelty of having to pit your wits against the top clubs four times in a season instead of the customary twice. Our opening League match was against my local side, Ayr. The game ended as a cagey 1–1 draw, and that was the pattern for our first five games, each one ending in a draw. We lost our sixth game at St Johnstone 2–1, but that was probably a blessing in disguise because thereafter we won and set ourselves up for quite a decent season, finishing fourth at the end of the campaign. One of my favourite results was a 6–3 win at Dundee, although beating Dundee United three times out of four and drawing the other game against them was also a bit of fun for me.

We also reached the semi-final of the Scottish Cup after knocking out Jock Stein's Celtic, Cowdenbeath and Hibs on the way. Rangers were our opponents at the last hurdle, with the game to be played at Hampden Park. They beat us 3–2 and went on to win in the final against Hearts, but we gave a good account of ourselves. It was an Alex Miller penalty which proved to be the one goal too many for us.

That semi final match of March 1977 still leaves a bad taste in my mouth, even after all these years. It was not just the penalty. We were two goals ahead at half-time and should have been home and dry, but the penalty decision knocked the stuffing out of us. It was what is politely called 'a harsh decision' – but there are other words to describe it. In the last twenty minutes we had gone from being 2–0 ahead, and cruising to the final, to losing 3–2. We left the pitch feeling totally shellshocked. I don't think that Rangers were helped by divine intervention, but I do feel that they had more than eleven players on their side.

The following season we met Rangers in the quarter finals of that same competition and this time they beat us 2–0 at Ibrox – although they themselves lost 1–0 in the final against Celtic. In the League, our away record let us down because we only had two wins away from home – both against Hibs. We were pretty solid at Fir Park, though, and suffered only two defeats.

Those early days at Motherwell were made all the more interesting because there was a compensation battle going on between the club and Portsmouth, who were due to pay something for the signing of Ian St John as their manager. Motherwell had not wanted to lose him and there followed a disagreement between the two clubs that dragged on for some time. The Motherwell chairman, a lawyer by the name of Ian Livingstone, a fine gentleman, kept us informed of the situation, and it finally transpired that Portsmouth could not afford to pay the compensation and, instead, offered any player on their staff in exchange for Ian St John.

The upshot was that I made several trips to Portsmouth to watch them and see if they had any player who might do a job for us. I believe that the compensation finally agreed was to the value of £30,000, although it was never confirmed. It was a fair amount of money in the mid-seventies, so I had to be sure that we were not going to be sold short.

Portsmouth had one or two decent players, but the only one that I thought might be any use to us was Peter Marinello. Now Peter had been with Hibernian until he was sold to Arsenal for £100,000 – a goodly sum in those days. Peter had been described as the 'new George Best', but, though he certainly had both the looks and the football skills, there was no way that he – or anyone else – could have stepped into the shoes of the world-class Best. I'm sure that the pressures of trying to live up to such an image did no favours at all for Peter Marinello and contributed to his being transferred from Arsenal to Portsmouth and being now at our disposal if we wanted him.

I reported back to Willie and the decision was taken to sign him. I found him to be a very nice guy, but he had some basic faults that several coaches at his different clubs had tried to remedy without success. One was that he would not remain wide to use the full width of the pitch. He would cut in far too quickly instead of staying out on the left wing as long as possible. Both Willie McLean and I used to get on to him about it, and he told us that Don Howe, his coach at Arsenal, used to say the very same thing to him. It was not deliberate awkwardness, just a bad habit of straying into the pitch and not being available in the open spaces on the wing. We warned him that if he played from the inside he was making himself a sitting duck for opposing defenders to clatter him.

Peter Marinello's other problem was that he could not cross a ball properly. He had great pace and he could take on and beat anyone at will with his obvious ball skills, but his final touch was poor, and so Willie McLean devised a simple exercise to help him. We would put a cone, or marker, a little way in from the corner of the pitch and Peter would practise running towards it and then putting the ball inside it before making his cross. It changed the whole angle of his last touch to 45 degrees and gave him a much better chance of putting in a good cross than if he was trying to put the ball over from paralell to the touchline. Willie had a very perceptive eye for football, and that simple measure certainly helped Peter Marinello. Some time later, when I was at Clyde, I used the same method to help Pat Nevin, and it is a tribute to Willie McLean that it helped Pat, and other players too.

Another memory of that period was our Scottish Cup fourth-round tie against St Mirren in February 1977. Alex Ferguson was manager of St Mirren then, and they were running away with the new First Division. For their visit to Fir Park they brought most of Paisley and, of course, Fergie was his usual self, intimidating everyone and confident of what he was going to do. We wound up our own players into battling mood with key St Mirren players like Frank McGarvey, Tony Fitzpatrick, Billy Stark and Bobby Torrance all delegated for special attention – which, I can assure you, they got. The St Mirren players didn't relish it and we beat them 2–1 – much to the annoyance of Mr Ferguson.

It is worth pointing out that Fergie did take St Mirren to the championship of the First Division that season, and thus gained promotion to the Premiership, so no doubt his famous scowl did not stay in place for long. Certainly Alex is another of those managers for whom the word 'defeat' is only applicable to other managers and their clubs. His track record speaks for itself, and is a reflection of his rugged determination always to have things his own way.

Of course, Willie McLean was delighted with that St Mirren result, and it was interesting to see the two faces of management – Willie with a grin from ear to ear, and Fergie with his grimace. I have always learned a great deal from managers and how they handle things, whether success or failure. Bob Shankly at Dundee, for instance, was very similar to his brother Bill. He never contemplated defeat – it did not exist in his mind, let alone his vocabulary. When it happened he rarely spent much time thinking about it but much preferred to move on to the next challenge.

A tip for any of today's players who might one day want to go into coaching or management – keep watching the guys who are in charge of you now. I learned from every person who ever took me for a training session or who was my manager. I didn't agree with everything, but the more you observe, the more characteristics you pick up, then the more experience you have to draw on when it becomes your turn in the driving seat. I would never presume to know all the answers, but I have certainly benefited from making a study of all the managers I have ever had the privilege of knowing. Another method of gaining insight vicariously is by reading autobiographies – maybe this one excepted!

At Motherwell, we had a groundsman, sadly deceased, who was famous for being one of the greatest characters in the game at that time. Andy Russell was his name, and there are many stories about him – most of which are true. One of my own experiences occurred the night that Celtic came visiting towards the end of the season when they were chasing their ninth consecutive championship. I remember it very well as it was a Wednesday night, and few people doubted that Celtic would clinch the title – probably on that very evening. Motherwell, of course, had other ideas.

Jock Stein arrived with his entourage of superstar players,

looking every bit the reigning kings of Scottish football. One of the first people Jock bumped into was Andy Russell, and he said to him, 'Well, Andy, and what's your park like tonight?'

Our groundsman answered in a fairly provocative manner: 'G'd enough for what's goin' on to it!' There was no way he was going to be fazed by the big boys from Glasgow.

Jock didn't really appreciate that reply but he was not going to let it spoil the party. We didn't know it at the time, but he had brought some bottles of champagne with him in readiness for the after-match celebrations. Celtic went into their dressing room and Andy Russell watched as their gear was being unloaded. It was then that he spotted the bottles of champagne and hurried down to the Motherwell dressing room where Willie was giving his pre-match talk. Willie hated being interrupted at this stage, but Andy insisted that it was urgent and so the manager broke his own rule and allowed him to deliver his message.

'Jock's got six bottles of champagne in there!' he revealed.

'Oh, he has, has he?' Willie turned to his players. 'There's no way he's drinking his champagne here at Motherwell!'

It was quite a game and we put three goals past them. Two of those goals, in fairness, were own goals by Celtic's Andy Lynch, but we still deserved the victory and, as the players trooped off down the tunnel at the end, Andy said to Jock, 'What are you going to do with your champagne now, Big Man?'

It didn't help the mood that Jock Stein was in at that moment, and he launched himself at Andy. The two of them were rolling around the floor, punching and shouting, really in a playful mood, in mock anger, until the referee – Ian Foote – separated them. A report went in to the Scottish Football Association but they decided to let the matter rest – which was probably the wisest decision, as it was a one-off incident and did no real harm.

That's not the only incident I recall about Andy Russell.

There was another occasion when a carpet firm, Maryhill Carpets, sponsored a game with Rangers at Motherwell. It was thought a good idea to have a red carpet for the players to run out on. Several days before the game this magnificent red carpet was delivered to Andy at Fir Park

When the big day arrived it was very noticeable that the carpet was somewhat shorter than it had been on the day of its arrival. Later, we found out that some of Andy's family had suddenly found themselves the better off for new lounge carpets. Still, Andy put out the remainder for the teams to come out on – which they did with due pomp and ceremony – then he began rolling it up.

Someone shouted, 'What're you doing, Andy? The referee's no' come out yet!'

Quick as a flash Andy shouted back 'I'm no havin' that b*****d Valentine walking on my mother-in-law's new carpet!'

There were some disillusioned full time professionals at Motherwell who wanted first-team action all the time. I never blame players for that. It shows that they care about their job. The problem is that you need to have depth in a squad but you cannot play everyone you have on your staff. Among the players were Lloyd, a goalkeeper from Liverpool, McClymont, Muir, McCabe, Pelosi, Leishman, Pettigrew, Stevens and MacLaren. They were all fine players – but frustrated. Some of them, like MacLaren, Stevens and Pettigrew, finally did become regulars in the first team, but others were destined for only occasional chances. I did my very best to keep them all a happy bunch because I knew what they felt like from my own experiences of being in the reserves, I believe it provided me with further education in the management of players as individuals.

We managed to keep our heads above water at Motherwell and probably would have won a few things but for some strange results going against us by the odd goal here and there.

As it was, we were 'nearly men' – a very difficult outfit to beat, but not quite good enough to actually win anything. With more capital to give us a wider selection of players I think we could have become a greater power in Scottish football. It is one of those things that have to be filed under 'we'll never know' – probably the biggest file of all time!

Football in Scotland in the mid-1970s was undergoing a transformation. There were still those who did not like the idea of the League being split into more than two divisions, each with fewer clubs, but the supporters seemed to like the idea, believing there would be more interest in the promotion and relegation battles. In general, people do not like change. My dislike, however, is of change for the sake of change. If there is a definite aim and purpose, then fine, I'll go along with it.

When Scotland set up its new League system I was not opposed to it, and I have to say that the changes that have taken place since have all been for the good of the game. In England, there were many moans and groans when the old Football League system was scrapped and the Premiership introduced, but it has proved to be a tremendous shot in the arm for the game. A huge rise in available money has meant that the facilities at grounds are so much better, world-class players are attracted, and everyone is on a better deal. The standard of football in England is higher, and England has become a force to be reckoned with on the world stage once more. I am sure that it all has much to do with the restructuring of the League.

In Scotland, there has been talk for a number of years of further restructuring, breakaway groups and all kinds of things. I'll go along with anything that gives us better football and co-ordinated youth development, just so long as that is the prime intention – rather than just a battle for power and money. There was no power battle at Motherwell. I had the best of both worlds – football with a great manager, a fine bunch of players and other staff.

My teaching work gave me the satisfaction of doing

something different from football and helping young people on the road to very different careers from those of the players I was working with at Fir Park. But my ambitions towards management had grown, and the day dawned when I was in the frame for another job in which I was to be the man in the hot seat. The club was Clyde. I had played against them a number of times and had been to their well-known Shawfield Stadium quite often. I felt a bit sorry for them because they had the reputation of being one of those clubs that seemed always to be either relegated or promoted. It had not been many seasons before that they had finished third in the First Division behind Celtic and Rangers, yet since those days in the late 1960s they had been relegated, promoted and relegated again.

Now I had the chance to follow in the footsteps of my old pals Stan Anderson and Billy McNeill and become manager of Clyde, and I really wanted to have a go. I remember saying at the time how amazed I was to see Clyde in the Second Division because, only a few seasons before during my early days at Motherwell, we had found them one of the hardest sides to play against and we had failed to beat them. Now they had slipped down two divisions in as many seasons.

One of the things I had to be assured of was that there would be no interruption to my education work if I became manager of Clyde. I have never been under any illusions about football and how it can leave you high and dry just when you have started to trust it. I have seen and heard of many players and managers who thought they were going along quite well only to have the rug pulled from under them unexpectedly. Had there been any problem with my continuing at Craigie College, I don't think I would have accepted the job but, as it was, there was no objection and so I shook hands on the arrangement.

I had managed all kinds of schools and youth teams and had been assistant to Willie McLean – but now things were beginning to get a little more serious. Suddenly Craig Brown was being described in the newspaper as 'Manager of Clyde Football Club'. I felt that I had just set foot on the 'yellow-brick road' to fame – or failure! A whole new chapter in my life was about to begin.

9

Off to Clyde

IT WAS A phone call from Billy McNeill that set me on the road to becoming manager of Clyde. Billy and I are old pals, as I have already said, and he phoned me to say that he had recommended me to the chairman, Tom Clark, to succeed him, as he had decided to take the job as manager of Aberdeen Football Club.

I felt honoured that Billy had done this for me, and it confirms what most people know about football – that it is an old pals' act. Clyde were in the bottom division at the time, and when I took over in July 1977 they had just finished in what was considered to be their lowest position ever – eighth from the bottom of the Scottish League. I don't think anyone can apportion blame for that. There had been a number of years of instability for one reason or another. Billy McNeill had been in charge for the last seven or eight games of the season, and before that Stan Anderson had been the manager. During Stan's protracted illness Bobby Waddell, Mike Clinton and Peter Rice had taken temporary charge. They were all good managers and coaches, but somehow it had just not worked out at Clyde.

Billy's influence had steadied things but there was a lot of work still to do and, when I began my stint in mid-July, I had sixteen players, three backroom staff and three scouts. Billy had told me that the players were very good as individuals at that level, but that they needed organising. He felt that I would not need to make many signings – if any – to win promotion from the Second Division.

When I asked Billy about the staff his response was very interesting. He told me that our physiotherapist, John Watson, was, in his opinion, the best in the country. John was also superintendent physiotherapist at Strathclyde Hospital in Motherwell. Billy said that he would have loved to have taken him to Aberdeen with him, but John had wanted to stay where he was in full-time employment at the hospital and part-time at Clyde.

Billy also told me that Clyde had a very fine and very dedicated commercial manager called John Donnelly, and that there was a very good coaching assistant in Stewart MacMillan, who could also take charge of the team for reserve-type games. I say 'reserve-type' games because Clyde did not actually have a second string at that time, but would field some of the less regular first-team players for minor cup competitions and friendly games.

I did not know any of the three scouts who were attached to the club, so I thought I had better enlist some guys whom I did know. Quite probably, the scouts who were already at Clyde knew what they were about but, as a manager, you need to have scouts who are exactly on your wavelength and know your thoughts on players. They are, after all, your eyes and ears. So I appointed Bob Weir and the late Andy Sawyers.

Billy was very thorough in his appraisal of the situation. He even told me that the club had a very good tea lady who also did the laundry, and one or two other things about the place. Sadie Donegan certainly lived up to Billy's praise of her.

Most importantly, Billy told me that if I was offered the job I should jump at it, because the Dunn family, who ran the club, were lovely people and had both integrity and dignity. To a great degree it was owing to the Dunn family that the club was held in such high esteem throughout the country.

Not long after the chat with Billy I received another phone call asking me if I would attend an interview for the job. I travelled to Shawfield Stadium, which was also a well-known Glasgow greyhound track. It was my first-ever meeting with John McBeth, who was the Clyde secretary. He was also the son-in-law of the chairman. From our first encounter, it was obvious that John along with his wife, Frances, was an extremely dedicated Clyde supporter.

In the years that followed, I have never ceased to admire the honest work that has been put in, both during my time and since, for Clyde Football Club. Mr McBeth is on the executive committee as well as being vice-president of the Scottish Football Association, and he is an insightful and tireless worker for the good of the game and for no financial gain.

So, John met me and I was then interviewed by the board of directors, who asked me if I would accept the post on a part-time basis. I readily agreed to this because it meant that my educational work could continue. I was asked to start immediately, and I must say that Motherwell were most understanding when I explained the situation. The then chairman, Ian Livingstone, was very sincere in his good wishes.

I had been training with much larger groups of players at Motherwell and it was a delight to be working with a smaller group at Clyde. I felt that it made personal attention much easier. At Motherwell I had often been involved with three sessions a day, but here it was much more concentrated with about four good sessions a week. The Clyde players were very enthusiastic and responded well.

The directors had made it clear that there was very little money available for players, but they said that they would do their best, and I would like to put it on record that they were as supportive as possible throughout my time at the club.

As Billy McNeill had told me, they had some good players. John Arrol was the goalkeeper, with Phil Cairney as his replacement. Bobby Ferris or Eddie Anderson was right back and at centre-half we had Joe Finlayson, with Jim Boyd at left back. In midfield were Brian Ahern, Bobby Harvey and Steve Archibald, as well as Gerry Marshall, Neil Hood and Joe Ward. Our front players included Sean Sweeney and Arthur Grant. Stan Rankin was my first signing, and Gordon Hamilton was our captain.

Anyone who knew anything at all about the game could see that we had quite a good squad, and it was still a bit of a mystery as to how the club had fallen into such a relatively lowly position. Unfortunately, these things do happen, and it was now my job to try to change it. I wanted to get the supporters more involved, to let them see that we meant business, so I invited them to come and watch training sessions. The response was quite good, and you could feel the spirit at the club starting to lift as the new season approached.

We had a particularly good pre-season friendly at home to Preston, which ended as a 1–1 draw – and which was Nobby Stiles' first game in charge of Preston. It confirmed that we needed more confidence in front of goal because we had controlled the game throughout and should have won. Friendlies are never as good as competitive matches to pinpoint your deficiencies, but when you are the new manager it gives you the chance to assess what you have – especially since most players want to make a good early impression.

The season began on 13 August 1977 with a 0–0 draw away against Albion Rovers. It was not an inspiring match but it did set the ball rolling. A week later we had our first home game, and I was delighted when we beat Stenhousemuir 3–0 in front of an improved home attendance. From then on we seemed to gather momentum, and it was not until our seventh game on 24 September that we suffered a defeat, and even that was partly due to our defender, Eddie Anderson, scoring an own goal.

By the turn of the year we had worked our way into a good position at the top of the table with just four defeats in our first twenty games. However, every silver lining has a dark cloud, and I was asked to see the chairman around that time so that he could explain our financial situation. He told me that the club had little money and that they did not want to go into the red – then he asked if I might be able to do something about it by selling a player.

I had only three players whom I thought might be worth selling from the point of view of bringing in enough money to make it worth losing them. I told the chairman so and named them – Joe Ward, Brian Ahern and Steve Archibald. Mr Clark asked me if I could perhaps contact a few people and see if I might be able to make a sale or two.

I phoned round several of my colleagues to gauge interest in my players. I promoted Steve Archibald in particular, because he was doing very well for us, and several Premier managers and their representatives came to look at him. I was told by one of them, a very well-known and respected manager, that Archibald would never make a top player.

It was Alex Stuart, manager of Ayr, who showed some positive interest, and we arranged a fee of £15,000 plus Jim McSherry – but the deal fell through because Jim, who has since become one of my best friends, refused to come to Shawfield, considering that our ground was not a football stadium but a dog track. I was disappointed, of course, and I phoned Billy McNeill to have a chat about Archibald. He advised me that he had used him as a sweeper and that he had been quite successful in that position. I could see the sense in that and I must now confess that the one thing I had never considered was to try him as a forward. We were well served in that position and I had therefore never needed to experiment, but he had scored goals for us from his midfield position.

After a bit of discussion with Billy, I agreed to sell him Steve Archibald for the princely sum of £20,000. I don't think Steve will mind me saying that he was to receive £3,000 as his share of the deal, which was to go through on 3 January 1978, after the New Year fixtures. The board pleaded with me not to play him in our two fixtures just before the transfer in case he should be injured and the deal collapse. However, I wanted my strongest side for the games against Albion Rovers and Queen's Park. Steve played well in both games and we took maximum points. Against Albion Rovers he even scored two of our three goals, so he had a very pleasing send-off with his old club consolidating a position at the top of Division Two.

Steve was delighted to find himself at Pittodrie, having broken through to 'big-time' football. I was very pleased for him too. To his credit, he never forgot his early days and later, when he moved to Tottenham, he sent wonderful boxes of chocolates to me at Clyde.

By accident, in a training match at Aberdeen, Steve played up front – and he was a revelation! Billy McNeill put him into the side as a striker and, of course, he took to it like that famous duck to water. Tottenham later paid more than £800,000 for him. In those days the transfer contracts were much simpler and there was no extra cash for Clyde when Aberdeen made such a profit on him. I like to think that I was quite a resourceful young manager, but I did not have enough initiative to dream up the add-on clause that has become commonplace in modern football finances. I did use it in later transfers, but not with Steve Archibald's move – so, to a certain extent, we got our fingers burned.

Having said that, the £20,000 that Clyde received was crucial, and the remaining players did not let the transfer make any difference to them. We had a very good second half of the season, including a 7–0 defeat of Meadowbank. Our home attendances gradually increased, and our best crowd of the season was our penultimate game at home to our Second Division championship rivals, Raith Rovers ironically managed by my mentor Willie McLean. Nearly two thousand supporters were in Shawfield for that game and we were very disappointed to lose 0–1 – only our second home defeat of the season, but a crucial game in which to fail.

On the last day of the season, just three days later, we were playing at home to Stranraer, and we really wanted to win this one – especially as they had beaten us at Stair Park. This time there were 1,200 supporters at Shawfield Stadium. We were a goal up through Joe Ward at half-time and then, in the second half, we took complete control and ended as 4–0 winners. Ward, John Brogan and Neil Hood each scored in the second half, and there were many celebrations at the end of the game – especially since our only rivals, Raith, had been beaten 2–0 at Dunfermline.

We were confirmed as champions, with Raith finishing on the same points as runners-up. The 21 goals scored by Neil Hood had made all the difference. The success had made a difference to our finances as well. The pools money was distributed on the basis of points gained during the season and, since we had done very well with 53 points, we had a good share. We also drew Celtic at home and away in the Dryburgh Cup and, with the money we earned from that, Clyde went from having nothing in the bank at Christmas to being in a very comfortable financial situation six months later.

Just as an aside, I was very pleased that Raith had been promoted with us because I had a great respect for their manager, Willie McLean. He had fallen out with the chairman at Motherwell but, after a short time out of work, Raith had snapped him up and he had soon knocked them into shape.

Ironically, our first League fixture of the following season was at home to Raith Rovers and we beat them 3–1. Our season began remarkably well, and by mid-September we topped the First Division table with five victories and one draw from our first six games.

Around Christmas-time we were still going well and were among the leaders, although we had dropped a few silly points.

I was still learning the trade, and I did receive one short, sharp lesson in mid-September 1978. We were playing away to Dundee and Eric Schaedler, their left back, tackled our best player at that time, Joe Ward, very crudely indeed – with the result that Joe had to be carried off. He was out of the game for most of the rest of the season. The referee was George Smith from Edinburgh, a man I respected both then and now, but I did not agree with his handling of that particular situation and I told him so.

A couple of months later he was put in charge of one of our home games and he came in and said to me, 'How are things, Mr Brown?'

I replied, 'Well, not too good, actually.'

'Why? What's the matter?' he asked.

'We've not yet recovered from losing our best player because of your incompetence a couple of months ago.'

I realised that I had overstepped the mark because he just walked away from me without saying another word. During the game, which was against Raith Rovers, he allowed what I thought was a blatantly off-side goal and I wondered if I had made a big mistake in saying what I had before the game – but to have suggested that Mr Smith was reacting to my statement would, I know, have been an unfair accusation against one of the most sincere officials in the game. Ever since, I have tried not to fall into the trap of criticising referee performances – although I must admit, to my embarrassment, that I haven't quite managed to stay on the straight and narrow as a World Cup qualifying match in Zagreb in October 1999 will confirm. More of that later though. I regret that falling-out with George Smith, who was an outstanding referee and is a very nice chap. Even the best of referees can make mistakes, though!

I was very upset about losing Joe Ward because he was our top player at that time, but later in the season I sold him to Aston Villa for £85,000. That, in a sense, was another mistake because I was naive enough – or perhaps cocky enough – to think that I could sell our best player and still replace him quite easily to maintain our form in the First Division. I didn't think that I needed to ask the board for any of the money we had received – I just relied on using reserve players. The consequence was that the second half of the season was very poor for us in comparison with the first half, and we picked up far fewer points. We finished in mid-table when we might have been challenging for promotion again.

It was an eventful first season in a higher division and I had continued my learning process. I was kicking myself for the fact that we could probably have done better, but the board seemed quite happy because we had increased our attendances and our transfer dealings had shown a good profit.

Around the New Year of that season, the Ayr manager, Ally MacLeod, left to become manager of Scotland. I was hotly tipped to replace him at Ayr, and I was interviewed by the chairman, Myles Callaghan, at his sumptuous home. He offered me the job on either a full- or part-time basis, and I was deeply honoured to be given the chance to be manager of my home-town club. I declined the offer, though, because I was very happy at Clyde, and felt that the club had much more potential still to be realised. I was also still lecturing at Craigie College and I thought it would be inappropriate to be lecturing and to be manager of the football team in the same town. Ayr had made me a very generous offer – certainly a great improvement on my income from Clyde – but I always feel that, in football, the satisfaction you get from working in an environment and with people you get on with is far more important than the riches of the game. Perhaps it would have worked out at Ayr, but I could not possibly have been happier than I already was at Clyde!

I had several other clubs approach me during my time with Clyde, but I am not going to name them. It would be unfair on the managers who were eventually appointed, and I have always tried to be as discreet as possible in all my dealings with clubs or people in this game. Players have talked to me about their business and personal problems over the years at both club and international level, and I have always kept their confidences.

Having said all that, there was one offer that came to me while I was at Clyde which I found to be both amazing and startling. It was an invitation from Ernie Walker, then the secretary of the Scottish Football Association, to meet him at the Haggs Castle Golf Club. When I got there, he went straight into the reason for the invitation and asked me how I would feel about becoming assistant to Jock Stein, who was by then manager of Scotland.

It was in the early 1980s, and Jock had established himself as the top man for Scotland. I was quite stunned at being asked, and felt deeply privileged even to have been considered for such an important post. However, I kept a level head and declined the offer. I did not think that I had sufficient experience at that time, and I was also concerned about job security. Scotland had gone through five managers in a decade and, if I had taken the job, it would have meant going full-time, and that would have meant the end of my academic career.

Some ten years after Jock Stein died, I was at a press meeting in Glasgow on the anniversary of his death and was asked if I had any Jock Stein stories to relate. I told them the story of Andy Russell's encounter with Jock, and also about how I had been invited to go and work with him at the SFA. The reaction from one or two of the journalists present was as surprising as it was disappointing. Their attitude seemed to be: 'Do you really expect us to believe that?' or 'Who does this guy think he is?'

There was never a problem in confirming my story because Ernie Walker was still around and would certainly have verified it, but it was the scepticism of those journalists that disappointed me. It was a clear sign of the age in which we live. It also highlighted the fact that when I was later appointed as Scotland manager, the appointment might have been made more acceptable. There are some journalists whose only quest in life is destruction and, even when you level with them, they still have to go one step beyond.

Jock Stein knew me well. In fact there was no one in football, especially Scottish football, whom Jock didn't know, but I believe that the person who had further recommended me for the job with him was a very good friend of his, Dr James Crorie. He was a very well-known legislator in Scottish football and had seen the set-up at Clyde and our methods of coaching and discipline. He was also, incidentally, an outstanding pianist. A favourite story concerning him was when one of our players, our striker Neil Hood, suffered an eye injury. John Watson, our physio, took him in, prepared the wound and shaved his eyelashes off so that the doctor could see where to apply the stitches. The doctor came in smoking a large cigar which he had to put out before he could get to work. He threw it into the pedal bin, not realising that John had been throwing swabs soaked in surgical spirits into it already. The flames shot up out of the bin and singed the hair and eyebrows of the good doctor, so that he was almost as bald as his patient when he came to put the stitches in. The boys used to joke that the stitches would be spaced about an inch apart when he'd had a few. Yet they loved and respected him – and with good reason, because he was an excellent chap and a very fine sports medico.

During my time at Clyde we had our ups and downs. I don't like to advertise the fact that we were relegated once during my spell at the club – but it is in the record books for all to see. We seemed to have a lapse of confidence, especially in goal, where I used four different goalkeepers in that 1979/80 season. I started the season with Dennis Connaghan, a really nice chap, whom I had signed from Morton. Dennis had a confidence crisis and I brought in David McWilliams from Airdrie. David was a former Scotland Under-23 international but he didn't excel either. I asked Bobby Clark, the ex-Aberdeen Scotland international, to come out of retirement, and he played four games for us before deciding that he really had finished his career. Bobby, who now coaches Notre Dame College in the USA, was grateful because it enabled his two sons see him play professional football. Then I brought in Greg Young. Goalkeeping changes like that have an effect on the entire team, so we lost our way and fell back to the Second Division along with Arbroath. If we had turned a few more of our drawn games into victories we would probably have been safe, but the lack of confidence went from defence to attack and we scored nothing like our usual tally of goals.

There was one highlight from that season, and that was a very creditable 2–2 home draw with Rangers in the Scottish Cup third round. We had played them earlier in the season at Shawfield in the League Cup and they beat us 2–1. The Clyde players were delighted when they were given a second chance in the Cup and, but for a penalty, we would have beaten them 2–1. As it was, the players performed extremely well and deserved the home draw. The replay ended in a 2–0 win for Rangers, both goals scored in the final ten minutes, but there was no disgrace in that.

The following season we were reassembling. We had a good crop of youngsters corning through, and it was time to introduce some of them to first-team football. As a result we did not win any medals during the 1980/81 season. We had a couple of good games in which we scored six against Montrose and against East Fife, but we gained the most satisfaction from seeing the younger players beginning to blossom.

When I was first at Clyde no strip sponsorship was allowed, but after a while some experiments in junior football resulted in the green light for teams to wear sponsors' names on their shirts. Along with our commercial manager, John Donnelly, I was thinking about where we might get some suitable sponsorship when an incident occurred that triggered off an idea. It took place in Polmadie Road, where the British Oxygen Company had some works. One night, as I was travelling to training, there was an explosion there and the road was soon blocked by police cars, ambulances and fire engines. The following weekend I picked up a copy of the local newspaper and found in it an absolute condemnation of BOC, which I considered to be very unfair because the incident had been a minor one, made to look much worse by the understandable presence of so many emergency vehicles. The whole thing escalated, with petitions designed to rid the area of the works. Local councillors became involved as their support was sought, and the whole matter became a major local talking point.

I saw this as a great opportunity, and drove over to their works and asked to see the managing director. After about an hour of kicking my heels I finally saw a guy named Gordon Moultrie, who was in charge. He was extremely pleasant and listened carefully as I put it to him that his company had alienated the local community and that a way of getting back into favour might be by doing something for that community. He asked me what I had in mind.

'The local school is John Bosco and I know the headmaster, John Mulgrew. I suggest that you give a donation to the local school, to Gorbals United Boys Club, whose president is Kenny Dalglish and whose leading light is Pat Harkins, Kenny's father-in-law – and how about sponsoring your local senior football team?'

He asked me if I had any figures in mind and I said that I had no idea what the board would accept, but I think I mentioned a figure of £10,000 for BOC to go on the team shirts. Remember, this was in 1981. He asked me to talk to the board, which I did the following night. Our elderly honorary president, Mr William P. Dunn, was there, chairing the meeting. I gave my usual report on the players and so on and then broached the subject of sponsorship.

Before I was able to get very far into my presentation, he interrupted me.

'I have to say that our jerseys have won the Scottish Cup three times. They are white and we don't want to deface them with advertising. They are sacrosanct!'

'But it's the coming thing, Mr President,' I pleaded.

He absolutely refused to discuss it, however. Also on the board was Professor Bob Jack, the professor of mercantile law at Glasgow University. He came into the conversation.

'Excuse me, manager, but you haven't mentioned money. Did you mention money to the British Oxygen Company?'

The old president-chairman had made it quite clear that there was no way he was going to agree to any sponsorship, so I replied, 'It doesn't seem now that the money is relevant – but I did mention the sum of £10,000 as being appropriate!'

The president-chairman now interrupted again and cried, 'Manager, I would put BOC on my bare torso for £10,000! Please carry on!'

So I did negotiate the deal and the upshot was that we became only the second club after Hibs, who had a deal with Bukta, the sports manufacturer, to use a sponsor's name in Scotland, with BOC brightly emblazoned in red on our shirts. That sponsorship only lasted for one year, but once again Clyde certainly benefited from moving with the times. The only reason we did not have the sponsorship renewed was simply that we were not high-profile enough. I was told that the company gained more publicity mileage from sponsoring a caber-tosser who regularly toured North America and Australasia demonstrating his skills. So the sponsorship of Clyde was not renewed by BOC, but was taken up by Solripe.

Talking of sponsorship, five or six years ago I was going to watch a game between Motherwell and Rangers. I drove into Ian Skelly's garage in Dalmarnock, from where we obtained our sponsored cars. I was talking to Stewart MacLaren, a former Motherwell player, who was now the sales manager for Ian Skelly. He asked me if I was going to the game and then told me to take a good look at the Motherwell jerseys. 'It will be the last time that you will see Ian Skelly's name on a Motherwell jersey!'

Naturally I was curious to know why, and he explained

that Ian had just sold his firm and, as he no longer owned it, the sponsorship was over. Stewart told me that Ian had received quite a few millions for the business – though he could not be specific as many differing figures had been mooted. As we chatted, a tea lady was pouring us a cup of tea each and I joked about how good it was that Ian had given all his staff £5,000 each as a reward for their loyalty. I noticed that she seemed to be taking some time pouring the tea, but her expression didn't change as I repeated myself. Finally she just turned to us and said: 'I must have been off my work that day!' – a typical piece of Glasgow humour.

We were into the 1981/82 season and our young players were beginning to grow in confidence. Pat Nevin in particular was becoming a bit of a show-stealer, but the whole side was gelling together very nicely. We were undefeated in our first eleven games. Then we suffered two defeats and a draw in consecutive games, which dropped us from top to second place in the Second Division. After that there were few blips, and we regained that top spot in mid-November and stayed there for the rest of the season. We were champions once again and back in the First Division.

The following season was one of consolidation once again. I have seen many teams go charging up the League and then come charging back down again, so I have always tried to keep cool in my team-building and not inflate the balloon so fast and so far that it bursts. That was something I learned all those years ago when I was taking my various sports courses.

We had a very interesting cup tie against Motherwell in the 1982/83 season. It was in the third round of the Scottish Cup and we were at home. The result was 0–0. The replay came a few days later, and it was quite a match in which seven goals were scored – and we hit four of them. It was a blow to Motherwell, who were a Premier Division side, managed by the great Jock Wallace, but we, of course, were absolutely delighted. Our Cup designs were short-lived, however, because we faced Partick in the next round. We played well and drew

2–2 at Firhill, and the replay was equally stirring with extra time needed since there were no goals after 90 minutes. The floodlights failed and the referee decided to abandon the match during extra time, so we had to play again. This time Partick set about us in a very businesslike way and beat us 6–0, with Mo Johnston scoring three – but it was still a Scottish Cup campaign to remember!

We were realists at Clyde. There were no great aspirations towards getting into the European Cup because we knew that was beyond us at that time. The club was simply not big enough for a sustained assault on such a target – but we were ambitious enough to want to improve constantly and better our position and our facilities. All that takes money, of course, and Clyde, like so many clubs, had to be self-generating. There was no one with a magic wand to come in and plant millions in the club's bank account and so we had to live on our wits – by developing and selling young players, or by commercial enterprises which helped to keep us apace of the rising costs of running a football club.

The cup ties against bigger clubs were a major help in keeping us afloat, and in the 1983/84 season we had a cracker against Aberdeen. It was not so much the 90 minutes of the actual game as the pre-match build-up which had Alex Ferguson giving me what for over the telephone. But that's another story ...

10

Fergie's Fury
and then to Mexico

THE HIGHLIGHT OF our 1983/84 season was probably the 5–0 pasting of Raith Rovers which came on the last Saturday of November 1983. Prior to that result we had been struggling for a while and had been bottom of the table for almost eleven weeks.

Managers will always tell you that injury problems, new players yet to gel, bad luck, the need to spend money and various other outside sources are to blame. Sometimes those are valid points, but other times they are textbook responses to journalists' questions. What the manager really needs is an excuse. However, our season really did get off to a slow start – on the opening day we were without five key players and I would say that it was mid-October before I was able to field our strongest team.

That 5–0 victory over Raith put us on a different road and we followed it with a 1–0 win at Kilmarnock, a 4–0 win at Airdrie and a 2-0 win at home to Meadowbank. Suddenly, we were walking around with wings on our boots. We suffered only one defeat in our next six games, and there was talk of us challenging for promotion. It was premature, of course, and we eventually finished in eighth place.

Aberdeen won the Scottish Cup that year by beating Celtic 2–1 at Hampden. On the way to the final they were drawn away to us in the fourth round, and we were determined to enjoy ourselves whatever the result. I wasn't going to let Alex Ferguson have things all his own way. He is a master of kidology, but this was one time when I saw the chance to wind him up a little.

On the Thursday before the game I was telephoned by North Sound Radio in order to tape an interview from my office. While my part of the interview was being done over the phone, Fergie was live in the studio. I knew that he would be listening, so I decided to have a little fun with him. He had already done his interview but was still in the studio when the radio reporter said, 'Have you any message for your old pal, Alex Ferguson?'

I replied, 'I have two things to say to Alex. One is that we will be using a Dunlop ball on Saturday, and the other is that we haven't rolled the pitch for three weeks!'

I heard a voice spluttering at the other end and then the sound had to be cut off because – I imagine – what he was saying was fairly uncomplimentary and certainly not for tender ears. A couple of minutes after the transmission was over, my phone rang again. It was Alex.

'You'd better not be playing with that * * * * * ball, and you'd better get that * * * * * pitch rolled!' he said.

'No way, Alex,' I replied. 'We're the home team.'

A bit of good-natured banter followed before the phone was put down. I knew from the previous season's Cup Final that Aberdeen had made some criticism of the Dunlop football. Jim Leighton was in goal for them and he didn't like the flight of the ball. Alex being Alex, he condemned it in the press.

So I had made a point of obtaining three Dunlop balls for our match. You try everything, of course, to give yourselves a little bit of an advantage over the other side. It is common practice throughout the game – although I would never take it to the lengths of what could be legitimately branded as cheating. As the home side you have the advantage of deciding upon how your pitch should be treated. If you make it a bowling green you play into the hands of a good passing side – as Aberdeen was at that time. You can keep the grass a little longer and level the situation by forcing the game to be played off the ground rather more if that suits you.

As it was, we unfortunately lost 0–2, with Aberdeen's Neale Cooper and Ian Angus scoring a goal each. They deserved their victory, and by the end of the season had picked up the Premier championship as well as the Scottish Cup. Our consolation was that we had given them a run for their money and had a crowd of 5,800 to see the Aberdeen superstars, who included Gordon Strachan, Willie Miller, Alex McLeish and Jim Leighton. It was certainly a worthwhile experience for our young players to play against them.

I was always on the lookout for new young players because we were never in a situation of being able to spend large sums of money to strengthen our side. We produced many good players, one of the most gifted perhaps being Pat Nevin. He was released by Celtic Boys Club for, it was said, being too small. Personally I hardly think that was likely. We managed to sign him from Gartcosh United youth team.

When Pat came to Clyde he was a revelation. His first game was a friendly against Sheffield United, and he looked absolutely brilliant. He was still a student at Caledonian University but he was also in our first team and very impressive. He was so impressive in fact that Andy Roxburgh listened to my recommendation that he play for the Scotland Under-18 side, took a look at him and picked him. That was some achievement for the seventeen-year-old Pat Nevin when you consider that Andy had the cream of the Premier Division from which to select his Scotland players at all levels. He had young players like Paul McStay, Brian McClair, Neale Cooper, Jim McInally, Brian Gunn, Davie McPherson, Eric Black,

Steve Clarke, Gary Mackay, Davie Bowman, John Philliben and others.

Andy was a bit sceptical when I told him that there was a young lad from our First Division that he could not ignore but, when he took Pat to Largs to join the rest of his squad for a trial match, he knew that he had made the right move. Pat did so well that he was in the Scotland Under-18 side that won the European Championship. Sadly, I could not be at the final between Scotland and Czechoslovakia in Helsinki, but everyone raved about Pat's performance at outside right and said that he virtually defeated the Czechs single-handedly. This was borne out by the fact that he was named European Youth Player of the Year.

That put Pat well into the spotlight, and a year later he went with Andy's Under-19 side to take part in the World Youth Championships in Mexico. I was delighted to hear that when Andy fitness-tested his players at Colorado Springs – their prechampionship camp – there was no one fitter than Pat Nevin. I felt that was quite a compliment to our training techniques at Clyde, as well as to his natural fitness. Pat had always been a player who took care of himself, lived well, trained hard and, in my opinion, a model professional throughout his career, which lasted seventeen or eighteen years.

We had Pat in the team for around two years, but it was inevitable that he would leave us because there were so many bigger clubs obviously interested in him. Ian McNeill, the assistant manager at Chelsea, came up to see us just before the Scotland Under-19s went to Mexico. He went to Pat's house in Barlanark in Glasgow and was there for hours and hours trying to persuade him to sign for Chelsea – which he eventually did for a meagre sum.

In those days there was no Bosman ruling and, even though Pat was out of contract, Clyde were entitled to receive something for the transfer. We asked for £180,000. It is rare for deals to run smoothly in football – clubs do not often reach instant agreement. Chelsea offered us £50,000, so the matter went to the first-ever international tribunal between the home countries. The meeting was held in Glasgow and Chelsea were instructed to pay us £95,000. I thought it was a paltry sum for such a highly talented youngster. I disagreed, at the tribunal, with Ken Bates, the Chelsea chairman, who was quite disparaging about the £40 per week we were paying Pat Nevin.

'You can pay players what you like, so why are you only paying him forty pounds a week?' Bates was obviously inferring that if the player was worth what we were asking we would be paying a lot more than that.

'We don't pay any of our players more than forty pounds a week,' I replied, adding that we did not pay the player what he was worth but only what we could afford. Bates then became very critical of Scottish football and I had to remind him that Chelsea had come up to Scotland to play Hearts, who were then in our First Division and had been beaten.

We were less than thrilled with the outcome of the tribunal. Not only was the £95,000 fee much too low, but it was decreed that Chelsea could pay in two instalments – half up front and the rest in a year's time.

Although Pat went for a miserly fee and what I considered to be poor wages, I'm pleased to say that he did very well for Chelsea and was instrumental in getting them out of the old Second Division of the Football League. He supplied the ammunition for Kerry Dixon to get the goals and later, when he renegotiated his contract, I think he had become much more shrewd and listened to advice. When he had first agreed to join Chelsea, Ian McNeill would not allow me or anyone else to advise him. He kept him at his house for hours until he signed. Pat learned quickly and fared much better with his next contract, and also when he moved on to join Everton, Tranmere, Kilmarnock and Motherwell where now he is the insightful Chief Executive.

So that was how Pat Nevin began his career with us. I was never in a position to spend big money on players and, as far as I can recall, I believe that the most I ever paid for anyone was £5,000. We were dependent upon player exchanges, free transfers and finding new talent. As a further example, when we dropped back to the Second Division I had to change a few faces and did some business with my old sparring partner, Willie McLean, who was then still at Ayr United. He wanted Brian Ahern and Jim Kean and we agreed a deal in which he signed them both and in exchange we received three players and £40,000. The players were Robert Reilly, Derek McCutcheon and Billy McColl. All three became useful members of the squad and Reilly in particular did very well for us. At the same time I obtained, on a free transfer from Kilmarnock, a guy called Jimmy Docherty, a small, spritely middle-to-front player who did exceptionally well for us. Another good signing on the same basis was Jim Dempsey, who had been with Motherwell. He did a great job for us.

That is the sort of wheeling and dealing that you have to do when you are in charge of a small club, be it in England or Scotland. Queen's Park was always a fruitful recruiting ground for me, and my old friend Eddie Hunter was the coach there. I always refer to him as mild-mannered and quietly spoken because he was just the opposite, and you could hear him all round Hampden from his place in the dugout. Eddie was attached to Queen's Park in one capacity or another for 30 years. I went to his club quite regularly and signed some super guys – players like Derek Atkins, who was an excellent goalkeeper but suffered a career setback when his leg was broken in an accidental clash with Mark Shanks of Ayr, Bobby Dickson and Ross McFarlane, who were a super servants for Clyde.

As I have already mentioned, we were promoted at the first attempt after making all those changes and more than held our own in the 1983/84 season. The 1984/85 season was almost a repeat performance, since once again we finished in eighth place in the table. At one stage we stood as high as third, and we were within a shout of promotion for most of the season. A 4–1 victory over Kilmarnock was our best result, although there were some excellent games against Motherwell, with whom we drew twice and won once in our three scheduled League matches. That was pretty good really, because Motherwell were ultimately champions of the division ahead of Clydebank, whom we beat twice.

I was nearing the end of my time with Clyde, although I didn't know that at the time. There was still the 1985/86 season ahead and we prepared as normal. We got off to a good start and were undefeated in our first eight games. We were in a healthy second place in the table when Airdrie beat us 3–0 away. We began to pick up more than our share of injuries at that time, and the loss of several key players, including Derek Frye, who had been our phenomenal top scorer for several seasons, meant that we struggled to field a consistent side. We gradually slipped down the table and looked in serious trouble for several weeks until we staged a late rally and lost only three of our last ten games. That succeeded in pulling us out of the danger zone.

It was during that season that the great Jock Stein died. It was in September 1985, and the story of what happened has been told too many times for me to repeat it here – although I would not want that to appear in any way disrespectful to Jock, with whom I came into contact very many times and for whom I had the utmost respect and affection. He was a one-off, and Scotland has never seen his like before or since.

The Scottish Football Association inherited a problem when they lost Jock. Who could replace him? The team had to beat Australia in a play-off to be sure of a place in the World Cup finals, but someone had to take charge with immediate effect. This was Alex Ferguson's cue to take the reins. He had been incredibly successful with Aberdeen, including winning the European Cup Winners' Cup, and it was no real surprise when he was asked to take the national team – at least until the World Cup campaign was at an end.

It was not the first time that Alex had been involved at

national level. He had assisted Jock Stein previously while continuing as manager of Aberdeen. Such arrangements can be difficult, because there can be conflicts of interest. Every manager wants his players to be internationals, but sometimes international fixtures can come at difficult times in that there might be very important club games within days of international matches. More than one player has developed a 'groin strain' that has suddenly disappeared after an international game. When a club manager is also heavily involved in the international set-up he has more than the usual soul-searching to do.

Alex successfully steered Scotland through the play-off, drawing 0–0 in Melbourne and winning 2–0 at Hampden. Scotland was on the way to Mexico, and Alex invited me to be one of his coaching team. I was certainly delighted to be asked and willingly accepted. There was still a lot of work to be done at Clyde during the summer, but since the tournament was to run from the end of May for a month, I would still be back in time for pre-season preparations.

The 1986 World Cup tournament was exciting, albeit short-lived. Before we left there was all the usual hype and build-up, and I think some of the media began to think that the Scotland squad had the ability to walk on water. When you consider that we were drawn in a group with three very strong opponents – Denmark, West Germany and Uruguay – the reality of the situation was that we would do well to keep our heads above water, let alone walk on it! When so much expectation is built up, failure becomes a total disaster, and with it the picking over the bones to apportion blame. We did not get past the qualifying group and the criticism aimed at Alex Ferguson was very unfair, even allowing for the fact that it is always the manager who carries the can.

Against Denmark, Roy Aitken had the ball in the net but was harshly adjudged to be off-side. The Danes won 1–0, and in fact they also beat West Germany and Uruguay, so Scotland's performance was by no means a disgrace. In the next game, Gordon Strachan put Scotland ahead after eighteen minutes, but the Germans stormed back to make it 2–1 and went on to reach the final. Berti Vogts tells me a story about that game; he was assistant to Franz Beckenbauer and was sent to spy on our final training session. Alex Ferguson had decreed it to be private so that he could try out some moves and also establish the fitness of Gordon Strachan.

When Berti was refused admission he exchanged a German jersey for a Coca-Cola man's outfit and his drink's stall. He thus gained entry to the stadium and viewed the entire session. To this day he still tells the story and refers to himself as 'the Coca-Cola man'.

Our final game was against Uruguay, who had previously drawn with the Germans before being given a 6–1 hiding by Denmark. Scotland had to win – there were no other options. In an explosive first minute the Uruguayans were reduced to ten men when Batista was sent off. Everyone except those of us on the Scotland bench rubbed his hands in anticipation but, despite tremendous pressure, the Uruguayans did not crack. A goalless draw meant that Scotland was out and the criticism was in.

It had been an interesting experience and I returned to Scotland a wiser man. They say that travel broadens the mind. Travelling and being involved in football broadens the back as well. At Clyde we were wrestling with the problem of finding a home as Shawfield was no longer to be available. A ground-sharing arrangement with Partick Thistle was agreed so our home games were to be played at Firhill Park. Their manager at the time was Bertie Auld.

Every July I went on the national coaching course at Largs, and 1986 was no exception. While I was there, after the Mexico World Cup, I was approached by Andy Roxburgh, who was the Scottish Football Association's Technical Director, or Director of Coaching. He told me that things were happening at the SFA which would affect him and, if he had his way, could also affect me. Andy was soon appointed as

Scotland team manager, and a week later he contacted me to ask if I would join him as his assistant and manager of the Under-21 team.

When you are used to the day-to-day running of a football club and the fixtures being week in, week out, it can come as a bit of a culture shock to take up a post in international football. Having control of the Under-21 team meant that my involvement would be greater than just following the manager around, and so I decided that it was time for me to take up this new challenge.

That ended my career in club management to date. On the subject of management, there is one point that I would like to make about the credentials needed for such a job. When I took over at Clyde, my very first game was a friendly against Preston. Their manager was Nobby Stiles. Nobby remained as manager of Preston for about four years, during which time the club was promoted once and relegated twice. Nobby is probably most famous for the magnificent part he played in England's historic 1966 World Cup win, and I have often reflected on the fact that none of that squad of superb players was ever a great club manager. Jack Charlton did OK and was, of course, a marvellous international manager – but none of the others seriously achieved much as club managers. They were, of course, the most successful British international team to date.

Doesn't that tell us something? Just because a player reaches the top of the tree in international football, it does not necessarily mean that he will make a great manager. Therefore, when there is a clamouring for a big name to be appointed as the new manager somewhere, perhaps it might be a good idea to look at his coaching and management credentials rather than what he has achieved as a player. The qualities that are required to make a tiptop player are not necessarily the same as those required to make a first-class team manager. There are exceptions, of course, men who achieve success both as a player and as a manager. Beckenbauer, Vogts, Dalglish and

THE GAME OF MY LIFE

Cruyff readily spring to mind. However, I don't think that top-class playing experience necessarily makes for a top-class manager. Of course, I'm bound to say that, but there are so many examples to support my viewpoint, men like Arrigo Saachi, who never played football as a professional at all, and Gerard Houllier, so successful at Liverpool.

The top countries in Europe are all now insisting on a mandatory coaching qualification before a job can be offered. This is certainly the case in Germany, where part of the course is six months of full study. It is similar in Holland as well as Spain, France, Denmark and Italy, where a coaching qualification is obligatory. UEFA are trying to extend that, and they have instigated a Pro Licence which will be standard throughout Europe and enable managers and coaches to work in any of the UEFA countries. In Scotland, with Frank Coulston at the helm, we have already started to comply with our Premier Division managers, assistant managers and coaches in the first instance. Already the Pro Licence is held by most of our top managers.

There will always be a few people who argue that qualifications are meaningless and that practical experience and a playing career are what really count in order to be a top manager. I'm not going to place myself in a seat of judgement, but I would say to these people that the courses are very good, and if they were to experience one they might change their minds. At the very least they would be able to see the benefits that a coaching course provides, even for someone who is a 'natural'. Significantly Sir Alex Ferguson, in his autobiography, uses the word 'inspirational' when referring to our Largs coaching courses.

Speaking purely from my own experience, I do feel that if it were not for attending the courses and keeping up with the latest ideas and developments, I would not have been at Clyde for nine happy years, or indeed be in my current position. To the people who instigated the very notion of coaching courses – I thank you!

To all who run coaching courses throughout the world, I extend my appreciation and offer my best wishes for a continuation of this vital addition to the professional game. Those who, mistakenly, feel that courses are of little value have, in my opinion, got the wrong end of the stick.

11

Reflections on Clyde

I CANNOT LEAVE the subject of Clyde without a few more recollections and observations. When I joined the club they were in the middle of the Second Division. When I left them they were in the middle of the First Division, and so I would like to think that, on the whole, I did well for the club. I had some great times at Clyde. I had some terrific young players and some very good dedicated older professionals.

The great thing about Clyde was that it was a family club with a wonderful atmosphere and the willingness of everyone concerned to pull together. It is something that I have remembered throughout my management career – that you must have a squad that is fully integrated, with no one rocking the boat or causing trouble, because that is cancerous in a football club dressing room. I have seen this throughout the years as a player and as a manager with both big and small clubs, and, of course, as an international manager, where you deal with the biggest of players in terms of status.

I think one of the contributory factors to the club spirit at Clyde was a fair distribution of everything. I have already indicated that our wage structure meant that everyone was near enough in the same financial stratum. Everyone was treated the same in other senses too, whether a youngster just starting out on his career or a well-seasoned professional. For instance, I have always been a great believer in team photographs that included everyone. I like to get everyone involved without identifying them as either a first-team, reserve or junior player. If you wore the shirt, you were in the team, and your position in the photograph had nothing to do with your standing, either in the game or at the club.

This was a psychological ploy I used even for a World Cup qualifier against Latvia in October 1997, at Celtic Park. I told the players that if they were successful in beating Latvia, and consequently qualified for the World Cup, they should acknowledge the supporters by walking round the edge of the pitch in a dignified manner, applauding the crowd. I also insisted that the substitutes should come off the bench, take off their tracksuits so that they were not identified as substitutes, and join in, and that there should be no shirt exchanges before that lap of honour. I did not want to see any of them going round in a Latvia jersey or putting on any daft hats, as I called them. I told them that if a supporter threw a scarf or flag, they should offer to hand it back and only accept it if it seemed that it would cause offence to give it back, and after accepting it to wear it or hold it with modesty and dignity. I wanted to see them conducting themselves with the same professionalism in victory as they would have done in defeat.

The point was that the substitutes were made to feel a part of the success. The substitute goalkeeper, Neil Sullivan, walked round with Jim Leighton, our first choice, demonstrating the essence of togetherness that was a significant factor in our victory.

At Clyde, I tried to maintain that same spirit. At the end of each season, at our last home game, I used to send the players out with large cards to hold up to each part of the ground. The message was simply a thank you, but I felt that it was important to express our appreciation to the supporters and not let them feel like outsiders. They were all a part of the club to me.

We did the same with the Scotland Under-16 side when we reached the World Cup final, to thank the fans for their tremendous support during that tournament.

Other happy memories from Clyde include the board, a fine bunch of gentlemen who genuinely had the club at heart in all their decisions. I did not agree with everything, of course – but I could never say that the board were not doing their best, as they saw it, for Clyde Football Club.

William P. Dunn was the chairman who became honorary president. Tom Clark was chairman while I was there, and it was certainly a sad day when he died. Ian V. Paterson replaced him as chairman. He was a solicitor and former County Clerk of Lanark, one of the most shrewd men that you could ever hope to meet. He didn't profess to have a great inside knowledge of football, but he was a very keen supporter. He was also a very keen businessman and very clever in a man-management sense. I think I used to drive him to despair sometimes when I did things that were quite natural to me. If I saw a tie-up on the floor of the dressing room, I would automatically pick it up. I would also carry kit-bags and do other things that he felt were unbecoming to a manager. I just like to muck in with the rest, but he didn't feel that this was good man management. Similarly, he believed that I should not always change into a tracksuit but should watch the training from a distance. I totally disagreed.

Having said all that, I learned a lot from him – much that has been of great value since then.

When Mr Paterson retired, I was offered a place on the board myself. I had no shares, but the chairman told me that it was not necessary as the constitution of the club dictates that there must be seven directors and not all need to be shareholders. He indicated that if, or when, shares became available I could have some.

I accepted, and I well remember my first game as a director. John McBeth was the new chairman, a very well-deserved appointment because of his and his wife Frances' unstinting work for the club. That first game was at Greenock Morton. I sometimes had the habit of sitting in the stand if there was a poor view from the dugout, which happened to be the case at Greenock. I was up in the stand when a Clyde fan shouted, 'Hey, Brown, now you're a director, how about getting us a new manager?'

They never miss a trick.

We were 3–1 up at half-time and I was feeling quite pleased with myself. Obviously my new dual capacity at the club was working wonders already. Those were not my feelings at the end of the game as we contrived to lose the match 4–3, adding insult to injury by failing from the penalty spot in the last minute when Derek Frye blasted the ball over the bar. It was a rare mistake from such a deadly scorer and it just about summed up the afternoon.

Becoming a director gave me a clearer insight into the workings of a club, and in particular the financial problems surrounding any football operation. It was quite interesting, talking to Chelsea Football Club, to find that their turnover around the 1981/82 season, when we were in discussion about the Pat Nevin transfer, was £1.4 million and ours was £140,000 – exactly a tenth. I found it quite an interesting parallel.

As a board member I did see the balance sheet, and it made me conscious of the fact that Clyde was a club that wanted to stay in the black. They never wanted to risk going into the red for any reason, and it made me all the more aware of the need to develop young players and sell them on. That brings me to another aspect of being a club manager.

I feel very strongly about people assessing managers solely on match results and not looking at the other aspect of the operation – keeping the balance sheet healthy. I have gone on record in the past as saying that the best managers are not necessarily the ones with the big cheque books at the prominent clubs. I have always said that men like Allan McGraw ex-Morton and Terry Christie, who is now at Alloa Athletic and used to be at Meadowbank Thistle, are worth their weight in gold. Another such 'wonder man' is Dick Campbell of Brechin City. These guys know what it means to have to balance the books, as did the Steedman brothers at Clydebank. I think at Morton, the combination of Allan McGraw and his former chairman, John Wilson, was a very good one. Their club was a perfect example to others as regards the development of young players and survival at a good standard. Similarly Clydebank, and hopefully Clyde, have been successful in staying afloat while still being reasonably competent on the football pitch.

One of the great benefits of managing a club like Clyde is that it teaches you the art of improvisation. We did not have luxury training facilities at our disposal and our Tuesday, Wednesday and Thursday training sessions had to be held on the pitch, which was not ideal if the weather was bad. In the summer we could go to nearby Richmond Park which ran alongside the River Clyde. The young players would carry our portable goals to the park and that's where we would train, watched by the passing dog-walkers. The players liked the environment of the park – except when the ball was kicked into the river. We had to hail passing rowers to retrieve the ball for us as our financial constraints were such that we could not just shrug our shoulders and wave the ball goodbye. It was a bit like our 'pitch' alongside the railway when I was a lad!

Footballs were very valuable to a club like Clyde. In fact, such was our financial position that John Watson, our physio, used to have a standard reply when players came to him for a bootlace: 'Left boot or right boot?'

It was a joke, of course, but not too far from the reality of the economics at a club like Clyde. John was an outspoken man in the dressing room. He would never allow anyone into the treatment room with his boots on – in fact he wouldn't treat anyone who had not had a bath. When I first went there he even had a swear-box – which was quite a shock to me since I had just left Motherwell, which was famed for its industrial language. When I was talking to Willie McLean a little while later he asked me how I was getting on. I told him that I was very happy and was quite struck by how polite and nicely spoken everyone was.

'No wonder they're in the f*****g Second Division!' said Willie.

As I said before, you had to be resourceful in many ways, especially when you were dealing with part-time players, who could be rather more difficult than full-time players. You had power of payment and selection over the full-timers, but with part-time players you only had the power of selection as most of them were in other full-time jobs and the money they earned from football was hardly of significance to them. They included some very intelligent guys, and they were not going to take what we would call 'snash' from the manager.

In a sense, dealing with part-time players is a bit like dealing with international players. They are financially independent. You have the same kind of scenario, so you must have a discipline and a fairness that are fully understood. In football, too much kindness is often misconstrued as softness, and that applies to part-timers as well as to full-time pros.

I always think that footballers represent a complete cross-section of the community. People have this misguided notion that they are not necessarily the brightest guys in the world, and they can be quite disparaging about the intellect of players. This is particularly prevalent in Scotland where, it seems, if you went to a rugby-playing school you would automatically be far more intelligent than someone from a football-playing one. To me that is total nonsense because I have met and worked with very many footballers who not only have great intelligence but also many academic achievements on their CVs. Others may not have academic triumphs, but they have a mastery of common sense and general knowledge. Saying that footballers are unintelligent is on a par with judging an entire community as being stupid.

A lot of the part-time players I worked with were deep thinkers about the game and I valued their opinions – although I do have to admit that one of my failings is that I am an autocratic manager. I am not at all democratic in terms of selection or debates about tactics. I have always taken my responsibility to the full and, while I will listen to someone else's ideas and thoughts with respect, I have invariably made up my own mind about things and been dogmatic to the point of being dictatorial.

Anyway, at Clyde we had to make do in training, and we had to keep on searching for players in the lower grades. To do that we had to keep abreast of what was going on in junior, youth and schools football. It meant that I was totally preoccupied with the game, going to match after match. In one week I attended no fewer than eleven games in the afternoons and evenings. It was an all-consuming hobby and job.

It did not stop at watching games either. As an example, Clyde had four different supporters' clubs, and I used to attend as many of their meetings as possible. The parents of schoolboys also needed time to discuss the progress of their sons.

The manager of a club like Clyde has to be a Jack-of-all-trades. In my case I had wonderful support from my two assistants. My first was Ross Mathie, whom I took from a junior side the attractively named Shotts Bow Accord. Ross was excellent, and years later I was happy to recommend him to Andy Roxburgh at the SFA. When he left I promoted a player, Rab Thorburn, whose commitment and involvement had greatly impressed me. Not only did he have a BSc honours degree, but he then added a Master of Business Administration degree. Rab was an outstanding bloke who had a great rapport with the players. I consider myself to have been very fortunate in having those excellent assistants, and I would urge any manager in a similar situation to make sure he is well supported to carry what can be a really heavy load.

I am sure that Alex Ferguson, currently Britain's best manager, would agree that a good grounding at a small club – as I had at Clyde and he had at East Stirlingshire and St Mirren before he went to Aberdeen – is the best possible apprenticeship. The different things that you have to do as a manager with one of the smaller clubs teach you much more about football than if you just come in at the highest level straight from playing.

I was in charge of the national side for the eight years, and I like to think that I have a sound knowledge of Scottish football. I have coached Under-12 teams at primary school level, Under-13, –14 and –15 teams at secondary schools, the Scotland Under-16 team that reached the World Cup final, and basically every level of domestic and international football except managing a Premier Division side. Yet my most valuable time was dealing with players and jobs of all kinds while I was at Clyde.

Mrs Mary Agnew was secretary at Clyde – a redoubtable lady who worked very hard for the club and was a valuable assistant to me with her tremendous ability to keep the paperwork under control. Even at a smaller club like Clyde, there always seems to be piles of it. I did a lot of typing myself, but she was a thoroughbred on the typewriter while I was a cart-horse.

Everything was brought to the manager's attention – problems with the carpark, laundry, ball-boys, police. You name it, and I have been faced with it. That is why I have always been so grateful for all the help that was available.

I have mentioned one of our doctors but, following Dr Crorie, we had Dr John MacLean – another fine medical man. I had to make sure that there was adequate medical and physio cover all the time. To be quite frank, I could spend the rest of the book talking about my duties at Clyde. Suffice it to say that I would not have missed a moment of it for anything.

bove: Captain of the St John's Grammar School football team. hat's me in the middle of the front row.

elow: Scotland/England rivalry! I played in the Secondary Schools iternational – you may recognise the young player on the left of the iiddle row. Back row, far right, is Billy McNeill.

Honing my ball control at Orchard Street in 1959.

Inset: This team picture was when, unfortunately, our Scottish side was beaten 4-3 by England. There are some familiar faces here – back row, second from right is Alex Ferguson and next to him on the right is Jim Cruikshank, formerly of both Hearts and Scotland. I'm front row, centr

THE NEW YORK SKYLINE
The symbol of America's greatness and liberty on entrance into New York harbor.

POST CARD

Sorry you missed this
experience Craig, but apart
from that you are so well
off at times as to enjoy such
a Trip, one has to be winning.
The condition are difficult and
opposition the usual Continental.
Best wish D. Shankly

Craig Brown Esq
30, Orchard St.
HAMILTON
LANARKSHIRE
SCOTLAND.

Above: Dundee FC in Iceland. I am in the front row, far right.

Below: Here is the postcard that Bob Shankly thoughtfully sent me from New York, when I couldn't make it over with the rest of the team because of my knee injury.

Happy days with Dundee. *Above*: Dundee's Championship-winning squad, 1961/62. Back row (*left to right*): Penman, Seith, Stuart, Liney, Wishart, Brown, Waddell. Front row (*left to right*): Smith, Hamilton, Ure, Cox, Cousin, Gilzean, Robertson.

Below: Me with team mates Doug Houston, left, and Ian Ure, right, at a coaching course in Largs. Ian and I were two of the Garvie Five, who had all sorts of fun.

he Dundee boys *en route* to Cologne in 1962. Little did we know how
ventful our fixture there would be! *Inset*: A young Craig Brown at
)ens Park before a vital League game.

Celtic v. Dundee, 1962. I outjump our keeper, Pat Liney, to head clear with Bobby Seith (Dundee) and John Hughes (Celtic) watching. In the background is the old 'jungle' at Celtic Park.

The legendary Hammy and the Hamsters. Back (*left to right*)
Hugh Robertson, Alex Stuart, Alex Hamilton. Front, myself and
Kenny Cameron.

Above: Motherwell FC in 1975. I was Assistant Manager and am seated front right.

Below: My first meeting with the Clyde FC players, July 1977.

I had a broad cross-section of players at Clyde and I always tried to ensure that morale was good. I like players to socialise and become friends. That doesn't mean that they had to go out, get drunk and run riot, but to hold social occasions that included their wives and partners. With this in mind, I had a kind of social committee, comprising three players who looked after that side of football life.

Berti Vogts, the former German national manager, set up something similar with his players. He had an executive committee for his squad. We have never done that with the Scotland squad, although there is a players' pool committee which looks after the squad's commercial interests under the directiom of Paul Stretford of ProActive Sports Management. It is very difficult to have a social committee when your players are spread around Britain.

We did not have that sort of problem at Clyde, of course. Our committee ran a social fund to which every player contributed a couple of pounds a week. This ensured that we had the money for our events. As an example, we might have a Saturday afternoon game against St Johnstone in Perth After the game we would have a dinner-dance, stay over and then have a round of golf on the Sunday morning before travelling home later in the day.

I found these events to be invaluable in the social integration of the group. Players like Neil Hood and John Brogan, together with the commercial manager, John Donnelly, were instrumental in organising events like that – golf days, and so on. Players who were there during my time – including much-travelled men like Steve Archibald – still tell me that their happiest days were with Clyde Football Club.

In 1978 it was Clyde's centenary year, and I was extremely proud to be manager of the club at that time. There were a great many celebratory events which involved players of both the past and the present, the supporters, and just about everybody and anybody who had been involved in any way. The club was granted a civic reception at which many former

Clyde heroes appeared, including Harry Haddock, a very famous name in Scottish football, Tommy McCulloch, Tommy Ring, John McHugh, Dick Staite, Sam Hastings, Jim McLean and a host of other great names from Clyde's past.

There were a number of players during my time who later became national and international stars but, to me, all my players were stars in that they did their best for the club. One of the most conscientious players I have ever met was Joe Filippi, and there is a little story attached to him and a game against Ayr. I signed Joe from Celtic for £3,000. He was a very good left back and he wanted to make a good impression against Ayr which was his home-town team. During the game he was a bit late in the tackle on an Ayr player. I knew it was a bad one and was not surprised when the referee, David Syme, demanded to speak to him.

'You were a bit late there, number three,' said the referee.

Joe was a very polite man, but he was also extremely quick-witted, and he replied, 'I got there as early as I could.'

The referee did not even smile. 'Name?' he snapped.

'Joseph Filippi.'

You could see that the referee was struggling with that one. Being aware that Filippi was not the most common of names, and trying to be helpful, I called out, 'Spell it, spell it!'

I heard Joe take my advice.

'Mr Syme, it's Filippi with two Ps.'

The referee jotted it down, looked the player in the eye and said, 'Well, Mr Filippi with two Ps, you're off with two Fs!'

I suppose that it doesn't always pay to be polite and helpful!

When I left Clyde in 1986 my two sons, Hugh and John and my young daughter, Val, were fans of the club. A few games after I had left, they were at a Clyde match with Kilmarnock. Clyde were playing really well and my two boys were as excited as the rest of the supporters in the 'away' stand. One of these supporters nudged Hugh and said, 'We've turned the corner since we got rid of that Brown.'

My son replied, 'Indeed we have. You're right there, pal!'

There was no way that he was going to admit who he was.

My sons have been brought up to enjoy the game and not to take it too seriously. As a professional, I have to take it very seriously, but I like to keep hold of my sense of humour to stop myself going 'psychedelic', as I call it.

To sum up my experience at Clyde, the hours spent on the training ground were of great value to me because I was not only doing my best for the club but was also continuing to learn my trade. If you are willing to admit your mistakes and to learn from them, then time spent at clubs like Clyde is time well spent.

12

In the Scotland Camp

WHEN THE OFFER to become assistant to Andy and coach the Under-21 team came in I was still lecturing at Craigie College, and at that same time Graeme Souness had become manager of Rangers with Walter Smith as his No. 2. I knew Walter well because he was one of the SFA staff coaches at Largs.

One morning at Largs, Walter approached me and told me that his chairman would like a private word with me. At this stage I had neither accepted nor rejected the offer from Andy Roxburgh as I was waiting to meet Ernie Walker, the then General Secretary of the SFA. However, when Walter told me that David Holmes wanted to see me I said that I couldn't see much point because the club already had a good coaching team in place. As well as Graeme and Walter, Don MacKay was there working with the reserve team. Walter was insistent that I meet his chairman, however, and so we arranged to have a chat at Ibrox at seven o'clock in the morning in the club's Broomloan Road stand. The reason that the meeting was so early was to give me time to get back to Largs for a nine-o'clock start.

David Holmes was waiting for me and almost immediately began to put his case. He told me that the club was in the process of rebuilding throughout, and that he had made quite a study of my career. As a result, he felt that it would be appropriate to invite me to join the board of directors of Glasgow Rangers. This was a very tempting offer, and an honour, which had to be considered seriously.

I gave it a lot of thought, of course. If I accepted Rangers' offer it would take me away from the coalface of working with players, as I would be mostly involved in administrative matters concerned with aspects of club development, in particular the apprentices, of whom there were more than a hundred at the club. I would be the director responsible for that and various other development avenues.

I found Mr Holmes to be a very persuasive, enthusiastic and determined gentleman, who was obviously very excited about the future of Rangers Football Club. After our meeting he was going off for a three-week holiday, but said that upon his return he would like to have my decision, suggesting that I might like to attend the pre-season friendly against Bayern Munich and talk to him then.

Walter Smith had given me some further ideas about Rangers and told me what he knew of the plans for the future and, as you can imagine, my head was extremely full. On the one hand I had the opportunity to join the SFA as assistant manager of the national team and manager of the Under-21s, and on the other was an exciting opportunity to join one of the biggest football clubs in the world in a challenging and responsible role. Meanwhile, I was still manager of Clyde and a lecturer at Craigie College. Thank goodness for golf!

Eventually the smell of the liniment proved to be too overpowering and I realised that I could not take a position that would deny me my fair share of that unique aroma and the atmosphere that goes with it. I telephoned Campbell Ogilvie, the Rangers Director-Secretary, and asked him to inform Mr

Holmes of my decision to decline the great opportunity that he had afforded me.

I accepted the position at the Scottish Football Association. I was involved with the pre-season training of Clyde and the move to Firhill because I had to work three months' notice at the college and the SFA were kind enough to allow me to work part-time for them until my notice reached its conclusion.

My first game in charge of the Under-21 side was against West Germany at Ibrox. The Germans fielded a very strong side and I knew it was going to be quite a challenge. The game was played on 9 September 1986, and I was delighted with a very resilient Scotland performance and a 1–0 victory, which was a great morale-booster for all concerned – myself included.

The team included several players who have since become household names. Henry Smith was in goal and in front of him were Robert Shannon, Joe Tortolano, Derek Ferguson, Paul Hegarty, Tommy Boyd, Steve Gray, Peter Grant, Gordon Durie, Kevin Gallacher and Ian Durrant. I also used Robert Fleck, Owen Archdeacon and Ian Ferguson, who were on the bench. The scorer? Kevin Gallacher. One might be tempted to add – who else? Kevin was a deadly scorer throughout his career.

Just over a month later came my second game in charge. This one was very different because it was against the Republic of Ireland in Dundalk, a European Championship group match. As was customary, it was being played the day before the seniors met in their group game. I was still at college at the time, and on the day of the match I had to finish in the early afternoon, catch a flight to Dublin and then be taken by car to Dundalk to meet up with the team. The side was near enough the same as I had used against West Germany, but I put Andy Goram in goal and added Gordon Hunter, Derek Whyte and Jim Duffy.

In our group were Belgium and the Republic of Ireland,

and I was keen that we should get our campaign off to a flying start at the expense of the excellent young Irish team. It was a very good game and at the end we had won 2–1, just the result that I wanted, and so, as you can imagine, I was highly delighted and considered that my journey had been well worth the effort. Shannon scored our first goal and Gallacher again hit the winner.

Having got off to such a good start, we then won the return game at Easter Road 4–1, Robert Fleck scoring a superb hat-trick and Ian Ferguson adding our other goal. Now we had to pull off a couple of good results against Belgium. The first match was in Bruges on 1 April 1987, and we were happy with the 0–0 draw. The return game took place the following season at Falkirk and we won 1–0, guaranteeing that we finished top of our group. It was Andy Walker who scored our goal.

Our senior side were not faring so well in our bid to reach the European Championship finals. In addition to Belgium and the Republic of Ireland, we also had to face Bulgaria and Luxembourg. Victories over Belgium, Bulgaria and Luxembourg were fully warranted. But there were too many other dropped points and, although Scotland were only two points adrift of eventual group winners the Republic of Ireland, it was a defeat by the Irishmen at Hampden that made all the difference.

Our Under-21 campaign continued, and we had to play England in a quarterfinal game. The first leg was at Aberdeen in February 1988. Paul Gascoigne was among the stars in the England team but it was Watford's Gary Porter who stole the show by hitting England's winner. That left us with an uphill task in the return a month later at Nottingham Forest's City Ground. We battled, but once again it was to no avail as a goal from Manchester City's David White won the night for England, and the tie, with a 2–0 aggregate score.

I am not one for excuses. If you lose you hold up your hand to be counted just the same as if you win. However, one of the problems of running a national Under-21 side is that you never know from one game to the next which players are going to be available to you. It is not just the demands of the clubs or the injuries, but also the demands of the senior team. On the day after our first leg against England, the Scotland senior team had a friendly match against Saudi Arabia in Riyadh and I had to give up one of my best squad members, namely John Collins. I'm not saying that he would have made a vast difference because that would detract from the performance of the other players, but in a match with so much at stake you like to have all your options available to you. I was disappointed about that but I understood Andy Roxburgh's reasoning. He was trying to build a squad capable of reaching the 1990 World Cup and he had to use friendly matches like these to assess all his options.

I think the game in Saudi Arabia was the only one I missed during my period as assistant to Andy, but I had other duties at that particular time.

Every manager must make it a priority to surround himself with good, loyal, knowledgeable colleagues, and at Under-21 level I selected Tommy Craig. He may have earned only one international cap but he was a good, inventive coach and well respected by the players. Tommy was my colleague throughout my time in charge of the Under-21 team. Our physio was my former Clyde colleague, John Watson. John had been promoted, as he had previously worked for Andy with the youth team. Our medico was Dr Craig Speirs of Greenock Morton Football Club. We later introduced a goalkeeping specialist coach in Jim Stewart, the former Rangers, Middlesbrough and St Mirren keeper.

The backroom staff are vital at whatever level you are playing. You have to get it right, and I believe that we had exactly the right set-up for the job during my seven and a half years in charge of the Under-21 team.

In 1992, we again won our group with only one defeat in our qualifying games against Bulgaria, Romania and Switzerland. Our quarter final tie was against what had now become Germany. We drew the first leg 1–1 in Bochum and then had a terrific return game at Pittodrie. The Germans were 2–0 ahead before Ray McKinnon pulled one back just before half-time. Herrlich then made it 3–1 to the visitors and set the scene for a storming second half in which Gerry Creaney, Paul Lambert and Alex Rae took it in turns to score and give us a 4–3 victory and a 5–4 aggregate.

Our semi final opponents were Sweden. The first leg was at Aberdeen where we were held to a 0–0 draw. I was not too disappointed as the Swedes had played a typically tight tactical battle to give themselves a clean sheet for the return match. I knew they could not play the same way at home and thought we might do better in Sweden. It looked, though, as if the tie was going into a stalemate situation, until nine minutes from the end when Rodlund scored the winner.

We had a very good Under-21 team at that time – Michael Watt, the goalkeeper from Aberdeen, Alan McLaren of Hearts at centre half, and Gary Smith of Aberdeen, who was also in the centre of defence. We also had Paul Lambert, who has since made quite a name for himself but was then with St Mirren, Brian O'Neil, who was with Celtic at that time, Eoin Jess and Scott Booth of Aberdeen, Alex Rae of Millwall, Gerry Creaney and Phil O'Donnell of Celtic and Duncan Ferguson of Dundee United. Many of those players have moved on to bigger clubs and bigger things.

Perhaps I should digress a little at this stage and explain something about myself. Everyone looks upon me as being a quiet sort of a guy who remains cool and calm even under the most stressful of circumstances. It's a nice image to have, and if it happens to be the reality then fair enough. However, I haven't always been like that. When I was at Clyde I was quite a wild man, always raving on the touchline and treating everyone else as a bitter enemy. I received a number of disciplinary letters from the Scottish authorities and I was always wound up like a coiled spring.

Some of that remained with me during my years with the

Under-21 side. I remember that, when we were playing away to Romania in the group match to qualify for the 1992 European Championship, I had occasion to speak to Tommy Craig, just before half-time, about Gerry Creaney's first-half complaints about some aspects of the defensive display. In fairness, Gerry had scored an excellent goal to put us ahead, but we were under the hammer after that as the Romanians tried to get back on level terms. Creaney was shouting abusively at his colleagues, and I told Tommy that I would speak to him at half-time – which I did in no uncertain terms. A few years later, Gerry Creaney was featured in one of the newspapers and, when asked for his most dangerous moment, said it was being confronted by me during that half-time in Romania.

Tommy Craig said that he was going to join in but that there was nothing left to say after my ten-minute barrage. Sometimes, in anger, we don't realise how loud or vitriolic we become. It is a fact that, as a football manager, you have to have an inner hardness because players understand that, and also because it is your head that is always on the block. You have to be determined that, if the axe is going to fall, it is because you have done something wrong and not because you have allowed others to do wrong on your behalf. You have to be single-minded and autocratic. Today there seems to be a measure of democracy creeping into dressing rooms, but I am of the old school – too autocratic. What I say is what must be, and then I will stand the consequences of being proved wrong.

Luckily we had a strong squad at that time, and indeed throughout my time in charge. We were officially placed third in Europe – our best ever and excellent for a country of our size.

Since the Under-21 games often coincided with the senior matches, I was able to go on spying trips for both my team and for the senior side. The Germans, for instance, tend to play the same way at all levels. In Scotland we tend to allow the coaches at the various levels to decide upon their own strategy.

My missions were useful for both teams and, if we found that a country played the same tactics at all levels, it made the Under-21 games all the more interesting when they were played on the eve of the senior games.

Four years after that 1992 campaign, Tommy Craig had been promoted to manager of the Under-21 side and his assistant was Alex McLeish, who was capped 77 times by Scotland. I have a little leg-pull with Alex when I see him. I ask him how many caps he won. I already know the answer, but then I say to him that probably there were seven corners per game, and he as a central defender would come up for most of them. Even allowing for staying back for a number of those corners it still means that he had something like five hundred scoring opportunities. Then I like to ask him how many goals he scored for Scotland. I know the answer to that one as well – zero. So how come, Alex, you still like to come up for corners? He has a ready response, though: 'I acted as a decoy for Kenny Dalglish!'

With Tommy in charge and Alex as his assistant, the Scotland Under-21 side once again reached the last four in the 1996 European Championship before going out by a single goal. It was another great achievement, showing the strength of the young players that we produced in Scotland, and totally vindicated the youth development programme we had. Dare I say that in England there was nowhere near the same level of success at Under-21 level over that same period of time?

The annual tournament in Toulon for Under-21 sides was something I enjoyed each year. It was a great experience for young players to get a taste of competitive football in a tournament situation, and helped to build up a squad for the European Championship games to follow. It also gave me the chance to watch other coaches in action and the opportunity to add to my own knowledge.

As an example, I watched the Brazil Under-21 team in Toulon. I know they have a very generous staffing arrangement for their teams. In World Cup finals, if they have 22 players they will most likely have 22 members of staff to take care of them. In Toulon, they had a coach just for warming up the substitutes. No sub was allowed to get into the game unless this coach was satisfied that he was ready. It was such a good system that in the Scotland set-up we have copied it. I think we were the only nation in the 1996 European Championship to employ a warm-up coach for our substitutes. I also think we were the only team to have our substitutes out on the pitch at half-time under supervision to prepare in case they were needed. Our physio, an excellent young man by the name of Philip Yeates, of Dunfermline FC, is known to everyone as Pip, and he took the responsibility of making sure that the subs were warmed up for action.

We continued that strategy throughout my time with the national team. We had seven subs on the bench and we could use any three of them, so we had to keep all seven ready for action. Our spare goalkeeper has his own coach, Alan Hodgkinson, to keep him in readiness for action. All in all we tried to keep ourselves well organised, and this stems in part from watching the tricks of the trade used by other coaches, and in particular those from the Latin American countries during my Under-21 days.

One thing I notice about the Brazilians is that they walk out hand in hand. If I asked the Scotland players to do that I know what sort of response I would be likely to get! The Latin Americans have a different view of such things, and they walk out brimming with confidence. You didn't see us doing that in the World Cup, though – the disparaging remarks I would have got from fans and players alike would tend to have had the opposite effect to the togetherness I tried constantly to achieve.

Talking of Toulon, Alan Shearer scored many fine goals for England in those tournaments, as he has for his country's senior team and his various clubs. I think I witnessed the best goal he has ever scored when I watched him in the final of the tournament against France in 1991. Shearer was already top scorer of the tournament with six goals in three games, but his winner in the final was quite sensational as he sent a scissors-kick volley into the net from twenty yards. It was a most wonderful example of striking play, and the goal was simply out of this world. Although we won two and drew one of our three games we did not make it into the final, but we did receive the tournament's Fair Play Award and we were very happy with that.

One of the big advantages in tournaments like that is that you get to know your players quite well before dealing with them in a senior situation. You can foster team spirit early on and teach the youngsters how to conduct themselves during a tournament, whether it be in a foreign country or within your own shores. One of the acid tests for young players is when you treat them to a pizza!

I know that dietitians will throw up their hands in horror, but we occasionally treated our young players to a pizza. We'd stop the team bus and they'd all pile out and pick whatever they wanted. That's when you find out who the 'big-time' guys are. Most pizza places have a list of 20 to 30 different types of pizza, and the majority of players are quite happy to select one off the board. The 'big-time' player will always be unable to find what he wants and have one made specially – which he feels will impress everyone else. It didn't impress those of us who were trying to get the coach on its journey again as quickly as possible, but it did give an insight into the character of the players under your control.

Some of them are tempted to get a wee bit too big for their boots. I can remember when we had trials for fifteen- and sixteen-year-olds at Stirling University. Each had an individual room, and I went round at eight o'clock knocking on the doors to wake them up. I made a mistake at one door and instead of knocking and saying, 'Up you get, it's eight o'clock', I said, 'Breakfast, breakfast!' instead. A sleepy voice inside replied, 'Just leave it at the door!' That young man is now a well-known player at a big Scottish club.

I will say that most young players do appreciate their opportunity and do not take anything for granted, but there is always the odd one that achieves status in his own mind long before it is bestowed upon him.

At one time you were allowed to play two over-age players in your Under-21 side, but that has now been stopped. It was a great help because it not only opened up extra options but gave you a chance to put some experience into your side and provide extra tuition for the young players. Alex McLeish was one of my over-age players, as were Stuart McCall, Andy Goram, Henry Smith, Jim Duffy, Campbell Murray and Paul Hegarty. We tried to include players who had a good sense of responsibility and I think it worked very well.

My time in charge of the Under-21 side was of great value to me. It allowed me to benefit from watching others as well as experimenting with my own ideas, and to gain further experience of coaching players for their country rather than for the more regular club fixtures. It gave me the chance to make a few mistakes which were not as costly as they would have been if I had done the same thing with the senior side.

I still think there is a strong case for more B international football. I believe there remains still a huge gap between the Under-21 side and the senior side, and a greater rise in status for B internationals would be the equivalent of having a reserves section in a club. A lot of players have a problem in making the transition, and I am convinced that the stepping-stone of B internationals would be of great value, as it did for Don Hutchinson.

As well as the Under-21 side I was also in charge of some youth sides, and we had some excellent results at these levels. In 1987, not long after I was appointed, the Under-18 side qualified for their World Cup finals to be held in Chile. Ross Mathie was my colleague – and he is now the Assistant of Football Development Director for the SFA and runs the various youth teams. The medical team was Dr John Maclean and Philip Yeates, both of whom have since been promoted and are now working with the national team. I like the Liverpool scheme of continuity, both in coaching and in medical staff.

Peter Donald was the official in charge of our party. He is now the efficient secretary of the Scottish Football League. Heading the delegation was John S. McDonald, a very well-known Highland League administrator, who was then chairman of the Youth International Committee of the SFA. John, or Jock as he's known is a very famous character in Scottish football. He once punched the late great Billy Bremner, and he was there when Mo Johnston and Charlie Nicholas returned to a hotel late and were disciplined. They did not recognise him, and Mo slipped a fiver into his top pocket when he opened the back door for them. Jock blew a gasket and gave them a loud dressing-down. Mo then asked him what he was going to do with the fiver.

'I am going to buy myself a large Macallan and water, thank you very much,' came Jock's reply.

In our group in Chile we had East Germany, Bahrain and Colombia. I told the players that if they did well and qualified we would have a night out at a world-famous disco, situated on the Pacific coast, called Topsy Topsy. I thought that while they were in the disco the staff could have a meal at a neighbouring restaurant.

We won our first game against East Germany with a 2–1 result and then drew 1–1 with Bahrain. We only needed to draw with Colombia and we would qualify for the quarterfinals. Sadly, at half-time we were two goals down and the Colombians were already celebrating. However, we were not about to give up easily, and when we reduced the deficit from the penalty spot I knew we could fight our way back into it – as indeed we did. The final score was 2–2 and we were through.

Among our players in that side were Alan Main, who is now goalkeeper at St Johnstone, Billy McKinlay of Dundee United and Blackburn Rovers, Paul Wright, formerly of

Kilmarnock, now Falkirk and Scott Crabbe, the former Dundee United, Hearts, Falkirk and Livingston striker who is now with Raith Rovers. Not many of the other players have come through to top-grade football, except perhaps Scott Nesbit and Brian Welsh, who were the two dominant centre-halves.

When we were flying out to Chile I met my old friend Berti Vogts in Amsterdam and I asked him how many players he had missing. I was surprised when he told me that none was missing because it was October and both the German and British seasons were in full swing with every available player being needed at club level. Berti explained that the president of the West German Federation had told the clubs that if their players were called up they would have to release them. I felt quite envious, because from the initial eighteen players I had selected no fewer than fifteen were not released to us. Players like John Collins, Paul Lambert and David Robertson were forced to drop out, so we went with a reduced squad because our clubs were not forced to release their players for the three weeks of the tournament. Knowing that your opposition is at its strongest does not help your confidence.

Having qualified for the quarter finals, we kept our word to the players and allowed them to go to this Topsy Topsy disco, but found to our horror that they would not be allowed in unless accompanied. The players all had to have partners. I asked one of the local representatives if they could find partners for all our players. They said that they would find them partners at the Catholic University of Valparaiso. We were staying in a beautiful place called Vina del Mar on the Pacific coast, and Valparaiso was the adjoining town where the games were being played. So a quest was started at the university to find eighteen girls to accompany our players.

We told the lads what was happening and gave them permission to wear their own casual clothes. They were told that their partners would be collected in small groups on the way and that they must each sit on their own so that the girls could select their partners. We thought that would be a fair arrangement for the young ladies.

Well, far from wearing jeans and so on, the players really put on the style and wore their very best suits. As for the aftershaves and colognes, the whole bus smelled like a mobile parfumerie. It was hilarious watching the faces of these guys every time the bus stopped to pick up another group of partners. Nobody, of course, wanted to be the last one selected but, in the end, it was Scott Nesbit who claimed that dubious honour, to the merriment of everyone else.

When we eventually got there it turned out to be an unusual disco. It was on three floors, and to travel upwards you were conveyed on a kind of big wheel, and to come down you slid on a mat.

Ernie Walker and Andy Roxburgh flew out to join us for our quarter final game in which we were facing the mighty West German team. We had been adopted by a girls' secondary school, and they had not only learned Scottish country dancing and poems for the occasion but also gave us a lot of vocal support. We were to be without them for the West German game, so Ross Mathie and I decided that we ought to enlist the support of a local school once again. It was a mixed school and we were warmly welcomed. We taught them a few Scottish songs and the inevitable 'Here we go, here we go, here we go'. They made flags and banners and gave us some great support in the stadium.

At the end of normal time the score was 1–1 and it was quite a game. We went into extra time and then lost Scott Nesbit, who was ordered off. The Argentinian referee then confounded everyone when we scored from the penalty spot through Joe McLeod, only to be told that the kick must be retaken. This time Joe failed and the game went to a penalty shoot-out which the Germans won 5–4.

It was a sad way to end the tournament, and it had happened to us twice – at this level and at Under-16 level. If you also take into consideration Gary McAllister's penalty failure in Euro 96, you can see why I am keen to ensure that we claim all our future results within normal time. I don't want to leave anything to the chance of failure which penalty kicks provide.

The Under-16s World Cup was held in Scotland in 1989 and, as the host country, it was up to us to maintain local interest in the competition. We did not start too well and were held to a 0–0 draw by Ghana at Hampden. We then played Bahrain and beat them. We got through our group and played East Germany in the quarterfinal at Aberdeen. We won 1–0 and faced Portugal in the semifinal. The Portuguese were coached by Carlos Queiroz, now South Afica's national coach, and it is interesting how many coaches of these youth teams have gone on to become managers and coaches of their senior teams, as I did.

The Portugal game at Tynecastle was watched by 28,000 with another 5,000 locked out. A Brian O'Neil goal gave us a 1–0 victory, and there we were in the final. We faced Saudi Arabia in front of a 53,000 crowd at Hampden. We went 2–0 ahead and looked to be in good shape, but the Saudis pulled one back and then we missed a penalty, which gave them renewed spirit. They scored again and we were into extra time. With no goals in the extra half-hour it was all down to penalties and, as I said before, we failed.

Nevertheless, it had been an excellent tournament and was a fitting tribute to the standard of youth football. I was very proud to have coached that team and to have been generally at the hub of football at this level. It was an excellent experience for me and, hopefully, I was able to make some small contribution to the careers of those young players.

13

Assistant Manager

ONE OF ANDY Roxburgh's early decisions was to appoint Alan Hodgkinson as goalkeeping coach. He managed to get Alan to come and coach our two chief goalkeepers of that time, Jim Leighton and Andy Goram. We also had Nicky Walker, Jonathan Gould and Campbell Money among those in the frame. Our Under-21 goalkeeping coach, Jim Stewart, worked alongside Alan Hodgkinson, and one of the reasons for the defensive success of the Scotland team was that we had such good goalkeeper coaching provision. It also took the responsibility away from Andy and me and enabled us to concentrate on the outfield coaching.

It was a busy time as you can imagine, but there is a rule that Under-21 matches played on the eve of senior games must not be more than a hundred kilometres from the seniors' venue. That makes it much easier to get from one game to the next, and for people like me to fulfil their role. Having been a player at Rangers and Dundee, where there were many international players, I did not feel out of place when it was my turn to walk into the dressing room of the national squad. I did not feel overawed, even though I had no senior caps myself. I knew what these chaps were about and felt perfectly comfortable with them, as indeed I like to think they felt with me.

After a year or two, many of the national side were players who had been with me earlier in the Under-21 side, but of course at the beginning this was not the case. It was a very interesting time. Andy knew his way around and he knew he had a job to do following the disappointment of the 1986 World Cup finals. He had the immediate task of getting the side through to the European Championship, unknown territory for Scotland as we had never qualified for the final stages before. He also had an eye on the 1990 World Cup and knew that he had to build a side that could keep up the momentum of Scotland's frequent appearances in the tournament.

Andy himself was a former schoolboy, youth and amateur international player for Scotland. His club experience was gained with Queen's Park, Clydebank, Partick Thistle and Falkirk. He was a striker and a deep-thinking player rather than one of those sent up front as cannon-fodder. He had been the SFA Director of Coaching for ten years before taking on the role of manager to the national side. The first couple of years of his career in charge were not easy. There was little opportunity to arrange a series of friendlies to test the water. It was straight in at the deep end to try to qualify for the European finals to be held in West Germany in 1988. The first Scotland game was at home to Bulgaria and it resulted in a disappointing 0–0 draw. Even the second-half appearance of Kenny Dalglish from the subs' bench for his final international cap failed to break the deadlock. There was little comfort in being unbeaten because in group situations you really need to capitalise on home advantage.

The next game was the one I have already mentioned. It was away to the Republic of Ireland and, once again, ended in a 0–0 draw. There was some relief when Luxembourg came visiting and we beat them 3–0. The picture was starting to look a little healthier, since we were unbeaten after three games and had not conceded a goal. All that changed when we then played our return game with the Irish Republic. I've already written about the 1–0 home defeat so I will not repeat it – it's far too painful. Andy remained cool and continued to study his players and coach them into his style. We went to Belgium for our next fixture. Remember that Belgium had reached the semifinals of the World Cup only a year earlier and still had the likes of Scifo and the Van der Elsts to lead their own assault on Europe.

At half-time we were faring quite well. Claeson had given the Belgians the lead after eight minutes, but Paul McStay levelled five minutes later. The second half became virtually one-way traffic, though, as Claeson completed his hat-trick. Vercauteren added another and we came home on the end of a 4–1 scoreline.

By now we only had two games left, and the chances of qualifying were very remote. We would have to win both games, and some disaster would have to befall those above us. The Tartan Army was given something to cheer about because our remaining games saw a very different approach and we took revenge over Belgium with a 2–0 victory. Ally McCoist scored in the first half and Paul McStay in the second. The game was played at Hampden, so there were a lot of happy Glaswegians in town that night, no matter what scarf they wore. There was an even better result to come because in our final game we beat Bulgaria in front of their own fans when Gary Mackay replaced Paul McStay at half-time and scored the only goal of the match. We did the Republic of Ireland a big favour because that left them in top place in the group and automatic qualifiers.

All sights were now on the 1990 World Cup in Italy. Yugoslavia, France, Norway and Cyprus stood between us and a place in the finals. One particular game that is outstanding in my memory was the home game against France on a wet night at Hampden. We had researched the opposition in the usual way, Maurice Johnston helping because he was playing for Nantes. We had the added incentive of Mo wanting to put one over on the players he was seeing every day in his club life. He certainly did that because we beat the French 2–0. It was a crucial game in that we wanted to keep up the momentum that had taken us into a good position in the group after beating Norway 2–1 in Oslo, drawing at home to Yugoslavia and beating Cyprus 3–2 in Limassol. Our goals against the French? Both were scored by Mo Johnston.

We were staying at Gleneagles to prepare for the France game and there were horrendous traffic problems in Cumbernauld as we were journeying to the match. In 1989 there were no mobile phones in everybody's pockets, so it wasn't easy either to get help or to phone ahead to tell anyone of our problems. Roy Aitken did have a mobile – but it was in his case in the luggage compartment of the coach. We pulled over and Roy phoned through to Hampden to tell them that we would be late. A police escort assisted and we were hurried through to the stadium. Even so, we arrived just 35 minutes before the kick-off which left little time for changing and final team talks. Players do not like to be at a ground too early, but this was carrying things a bit too far. It was an excellent performance, though, with a sense of passion and urgency lifting the players above the muddy conditions to great heights of international football.

After beating Cyprus 2–1 at home we then had to travel to Zagreb to play the strongest team in the group, Yugoslavia. Gordon Durie put us ahead in the first half and all was going well until the 54th minute when Katanec equalised. We were then seriously under the hammer and our defence went to pieces to the extent that first Steve Nicol and then Gary Gillespie scored own goals. I don't think the Yugoslavs could believe their good fortune.

There's a story attached to that game as well. As you may be aware, players are accommodated two to a room on these trips and they are told that they must not lock their doors in order that they can be checked on at any time. There was one player on that trip who nobody wanted to room with because he had a problem with flatulence – quite an overwhelming problem it was too. On the night before the game I did my rounds of the hotel, but when I came to his door I found it to be locked. I knocked and waited for a few minutes until the door was opened by the flustered-looking player who was wearing bulging boxer shorts. I asked him what was going on and checked that he was alone. Rather red-faced he told me what he had been doing. I'm not going into any detail but many a referee has been branded guilty of the same act by fans all over Britain.

The next day I was making my contribution to Andy's team talk and went through the list of Yugoslav players, which included Ivkovic, Spasic, Baijic, Stojkovic and others with similar-sounding names. Finally, I turned to the said player and added, 'There's another guy who needs taking out of the game, W. . . . ovic!' The player was one of our England-based men, but I don't want to embarrass him further so I'll keep his name under wraps.

In a sense we could afford to lose to Yugoslavia, but we didn't want to have a similar result against France, who would be including Eric Cantona in their side. Andy was worried about the outcome of this game, and I think it was a masterstroke on the part of Ernie Walker of the SFA when he called Andy and me to one side at the hotel shortly before the game. I think he could see that we were both a little worried by the situation because he gave us this morale-booster.

'You've done a fine job, guys, no matter what the result of this game tonight in Paris. I'm going to recommend that you get a new contract to the European Championship of 1992. I know the President approves so I hope you will be happy with that.'

It was not relevant to our match preparations but it certainly gave us both a great psychological lift – in particular

Andy, who was, of course, in the hot seat. Ernie had done the same thing back in 1986 when we were in Mexico for the World Cup. On the morning of our final game, against Uruguay, Alex Ferguson and the backroom staff were having our breakfast in the prison camp in which we were staying. The players had nicknamed the place Alcatraz because it was very remote and pretty spartan. Alex had a worried look on his face before he left the table, but he looked a much happier man when he came back. We asked if there was a problem, and Alex told us that Ernie Walker had told him that, regardless of how the game went, it was felt that he had handled the campaign very well and that it had been a useful exercise notwithstanding. He had congratulated him on the attitude of the staff and players and thanked him for all he had done.

No matter how experienced a manager is, a pat on the back at times like these can be a great morale-booster and can lighten the load, improving your approach to the game ahead. It takes a good official to recognise the need for that kind of help.

We had scored first in each of our group qualifying games up to now and we wanted to keep that momentum going. Andy told the players to keep their heads against the Frenchmen, who were in need of maximum points if they were going to stand any chance of reaching Italy.

It was interesting that although Eric Cantona played as an attacking midfielder for Montpellier, the French national coach, Michel Platini, elected to use him as a striker. Richard Gough almost scored with a header early on in the game but all too soon we were on the defensive and Deschamps put France ahead after 25 minutes. We pulled ourselves together, though, and we were not too unhappy at half-time. We felt that we were a match for the French and could get back on terms. The second half proceeded with Scotland mostly on the offensive. When Di Meco lunged wildly at Mo Johnston, the referee had little option but to reduce the French to ten men. We continued to press but Ally McCoist was having one of those days when the ball would hit the side-netting or the paintwork off the bar, but just would not go in. Cantona suddenly found himself alone with just Jim Leighton to beat and could not resist making it 2–0. In the last minute Steve Nicol scored his second own goal in as many games, and we trooped off with a 3–0 defeat hanging round our necks – a scoreline that flattered the home side, but it was still a result, and one that did us few favours.

We had to get a result against Norway to clinch our place in Italy. There was a danger that, having leaked six goals in our last two games, we might still be suffering from the same problem, even allowing for the fact that we had scored half of those goals ourselves. There was a little extra pressure because Jim Leighton was going through a bit of a difficult time – especially since we had been forced to leave him out of the side for the Yugoslavia game as he had sustained a back problem while kicking a ball in training. He was with Alex Ferguson at Manchester United at this time, and Alex was reported as saying that Andy should assure Leighton that his place was safe in order to settle his nerves.

A journalist raised this point at a press conference and Andy parried the suggestion by pointing out that he did not pick other managers' teams and therefore he did not expect them to pick his. It was a fair point, but the next day there were newspaper headlines screaming that Andy was telling Alex to shut his mouth. Alex was soon on to Andy, and I was in the room when the phone rang. I picked it up and, before I could say anything, there was a torrent of abuse. I finally managed to interrupt and explain that it was me he was haranguing, and I tried to point out that Andy had said nothing at the press conference resembling anything like what had appeared in the newspapers. Alex was not a happy man and growled on a little more before Andy was able to take his call.

Some time later there was a need for someone to go to Old Trafford to watch some players – and guess who that someone was. Right in one – I was the guy! I had always been well received at Old Trafford before and knew quite a few of the staff, so there was no problem in arranging my seat. When I got there I was told to go to Fergie's office because 'he'll be pleased to see you'.

Oh no he won't, I thought, but I went there anyway. There were a number of people already tucking in to pre-match sandwiches. I looked around the room but could see no sign of Alex. A minute or two later I heard his footsteps and he appeared at the door. He looked straight at me and I waited for the explosion.

'Hello, Broon, how are you?' he enquired very politely. The previous matter was never mentioned and has never been spoken of since. It is another example of the Jekyll and Hyde character of one of the world's greatest club managers.

The Norway game attracted 64,000 into Hampden. We needed to draw at the very least, while the Norwegians were playing for pride only. As it was, Jim Leighton was in the side and equalled the record of 55 full caps for a Scottish goalkeeper, which was then held by Alan Rough. There were a number of our regular players missing because of injuries, but the team set about the task with a strong will. The supporters were terrific and roared the side on almost throughout the first half, even though the breakthrough goal was becoming more and more elusive.

The referee was looking at his watch and Andy and I were already well into our thoughts about what to say to the players when Maurice Malpas sent a long clearance up the field. It found Ally McCoist. Thorstvedt, the Norwegian goalkeeper, sensing the danger, rushed out of goal and Ally sent one of the finest chips from 25 yards I have ever seen – straight over his head and into the net. Hampden went wild.

The second half was fairly even with both sides hitting the woodwork but, in the last minute, Erland Johnsen let fly with a hopeful shot which dipped and swerved wickedly past Jim Leighton and into the net. It was agony to watch. Suddenly the scoreline was 1–1. We were put out of our misery a moment later when the referee ended the game. There was no misery on the terraces, though. The Tartan Army had been celebrating for some time and after the game, in the dressing room, we were able to join them in toasting the 1990 World Cup.

I mentioned earlier that when I took the youth and Under-21 sides I greatly valued the local support we were given in tournaments. Andy had the same view, and before we went to the World Cup it was decided that we should take the players to Genoa where we would be playing two of our group games, against Costa Rica and Sweden. Our other game would be in Turin against Brazil. Yes, Brazil again!

The idea was that we would travel out to Genoa to take in their local derby game against Sampdoria and be introduced to the crowd. Liverpool had other ideas. Kenny Dalglish was manager at Anfield and he did not feel inclined to allow Steve Nicol or Gary Gillespie to come on the public relations trip. Andy was not at all happy about this because he felt that it was vital for as many of the players as possible to attend. I can vouch for the fact that Andy was never a junket man. He would only make trips that he felt were necessary. As well as being a PR exercise, it was seen as a great chance for the squad to see for themselves what the ground was like and what the atmosphere would be. It also gave us another chance to have a look at the five-star Grand Hotel Bristol in Rapallo, which was to be our luxury base for the tournament.

Andy was so annoyed at the non-appearance of the Liverpool players that he dropped them both for the friendly against Argentina, who were then the reigning world champions. It was a prestigious game and everyone wanted to play in it, but Andy was not going to allow sentiment to get in the way of discipline.

The friendly was watched by about 52,000, and Scotland gave a great account of themselves against the superstars of Argentina. Maradona was not in their side, but players like Caniggia, Batista, Valdana and Monzon were very much in evidence. It was a great night for Scottish football because a

Stewart McKimmie goal proved to be the only one of the night, and we were given a great morale-booster by beating the then kings of world football. For once I think the England fans were on our side as well, since they were still seething over Argentina having knocked them out of the World Cup in 1986 with that infamous 'Hand of God' goal by Maradona.

Our preparations for the 1990 World Cup could not have been better. I was working alongside Andy throughout and we went into the competition fairly confident of being able to do well, even though we had been criticised for a couple of poor performances in the other friendlies – losing to East Germany and Egypt and drawing with Poland. The latter game took our own-goal tally to four, something of which we were reminded at every opportunity.

We travelled to Malta to acclimatise and play our last warm-up match before going to Italy. We won 2–1 with goals from Alan McInally and we now felt that we were as ready as we were going to be. There were a number of worries, however. Mo Johnston had been scoring all season and was one of our main hopes for goals, but he had torn a stomach muscle and it was touch and go right to the last minute. We also found out at the last minute that Ally McCoist had been nursing a hamstring injury but had been keeping it quiet in the hope that it would go away. Alan McInally's arm had been in a sling for several weeks, and Gary Gillespie was another hamstring victim. Murdo MacLeod was another worry because he had been suffering from a bad groin strain and he actually returned to his club, Borussia Dortmund, for intensive treatment to get him fit for the tournament. There were various other niggling injuries which meant that we had rather a patched-up squad, but it was felt that we had to take a gamble.

I am the sort of person who likes to learn something every day, and I was certainly still learning each day from the activities leading up to the 1990 World Cup. Andy was very similar to me in background and in fact had once been the youngest headmaster in Scotland. We were usually on the same wavelength, but at the end of the day he was the man with his head on the block, ready to take the brickbats or the bouquets. I was merely riding shotgun, but it was a very interesting journey and a great apprenticeship, even though the thought of one day stepping into his shoes had never, at that time, entered my head.

At last our big day, Monday, 11 June 1990, arrived, and there was another setback because we were not allowed to wear our familiar blue shirts. Since Costa Rica wore red it seemed a little odd that there should be any sort of problem but, apparently, the concern was over television coverage and the fact that the Third World was still watching football on black-and-white television sets. We were considered to be the 'away' team so we were ordered to wear our second strip of white with blue-and-yellow hoops.

It is now a matter of history what happened when we played the Costa Ricans. We are still reminded quite frequently that we lost to the underdogs. It was agony to watch. The Costa Ricans were very fast and specialised in one-touch football that avoided physical confrontation. Having said that, they had just one shot throughout the first half, while Johnston and McCoist both went close at the other end.

The dressing room at half-time resembled the medical tent on a battlefield. We had several players nursing knocks, but Richard Gough was the most seriously hurt. He had aggravated a long-term foot injury and was able to take no further part in the game. We realised that he was going to miss more than the second half. In fact, Richard went home for treatment – his World Cup was over.

Stewart McKimmie replaced him but barely had time to break into a sweat before we were a goal down. The second half was only four minutes old when Costa Rica's Cayasso was set free and cleverly shot straight into the net. After that, the wall went up in front of their goal and, despite shot after shot, we just could not score. The Argentinian referee refused what looked like a blatant handball and, when the final whistle was blown, the unthinkable had happened.

The press tore us apart and the Tartan Army let us know what they thought of it. Andy described it all as a 'bad dream', and I could not describe it any other way. That result has haunted us ever since. Nobody has ever taken into account that Costa Rica lost only 1–0 to Brazil and then beat Sweden. No excuses. We had 80 per cent of the play and should have won. It was a poor performance, but in a sense it is an insult to the Costa Ricans just to castigate Scotland and not acknowledge their ability in reaching the second round.

Our next game was against Sweden. With Brazil still to come, we just had to get a result from this one. We made a few changes, some enforced and some tactical. Morale was very low after the Costa Rican débâcle and the press overstatements. We had to work very hard to restore team spirit, and this is where I would like to pay tribute again to the Tartan Army. They had aired their views on our previous result but were in full supportive voice when they turned up for our game against Sweden. The players were bubbling by the time they left the dressing room. They were determined to silence their critics, and we worked hard in getting them focused and I undertook my usual task of dissecting the opposition. The players were given such a magnificent reception by their supporters that you could see them visibly lifted.

If the Costa Rica performance was poor, then the display against Sweden was great. Robert Fleck was a late choice for the squad. He had not been a first choice and was on holiday in Yugoslavia before getting the call to join the squad. He played very well in this, his first World Cup game, and was involved in everything. Stuart McCall scored our first goal after ten minutes when he met a Murdo MacLeod corner.

It was a battle of tactics as much as anything else, and we played our ace sub cards of Paul McStay and Ally McCoist at just the right time. Roy Aitken, our captain, also kept up the momentum, and it was his endeavour that led to our second goal. Roy latched on to the end of a great piercing pass from

Fleck, the goalkeeper parried his fierce shot, and as Roy went for the rebound he was fouled by a defender. Mo Johnston converted the penalty and even a late goal from Sweden did nothing to detract from the result and a performance that we felt must have given our next opponents, Brazil, something to think about.

We moved camp to St Vincent and made our preparations. A draw would benefit both teams but there was no way that we were going to shut up shop, even against the Brazilians. We adopted a sweeper system because it suited the occasion, but we were seeking maximum points if possible. Brazil were described by the media as 'subdued', and it is true that they did not seem as zestful as usual. However, their skilful passing was not below par and we knew that we were in for a game of the highest standard.

There were nine minutes left when Brazil struck. Jim Leighton made a good save, but the ball bobbled in the mud. The loose ball was picked up by Muller, who had no hesitation in sending it into the net. A little later, Mo Johnston had a great chance to equalise from six yards out – but he fluffed it. Devastated, he lay prostrate in the mud, symbolic of how we all felt.

The game ended and we were out. Yet again, Scotland had failed to get past the first round. Andy had little to say except that he felt sorry for the supporters, who had all been brilliant. The media raised the usual questions over Andy's future, but there was never any serious thought of changing the set-up. I felt the same as everybody else – extremely disappointed – but I was already looking at another quest.

Scotland had never before appeared in the finals of the European Championship, but I genuinely believed that we had the capacity to change all that.

14

Europe and Beyond

THE DUST OF the World Cup disappointment still hadn't settled when the campaign for Europe began. In our qualifying group were Switzerland, Romania, Bulgaria and San Marino – who were expected to be the whipping boys. We knew that the others were not going to be push-overs by any means, and I was soon on my travels to spy out the opposition.

The Scottish public were in mourning for our World Cup appearance when we began the trail to Sweden 92. I think they must have been waiting to see how we would shape up because only 12,801 turned up at Hampden to see our opening game against Romania. Our visitors were well organised, as we expect from the eastern European countries. Our players were a little nervous and took time to settle – too long in fact because, in the thirteenth minute, Catamaru put Romania ahead. Our players protested that there had been an infringement but their claims went unheeded. I looked across at Andy Roxburgh but his face was as expressionless as usual. His mind was already into the next phase of the game.

Far from making matters worse, the goal actually spurred

the Scotland side on and, just before half-time, our efforts were rewarded when John Robertson scored the equaliser. You could sense the relief all over Hampden, and at half-time the players were in a much better mood. Around midway through the second half Ally McCoist scored a fine goal to make the final score 2-1, which got us off to a flying start.

A month later Switzerland were the visitors to Hampden and the score was the same. It was John Robertson who broke the ice once again, late in the first half with a penalty. Gary McAllister, with his first goal for Scotland made it 2-0 early in the second half, and even when the Swiss pulled one back there was never any serious danger that we would let it slip. The Scots went home happy. The Hampden crowd had topped 27,000, and the feel-good factor was creeping back.

We were off to Sofia for our next group game. Bulgaria had beaten Romania 3-0 away, so we knew that this was going to be our toughest test thus far. We were not expecting to get off to a flying start, but in fact we did when Ally McCoist put us ahead in the ninth minute. The Bulgarian fans were silenced, but the Tartan Army became even noisier, and it was certainly looking like we were in with another chance of victory. However, a second-half lapse let the Bulgarians through, and in the end we had to settle for a draw. I have to say that when the home side attacked they were very threatening indeed, and it was a credit to our defence, and in particular Andy Goram in goal, that we came away with a point.

We were at home for our next game, and it was the return with the Bulgarians. We were at the top of the group and good value for that position. The game was not exactly a bundle of fun for the spectators. The defences dominated and there were rare scoring opportunities – until the second half when John Collins replaced Gordon Strachan with ten minutes left. Then, within a very short space of time, he headed home a delightful cross from Brian McClair. The place erupted and we were on our way again. The party was pooped, though, by a bizarre late goal in which the Scottish defenders, to a man, stood appealing for off-side while the Bulgarian substitute, Kostadinov, gently placed the ball into an empty net. There was barely time to restart the game and we were all a bit shellshocked, although words were spoken in the dressing room about one of the very basics of the game – namely, playing to the whistle. Probably the player was off-side, but it is the referee who has to make that decision and not the players or anyone else.

San Marino came next, and that was a game both to forget and to remember. The part to forget was the fact that we only won 2-0, while other sides had fired six or seven past the minnows of the group. Our first goal didn't come until well into the second half when Gordon Strachan put us ahead from the penalty spot after Pat Nevin had been fouled. A few minutes later it was a cross from Gordon which helped Gordon Durie make it 2-0. It was an adequate, but not a great, performance in heavy rain on a pitch that became more of a bog as the game wore on. For me, the aspect to remember and savour was the role of the Tartan Army, who once again did us proud. There were only 3,512 people on the terraces, and I am convinced that 3,500 of them were from Scotland. Despite the conditions and the lacklustre performance from both sides, the supporters made it seem like a home game.

By the time we travelled to Switzerland for our next group game we had slipped from the top place, replaced by the Swiss who had beaten San Marino 7-0. We were stunned when the Swiss raced into a 2-0 lead in the first half, and Andy had a few words to say at half-time. We had paid the home team too much respect. Gordon Durie led the charge in the second half and scored a goal within two minutes. We battled away, and with seven minutes left, Ally McCoist popped up for another of his vintage goals, and we were more than happy to come away from Berne with a 2-2 draw.

We were away again for our next game and had to face Romania. We were now at a crucial stage in these qualifying games and every goal counted. The 30,000 home crowd played

their part in cheering on their side, and we were grateful that
we had done our defensive homework because the Romanians
worked hard to break us down and threatened to run riot if we
caved in. We were doing fine, even though we were under
intense pressure. Unfortunately, Gordon Durie lost his head
momentarily in the 73rd minute and gave away a penalty when
he handled in his own area. It was one of those things that can
happen to anyone. Gheorghe Hagi, the Romanian superstar,
scored from the spot and his side then shut up shop for the rest
of the game.

It was a blow to our qualifying hopes and we knew that
we had to go for gold against San Marino in our final group
game. The crowd of 35,170 at Hampden was almost exactly
ten times the crowd that had witnessed our previous encounter.
The Tartan Army was in party mood because they knew that
we were in with a very good chance of qualifying for the
European Championships for the first time ever. Bulgaria and
Romania still had to play each other but nobody was prepared
to think in terms of Scotland not making it after coming this
far.

Within ten minutes Paul McStay had opened the scoring.
Richard Gough added his name to the score sheet and then
Gordon Durie made it 3-0 by half-time. We told the lads to
keep plugging away but not to change the tempo at all, and
Ally McCoist made it 4-0 midway through the second half. I
think the fans wanted a goal riot, but it is never that easy and,
in the end, we had to settle for 4-0 and wait for the final group
game a week later in which we hoped that Bulgaria would do
us a favour against Romania. Hagi, uncharacteristically,
missed a penalty, but Popescu gave the Romanians a 1-0 half-
time lead. Time stood still in the second half until Dirakov
made himself a Scottish hero by scoring the equaliser. The
score remained at 1-1, and we were through to the European
Championships for the first time.

Meanwhile, the coaching at Largs continued apace and the
facilities became much improved. Some of the improvements

came before the 1990 World Cup when the pitches were dug up for renovation. That year, for the first time since I joined the coaching staff in 1969, we had to go to St Andrews, where we took advantage of the excellent facilities of the university. They certainly did their best for us and made us very welcome.

In my coaching group was an international player who had been enjoying a remarkable career but was now apparently coming close to the end of his playing days and doing his best to obtain the highest possible coaching qualifications. He was none other than Gordon Strachan. He sailed through his A Licence award.

So, Andy Roxburgh had become the first manager to take Scotland into the European Championship tournament. It was no more than he deserved because he was always a very hard-working guy, always very methodical, and a great talker. He put a lot into motivating his players. After the World Cup defeat by Costa Rica, for instance, he restored morale by showing a video of great Scottish sporting achievements.

He also used to pick themes for his team talks. I remember him asking the players if they would like to win another cap. It was his way of putting it into their heads that their international careers lasted as long as the quality of their performances. Unfortunately, when he came to Alex McLeish, he came upon a player who was just about to earn his 50th cap, a place in the Hall of Fame, and a ticket for life to every Scotland home international. So when Andy asked Alex if he would like another cap, Alex was quick to nod his head. I couldn't resist a joke and said, 'Well, you'd better weigh in with a bit of cash, then.' All the players laughed, but Andy didn't and he had a word with me later about 'ruining' his team talk.

To get ready for Sweden we played several friendly games. We beat Northern Ireland 1-0, and then we drew 1-1 with Finland before going to the USA, where we won 1-0 in terrific heat in the Mile High Stadium in Denver. We then beat Canada 3-1 in Toronto before flying back to Europe and a 0-0 draw in Norway – our final preparatory game before the European Championship. A lot of people still think that this kind of travelling taxes the players before a major competition, but believe me it has quite the opposite effect. It gives them the chance to play a few games together and focus on the job ahead and, at the same time, distance themselves from the domestic season they have just completed. Because the guys are together all the time it also helps to build team spirit and cements their friendship and loyalty to the squad.

Our group for Sweden could hardly have been more difficult. We had to play Holland, the defending champions, Germany, the world champions, and the CIS – who had only just changed their name from USSR and had come through their qualifying matches undefeated. However, we were undaunted and in buoyant mood as we took the pitch to play Holland in the Ullevi Stadium. The scoreline tells everyone that Holland won 1-0, but it does not give a full and true account of the story. Holland were very impressive in the first half with Van Basten, Gullit, Rijkaard and Wouters on top form. For Scotland, Gary McAllister, Paul McStay and Stuart McCall were also in good form, and at half-time there was still no score.

In the second half we exerted some pressure of our own, and while the first half belonged to the Dutch, the second half was unquestionably under Scottish dominance. It was really against the run of play that Dennis Bergkamp scored the only goal of the game and sent us from the pitch beaten but unbowed. We won many friends with the quality of our play, the determination and the character shown – not only by the players but by the Tartan Army, who had been magnificent representatives for Scotland.

On to the next game and Germany. Once again the Scotland side fought bravely and gave the Germans a severe fright. But for the brilliance of Illgner in the German goal, I am sure we could have been two goals ahead in the first ten minutes. As it was, the Germans composed themselves and took the initiative through Riedle to make it 1–0 at half-time. We suffered a cruel blow early in the second half when Effenberg's shot hit the boot of Maurice Malpas and soared into the air. Andy Goram, trying to change direction, slipped and could only watch helplessly as the ball sailed into the net. To their credit, the players did not give up, and when the final whistle went the Germans smiled more with relief than with delight.

We were thus eliminated from the competition and had not yet scored a goal. We still had to play against the CIS and really wanted to wave goodbye to Sweden with a flourish. Our performance was probably the least impressive of our three games – but the result was excellent. After six minutes, Paul McStay fired in a 25-yard shot through a ruck of defenders which Kharine, the CIS goalkeeper, did not see until it hit a post, ricocheted to the back of his head and bounced into the net. Just over ten minutes later Brian McClair tried a long-range drive. It took a slight deflection and went in, which made Brian particularly happy as it was his first goal for Scotland in 26 appearances. When Pat Nevin was tripped during the second half, Gary McAllister made no mistake with the penalty and at the end of the game we had won 3–0.

The Scottish supporters were out in force and the players went to them to show their appreciation for the tremendous backing they had received and for the fact that the Tartan Army had become the characters of the championship – a lot of fun and well behaved.

There hardly seemed time to breathe before the World Cup qualifiers were underway. Once again there were some tough games to come as we were drawn in the same group as Italy, Portugal, Switzerland, Malta and Estonia.

The first match was away to Switzerland in Berne. It would be an understatement to say that it was a disaster. It was in fact a total disaster. Not only did we lose, but Richard Gough was himself sent off for an instinctive hand ball. Our campaign was certainly off to a bad start with a defeat and the prospect of having one of our most experienced players suspended.

Our first home game was against Portugal at Ibrox, and they proved to be a handful. They were fast and very tricky and we were under pressure for much of the game. We just did not seem able to get into the game, and were grateful at the end for our first point from the 0–0 scoreline. The Portuguese were a little disgruntled at having two penalty appeals turned down, but that's football for you.

Less than a month later we were at home again, and this time it was Italy who were the visitors to Ibrox. Franco Baresi came out of retirement to boost the Italian campaign, and they were the favourites to win the group. They were also favourites to win at Ibrox, but I found them less than convincing. The usually solid Italian defence was nervous and at half-time we felt that the points were there for the taking. Despite several good opportunities, the ball simply would not go into the net and again we ended with a 0–0 result. It was beginning to be a worry. We had two points from our three games and had scored only one goal.

It was three months before our next game in February 1993. Once again we were at home, this time to Malta. A lot of people decry the Maltese, but they are not an easy team to beat, especially on their own ground. When they visited Ibrox they were out for damage limitation. Ally McCoist put us ahead after fifteen minutes, but it was not until midway through the second half that he made it 2–0. Pat Nevin added a third near the end.

At last we had a victory, and some goals, and our record suddenly looked a little more respectable, with a goal difference in our favour and one defeat in four games. The prospect of a trip to America for the 1994 World Cup had not entirely faded.

We knew it was going to be a tough job getting a result from Portugal in Lisbon in April 1993, but we felt that it was not an entirely hopeless task. If we pulled something off, we were still in with a shout for the World Cup finals. It was obviously a very important game for us.

Leading up to the game there was quite a bit of hassle because we had a large representation from Rangers at the time. In fairness, Rangers were doing very well, both in Europe and at home, during this time. They had gone something like ten games without defeat in Europe, including that wonderful tie against Leeds United which they won both home and away. They were certainly in exceptional form and you cannot ignore players who are part of a success like that. The McCoist–Hateley partnership was outstanding.

In the Scotland squad we had Goram, Gough, McPherson, McCall, McCoist and Durrant. The Scotland game was sandwiched between European Cup games against Marseille, so there was a lot of pressure on those Rangers players to peak several times in quick succession. In hindsight, it is easy to see why there was not full concentration on the Scotland match from those players, who were in the middle of a very tense and important European tie.

I'm not making excuses for the players involved, they don't need my help, but you have to be fair and say that the timing could not have been much worse. I don't go along with what Richard Gough later said, blaming our defeat in Portugal purely on tactics. It's a question of 'Well, he would say that, wouldn't he?'

Richard said that we had been told that Rui Barros, the little midfielder with Monaco and Portugal, would not be playing. I can confirm that. The information came as the result of a conversation I had in the car when I was travelling back from the Under-21 game. In the vehicle with me was Bobby Robson, at that time coach of Sporting Lisbon. He told me that he didn't want to be disloyal to Portugal, which I can believe because Bobby Robson has always been an outstanding gentleman, but he marked my card to the effect that the Portuguese choice for that midfield position would be Figo. He didn't volunteer the information. I had to ask him.

I reported back to Andy what Bobby had said. What later crept into the newspapers was that we had taken the advice of a taxi driver. The mischief makers who misreported it had no idea that my 'cabbie' was an official of the Portuguese Football Federation and that my 'informant' was Bobby Robson.

We had prepared for a team that included Figo instead of Barros, but had plenty of time to advise our players of the change before it was too late. I asked Carlos Queiroz, the manager of Portugal, whom I knew, what had happened to make him pick Barros.

'He failed a urine test yesterday, and again this morning – but at four o'clock this afternoon he was OK,' said Queiros. He went on to explain that Barros had been taking antibiotics for a heavy cold and that he had not wanted to risk any misunderstandings. As a result, the Portugal manager had prepared his team without Barros but had drafted him in later in the day.

I can assure you that Andy Roxburgh sat the whole Scottish team down, more than an hour before the kick-off, told them that Barros would be playing, and made arrangements for dealing with him. The point is that there is no doubt whatsoever that the team was fully informed of the situation. I was there – I know.

Nevertheless, the newspaper headlines read that a taxi driver had supplied Scotland's tactics for the game, which was, of course, absolute nonsense.

Within a few minutes of the game starting, Barros made his presence felt by scoring at the near post. They quickly settled and the rest of the story is now history. Cadete scored twice, Futre got one, and Barros scored another to make the final score an embarrassing 5–0. Scotland simply did not perform. Nothing went right and we were pretty dejected, I can tell you. Worse than all that, this was also the game in which Ally McCoist broke his leg. It was a shock to us all. We were 3–0 down when it happened and Ally was carried off.

He was examined in the dressing room and the general opinion was that the leg was broken. However, you can't keep a man like Ally McCoist down for long. He remained cheerful and refused to blame anyone for what had happened. When the game ended, his teammates rushed to the dressing room to see how he was. He was lying on a table with his leg in a splint, waiting to be X-rayed properly.

'How are you doing, Alistair?' someone asked.

'Och, it could be worse,' replied McCoist, with a grin. 'We could have lost five–nil!'

Needless to say, Ally didn't know the final score at that stage. When he flew back to Scotland, Andy travelled with him, journeyed on with him to the hospital and stayed with him until the results of the X-ray were available. I have known other managers who would not even bother phoning to see how a player was.

That injury was a major blow to Ally's career at that stage because he had been in such incredible form. He is also such a great character that it was sad to see him invalided. Happily, he bounced back and I had the privilege – and the benefit – of selecting him for his Scotland comeback.

After that hammering from Portugal we had to pick ourselves up, because we still had two more World Cup games to play before we could say that the season was over. On 19 May, just three weeks after that last game, we were away to Estonia. We could not afford to lose this one, not only from the point of view of the World Cup place, but also for general confidence.

Estonia proved to be a tough nut to crack, but Kevin Gallacher demonstrated once again what an excellent player he was when he scored just before half-time. You could see the tension lift and the dressing room was very lively during the interval. John Collins made it 2–0 about a quarter of an hour after the restart, and then Scott Booth scored our third with ten minutes left. The journey back home was much happier.

Two weeks later we met Estonia again, this time at

Pittodrie. As has been proved more recently, you can never underestimate teams like Estonia. They are the underdogs most of the time and have nothing to lose. They are also greatly underrated, and that puts a lot of pressure on their opponents, who always carry the burden as favourites to win the game. That great club and country servant, Brian McClair, put us at ease with a goal after sixteen minutes. Pat Nevin made it 2–0 before half-time, but then we lost our sense of direction somehow and when Bragin pulled one back after about twelve minutes of the second half, things looked as if they were drifting. With just under twenty minutes left we were awarded a penalty which Pat Nevin converted. The score was 3–1, but it was not a vintage performance, and we were all concerned about our remaining group fixtures.

We were back at Pittodrie on 8 September to play Switzerland. They had beaten us 3–1 a year earlier in the first fixture of the group. Roy Hodgson, now with Udinese in Italy after spells with InterMilan, Blackburn Rovers and FC Copenhagen, was in charge of the Swiss, and he had developed a very good side. They had beaten Italy at home and drawn with them away, so we knew that they were possibly the greatest threat to our ambitions. We had to win – it was as simple as that.

After a very tense first half, John Collins gave us the lead with a great goal in the 50th minute. The celebrations started – but too soon, as it happened. The referee awarded the Swiss a penalty and Bergy put the ball past Bryan Gunn. The last twenty minutes dragged by with little hint of another goal, and when the final whistle went we knew we were out of the World Cup.

I looked at Andy's face and his expression matched my own. He had been in charge for 61 games, equalling Jock Stein's record. He had earned much applause and recognition for his Scotland squad, but now it looked as if it was time to reconsider his future.

A few days later Andy resigned. The SFA International

committee did discuss it with him with a view to changing his mind, but he explained that he felt that his team had died during that game against Portugal. He had made up his mind and that was that. I believe, though I do not know for certain, that Andy had many offers on the table – and indeed he has since become UEFA's Director of Football Development, a very responsible job and one that I know he enjoys immensely. As technical director of UEFA he is responsible for 51 countries, and I have attended many of the courses he organises and presents for coaches. All the top coaches attend, and Andy Roxburgh is well respected by all of them.

Having failed to get Andy to change his mind, the committee called a press conference which Andy agreed to attend in order to formally announce his resignation. At that same press conference it was to be announced that I was being temporarily put in charge. Looking at it from my point of view, it was not the greatest compliment I have ever been paid. I had taken the Scotland Under-16 team to the World Cup final, the furthest it had ever gone, the Scotland Under-20 team the furthest it had ever gone, and the Scotland Under-21 team the same. The committee knew my record but with sometimes five to six weeks between meetings I had to be patient. I did not complain because that is not my way, but I was a little disappointed at the delay.

I was left to get on with the job, with little attention being paid by anyone to my track record. As well as my successes with Scotland I had won two championships with Clyde and had a very good pedigree in the transfer market. I was not exactly a novice to the job, but I felt uncertain about my future.

15

So There I Was ...

SO THERE I was, holding my head in my hands with my whole past life flashing before me, wondering if I would not have been better off pursuing my career in education rather then subjecting myself to this torture. The Olympic Stadium in Rome is a huge place, but there is absolutely nowhere to hide when something goes wrong. Remember that we were playing for nothing but pride because we could not qualify for the World Cup even if we had scored a hatful against Italy that night. I had to forget all about what had happened before, and the fact that everyone was calling for a former international star to take over as manager of Scotland. I was partially ignored in all the speculation – which showed exactly how the media thought of me. I was not there to prove any points to anyone, just to get the best result possible for the players and my country. The rest was up to everyone else.

There were more than 80,000 fans in the Olympic Stadium and Italy had to win their last two qualifying games to guarantee a place in the World Cup of 1994. The scene was set for us to be sent home with our tails between our legs. We had lost our previous game in Portugal 5–0. Andy Roxburgh, after the match, simply said, 'A team died out there!' It is not easy to lift players after a result like that. If they have lost by the odd goal they are often more determined to do better next time – but a heavy defeat can be a wipeout in more senses than one.

I was thrust into position when Andy Roxburgh resigned and the SFA were in no rush to replace him – mainly because they wanted to make sure of making the right move for the right man. So, there I was, the temporary manager of Scotland. It was not the most flattering position for me to be in, but I had been asked to hold the fort while the SFA committee was deliberating and that is exactly what I had planned to do. I had no idea what would happen when the new man took over, but I suspected that I would probably be visiting the Jobcentre to see if anyone wanted a football-mad teacher with a dodgy knee.

I prepared the team as thoroughly as possible with the assistance of Murdo MacLeod, himself a former Scotland international. Part of the preparations for a match involve taking a good look at the opposition. In big business it is common practice to study your competitors, and I believe that the same should apply in football. Never dismiss your opponents as irrelevant. No matter what the game, or who is opposing you, you still have to win, and you have to do so by defeating that opposition. You need to know them in order to achieve that.

The preparation doesn't end the day before the game. It is important to watch even the warm-up of the other side, and I did exactly that. The Italians worked very hard on their warm-up for this important game. They were on a rubber-floored indoor pitch about the size of two goal areas put together. They were put through their paces very thoroughly and very strenuously. I saw the sweat dripping off the ponytail of Roberto Baggio and running down his back, soaking his T-shirt.

When they took the pitch just before the kick-off, they

were very loose and alert for the game. I stood at the side of the dugout on the running track that went around the pitch and watched what was going on. When the whistle went for the start of the game they tore into us like a team that had already been playing for a quarter of an hour. Within four minutes they had taken the lead. A well-worked throw-in saw the ball go to Baggio. He ran a few yards and sent the ball straight to Donadoni, who wasted no time in putting it past Bryan Gunn. We were caught completely cold as Rome went crazy, with the Italians taking another step nearer to the World Cup finals.

To their credit, the Scotland players did not allow their shoulders to sag. In a sense it would have been understandable if they had. In your previous game you are beaten 5–0 and now, in your next game, you are a goal down within minutes. I thought at the time that Bryan was a bit unfortunate to allow Donadoni's long shot to go past him.

We were restricted for the next twelve minutes to rare attacks as the Italians decided to make a romp of it. In the sixteenth minute Roberto Baggio, playing in an inside right position just off the front, sent a beautiful ball to Casiraghi. He got there just before our centre-back, Brian Irvine, and angled his shot across the goalkeeper and into the net. So just imagine that it is your first international in charge and you are two goals down within such a short space of time. There is still an hour and 14 minutes to play against one of the best teams in the world, on their ground and in front of 80,000 Italian supporters.

I felt a kind of numbness and bewilderment for the first and only time. I wondered why I had involved myself in this situation at all. Fortunately we settled down very quickly after that and played with some composure. We had nothing to lose and, once again, I have to praise the players for keeping their heads. They drew strength from their situation and contained the Italians for some time. I watched them growing in stature all the time. Even the home fans were beginning to quieten down just a little. Then Kevin Gallacher pounced on an opportunity and sent the ball over the head of Pagliuca in the Italian goal. Suddenly it was 2–1 and we were back in the game. It certainly silenced that very volatile Italian crowd.

At half-time we tried to pick things up a bit and inspire more of the same from the players. They were quite cheerful and couldn't wait to get out for the second half. Gordon Durie and Gary McAllister were winding everyone up as well. I don't know how things were in the Italian dressing room, but there was no lack of spirit in ours at that time.

Perhaps this is the right time for me to explain that I had shocked a lot of people by leaving out Paul McStay. Paul, of course, was, and still is, a legend in modern Scottish football, and had been capped for his country more than 70 times. Dropping him from the starting line-up was leaving myself wide open to the most abusive criticism that you can imagine – though not from the player himself, I hasten to point out.

I have a policy about handling players. On the Monday before the game we were leaving the Gleddoch House Hotel, which had been our base before flying to Italy. I took Paul McStay to one side and told him that I didn't think he had been playing particularly well lately and that I would not be naming him in the starting line-up. I also said that I knew how much he wanted to play against Italy in Rome and that, if it was appropriate, I would send him on to the pitch from the subs' bench at some stage of the game. I told him that I could not guarantee doing that and we would have to wait and see how things went. I wanted him to realise that he was still an important member of the squad. I simply wanted to reassure him that I had not forgotten him and that he was still a very valuable player to me.

Earlier, there had been much press talk about who would be given the captaincy for the game. Although I was only in temporary charge, I had decisions to make and the authority to make them. Would I choose Paul McStay or Gary McAllister as captain? That was the question the media wanted answering. I try to give the press a story every day, because I know they have a job to do, but I was being pushed to name my captain before I was ready to do so. You can imagine the headlines when I told the press that Paul would not be playing other than from the subs' bench. Gary had obviously got the job and I was, of course, in a no-win situation. If I had picked Paul I would have been told that it was time for a fresh start – if I didn't, then I was making a big mistake by not keeping to a stable captaincy. Those are the sorts of things that you learn to live with when you have responsibility – and especially so when you are in the spotlight as manager of Scotland.

Well, at half-time I thought about bringing him on, but I decided against it. I decided it would be better to leave well alone. Sure enough, the second half kicked off and we were playing really well. We were seriously unlucky not to equalise when Gordon Durie fired in a tremendous shot that had 'goal' written all over it before it hit the shoulder of his teammate Ian Durrant and ricocheted just wide. We had come desperately close to making it two goals each and it was clear that the Italians were becoming worried. Their football was not flowing as well as it had during the first quarter of an hour of the game. I did bring Paul McStay into the game with about twenty minutes left, and he played his part in keeping our tails up.

As inevitably happens in games like this, the matter was finally settled when the Italians had a breakaway as we were piling more pressure on them. They raced away down the right with a good fluid move which ended with Stefano Eranio – who, in May 2001 received a marvellous standing ovation and goodbye from the fans in his last game for Derby County against Ipswich Town before returning to Italy – collecting the ball just inside the area and making the score 3–1. You could see the relief among the Italian players and hear the same from the mass of supporters. It was an excellent goal, but it did feel a little cruel after so much effort had been put in by the Scotland team.

So, we lost my first international and I think the media

were left a little bemused. Some representatives would very much have liked to have been vitriolically critical, but they could not really fault the performance.

The only thing that annoyed me was when one well-known newspaper sarcastically wrote that the Italians had not even bothered to come out on to the pitch to warm up before the game. It shows just how ill informed that writer was because I had watched their rigorous work-out indoors before the game with my own eyes. It was suggested that the Italians treated us with disdain, almost contempt, by not bothering to come out on to the pitch. Because our journalists had not witnessed what I had seen, some reported that the Italians had opened the scoring without even breaking into a sweat.

Believe me, those Italian players, and their coaches, gave us a lot of respect both before and after the game.

Anyway, that was my first game in charge. I returned to Scotland amid the whirlpool of speculation about who was going to be the new manager. All the newspapers were listing likely candidates. Names like Dalglish, Ferguson, McQueen, Bremner, Jordan, Strachan, Miller and Souness were widely touted, with each newspaper picking its own favourite. Brown was still not getting much of a mention, although there were a few reporters wanting to ask me who I thought would be the best man for the job. Only a few asked me if I fancied it.

Mind you, I really wasn't sure if I did fancy it. I hadn't really given the prospect much thought. I had been too busy getting the trip to Rome organised and being at the match to think of much else. With the game over I felt much better. We had done well even though we had been defeated. I still hadn't gone as far as thinking about having the job myself, but I had gained some satisfaction from the fact that the players had come off the pitch with their heads high – and that meant a lot to me.

There were many lessons I had learned from that first game, and I had also renewed my acquaintance with the Tartan Army. I must tell you a few things about those great Scotland supporters who will follow the team anywhere and everywhere – sometimes even without a ticket for the game.

I have been a Tartan Army man myself. It was at the time I was playing for Falkirk, and the club decided to take us south by bus as a treat to see the game against England on 10 April 1965. We arrived in London on the morning of the game and the club secretary, Charlie Taylor, handed us a ticket each and a ten-bob note to buy a meal. You could get a pretty decent meal for ten bob in those days.

A group of us, including Doug Baillie now of the Sunday Post and John Lambie, who was later to become manager of Hamilton, Partick Thistle and Falkirk and now Thistle, headed for the centre of London to have our meal. We found a pretty top notch restaurant and the food was very good. The only problem was that the service was very slow and we had limited time because we still had to get to Wembley. In the end we hit the panic button and didn't wait for our sweet but left the restaurant. Since I was last to abandon the table and since my conscience was bothering me, I put everything I had from my pocket on a plate – all of £3.76 – and ran after my pals!

The game at Wembley was a cracker. The final score was 2–2 and we watched Ian St John and Denis Law get a goal each. My old pal Billy McNeill was there in the heart of the defence as usual, and I think even the England fans would admit that they were a little bit lucky that day not to have been well beaten. Our fans were superb. Unless you have travelled with them, you might not realise that they are the most passionate, noisy bunch of guys you could ever muster together. At matches they are tremendous, and they always bring the place to life wherever they go. You rarely see them engaged in battle, either. They go to support their country and to have a good time while they are doing it. Their idea of a good time does not include being baton-charged and thrown into a cell for a few days.

There are known characters among them too, and one of these made his presence felt on that trip to Rome. We were staying at the Sheraton Hotel, about fifteen miles outside the city. It was the eve of the game and the players had all gone to bed. I was having a drink and a chat with the other members of the Scotland entourage. I suppose it must have been about half past ten or eleven o'clock. Suddenly we heard a bit of a commotion in the hotel foyer. We were in the lounge but could still hear the noise quite distinctly. There were four of what we might call 'the lads' in their kilts and T-shirts, and they were carrying cans of 'refreshment' in this very posh hotel.

The hotel staff were excellent and they treated us very well, and while 'the lads' were not intent on causing any harm, they were certainly disrupting the atmosphere and causing some alarm to many of the other guests. They found us in the lounge and they all wanted to come and shake my hand and wish us all the best for the match. Of course, they didn't do all this in a whisper, as you may imagine. In truth, they were also looking for tickets. They had made the journey to Italy on spec, hoping that they might be able to get some tickets when they arrived in Rome.

One guy I recognised was John Grigor. Now John is a very conscientious Scotland supporter. He is a member of our travel club, which has more than 12,000 members, and he is also a great organiser of bus trips. I have seen him at games all over the world wherever Scotland have been playing. He would hire a submarine to get there if he had to. He once ordered the driver of his bus to tuck in behind the police-escorted team coach in Belarus and thus enter the executive parking area.

On this particular night, John and his pals had imbibed a few too many. I jumped out of my seat and went over to them, shook hands, talked to them a little and ushered them back out of the hotel and into the carpark. They departed quietly enough after that, and I guess they found some tickets somewhere. I didn't have any for them – I rarely do. They did embarrass us because they had taken a bit too much liquor on board, but I'm sure they were the first to realise it afterwards.

To all members of the Tartan Army I would say to you that your support is appreciated much more than I can ever hope to explain. You are an important part of the squad wherever we go. However, please remember that we have to try to keep some kind of a peaceful atmosphere at our hotels – especially on the eve of a big match. Most managers will tell you stories of the opposition supporters trying to give you a bad night's sleep before a game. We can do without our own supporters doing the same – even with the best of intentions. Get a good night's sleep yourselves so that you are match-fit for when we need you – at the game!

We arrived home amid speculation about the new manager, as I have mentioned, but still there was one newspaper trying to get something else going. I was told that a newspaper had offered Paul McStay quite a large sum of money to vent his anger about my decision not only to have him on the bench at the start of the game, but also to relieve him of the captaincy.

It says a lot for Paul's character that he refused the newspaper's offer. For my money that is a great tribute to the man's tremendous loyalty. A lesser person might well have taken the money and given the newspaper what it wanted to hear. Paul didn't, and I admired him for his honesty, integrity and loyalty.

The decision I took with regard to Paul had been an honest one and I had been open and quite frank with him in telling him of my decision. I hadn't asked someone else to tell him or even kept my mouth shut and let a team sheet do the talking. Of course, the matter was not totally forgotten by the Celtic fans, who worshipped Paul!

Some months later I went to watch Celtic play in a European tie against Cologne at home. I parked my car in the school carpark, which is adjacent to Celtic Park, and I had to walk into the stadium. It was like running the gauntlet. Sometimes the supporters just want to shout your name, but on this occasion I was called by various names as I walked through the crowd – some of whom had even climbed up on the railings to make sure that I heard their voices. They had not forgiven me for my Paul McStay decision. I was shouted at and spat upon. When I got into the ground I sat next to Kevin Kelly, one of the directors. In front of the directors' box there was this huge chap wearing a Celtic scarf. As soon as he saw me he turned round and gave me some terrible abuse: 'You should be at Ibrox, watching that Durrant and that Ferguson in the Rangers reserves. What are you doing here watching us?'

I had already had one supporter tap me on the shoulder and say, 'By the way Craig, Paul's wearing No.8!' so I was getting a bit fed up with all this. You can never show it, though. In situations like that you just have to take it. Anyway, when this other guy was hurling abuse at me, Mr Kelly turned to me and said, 'I'm glad you're here. Otherwise it would have been me and the other directors getting all that.'

My embarrassment was increased when, about three minutes from the end, the very loud Celtic Park Tannoy came into play. There was the usual ding-dong, ding-dong, but instead of an Avon lady at the door there was a very clear voice saying, 'Ladies and gentlemen, tonight's sponsor's choice for man of the match is Paul McStay of Celtic!' The crowd roared its approval and I received another torrent from this guy in front of the directors' box. Paul had given me the best possible response to my not putting him on from the start in the Italy game by turning in a blinding performance for his club as I sat in the stand. The relationship between the Celtic fans and the board was not very good at that time, so I think my presence had served to take some of the pressure off them. No wonder the directors always welcomed me back to Celtic Park!

For the record, I have always had the highest regard for Paul McStay and his exemplary playing style. I don't think he has ever committed a dirty foul in his entire life, and he has always trained well, worked hard and played at the top of his game. He was a magnificent midfield player for Celtic and for his country, always contributing his best and scoring some great goals into the bargain, and he deserves the greatest respect possible. I will be eternally grateful to him for his attitude towards my decision at that first game in charge. I hold him in as much repect as I possibly could anyone, and I hope to a degree that it is mutual. What a role model he has been, and still is when he works with our youth international teams.

The Paul McStay incident throws up another interesting point. How do you tell players that they are dropped – especially international players with great reputations? Do you hope that they will find out by some devious method? Do you phone them in advance and hope that you will not have to face them? I decided that there was only one way for me – the way that I had seen other managers, whom I have respected, tell players that they are out of the side for a particular game.

One thing I didn't want was a repeat of something I had witnessed in 1990 when we were preparing for the World Cup in Italy. We were staying in the Hotel Bristol and we were on the training ground in Rapallo. Andy Roxburgh elected to tell Ally McCoist what was happening. I do think it is the best policy to tell players your decisions in a football context rather than in the office. As a manager at club level I always used to have end-of-season talks with my players on the training field. Some I would have to tell that they were being released, while others would be offered new terms. Either way, I always thought it was better for both parties if it was done on a man-to-man basis in a football environment.

I have already mentioned that when I was given a free transfer I received the information written on a piece of paper in a very impersonal manner. I know how I felt about that. I have always tried to be as courteous as possible to players and others, whatever their situation or status.

To go back to Andy and McCoist, we were at the training ground and most of us were already on the bus waiting to go. What was delaying us was a discussion between Andy and Ally after the manager had told the player that he would not be playing. When you try to talk to a player in the hotel, you cannot go to his room because he usually has a room-mate. He could come to your room but that is a bit too formal for me, and therefore it can be difficult to find somewhere private enough to break the news. It's tricky – but you have to learn to handle it if you are going to be in charge of players. I have also learned that you have to talk straight to players. They don't want to be mollycoddled or listen to a lot of excuses. Talk straight to them and let them know exactly where they stand. Be honest and truthful – it is much better that way. I never say that another player is a better player than the one I am talking to. I always say that, for this occasion, I think that player so-and-so is a more appropriate choice.

Another aspect to take into consideration is the role of the press in these things. If you are straight with your player and he is an honourable person, then he will not let you down. It is advisable, I have found, to talk to the player about what is going to be said to the press. I usually tell them that I am going to say such and such a thing, and then ask the player if he would agree with taking that line. We can then discuss it until we arrive at a uniform response, so that we don't find ourselves falling out over a newspaper discrepancy in our story.

So, there I was, back from Italy with a defeat under my belt and some abuse ringing in my ears. I did not know what the future held and could only read the newspapers the same as everyone else to see if there were any new developments in the supposed quest to find a really big name to take on the mantle of Scotland manager. My first match as caretaker had been a great experience and, as always, I had learned a great deal too.

We still had one more game to play in the World Cup qualifiers – away to Malta just over a month after the Italy game. I expected that I would probably still be in charge for that one because the SFA officials were not rushing to name my replacement. I had no idea that the Italy game would be my first and last as caretaker manager.

16

The Job's Mine

BEFORE THE MALTA game the speculation about who would be named as manager was still going on, as you would expect, and there were times when I thought that perhaps I had become invisible because my name seemed to just disappear from the scene. I was determined that, even if I was in charge for just a month or so, I was going to make the most of the experience. I decided to make a temporary appointment of an assistant, and the man I chose was Alex Miller.

Alex is someone I respect greatly. We had been on many courses together and I had no doubts that he knew his stuff and would be a great asset. He was a guy with a huge knowledge of the game and its personalities. I knew that we could work together because he was a man of integrity and knew what hard work was all about. I made an informal phone call to him to ask how he felt about the possibility of joining me in the Scotland set-up – possibly for just one game, because I had no idea what was likely to happen after that. Alex spoke to his chairman, Mr Douglas Cromb, and then agreed to the arrangement, and we both began work on the preparations for our trip to Malta.

We were due to leave for Malta on the Monday, with the match being played two days later. At the hotel, on the day before the game, I was called to the room of the chairman of the SFA international committee, Mr Yule Craig, former chairman of St Mirren. He was a man who commanded respect and he certainly got it from me because I knew that his heart was in the game and he wanted the best for whatever he was involved in. Alex Miller and my pal Alex Smith had both been managers of St Mirren while he was in charge and had nothing but good things to say about the man.

I went to his room knowing that whatever dealings I was to have with him would be honourable, and therefore I was in no way apprehensive when I knocked on his door. He called me in and I sat down with him and Chief Executive, Jim Farry. He smiled and came straight to the point.

'How would you like to stay in charge of the team up to and including Euro 96?'

I have to admit that, although I knew we would be discussing some aspect of the job, I was totally unprepared for this. I was pleased, of course. It felt the same as if I had been picked to play for my country. We sat and talked it over for a while, agreed terms and shook hands.

The official announcement had still to be made and so I couldn't share the news with anyone at that stage. The players were talking all the time about who the new boss was likely to be, and of course this fuelled further speculation in the newspapers. It was not until the players were changing for the match that the then president of the SFA, Mr Bill Dickie, vice-chairman at Motherwell, announced to everyone present that I had been appointed. There was spontaneous clapping in the dressing room. Gary McAllister came straight over to me and said, 'You've come a long way since you were teaching at Belvidere!'

'And you've come a long way since you were a pupil at Keir Hardie Primary School,' I replied. The two schools were situated close to each other in Belshill where Gary was a pupil and I was a teacher. Gary was the first person to shake my hand. The other players subsequently joined in the congratulations and handshaking – and then they went out and won the game 2–0!

The team for that Malta game was Leighton, McLaren, Hendry, McKinnon, Irvine, Durrant, McAllister, McKinlay, Nevin, Ferguson and Gallacher, and we used Boyd and Booth as our substitutes. Billy McKinlay and Colin Hendry scored a goal in each half – it was Colin's first goal for his country. The Ta Quali stadium had a crowd of 8,000 and the date was 19 November 1993. That's for the benefit of all you statisticians.

We finished fourth in our group of six, having won four and drawn four of our ten fixtures. It could have been much worse but, there again, it could have been much better too. Italy and Switzerland were the qualifiers from the group. I was pleased with our performance and I like to go back to Malta because I have friends there – wonderful people like Father Hillary, former technical director, Philip Psaila, a recent national coach, and Joe Mifsud, the president of the Malta FA – and because it now has a special place in my memory. We have been back since for a friendly match where we won 3–2.

It was useful to me to have players in the squad with whom I had worked before at club level. Pat Nevin was an excellent example. He was a player with tremendous skill, a good brain, and the desire to please. Ian Ferguson was another – a very misunderstood player in my opinion. Ian is a quiet teetotal guy who changes into a Mr Hyde character on the football field, where he becomes an aggressive, snorting and snarling kind of player. You would never believe that he was the same person. These two players I knew well, both from my club days and also from the Under-21 team, where many served their international apprenticeships.

Before beginning our campaign to reach Euro 96, we had a number of friendly matches in which to experiment and get settled in to a new way of football life. I had taken a conscious decision to play the way I had been playing the Under-21 side –

a way that had already proved itself successful. In 1992, for instance, against Germany, I had favoured a 3-5-2 system and I liked it. It was never 5-3-2, always 3-5-2. I do not use the term wing-back and never have done, but I suppose that it is not a bad description of how I used my wide midfield players.

I adapted this system from watching the Germans, whom I consider to be the most efficient in Europe. In those early days I used Stewart McKimmie and Tom Boyd as wide midfielders. I told them that their priority was defence but that they must have a midfield mentality and attack where needed. The system gave us a five-man defence when we needed it, and wingers when we were on the attack.

Some of our most excellent players were midfielders – McAllister, McCall, Lambert and Collins among them – and we needed to play to their strengths. It was our best department, and we did not want to have that sort of talent sitting on the sidelines if we could find a way of harnessing it and using it in a suitable system. Our central defenders were men who played in that position every week with their clubs, including Craig Levein now manager of Hearts, who was the man I had as the original free defender. It was a great tragedy that Craig had to give up the game, because he told me that he was very happy with the role I had given him. He felt that it used his particular abilities to the full. He was certainly a very skilful player who could adapt to every position. No wonder he enjoyed himself so much. With Craig hurt, I decided to give Colin Calderwood a chance. I had watched him and admired his style for some time, and Lou Macari, his former manager at Swindon Town also chipped in a recommendation – so Calderwood got his chance and took it very well indeed, his first game being in Moscow with a 0–0 draw with Russia.

Alan McLaren was another great talent whom I had admired since seeing his performances in the Under-21 side. He was being tipped by Walter Smith as the Rangers captain of the future, and I also tipped him to become Scotland's captain one day.

Regrettably Alan has also had his share of injury, but sadly we have heard the last of him as a player. He was in my squad in those early days, as was a man I have already mentioned and can only mention again as Mr Reliability – Colin Hendry. What a player!

All in all we had problems with central defenders because of various injuries, and it was expressed to me by more than one person that Richard Gough should be recalled. I had other ideas, though, and, even though Richard had stated in public that he would be available to play for Scotland now that Andy was no longer manager, I decided he would not be playing in the team.

Of course, we had problems with our striking positions too. The stars in my time were of course Maurice Johnston and Ally McCoist, who had formed a very good partnership. Johnston had dropped out but we still had McCoist, although he was not then available because he was still recovering from a broken leg. We tried various people in various permutations. I used Duncan Shearer, Andy Walker, John McGinlay, Kevin Gallacher, Darren Jackson, Gordon Durie, John Spencer and others, but it was difficult to find a regular scoring partnership. That brought some criticism in the early days that we were well able to defend but that we couldn't score goals. I couldn't really argue with that because the scorelines were there for all to see, and we were not scoring as many as we should have been, even though each of those players was, in my opinion, of the highest standard.

So the structure was modelled on the German example, and I think subsequent achievements have proved that it was the right decision. Alex Miller went along with me, even though the system was alien to what he was using at club level. In his typical professional manner he soon adapted and coached it the way I wanted it to be coached. Alex usually preferred to use a 4-4-2 system with his club work, but he was happy to support my choice of system.

Of course, there has been a lot of criticism of Scottish

goalkeepers over the years. I think that it is totally unjustified. The guy wearing the No.1 jersey is probably the most important on the pitch because he has not only to be the last line of defence but also has to give confidence to the entire side. In our Scotland set-up we had Alan Hodgkinson as goalkeeping coach and, for my money, he is one of the best in Europe. I am sure that our excellent defensive record in recent years is a testimony to his coaching. Yes, he is an Englishman, and he was capped by his country five times, as well as having a career spanning more than six hundred senior games with Sheffield United. He has probably never been more appreciated than he was as part of the international scene with Scotland. Alan certainly not only knows his business but also has the capability of teaching others in a way that they can both understand and relate to. Nobody jokes about Scottish goalkeepers any more. These days we have the reputation of being a difficult team to beat and that is, in no small way, because of the quality of our keepers.

Alan not only takes charge of our goalkeepers but also takes responsibility along with Jim Stewart for coaching the coaches of goalkeepers, and is involved with the judging of those coaches for their diplomas.

As you can see, I was gradually getting my staff together and had a fair basis of assessment of the players at my disposal. There were also players who were often brought to my attention who had Scottish parentage but had not actually been born in Scotland. We have a good system to make us aware of such players and to keep an eye on their progress.

I thought we needed someone with greater international experience because neither Alex Miller nor I had been capped at senior level and we felt that was a deficiency in our set-up. Tommy Craig had been my colleague in caring for the Under-21s, but even Tommy – great player though he was – had only been capped once by Scotland. To compensate for our inexperience as international players we brought other coaches in to help. Willie Miller was one. He was then manager of

Aberdeen and had been capped 65 times. Another was his former Aberdeen teammate Alex McLeish, who had 77 caps to his credit. Murdo MacLeod I have already mentioned and he was still with us. Tommy Burns came in as well, and like Andy before me I put him in charge of the 'B' international side. I invited other managers to join us as guests for our away matches, which gave them an insight into what we were trying to do. Walter Smith, Jim Jeffries, Alex Totten, Bobby Williamson, Josef Venglos and Lou Macari are just some who accepted the invitation. It also provided us with extra brains for our think-tank, because I have always had a listening ear and will consider any advice that anyone has to offer. Besides these things, it helped to develop an understanding and a good relationship between the national coaches and the club managers. I believe that it has resulted in an excellent comradeship between managers at all levels in Scotland.

The staffing situation was an important one and I gave it a high priority in my first moves as the new manager. The medical team too had to be of the highest quality. International sportsmen are rather like thoroughbred horses – they should have only the best. You never see top racehorses roaming over pieces of balding common land scavenging for food and grabbing a little bit of exercise only now and then. They have the very best in treatment, training, diet and facilities – and that is how international footballers have to be treated.

With our World Cup commitments finished we were now in the business of being sparring partners to those countries who had made it to the USA. We also had the draw for the European Championship to look forward to and the added incentive that the finals were going to be held in England – probably the shortest possible journey for the Tartan Army to have to make to accompany us. The draw for the qualifying round was made in Manchester on 22 January 1994. For me personally it was an exciting moment because I was there for the first time as manager of my country and, as such, I was rubbing shoulders with some of the biggest names in European soccer. One thing I could guarantee was that we would not be coming out of the same hat as England because Terry Venables and his men had the luxury of not having to qualify since they were the host country.

There were a few complaints about the way the draw was handled – mostly from those media representatives who struggled to get into the place. The draw was being televised live from the theatre of the Granada Tour – the visitor centre attached to Granada Television. Not everyone from the media was able to fit into the venue, and so an overflow room with a video screen accommodated the rest, and I think it was from there that most of the moans originated. Some of those not in the actual theatre probably felt that they had been slighted.

The stage-managed draw threw up some interesting match prospects, but I was concerned only with where we would land. As it was we fell into Group 8, the last on the list. In that same pen were Russia, Greece, Finland, the Faroe Islands and San Marino. As the names come out you don't really take in what is being said. It is only when you look at the list later, several times, that you start to realise the implications.

Russia and Greece had both qualified for the World Cup, which meant that they were certain to provide us with stiff opposition if we were to qualify for Euro 96. Finland have never been push-overs, the Faroe Islands meant a demanding journey, and San Marino had given England a shock just a couple of months earlier when they had scored in nine seconds. No, nothing could be taken for granted in this group. We had to finish in one of the top two places and that was not going to be a simple task.

The European Championship was then forgotten for a while as the full force of international publicity focused on the World Cup, covering it from every possible angle months before it actually began. In Scotland, though, we continued with our rebuilding programme.

The rebuilding included the first stage of the overhaul of Hampden Park, and we were to be hosts to Holland in a match to mark the reopening of the great stadium, which had been out of commission for two years as it was given a £12 million face-lift. Like most Scotsmen I have always loved Hampden. The place has now been given another face-lift and is the headquarters of Scottish football, including the offices of the Scottish Football Association. It looks splendid now, but then it has always looked magnificent to me. Anyway, on 23 March 1994 Holland arrived to help with the celebrations.

We prepared for the game the same as we would for a competitive match. Holland had qualified for the World Cup from the same group as Norway, which meant that they had played a part in eliminating Graham Taylor's England with a 2–2 draw at Wembley and a 2–0 victory in Rotterdam. The Dutch players were keen to prove that they were worth their place in Dick Advocaat's squad, so we knew they would not be coming along just for a kickabout. I wanted to start my preparations for the forthcoming European qualifiers, but I decided against any dramatic changes to the squad. Gary McAllister remained as captain, a job he was well suited to.

The Dutch were a class act with players like Dennis Bergkamp, Ed de Goey, Frank Rijkaard, Bryan Roy, Marc Overmars, Aron Winter and Frank de Boer in their side, along with other great names. Bryan Roy scored the only goal of the game about midway through the first half, and probably, to an independent onlooker, Holland had control of the game. However, the Scotland players gave a good account of themselves and I was encouraged by what I saw. I took advantage of it being a friendly to use four substitutes, and I learned a lot from seeing my players in action against another of the best teams in the world. Holland had lost only one of their ten World Cup games and had averaged virtually three goals a game. I was not unhappy with that final 1–0 scoreline, and the 36,809 in Hampden Park that night were well aware that they had seen a creditable performance.

It was my first home game as manager of Scotland and I would have liked to have recorded a victory, but it was still early days and I did not mind forgoing the luxury of victory in a friendly in order to prepare for victories at a later date. A month later we were on the road again this time to Austria for another friendly. The Austrians had failed to qualify for the World Cup so they were keen to save face in front of their own fans – and 35,000 of them turned up to watch them do it.

There was a cold edge to that Wednesday evening in Vienna. Our hosts were quietly confident but then so was I, and I hoped that I had instilled some of that confidence into my players. I had decided that it was time to give John McGinlay the chance to wear a Scotland shirt. He had been playing well at club level and you can never have too many striking options, so I included John in the squad and told him that he would almost certainly get his chance.

It can be very difficult to decide whether to put a new player straight into the side from the start of a match and be prepared to substitute him later, or to keep him on the bench and use him at an appropriate time in the game. Every player is an individual and you have to know what decision will get the best out of him. McGinlay was old enough and mature enough to be given a place in the starting line, and so that is exactly what we did.

Austria went on the rampage from the start and threw everything at us. It probably worked to our advantage because, if you can soak all that up at the start and wear the opposition down both physically and mentally, you will get stronger as they become weaker. In the twelfth minute it began to look as if we had made a mistake in our thinking. Austria took the lead through Hutter and we had a hill to climb, as they say. We fought back manfully and I was very pleased with the work-rate and the leadership of Gary McAllister, who refused to let any of the players have anything less than a totally positive outlook.

The hard work was rewarded in the 34th minute when John McGinlay announced his arrival with an excellent equalising goal. I was very pleased with him. You can't get much better than scoring on your international debut. The Austrians were taken aback by the effort put into our comeback and they seemed to have little answer to it. Their attacks floundered time and time again on our rock-like defence. Then, on the hour, the unthinkable – if you were Austrian – happened when Billy McKinlay made it 2–1.

With a quarter of an hour left I sent Duncan Shearer on to replace John McGinlay. I wanted to give Duncan his debut and see how he coped at international level. The Austrians did their best to get back on terms but our defence held and they became more and more depressed as the game wore on. When the final whistle blew, we had won 2–1 and I had gained my second victory as manager of Scotland.

We owed Holland a return visit and the fixture was scheduled for Utrecht on 27 May 1994, Holland's last game before the World Cup opened on 17 June. Once again, there were no half-measures from the Dutch. Jan Wouters was back as captain and Ruud Gullit was also back in the side along with Ronald de Boer. Brian Roy had inflicted the damage on us in the match at Hampden Park but we were going to do our best to keep an eye on him this time.

The home fans were keen to give their men a good send-off before they went to the USA, and they were certainly given something to cheer on the quarter-hour when Brian Roy slipped the leash we had put on him and put Holland into the lead. I was pleased that we did not buckle but kept our game going for the rest of the first half. The Dutch supporters had been expecting a slaughter but, in spite of tremendous home pressure, it was not happening.

I gave instructions at half-time that we were to stick to our game and not allow the Dutch any more freedom than they had already had. The game had just passed the hour mark when Peter Van Vossen struck to make it 2–0. Once again, though, we kept our heads and did not allow our shoulders to sag. We were having our moments at the other end but, with no disrespect to those players who were taking part, we were definitely missing the extra golden touch of Ally McCoist, who was an expert at turning a half-chance into a goal. This was a significant game for the home side also because after an alleged disagreement with Dick Advocaat, Ruud Gullit walked out on his country at half time. He was never to wear the famous orange shirt again.

I have always had great admiration for the Dutch and their football and they were not at all flattered by the scoreline when they were gifted an own goal from Brian Irvine in the 71st minute. I waited five minutes and then sent Duncan Shearer on for the last quarter of an hour. The fresh legs were just what we needed, and within five minutes Duncan, from a great pass by Eoin Jess, had pulled one back for us with his first senior goal for his country.

The last ten minutes or so were cut and thrust but there was no further change in the scoreline. In the history books it will show that Holland beat Scotland 3–1 on that night in May 1994, but it was a brave performance from the Scottish players. We had actually scored two of the four goals in the game – and that told me that we were able to mix freely with the best and give as good as we got. It also told me that we should never take on a match long after the end of the season when the players were out of training. This knowledge was used later when we had to play vital qualifying matches in the Faroes and in Minsk.

By the time the season had come to an end, all eyes were glued to the World Cup – mine included. I was particularly keen to watch our European Championship rivals, Russia and Greece, as they took on the best of the world in their attempts to win the crown. The Greeks were largely unimpressive. They had some dangerous-looking players, but they did not perform as a unit as well as most other sides, and it was no surprise to me that they were among the first to go home.

Greece lost each of their group games against Nigeria, Bulgaria and Argentina to finish bottom of the mini-table with ten goals against and none scored. Back home in Greece there was a massive amount of criticism, and some of the Greek players were apprehensive about going home to a welcome that was to be less than a hero's. That is the pressure in football. One minute you are a hero for reaching the World Cup finals, and the next you are almost Public Enemy No.1 for not being successful.

The Russians were in Group B with Brazil, Sweden and Cameroon. They also had a difficult task and were beaten by both Brazil and Sweden. They did take some consolation from recording the biggest score of the tournament when they beat Cameroon 6–1, but it was too late to get them past the group stage and they, like Greece, caught the early plane home.

I was always brought up to take a good look at the opposition, whether it was at club level or internationally, and the World Cup tournament gave me plenty of chance to observe these two nations, against whom we had to pit our wits in the European Championship qualifying group. I watched Greece and I watched Russia, and I knew that they were capable sides. But I also saw Holland win their group and then beat the Republic of Ireland 2–0 in the next round before going out at the quarterfinal stage after a tremendous tussle with Brazil, who won the game 3–2. Brazil had been 2–0 ahead and then Holland had fought back to draw level before that final killer goal from Branco. Brazil went on to win the World Cup, but Holland had given them a run for their money and it made me remember our performance against that same Dutch side.

As I contemplated these events and considered that I had now won two and lost three of my first five games in charge of Scotland, my thoughts turned again to Euro 96. We would soon be starting our campaign for a place in the finals. It was not going to be an easy passage, but the more I thought about it the more confident I began to feel. My agreement was to be manager of Scotland up to and including the European Championship, and I was determined to do my best and make the most of this great opportunity.

17

The Euro Challenge

THERE COULD NOT have been a much greater incentive for getting to the European Championship than the fact that it was being held in England. Scotland's chances of ever staging the tournament, will come, hopefully, as a result of our 2008 bid. The next best thing is to take part in the tournament when it is being staged in England. We did not qualify for the 1966 World Cup, but we were determined to take part in Euro '96.

Our qualifying group was a tricky one. Greece had qualified for the 1994 World Cup and therefore it would have been a mistake to dismiss them lightly. San Marino and the Faroe Islands were no longer the push-overs that they had previously been labelled. Finland were a team of excellent players and very unpredictable, and then, of course, there were the mighty Russians.

As part of our preparation, I travelled to Casablanca to see Finland in action against Morocco. It was a very revealing experience because my cab driver asked if I would like to see some street or beach football and, when I agreed, he showed me what must have been thousands of youngsters playing.

Their enthusiasm was tremendous, and showed that you don't have to go to Brazil to find tomorrow's stars playing in the streets.

The campaign began in September 1994, and a trip to Finland. I was able to field a fairly strong side, as could be expected so early in the season. There was no Ally McCoist because he was still recovering from a broken leg, but Duncan Shearer was a reliable striker and I decided to give him the chance to get us off to a flying start. Within 29 minutes Duncan had put us ahead after a magnificent move that involved 21 passes. We were on our way. John Collins scored our second after the break and we left Helsinki with maximum points and a lot of smiles. A month later we were back at Hampden Park for the visit of the Faroe Islands. I have a lot of respect for countries like the Faroes. They never have any major successes but they are more than happy just to be involved. They love their football and they are always very good-natured and hospitable. If anything, they are perfect examples of what this great game is all about.

At Hampden we beat them 5–1. John McGinlay scored after four minutes, Scott Booth made it 2–0 half an hour later, and John Collins struck just before half-time. It was Billy McKinlay who made it 4–0 in the 61st minute. He had only been on the pitch for a few minutes after replacing Cohn Hendry, who had taken a knock. John Collins made it 5–0 but then we went to sleep in defence and allowed Muller to pull one back. I was not happy about that because we had been sound in defence and to me every goal counts, whether it is for or against.

When the Russians visited Hampden for our next qualifying game we were well aware that this was likely to be one of the most crucial games in our quest to reach the finals. Even though the break-up of the old Soviet Union had rendered some players unavailable to Oleg Romantsev, the Russian coach, he was still able to select a formidable side.

I had been to the 1994 World Cup just to watch our

European opponents Russia and Greece, and I saw the Russians give an impressive display against Brazil. Amazingly, when I sat down in that 70,000-seat stadium in San Francisco, I was next to an all-American guy complete with baseball cap, reflector sunglasses, denims, the whole works. I had been sitting there for some time before I realised that this 'all-American' guy was actually Walter Smith, the Rangers manager. I had not recognised a man whom I had known for years. Mind you, I don't think his own players would have recognised him either. I was not alone because, after the game, we bumped into Alex Ferguson or Sir Alex as I now have to remember to call him and, as a joke, I introduced Walter as an American pal of mine. Alex didn't recognise him either.

At Hampden, Scott Booth put us ahead after nineteen minutes, having received a wonderful pass from Gary McAllister. Radchenko equalised six minutes later and the game became a stalemate. The Russians were obviously happier with the result than we were. I was disappointed that the territorial advantage had not turned into goals. I was not displeased with the defence, who had contained Andrei Kanchelskis and his teammates very well. However, we could and should have won.

Greece were having a good run at this time. They had won each of their three games and had scored eleven goals with only one reply. Admittedly, they had played what had been described as the 'weaker' teams in the group, but you still have to score goals and win games.

It was a harsh penalty decision against Colin Hendry which settled the match in Athens. The game was just eighteen minutes old, and no matter how hard we tried we could not get level. Hendry was alleged to have tripped Alexandris, the Greek winger, but it was a highly debatable decision. Later in the game we lost Andy Goram with an injury and I had to send Jim Leighton on to replace him. It was quite a turning point for Andy Goram because he took no further part in the group games and made only two brief appearances for Rangers during the rest of their season.

We were becoming quite concerned now because our next match was to be against the Russians in Moscow. The game was not scheduled until March, but I went early in the New Year to Moscow to check a few things and was telephoned there by Iain Ferguson, who was then sports reporter on the Daily Record. He had some really good, relevant news for me as he revealed that, in his newspaper's poll, only 8 per cent of supporters wanted me to be the Scotland manager. Kenny Dalglish had polled 28 per cent with 21 per cent going to Alex Ferguson. Gordon Strachan was third and I believe I came after him.

I suppose I was expected to make some peevish remark in response, but I was not going to fall for that one. You can twist statistics any way you like, so I just said how interesting it was that, when you looked at the percentage polled by Alex Ferguson, it showed that 79 per cent did not want Scotland to be in the charge of the best manager in Europe. Needless to say my words did not appear in the newspaper – there was just a piece about my lack of popularity. You are supposed to ignore these things and just soldier on, which you do, of course, but it does not help you to feel good about your work.

I was in Russia with Willie McDougall, who is our security officer, and we were well looked after by the Russian representative, Sergei Kussainov who was actually their top referee. On the way back we were held up at the airport where there were massive queues in the passenger area. Our embarrassed host took us past the queues and we found ourselves at the front, forming a new queue. When members of other queues decided to join us they were waved away, and you can imagine that there were more than a few people disgruntled by the whole affair. Our host explained that we were VIPs. A lady with a London accent became even more indignant. 'VIPs indeed! Who are you anyway?'

Quick as a flash, Willie answered her, 'Glasgow police –

and this is my prisoner!'

'Oh my God!' cried the woman, and she vanished into the crowd, convinced that she had just confronted a hardened international criminal rather than a football manager.

Willie is very conscientious on these trips. He leaves no stone unturned. He does not just look at the facilities for the players but those for the supporters also, to make sure that they have the best facilities possible.

My own brief is to check on the size of the pitch, the type of grass, the dressing rooms, training facilities, and of course our accommodation. At the hotel I check the air-conditioning, the quality and size of the beds and the linen used, and the catering. If necessary we take our own chef, Tom Kirkpatrick, but in Moscow that was not needed at all. Everything was very good indeed.

The game took place at the end of March. Our Under-21 team had played the night before and won their game, and that gave us a lift. Our chief enemy was the weather. Moscow was still in the icy grip of winter at that time, and we had the coldest training sessions I can ever remember, with snow as well as freezing temperatures. George Scanlon, the linguist who has acted as interpreter for Andrei Kanchelskis among many others, was with us, and I think he was feeling the cold along with the rest of us.

Tom Boyd was given the job of keeping Andrei Kanchelskis quiet for the 90 minutes and he did a great job – very positive. In fact he did his job so well that there was a real possibility of him scoring a couple of goals himself. It was 0–0 at half-time and remained that way for the rest of the game. I was very pleased with the performance. Some might say that we could even have won it, but not many teams go to Moscow in those conditions and get a result.

One of the things I have learned in my job is that you never underestimate San Marino. Our next game was away to them at the end of April 1995. There is no point in denying that we struggled, and it took a special bit of magic from John

Collins to get our show on the road. We seemed to be labouring against a team that did not have a great reputation but, believe me, San Marino can be an awkward side to beat on their own ground. It was them who frightened England to death with the fastest goal in World Cup history a few years ago.

John Collins turned it on in the nineteenth minute, though, when he took possession and went on a run that was a slalom through an obstacle of challenges. His finishing touch was to round the goalkeeper, Benedettini, and put the ball in the net. It was a magnificent goal. We struggled to add to it, though – until about five minutes from the end when Cohn Calderwood met a cross from Gary McAllister and gave us a 2–0 scoreline with his first goal for his country.

We were relieved when that game was over. I don't think our supporters were too impressed with the performance, but it was a victory nevertheless, and we knew there would be better days against higher-profile opposition.

Our season ended in June with our next European qualifier, this time away to the Faroe Islands. Before that, we flew to Japan to take part in the Kirin Cup. We had just two games to play, but it gave us the chance to keep a squad together and introduce some of the younger players to senior international football. We drew 0–0 with Japan in Hiroshima in a game that remarkably saw two players sent off, including our own John Spencer. A few days later we played Ecuador and beat them 2–1, with goals in the second half from John Robertson and Stevie Crawford.

The Kirin Cup trip was criticised by some, who felt that it was a long way to go just before a crucial European game. However, we had done our homework and knew what we were getting into. The facilities out there were excellent and we were able to train every day. Our fitness expert, Roger Spry, travelled with us. Far from being a taxing event, it was more like going to a training camp. Wales had been there in the past and we made some enquiries about their experiences. So we were well informed before we decided to accept the invitation to go to Japan, and I am convinced that it did us a lot of good.

We had only a brief respite before travelling to the Faroes. It can be a tricky flight, mostly because the landing strip is a little on the short side and the pilot has to get his approach just right. Sometimes they have to circle several times before going into a descent that is not unlike a white-knuckle ride at a theme park. For the uninitiated, when you played away to the Faroe Islands you then had to land on one island, live on another, and play on a third, so it was quite an experience. Now they have a fine new stadium in Torshaven which eliminates the tortuous travel arrangements. The hospitality is excellent because the people are always pleased to see you, and I must say that, after that flight in, we were more than pleased to see them as well!

The game was the old story. We were 2–0 ahead at half-time, thanks to a Billy McKinlay goal in the 25th minute followed by one from John McGinlay four minutes later. There were no further goals, which gave rise to a few critical comments once again. I understood the sentiments, but it did not matter if we had scored two or ten because under UEFA rules the goal difference against these smaller nations would not count in the final group reckoning.

We said our goodbyes for the summer and I went on my travels again. I had coaching engagements in Canada and America, and a UEFA commitment in Geneva as well as the courses at Largs. While I was in Minneapolis I saw the future of football in the United States. I attended a youth tournament for the USA Cup, which involved 675 teams and 43 football pitches. Anyone who believes that soccer will never get off the ground in the United States had better think again. There is a coming generation who love the game and, more importantly, have a lot of talent.

Greece were our visitors at Hampden just after the season started, and for one player at least it was going to be a fairytale evening. It had been more than two years since Ally McCoist had broken his leg against Portugal. He had experienced a number of setbacks but now, at last, he had been able to prove his fitness, and I was delighted to welcome him back to the squad.

I could not take the risk of putting Ally into the starting line-up, but he was on the bench. We had a setback when both Colin Hendry and Alan McLaren failed fitness tests, but I called up Tosh McKinlay and he fitted in perfectly.

We managed to meet at 11 a.m. for a training session at Hampden and when I arrived I was met by Andy Goram, who told me that he didn't feel fit enough or mentally attuned to the game. There was a suggestion that the real problem was that the game fell between two vital Rangers matches – but that has never been confirmed.

I spoke to Andy and put it to him that since he would probably be playing in the forthcoming Rangers European Cup game, it would not look too good for him to drop out of our match unless he went and explained it to the press himself. I was quite firm and told him that I was not prepared to make his excuses for him.

We spoke to Alan Hodgkinson and he tried to persuade Andy to do a little training, but really we both knew that there was little use in trying to cajole a player whose mind was simply not on the game because we would be going out at a disadvantage. There are those players who want to be talked into playing, their supposed injury being simply an excuse for the need to feel wanted as you persuade them to play. I've never found that at international level, but it certainly happens at club level. My policy is that I will never beg any player to play.

Anyway, we held a press conference and the media guys were quite shocked when Andy talked to them. I was not left with a serious problem in the goalkeeping department because I had the ever-reliable Jim Leighton with us. The press kept pushing me for the real reason for Andy's sudden withdrawal. I explained that I knew no more than they did, and that I was not a psychologist who could look inside Andy's head.

Predictably, the following day's tabloid headline was 'You Need A Shrink Andy – Says Brown'.

I was a bit upset about that because I had said nothing of the sort. Knowing Andy's character, I had no doubts that he would laugh it off, but I was worried about his family as I did not want them to be offended.

A few days later I was talking to Walter Smith on the phone and he told me what had happened in the Rangers dressing room. Ally McCoist and Ian Durant had obtained a straitjacket and had hung it on Andy's peg. Walter thought it was hilarious, but I was a little concerned. Fortunately the story faded away in the end.

Greece had little room for manoeuvre up front as our defenders kept control. We were having a few problems in attack ourselves. We were creating chances but it seemed we could not get the all-important goal. At half-time I told the players not to get over-anxious, keep plugging away and the goal would come.

With nineteen minutes left I sent on John Robertson and Ally McCoist. Ally was thrilled because he had missed fifteen internationals as a result of his injury. Now, at last, he was back in the shirt. Within 60 seconds he had headed a terrific goal from a John Collins cross. Hampden erupted as we all came to our feet. What a spectacular comeback! Never mind Roy of the Rovers – we had Ally of the Rangers!

That goal was the only one necessary. We beat Greece 1–0 and went joint top of the group alongside Russia. We had an excellent chance of reaching Euro 96.

Before the Finland game, their coach, Jukka Ikalainen, was reported to have said that we were likely to qualify on luck and, of course, I was expected by the newspapers to respond to this. I just said that we would show whether or not we were lucky by putting the ball into their net. Once again, this was taken as fighting talk when it appeared in print. I'm pleased to say that most of us coaches know each other well enough to understand what has really been said without all the embroidery. Very often, supporters are surprised to see opposition coaches enjoying a joke together when, according to the media, we are supposed to be stabbing each other in the back. The truth is that there is a great camaraderie among coaches – much the same as you would find on Death Row!

Again, we had a few injury problems before we faced Finland. Duncan Shearer was unable to play and Darren Jackson was a worry. I recalled Scott Booth, and it was fitting that he celebrated his recall with an excellent goal after ten minutes. It was the only goal of a game that was businesslike rather than exciting.

Our final game was to be at home to San Marino, but before that we had a friendly in Sweden. On the same day Russia were playing Greece, and if the Russians won then we were guaranteed qualification.

Sure enough, Russia won a very tense battle 2–1 and, as the news filtered through to us in Stockholm, we were beaten 2–0 by the Swedes. It did not seem too much of a disaster. We used the game to experiment with players, while Sweden, who had not qualified, were playing for pride. One worry was seeing Gary McAllister carried off with what appeared to be a severe ankle injury, which fortunately turned out to be not too bad.

I think everyone wanted to play in our final game at Hampden against San Marino, and certainly the Tartan Army made the occasion a real party.

There was only ever going to be one result but, to their credit, the San Marinese gave the game their best shot. Eoin Jess scored our first on the half-hour and Scott Booth made it 2–0 moments before half-time. The second half was three minutes old when I decided to send Ally McCoist on. Within a minute he struck again and made it 3–0. Pat Nevin made it 4–0 and then we were given an own goal by Francini to make it 5–0.

The supporters applauded the players and the players applauded the supporters. They had come a long way together

in the ten qualifying games, and the road to England lay ahead
– but for now it was party time!

There was excitement at having qualified for Euro 96, but
it was nothing compared to the buzz that ran through Scotland
when the group draw was made and we fell into the same
frame as England, Holland and Switzerland. I was at the draw
ceremony and I could not believe my ears. I was almost lost
for words when interviewed for television. Of course, the
England coach, Terry Venables, more than made up for my
inadequacy.

The draw not only brought our two nations together to
resume the traditional clash that had been shelved since 1989,
but also put us into the category of underdogs. The
bookmakers rated only Turkey below us of the sixteen
competing countries. That did not bother us at all. We were in
the tournament by the front door and we had every hope of
making our presence felt.

There was also talk of how great the financial incentives
were for the Scotland players. I found that distasteful because
the players who pull on the Scotland jersey do so for pride. In
my total of fifteen years as assistant manager, and manager, I
had never once heard money mentioned. These guys are all
well-paid club professionals. They do not need financial
incentives to play for their country.

Our warm-up programme included a friendly against
Australia at Hampden in March 1996. They were a difficult
side to break down, but Ally McCoist scored in the second half
and that was the only goal needed. A month later we travelled
to Denmark and were beaten 2–0. I have never been concerned
about defeats in these games. They are all about
experimentation.

In May we set up camp in the United States and played
two games. In New Britain we lost 2–1 to the USA. Gordon
Durie scored for us but the Americans netted in each half. A
few days later, in Miami, we lost 1–0 to Colombia with
Fausnno Asprilla getting the all-important goal after he had

come on as a substitute. The important point was that the squad had been prepared properly, not just in playing but socially as well.

Our first Euro 96 game was at Villa Park, and there was a terrific atmosphere at the stadium when we arrived. Holland were our opponents, and they were among the favourites to win the competition. We were determined to at least contain them and the 0–0 scoreline verifies that we were successful.

The Dutch came at us like an express train immediately the game started. Andy Goram made a wonderful reflex save from Seedorf. Stuart McCall brilliantly tackled the same player when he was in a likely scoring position and John Collins cleared from the goal line. That was the frantic start to the game. I think it did us good to be woken up so early. That flurry of activity had the same effect as a bucket of cold water in the face.

We had our moments in attack. John Collins had a fierce dipping shot punched away by Van der Saar and, in the last minute, Gordon Durie almost snatched a winner. As it was, the Scotland team had played its heart out and suddenly the rest of Europe realised that we were not there just to make up the numbers.

Of course, the big game was against England at Wembley. We were very keyed up for this one, perhaps too much, but it meant a lot to us. On the way to Wembley there was a great atmosphere on the team coach, and that was echoed by the fans inside the stadium.

The first half was almost like a sparring round, and I felt that we had the better of the exchanges. There were no goals, and at half-time I told the players to keep up their work-rate on the tiring turf and keep plugging away. I was very disappointed when Alan Shearer found space to head home in the 52nd minute, but we did not let our shoulders droop and only a wonder save by David Seaman prevented Gordon Durie from equalising.

When Tony Adams brought Gordon Durie down in the goal area, time stood still for a while. We were awarded a penalty and you could have heard a pin drop as Gary McAllister stepped up to take the kick. Another great, or lucky, save from Seaman denied him, and I could not help but remember the penalty that Gary had scored in the 1992 tournament in our 3–0 win over the CIS. I would willingly have exchanged them.

With eleven minutes left, Paul Gascoigne came to life and scored a superb solo goal to make the final score 2–0. We were disappointed but had nothing to be ashamed of. We had forced eight corners to England's two and that was basically the story, except that they had the points and we didn't.

I was very conscious of the fact that we had not scored in either game. There was still a chance that we could create a little bit of history and go into the next round. We needed England to give Holland a beating and ourselves to beat Switzerland.

Ally McCoist gave us the first bit of magic with a great goal after 37 minutes. He ran to the bench and we celebrated together, along with the Tartan Army. News reached us that England were winning 4–0. If it stayed like that we would go through. The magic spell was broken when Patrick Kluivert scored a late goal for Holland and improved their goal tally sufficiently for them to finish in second place in the group. We savoured our victory over Switzerland, where we had fourteen shots on target and our ten corners, but, at the end of the day, we were packing our bags. The dedication and commitment shown by all the players was summed up by the actions of John Collins. John's transfer to Monaco had led to a problem with his insurance. To ensure that he could play he had to pay the premium himself; a substantial amount of money which far outweighed his playing fees and left him well out of pocket.

The European Championship had been exciting and a wonderful event for us, but now it was time to look ahead to a new challenge. When the 1996/97 season dawned, we would be on a different road. One that could lead to France and the 1998 World Cup.

18

The Road to France

AUSTRIA, SWEDEN, LATVIA, Belarus and Estonia stood between us and a place in the World Cup finals in France in the summer of 1998. Only the top country would definitely go through, and there were various permutations and possibilities for those placed second in their groups. One would also go through, while the other eight would have to play off for the four remaining places.

Our road to France began with a journey to Vienna. It was expected that Austria would be one of the toughest opponents in our group, though to me they all looked difficult. There is no such thing as an easy game or an easy opponent. I recalled Duncan Ferguson to the side, but I did not want to make any drastic changes to the squad that had performed so well in our European campaign. The Austrians were lively, as you would expect from a home team playing their first World Cup match of a new challenge.

Our defence held and we were very pleased to come away from one of the two strongest teams in our group with a point and without conceding a goal. There were even times when I thought we might sneak a goal, but when the whistle went at 0–0 I felt that we had done a professional job and that was all that could be asked.

Our next task was to travel to Riga to meet Latvia. The trouble with so many of these recently emerged countries is that they are still an unknown quantity and can give you quite a shock if you are expecting them to be just also-rans. We made no such mistake in our match preparations and worked towards the fixture just as we would if we were playing Germany, Holland or any of the other leading lights of world football.

Again we gave an assured performance. John Collins scored for us in the eighteenth minute with a fine free kick straight from the training ground and we kept plugging away for the next hour until Darren Jackson made it 2–0 in the second half. The score remained that way and, once again, we returned home like businessmen who have just done a successful deal. I have always tried to coach patience and the realisation that there are 90 minutes in which to play. I think our performances during the World Cup demonstrated that patience a number of times, and this game was one of those times. The players set about their task in a methodical manner, kept their heads and were rewarded for their professionalism.

With those two games under our belt, we were in good spirits when we travelled to Estonia for our next game just a few days later.

The visit to Tallin proved to be a complete farce and a waste of time. We had been there before in other qualifying matches, but there was nothing quite like this one. In fact, there has probably never been one like it in the history of the World Cup.

The argument was over floodlights. We had seen the floodlights and knew that they were just not up to standard. The FIFA officials agreed with us and we were told that the kick-off would be brought forward. There had been some earlier controversy about what time the game was to be played.

We were happy to play at whatever time we were told. But the notion of playing such an important game under temporary floodlights, which did not illuminate the pitch adequately, was not only ridiculous but also against FIFA World Cup rules.

We turned up at the revised kick-off time. When it became obvious that Estonia were not going to be there, we sought further guidance from FIFA and were told to prepare for the game and kick off. If Estonia were not there, the referee had instructions to start the game and end it as soon as the ball was in play.

We followed the directive, as did the match officials. Later we were told that Estonia had appealed and that the game would have to be replayed. Thus the team that had complied with FIFA rules appeared to be penalised, while the team that didn't had a second chance. It was a bizarre situation made all the more ridiculous because there were those who blamed us for not wanting to play under lights that looked more like the sort that illuminate motorway roadworks.

It was even more galling when it was also suggested that we wanted the game cancelled because Gary McAllister was suspended. Since our next game was against Sweden we would have preferred him to have missed the Estonia game. As it was, we were without him for a key game, so that misinformed argument is easily nullified. It does annoy me when people sit at their desks passing judgement without having any first-hand knowledge of the facts.

We returned home and then took on Sweden at Ibrox on 10 November 1996, before a crowd of 50,000. What a game it turned out to be! The Swedes brought their strongest side and went for maximum points. Their early enthusiasm proved to be a mistake because a gap opened up in their defence and, after eight minutes, John McGinlay put us ahead with a superbly-worked goal.

After that it was time for our defenders to shine as Sweden threw everything at us. Jim Leighton was in great form and dealt with anything that broke through our tight defence. The minutes ticked away and in the end McGinlay's goal proved to be enough. Ibrox celebrated, and I felt a great deal of pleasure when I saw that we were top of the group.

The Estonia game was finally replayed in Monaco in February 1997. There is no doubt that we were below par, and I wonder if the players found it hard to get to grips with the game, feeling that they should not have been required to play it. The final score was 0–0 – the least said the better.

We had not seen the last of Estonia because, a month later, we played them at Kilmarnock in our group return match. It was an unspectacular match, but again a competent and professional performance. Tom Boyd scored a first-half goal and our pressure in the second half forced Meet of Estonia to concede an own goal. We were happy at 2–0.

Now we had to play one of our chief rivals again. After our draw at the start, Austria had won their next two games, including a victory over Sweden in Stockholm. Celtic Park was packed for their visit in April 1997, and our supporters were in good voice.

The game lived up to expectations. Austria had come looking for victory, but so had we. It was a great night for Kevin Gallacher, as he played out of his skin to get us the points. He scored a brilliant goal in the 25th minute which would have taken the roof off the stadium had there been one. In the 77th minute he repeated his performance and, at the final whistle, we were 2–0 victors and seven points clear in the table.

I was very pleased for Kevin because he was another player I had known from his Under-21 team days, and he had battled back from severe injuries to regain his place in the Scotland side.

We needed that cushion at the top because we had played more games than the others and we were yet to play away to Sweden – which was, in fact, our next date, just a few weeks after the Austria game. At this stage we had not conceded a goal in the qualifying games, but we knew that our defence would have to be in top form against Sweden.

Everything went according to plan until a minute before half-time when Kennet Andersson gave Sweden the lead, to the delight of the majority of the 40,000 crowd. Back in the dressing room we had to repair the psychological damage of going a goal down, but I have to say that there is always a strong will in the Scotland camp and our heads are never bowed for more than a passing moment.

We battled away in the second half and gave as good as we received, but there was a brief spell of shakiness in our defence, and Andersson was in for a second goal. We bounced back again and pushed the Swedes for most of the remainder of the game. Kevin Gallacher finally scored another of his excellent goals and we came close to the equaliser several times. Eventually we ran out of time and settled for the 2–1 defeat, our first of the competition.

There was just one more World Cup game after the end of the season, and that meant a trip to Minsk to play Belarus. The game was fairly uneventful except that everyone worked extremely hard and we came away with a 1–0 victory, thanks to a finely executed penalty by Gary McAllister. At the end of the sseason 2000/1 Gary had such a startling influence on Liverpool's Treble Cup success, scoring vital free kicks and penalties under pressure but for my money his most significant penalty was this one as it effectively sent us on our way to France '98. We were all delighted when we flew home. We had terrific support from the players who made the trip but did not take part in the game. Possibly they deserve even more credit than those who did play.

I remember putting Billy Dodds on with just a few minutes to go. He was desperate to get into the game, preferably from the start. I expect 90 minutes' work from substitutes, even if they are only on for ten minutes. Billy Dodds is just the sort of player for that work-rate. Gordon Durie and Gary McAllister were both extremely tired, and Paul Lambert and Kevin Gallacher were also absolutely exhausted. All the players had answered the call and had not been found wanting.

The performance was warmly applauded by the five hundred or so members of the Tartan Army who had made the trip to Minsk. I had been to a Sweden away match and noted that they had taken only about a dozen fans. It says something for the loyalty, dedication and passion of the Scotland fans that there is almost always a large presence whenever and wherever we are playing away.

After the summer break we had to prepare for the run-in with games against Belarus and Latvia. The matches were scheduled to be played at Aberdeen's Pittodrie Stadium and Hibernian's Easter Road ground. I felt that, since these two games were so important, they ought to be played in Glasgow. I spoke to the SFA president, Mr McGinn, who was with Jim Farry, the Chief Executive, and put my case. They agreed to discuss it, and then came back to me to ask if I would settle for just one venue change. I said that I didn't mind the Belarus game being played at Aberdeen, but that the all-important final fixture against Latvia should be switched to Glasgow.

Eventually I was told that the Latvia game would have to remain at Easter Road because the agreement had been signed and that was the end of it. I was disappointed, of course, since I firmly believed that the final game should have as many Scotland supporters present as possible.

As it was, the Belarus game was scheduled for the Saturday on which the funeral of Princess Diana was to take place, and the game was subsequently postponed for 24 hours, as I will describe later.

We were training at the ground of Highland League side Cove Rangers, thanks to the co-operation of Alan McCrae, an SFA council member and owner of Cove Rangers. Because of the death of the Princess, most of the players were making arrangements to visit churches and so on, but we still had to train.

Before the game there was a very moving moment when a

piper played a lament on the pitch while everyone stood in silence. The players were a little subdued, but they seemed very determined as they carried out what is a tradition in the Scotland dressing room shaking hands. For as long as I can remember, everyone has shaken hands with everyone else before an international. There is often a lot of shouting too, but not on that day.

Just to give you some idea of what it is like inside the dressing room before an international match, picture a scene with guys changing, some changed already, others stretching and warming up a little, some joking to keep their nerves under control, some starting to shout. If Colin Calderwood is there, you will find him shouting at himself and slapping himself really hard. There are those who prefer to be quiet.

I do not believe in last-minute team talks, but Alex Miller, Alan Hodgkinson and I would go round the players individually, offering a word or two of encouragement, or a reminder of some previously discussed point. We have a habit of putting charts of set pieces on the wall, and we might take a player to one just to give him a little reminder of a move or a position.

We liked the substitutes to look immaculate. They decided for themselves if they were going to wear tracksuits or jackets, but they must all wear the same and be uniform in their appearance. In my time, the number of substitutes has grown from two to seven, so there was less space in the dressing room and more players to speak to.

From about half an hour before the game I didn't like people who are not directly involved in the game anywhere near the dressing room. That included players who were not playing. We encouraged players who have been injured and might otherwise have taken part to look in and wish their colleagues well – but not after my half-hour curfew.

I admired the tremendous attitude of Colin Hendry, who was injured and could not play in the Belarus game, when he flew to Aberdeen just to watch the match and flew straight back afterwards. A great example of his support for the national team.

Gary McAllister and John Collins were in charge of set pieces during the game, and before the Belarus match I reminded them of a move that had been highly successful against Latvia, resulting in John scoring a terrific goal from a free kick. I said that Belarus would have seen that and would not allow the same situation to arise. These were famous last words because, early in the game, we did get a replica situation. This time it was McAllister who had the shot. The goalkeeper parried but the ever-alert Kevin Gallacher was there to follow up and put us ahead.

The tension drained out of the team and the crowd immediately, and the fans began to enjoy themselves. At half-time McAllister and Collins came to me very pointedly and said, 'Aye, that one's not going to work, is it?' – reminding me of my advice before the game. It was rare that they went against my instructions, but on that occasion I was glad that they had.

Gary indicated that he had had a recurrence of his knee trouble, so we watched him for a few minutes into the second half before sending on David Hopkin to replace him. What a fairytale it was for him. I had seen him in a Crystal Palace Nationwide League match against Queens Park Rangers, and he had been highly recommended to me by Dave Bassett, who was then his manager. I was impressed by him, and he certainly lived up to all the praise Dave Bassett had heaped upon him. I had seen him before several times, but never playing as well as this.

He made his debut by replacing McAllister and he scored two goals. It was sensational stuff and I was delighted, both for him and for the team. Kevin Gallacher scored another between David's goals and we were having a good time. It might seem strange, but I became concerned when we were 3–0 ahead and conceded a penalty. Petr Katchuro scored from the spot and ruined one of our many clean sheets. It was only the third goal that had been scored against us in the nine games that we had played – but every goal lost is like a flesh wound.

I was, and I am, proud of our defensive record. In our Euro 96 campaign we conceded only three goals in our ten qualifying matches, and in this World Cup campaign we had done the same. There are not many teams with such a record. In all competitive games since I became manager we had conceded just eight goals and lost three games. I think that is why we were seeded for the European Championship draw for the 2000 competition.

All eyes were now on the Latvia game, our last of the competition. We knew that we would stand a good chance of getting through as the best runners-up if we beat Latvia. Public pressure demanded a change of venue, and the SFA quickly amended their plans. I wrote to my old friend, Lex Gold, the then chairman of Hibernian and now in that role with the SPL, thanking him for releasing us from having to play the game at his Easter Road ground.

There was great anticipation when we played Latvia at Celtic Park on 11 October 1997. It was a sell-out, of course, and covered live by Channel 5 television. I was very happy to remember the request of Janis Mezeckis, the general secretary of Latvia, who asked me for a Scotland jersey for his son. Later, he told me how delighted his son had been to receive it.

As everyone knows, we won the game 2–0 with an excellent goal from Kevin Gallacher and a very well-earned one by Gordon Durie. We were delighted with the result and we also had a secret celebration laid on for Dr Stewart Hillis, our medical man, who had just gained a professorship. Win, lose or draw, we had arranged to take him for a meal that evening.

At the same time, Spain were playing the Faroe Islands in an evening match and, had there been a shock result, our standing would have been affected, so we were eager to hear the result.

We went to a restaurant in Cumbernauld. Professor

Stewart Hillis thought he was just going for a meal with his colleague, Stewart MacMillan, and it came as quite a nice surprise when all the Scotland backroom staff showed up dressed in our team uniform. I'd had a silver salver engraved, which I presented to him. We were delighted to have a professor among our backroom staff.

Around this time, I received a letter from Paisley University, which now includes the Craigie College campus. The letter informed me of a possible honorary doctorate, and I felt highly honoured and flattered to have such an award bestowed upon me. I received it at a degree ceremony just after the World Cup.

The news came through that Spain had proved their superiority over the Faroes – we were definitely finalists in the 1998 World Cup. The next morning there was a press conference at Glasgow Airport because I, and David Findlay, head of the International Department of the Scottish FA, were about to fly out to France to look at possible accommodation. I had refused to entertain such a trip until I knew that we were definitely going to France as finalists – but now it was time to start on the next phase of our quest for the World Cup.

While in France, we took the opportunity to go and see our Under-18 team in action in a tournament, and we were delighted to see Ross Mathie's team beat Denmark 5–0. It was a very good result because the Danes are one of the strongest sides in Europe. The Scotland performance was excellent and we were especially pleased to see the new generation of Scots on their way to becoming senior internationals in some style.

We later played a friendly against France in which they narrowly beat us, but it served, I believe, to give us a further taste of what to expect in the summer of 1998.

Since then I hardly stopped travelling. I am at home so little that our postman thinks I'm a burglar when he sees me. But the reward for all this was the honour of carrying the hopes of my country into the 1998 World Cup finals. Believe me, it was all worthwhile.

19

The Draw

WE DON'T WANT BRAZIL!

That was one of my statements before the World Cup draw took place in Marseille. I expect every manager or coach said exactly the same thing. Having Brazil in your group would virtually mean that you would be playing for second place. To be honest, I was not in particular dread of anybody, because you have to respect each and every country that has qualified for the finals of the World Cup. The hosts will have the full backing of their supporters, so there is no way that they can be taken for granted. The champions are keen to hang on to their crown so they will be no push-over – and all the other countries had to fight for their places too. Given the choice, though, I would not have selected Brazil to be among the countries in our group.

The French were keen to make a spectacular event of the draw and among the attractions was a 'Europe against the Rest of the World' game which experienced its own hiccups. The sides were to be made up of representatives of the various countries taking part in the World Cup finals. Gary McAllister was our obvious first choice, but he had been forced to withdraw because of injury. Darren Jackson was next on the list but the Celtic coach, Wim Jansen, did not want him to play because he wanted him in his squad for a game against Kilmarnock at the weekend.

I must say that Gordon Strachan, Gary McAllister's manager at Coventry, was keen that Gary should take part. Gordon had himself twice played in such a game and knew what an honour it was for the player, his club and his country. Coventry had even arranged for a private jet to fly him back, but Gary was simply not able to take part because of his injury. I was instructed by FIFA to find a striker replacement for Gary, and I thought of Ally McCoist or Gordon Durie, but both of them were also carrying injuries and Walter Smith suggested that it would be unwise for either of them to play. I told FIFA that I would try for Darren Jackson.

All this was happening on the Tuesday before the World Cup draw which was scheduled for Thursday, 4 December at the Stade Velodrome – which was also where the game would be played. FIFA jumped the gun and sent a fax to Celtic with instructions to the player advising him on travel and meeting arrangements. Celtic, naturally, were a little surprised, and Wim Jansen put the brakes on. I did not blame him for that – I only wish that FIFA had waited until I had spoken to them again before taking it upon themselves to contact Celtic. It would have saved a minor misunderstanding.

When I met Gordon Durie at Hampden during the launch of the Scottish Gas sponsorship of the Scottish international team, he indicated to me that his injury had responded to treatment and that he felt fit. I contacted Walter Smith again that Tuesday evening and asked if Gordon might be available after all. The Rangers manager confirmed that Durie had improved and that he would be prepared to let him take part rather than have no Scottish representation in the side. It helped that Rangers did not have a fixture until the Sunday. I contacted Gordon, who was thrilled at the opportunity. He postponed a charity appearance and the day was saved – but it had been a near thing.

I know some people might say that it was not worth the trouble but, if you were an established international player like Gordon who had the chance to be honoured by Europe, you would think it was well worth it. Also, I'm sure that nobody would want Scotland not to be represented in an historic match that would have been played with or without a Scotsman in the side. I was tempted to put on a pair of boots myself ... well, no, not really!

On the following morning I was up early at my home in Ayr to drive to the airport to meet up with my colleagues for the flight to France. The party included Jim Farry, the Scottish Football Association Chief Executive, David Findlay, our international head of the department, Willie McDougall, our chief security officer, Jack McGinn, President of the SFA, Doug Smith, chairman of the International Committee, and Maurice Brannan, manager of The Travel Department, which is affiliated to the SFA. We met at Glasgow Airport at 8.40 in time for a 9.30 flight to Gatwick, where we were due to pick up a flight to Marseille.

I had a look around the duty-free shops and then realised that the England party was also there to catch the same flight, so I went and sat in the lounge with Glenn Hoddle. We had a few laughs about the prospect of us being drawn in the same group – a prospect on which the press had already used up quite a few columns. David Davies, who looked after PR for the English FA, was also there, and we enjoyed a bit of good-natured banter before boarding our plane.

The plane was full of journalists, and it struck me that the World Cup finals had almost already started even before we arrived in Marseille. The flight didn't take too long and I talked with one or two members of the press, including Paddy Barclay, a well-known Scottish journalist. After disembarking we shared a bus with the English contingent as we were taken to our hotel, the Mercury. Even I began to feel the pangs of anticipation as the draw loomed ever nearer.

There were several other delegations at the hotel, and there was also quite a press pack. Among those I spoke to was Archie MacPherson, who was commentating on the Europe versus the Rest of the World game, and I was able to mark his card about the Gordon Durie situation. I have mentioned Archie before – we go back a long way. As well as updating him on the football news, I was able to tell him how his sister was doing, because I had been in Bahrain just a week earlier for the Awali Caledonian Society's St Andrew's Night celebrations. I had been a guest of Archie's brother-in-law Bob Ferguson and his wife Mary – Archie's sister. They had treated me very well indeed in Bahrain, and I wanted Archie to know how much I had appreciated it.

After checking in at the hotel and changing, our next stop was the Palais du Pharo for a reception and a meal. There were many famous faces there, of course, including all the powers that be at FIFA. In charge of the proceedings was Claude Simonet, the president of the French Football Federation. With him on the stage were Michel Platini and Fernand Sastre, the joint presidents of the French World Cup organising committee. The mayor of Marseille, Jean-Claude Gaudin, was our host. The speeches, which included a few words from Joao Havelange, president of FIFA, were not too long-winded, and then we were shown to our tables for the meal.

I hope you can picture how it was. There was a sea of people, and every now and then you would pick out a familiar or famous face. Everyone was being very friendly and diplomatic – but some of that diplomacy went out of the fenêtre when we were shown to a table that we were obviously intended to share with the England delegation. Upon it was written 'Great Britain'. For some time there has been a move by some of our European friends to have the home nations lumped together and, just for a moment, we wondered if someone was trying to tell us something. We also discovered that there were not enough chairs to go round. The mystery was solved when someone realised that there was another table with Ecosse on it. So we went to our Scotland table and left the English with their Great Britain table.

As usually happens at these events, I kept bumping into people I knew – fellow coaches and their assistants. The fraternity among national coaches is very good – probably because we understand each other's problems. Our table was visited by Warren Mersereau, who was in charge of Umbro US and was then one of the top executives of Adidas in Amsterdam. Warren is a wonderful guy whose support of Scotland goes back a long way. He takes his kids to Scotland games as often as possible and brought them to the final qualifying game against Latvia, at which he was jumping up and down as much, if not more, than they were. So you see, Scotland has fans in high places. Werner Kern, also of Adidas, and now Youth Coach at Bayern Munich, was with Warren, and it was good to see them both among the many other high-profile personalities.

Warren told me that his ten-year-old son, Davis, was thrilled not just by the game and the result, but also because he came away with the autographs of both Ally McCoist and Rod Stewart. Berti Vogts, the German coach, and I had sat together on the bus taking us to this function, and he had been singing the praises of Paul Lambert, who had been playing with European champions Borussia Dortmund. Berti told me that if Paul had been German he would have had no hesitation in naming him in his squad for the World Cup. High praise indeed.

After the meal Berti and I talked again, and he told me some of his preparatory plans. His squad was to stay in Nice throughout the tournament and would travel from there. Before the tournament, during the mid-season break in Germany, he planned to take his players to Saudi Arabia for a game or two. He also told me that his goalkeeper, Kopke, would be the German player in the European squad for the celebration match. I hope this gives some insight into the fact that managers and coaches are not always at each other's throats at these competitions.

We all have a job to do and there is always some kidology before a game, but in general there is a strong feeling of camaraderie.

The Dutch coach, Guus Hiddink, congratulated us on qualifying and praised us on our performance in the friendly against France, as did Bo Johansson, the coach of Denmark, with whom I travelled back to the hotel. We discussed the form and recent performances of some of his players who were involved in the Scottish Premier League, and I was able to confirm some of his thoughts about them. He told me that Denmark too would be based in the south of France, at a complex near Marseille.

Before the day ended I was interviewed by the BBC and then had a further discussion with my Scottish Football Association colleagues. It had been a long day and I was quite happy to get to bed!

When I awoke next morning my mind focused immediately on the day ahead. By the time I got to bed again we would know exactly what kind of a passage we were going to experience in our bid to be the first Scotland squad to get past the early round of the World Cup.

The rest of the Scotland delegation was also up and about early, and by nine o'clock we were breakfasted and on our way to look at a possible hotel complex near Avignon, which we were hoping would provide us with the ideal base for our World Cup challenge. We were met by the mayor of St Remy, which is near Avignon, and he could not have been more welcoming, especially when we told him that it was almost certain that this would be our choice as a base.

I had already been to St Remy, and I was happy with the facilities that would be available to us. My colleagues were equally impressed, and we were able to confirm that we would definitely be taking Scotland to St Remy. I was glad to get that settled in my mind, and I think the mayor and his colleagues were even more delighted. They were genuinely nice people and I knew that they would all do their best to take care of us while respecting our need for privacy.

We returned to our hotel in Marseille and prepared to go to the Stade Velodrome for the match in which Gordon Durie was playing. If anyone is thinking that we were away on some kind of holiday, let me assure you that we were extremely busy. In addition to that, it was very cold indeed, and we were all forced to wear heavy coats. If I had been choosing a holiday destination, it would have been somewhere a little warmer than Marseille in December.

At the stadium I sat near Berti Vogts and Bo Johansson, and also the French coach, Aimé Jacquet, with whom I had a few words. At one end of the ground the stage was set for the draw to take place a little later. The rest of the stadium was filled to capacity.

The game itself was quite entertaining. Ronaldo was in good form and seemed to be at the centre of all the Rest of the World's attacking play. Europe opened the scoring after just two minutes when Romania's Marius Lacatus planted the ball in the net. However, the Rest of the World side took over from that moment. Antony de Avila of Colombia scored the equaliser in the seventeenth minute, latching on to a through ball from Ronaldo, who himself put his side ahead six minutes later, and then set up two goals for the Argentinian, Gabriel Batistuta, before hitting another goal himself just before half-time.

With the Rest of the World leading 5–1 at the interval there was not much time to talk about anything else as we sampled the Marseille hospitality. The security had been stringent earlier in the day, but I must say that, when we all left our seats for the hospitality suite, everyone had to pass through the crowds, and it struck me that this showed a certain lapse in the arrangements. I wasn't bothered too much for myself because nobody would know who I was anyway, but men like Joao Havelange are high-profile people who are not universally popular and therefore could be the target for an assault. This was very possible as he too had to jostle with the half-time crowd, pushing towards the hospitality suite.

Gordon Durie made his appearance when the second half began. He had replaced Patrick Kluivert of Holland. I was surprised to see Gordon playing in a midfield role but he acquitted himself well. Europe pulled a goal back through the Frenchman Zinedane Zidane, and that pleased the home fans. There were no more goals and the game ended with everyone still speaking to each other. England's representative, Paul Ince, had played well so Glenn Hoddle was as happy as I was, although I was still puzzled that FIFA had chosen to play Gordon Durie in midfield after asking me to supply a striker.

Not long after the game had ended it was time for the draw – and all the pomp and circumstance normally associated with such occasions. The draw was controlled by FIFA's general secretary, Sepp Blatter, with the eyes of all the world upon that windy stage in Marseille. There were several personalities introduced to take part in the draw, with the players who had just participated in the game also being reintroduced as they took their places on the stage. The various national coaches were introduced. As one who has never liked being in the spotlight, I hated that moment – but it is part of the job and you have to make the best of it.

Finally, the draw got under way and the moment of truth had arrived. Brazil were in Group A and everyone wanted to avoid them – me included, as I have already stated. Naturally, we were also drawn in Group A, along with Norway and Morocco. I felt that it was a great honour that we should be involved in the opening game of the 1998 World Cup – even though it did mean that we were to be pitched against Brazil.

I was asked for my comments by the television contingent immediately after the draw and I had to repeat myself when I said that we had wanted to avoid Brazil but, having had no choice in the matter, we would do our best to upset them. We've played against them three times in past World Cup tournaments and have never succeeded in beating them – but that would count for nothing when we were to meet them again in France. If we had beaten them on each occasion in the past, it would still count for nothing. Our quest would be to restrict the damage, get the points if we could, and then concentrate on taking at least second place by virtue of successes against Norway and Morocco.

When you are involved in a draw like that, you do not have too much time to consider the other groups – but I felt that England did not have a bad draw. A successful first round against Romania, Colombia and Tunisia was very much on the cards for them, and I was sure that Glenn Hoddle would have much preferred to be in his Group G than in our Group A. At least we were not drawn in the same group.

There were more press interviews to follow for all concerned, and I was reminded that we had drawn 0–0 against Brazil in the 1974 World Cup. I am never quite sure how to respond to points like that because – and I don't want to seem disrespectful to the people who were involved in that game – it has no relevance whatsoever to a match nearly a quarter of a century later. It is rare for two teams to record the same result twice in a season, let alone in international matches which have generations of players between the fixtures.

Back at the hotel we discussed the matter and work started on arranging warm-up friendly matches. Everyone does this at gatherings of this type. National coaches very often get their heads together to suggest the fixtures and then hand over to the admin men to make the necessary arrangements. I was no different, and had already met with Steve Samson and set the wheels in motion for us to visit the USA, who were also keen for some friendly matches before the World Cup.

I finally slumped into bed at goodness knows what hour and reflected on a very full, interesting and exciting day. I didn't have much of a problem getting to sleep, although I did keep seeing those famous Brazilian shirts flashing in front of my eyes. The next day I was on my travels again – but not back to Scotland as yet. Knowing that we would be playing in Bordeaux against Norway, I went there to check out the hotel facilities. We would be based as arranged in St Remy, but we still had to have other hotels near to the grounds for the actual matches. Our base would be for match preparations. I realised that we would probably be flying to the games from our base, and I like to check out the facilities and travel arrangements personally. Maurice Brannan came with me to Bordeaux because he has the professional travel expertise and he also wanted to check out the arrangements.

On the same flight was Alfred Ludwig, the general secretary of the Austrian Football Federation. He was also going to sort out his team's arrangements for the World Cup. Austria were to be near Bordeaux even though they would not be playing a game there. That's the way it goes in tournaments like this. You cannot leave your arrangements too late, but there is no way of knowing how far you will have to travel for your matches. I'm delighted that Austria qualified. We had taken four points out of six from them in our qualifying group but their attitude did not change. They never fail to demonstrate the spirit of friendship that international sport should foster.

Michel Laffont was our contact at Bordeaux as he was the co-ordinator of the Bordeaux site. He had the enviable job of being appointed by the French Football Federation to look after the visiting teams. We made our first choice of hotel and hoped that confirmation would follow within a few days. Just in case, we took the trouble to check out alternatives – you never know when things may go wrong.

Having achieved all that, we travelled on to Paris for another hotel inspection. Since we were to play our first game at St Denis – and it was to be such a high-profile game – I wanted to ensure that everything would be first class, and I did not want any delays in the arrangements. We found suitable alternatives, and now things were beginning to take shape.

We now had the potential of hotels and facilities in Bordeaux, Paris, Lyons or St Etienne, and I was happy to travel home to Scotland, an older and wiser man but with still more questions ringing in my ears about our game against Brazil. It was the Sunday when I arrived back, and I took off to see Rangers play Hibernian and win 1–0 – but it is a day I shall never forget for a very different reason.

I was shocked to hear on the radio about the sudden death of Billy Bremner. I received numerous press telephone calls requesting tributes to Billy and I was pleased to talk about him – although I wish the circumstances had been different. I had previously had the privilege of writing the foreword for Billy's book on Scottish football heroes. That it was a privilege I appreciated even more when I heard the gravely sad news about his death. What a great player and what a great man. He was a one-off, never seen before or since.

It was a very sad day, and I shall always remember it as the day when Scotland lost a national hero.

That evening I was in Dundee for a charity dinner to help raise funds for St Joseph's Junior Football Club. My good friend Jim Leishman was MC, and Tommy Docherty and Willie Allan were speakers. Of course, Tommy was recalling his days in charge of Scotland and remembered the time he had travelled down to see Billy Bremner to ask him to be captain. He also spoke about the time in 1972 when Scotland were invited to take the place of England in a tournament in Brazil. The countries involved were all previous World Cup winners and, when England could not go, we were the next choice. Scotland made it to the semifinals – which was no mean feat. Tommy turned to me and said: 'You've no need to worry about Brazil, Craig!' It was typical of him to be both topical and supportive, as he always has been.

I was sitting near John McCormack, the then manager of Dundee, now of Queen's Park – and Dundee's superb youth coach, Kenny Cameron, and we had quite a blether with Tommy Doc. It was a very enjoyable evening but, as you can imagine, by now I was pretty tired as I had been going non-stop since the Tuesday, with only a few hours' sleep in each of the hotel rooms along the way.

The next day I was on my travels yet again. This time it was to London to take part in a sports chat show for BBC Television. The show was presented by John Inverdale, and Alan Hansen was also on the show – so the Scots were back in town. The following morning I flew to Aberdeen to help put together a video of the Scotland qualifying matches. Brian Hendry was overseeing the project, which was to supply the visual material I required for a coaching stint in America a few weeks later.

That same evening I took in the Aberdeen–Celtic game. Next morning I was back in my office in the Scottish Football Association headquarters for more meetings and the inevitable paperwork.

In little more than a week I had given countless interviews, toured a vast area of France, taken in three football matches, visited any number of hotels, and performed a multitude of other functions. That's what life was like when you were the national coach for Scotland. I was not complaining. For me, it was the best job in the world, and I enjoyed every minute of it. It was not every job that gave you the chance to take on the mighty Brazil in the opening game of the World Cup.

Before the draw I said that I did not want us to be in their group. But I could hardly wait.

20

Squad Selection

TO TRAVEL TO the World Cup in France '98, at least two charter aircraft would have been required – if I had selected every player recommended to me by fans and the media, that is!

No one could possibly imagine the amount of advice I received from the time of the draw until the final date for squad selection. Most journalists have their favourite players and, naturally, wish them to be included. Some players themselves ghost articles for newspapers and thereby have a link with that particular publication. So it is easy to be influenced if you are not determined in your mind to ensure that the players whom you decide to pick are the ones who are eventually selected. In this regard, I always consulted with my coaching colleagues, Alex Miller and Alan Hodgkinson, but tried to disregard others who have power but not the ultimate responsibility.

Prior to the draw in Marseille, we had played a game against France in St Etienne. Not having to qualify for the World Cup, the French were seeking opponents for friendly matches and we felt honoured to be invited to compete against them, although at that time they had not built up the huge reputation which they deservedly have today. As it turned out, St Etienne was a useful venue for us because we were to find later that our final ill-fated Group game against Morocco was to be in the same stadium.

As usual, we had a number of withdrawals but we managed to put out a fairly solid side against the might of France. Coach Aimé Jacquet, whom I hadn't known previously, was extremely welcoming and courteous to me. We had a lengthy chat as the players warmed up and I suspected that he was feeling the burden of having to ensure that the home nation put up a creditable performance in the Championship. Little did he or I know that France some months later would be worthy world champions.

The lads in the squad were a bit tired of hearing me say, 'If you're fighting the Indians, what do you do?' By then, they all knew the obvious answer: 'You kill the chief!' So, unusually on this occasion, I thought I'd give some responsibility to the players and ask them who the chief was in the forthcoming match. Deschamps, Desailly, Djorkaeff, Vieira, Thuram, Lizarazu, Blanc … all sorts of answers were forthcoming, but the one I looked for wasn't mentioned. Trying not to be too smug, I said, 'You haven't a clue! I'll tell you who the chief is – he is wearing number 10 and his name is Zidane!' Then I looked around the group for a 'hired assassin' and said to Billy McKinlay, nicknamed Badger, then of Blackburn Rovers, 'Badger, your job is Zidane. Make sure he doesn't get one kick at the ball.' Then I'm told, I reverted to my other favourite phrase: the players had to give him a 'heavy slap' – nothing dirty, but close, strong, attention.

Billy was unfazed by this responsibility but did say to me, 'You're asking me to go in hard. What if I mistime things a bit and get ordered off, a red card?'

My reply was quite straight forward, 'Don't worry about that Badger, they'll miss him more than we'll miss you!'

OK, the story is a bit apocryphal, but the lads got the message.

The game started very brightly for us and for the first half-hour things were very even with Zinedine Zidane predictably subdued. Then the inevitable happened. Laigle, who cannot normally get into the starting line-up, broke down the left and fired a vicious shot from a narrow angle high into the roof of our net past Neil Sullivan. One down after 34 minutes, certain thoughts go through your head – do we try to hold until half-time, or do we look to get a quick equaliser?

Naturally, the latter suggestion is preferable so I looked along the Scottish bench and saw Matt Elliott. Well, I didn't know he was a striker at the time! Then, next to him, was Ally McCoist, so I advised Ally to warm-up which he did with his usual enthusiasm. While Ally was warming up on the grass behind the stand-side linesman (I prefer to call these guys linesmen rather than assistant referees), Zidane stopped the ball from going out of play by tramping on it on the line. Just at that point, in came his marker with a really fierce tackle which resulted in the French playmaker hitting the ground with a thud. Billy McKinlay had done his job, but just a little over enthusiastically! The next rule, of course, was to apologise to the player first and then to the referee. Billy did just that using his only French word, 'Pardon! Pardon!' Zidane was not impressed and waved him away, but the referee, from Spain, beckoned Billy in the opposite direction. His English was good and we heard him say, 'You were a bit late there, Number 8.' Billy politely said, 'I got there as early as I could, ref!'

We waited with keen anticipation to see whether a red or yellow card was to be shown and, much to our relief, the referee showed only a yellow to Billy. That, naturally, was the signal for me to change the marker and I then delegated Craig Burley to give the close attention which Zinedine Zidane's talents merited.

As half-time was approaching, an amazing thing happened – we equalised! Indeed, it was a fine goal executed as a result of a pass in the inside-right position. I repeatedly emphasise to our players that the best ball in the game is usually between a left-footed left-back and a right-footed left-centreback. The idea is to put both these defenders in a position of discomfort having each to defend a carefully weighted through ball with his weaker leg. We have scored many goals from moves in this position, such as Gary McAllister's first goal for Scotland against Switzerland; John McGinlay in an away friendly in Austria; Scott Booth at home against Russia; Craig Burley's goal against Norway in the World Cup; and, more recently, Billy Dodds' opening goal against Belgium in the 2–2 draw at Hampden.

On this occasion in France, Craig Burley's immaculate pass found Kevin Gallacher in our favourite inside-right position. His cut-back between Marcel Desailly and Laurent Blanc was met at the penalty spot by the on-rushing Gordon Durie whose blistering shot hit the net behind Barthez.

Our fans behind the goal celebrated in great style with two of them, in fact, being caught on television giving a rear-view of what a Scotsman has under his kilt. Incidentally, this caused our then Chief Executive, Jim Farry, some consternation as his wife, Elaine, had told him of the television pictures before we left France by calling him on his mobile.

Anyway, I was delighted and punched the air which was, I'm told, my usual method of celebrating a Scotland goal.

At this point, I remembered there was very little time left until the interval, and we still had a certain Ally McCoist warming up. There was no need for him now as we'd got our equaliser earlier than I had anticipated. So I waved him back from his labours behind the aforementioned linesman.

McCoist, and only McCoist, could possibly have behaved as he did. On returning to the bench, rather than immediately sitting down, he came to stand right in front of where I was sitting and bent down until we were face to face. With any other player, I might have thought there was a complaint but I was totally bemused by Ally's actions. As I moved my head from side to side to watch the play, he did likewise, thus blanking my view of the action. Eventually, he noted my irritation and he backed off with a typical McCoist riposte: 'I see it and I don't believe it.' Whilst still trying to concentrate on the game, I replied, 'What's that?'

His reply was wonderful. 'Durie, two goals in six years, eh?' And as he walked to his seat on the bench shaking his head, he said, 'Prolific, bloody prolific!' That's another perfect example of the McCoist humour.

This was the same McCoist who, on 14 June 2001, playing in a celebrity-amateur tournament to open the new Kintyre Golf Course at Turnberry, hooked his ball off the tee narrowly missing me on a parallel fairway. I was in the company of three excellent colleagues from an Aberdeen oil company, Brown and Roots, captained by Duncan Skinner, when the bold Ally came running across from behind a bush and jumped on top of me to tell me that the hooked shot was intentional – a deliberate attempt to knock me out for not taking him to the World Cup Finals in France!

Many people did think that I was wrong to omit Ally, but the decision was made genuinely and sincerely and was largely because I felt that the calf injury which had been troubling him all season had reduced his mobility and that a younger player, Scott Booth, would be more productive. Ally, himself, has been reported since saying that it was a major disappointment. I have no reason to doubt this, but I do admire him for his honesty, and for the manner in which he dealt with the disappointment.

There was a totally erroneous story in a daily newspaper the headline of which was something along the lines of YOU'RE FINISHED ALLY, SAYS BROWN. At no time did I ever make such a statement and, in fact, the writer did apologise on my voicemail in my room in New Jersey, USA, when it appeared. Ally, in his own Sunday paper column, was asked to comment and, in a typically diplomatic manner, he said that he would be surprised if I'd made such a remark. This is the Ally McCoist, a guy who bears no grudges and who is a fervent Scotland fan.

In fact, in his last game for Kilmarnock against Celtic in May 2001, while I was summarising for Radio 5, Ally found out that I had said that he had missed a palpable chance in the first half. He phoned me to advise me that it wasn't a real chance because by the time he got there it was only a half-chance! Irrepressible!

To return to the game in St Etienne, I think of it as a creditable performance although we eventually lost when Craig Burley conceded a penalty and Youri Djorkaeff scored. I genuinely felt that the 2–1 scoreline flattered France, so we were beginning to look towards the World Cup with more optimism.

We had two more friendlies to play before we picked the final 22 for the big event in France. A home defeat, 0–1 to Denmark, was disappointing, especially as the Danish goal was scored by Brian Laudrup who took advantage of an uncharacteristic piece of slackness on the part of Christian Dailly to drive home an excellent winner for his country. I should point out at this juncture that Brian Laudrup, and more recently Henrik Larsson, have been wonderful examples of foreign players competing in the Premier League in Scotland. Whilst I think that there are too many foreign players of moderate ability, there is no way anyone could dispute the contribution which Messrs. Laudrup and Larsson have made to the quality of the domestic game in Scotland.

Our next friendly was at Easter Road, the home of Hibernian FC, against Finland. With Rangers, Celtic and Hearts all competing for the Championship in Scotland, I promised managers Walter Smith, Wim Jansen and Jim Jefferies that I would use players from their clubs sparingly. I often had to negotiate with managers, but I only did so regarding fit players and not, obviously, ones whom we withdraw through injury. I should emphasise that it is, in spite of some newspaper reports, the National Team Doctor who eliminates players, although I did read sometimes that a club has withdrawn so and so from action. The rule is clear-cut that if a player is summoned to appear, he must do so, and if he fails to respond to the summons the FIFA five-day rule can be applied. So on this occasion we were without a number of recognised players but, in fairness to them, I always liked to add to the cap tally, which meant so much to so many of the lads. It was for this reason that I put men like Tommy Boyd and Paul Lambert on the bench, to enable me to include them as substitutes at a time when they would be unlikely to risk fatigue or injury. I recall that I deliberately omitted David Weir from proceedings, and the only 'Old Firm' guy I started with was Darren Jackson, who was not featuring too often in the Celtic line-up at that time.

Our experimental three-man defensive unit was caught out early on when Jonatan Johansson, then of Rangers, and currently at Charlton Athletic, outstripped Matt Elliott and scored a fine goal for the visitors. Our equaliser from Darren Jackson was well deserved, but I received predictable criticism from the Scottish press who, once the match starts, often fail to take into consideration that the team is experimental for a number of reasons. On this occasion, it was the deliberate omission of players as well as some call-offs from injury.

Richard Moller Nielsen, a good friend, was coach of the Finland side and we both agreed beforehand with the referee that we could each use all seven substitutes. This was a sensible arrangement because, towards the end of April, things were beginning to become very tight in terms of the Championship in Scotland. I'm afraid that our Chief Executive at the time, Jim Farry, did not take too kindly to the fact that we put on two more substitutes than he had envisaged in the original match arrangements which were consistent with the laws of the game at that time. I was questioned on this, and particularly upon the fact that, to give Tom Boyd a deserved cap, I put him on with three minutes remaining. There was some justification for complaining about the number of substitutes used because it was distracting for everyone to have a revolving door at the halfway line as players were going off and coming on. However, from a technical point of view, it made good sense and I'm glad that, eventually, it was conceded that the Finland coach, Richard, and I had acted sensibly. That meant that in March 2000, when the European Champions, France, came to play us in a friendly match at Hampden, there was no problem when Roger Lemerre agreed with me and the referee, Mr Pedersen of Norway, that all 20 French players could be stripped for action and that seven could be used. If it was good enough for the World Champions, surely it was a sensible suggestion for us as well.

The provisional 22-man squad had to be selected before we left for our preparatory visit to America to play Columbia in New York and the USA in Washington. I did say that I was receiving plenty of advice around this time because, traditionally, it is a slack period for journalists. I made a flying visit to Miami to see Brazil take on Jamaica in a friendly match only to find that there were no fewer than nine Scottish sports writers 'suffering' in the heat of Florida. We saw Junior Baiano commit a very bad foul which was necessary because of his sluggishness on the turn. I identified the central defence as the weakness in an otherwise solid and impressive Brazilian side and I noticed the new position occupied by Dunga, in front of the two central defenders, and the superb form of Ronaldo. I had only a brief word with Mario Zagallo, the Brazilian Coach, whom I had met briefly at the World Cup draw. It's strange, but I often have a great deal of sympathy for the Brazilian coach. This may seem a bit of a paradox as he usually works with the best players in the world, but the level of expectation is enormous. I even heard Carlos Alberta Parreira being booed when his name was announced at the start of the World Cup Final against Italy in 1994. Mr Zagallo certainly did not look a happy man as the huge media core following Brazil were far from pleased with the performances in his preparatory matches.

Not only did the press make representations prior to the squad announcement, players whom I met would also often put in their tuppence worth, sometimes for a pal, but surprisingly quite often for themselves. I experienced one example of this when speaking at a function at Parklands Leisure Centre in Newton Mearns. Stuart McCall, who was in the audience, spoke to me afterwards and told me how anxious he was to be in the squad and how he would be particularly effective against Norway. Stuart felt that it would be his type of game. While I didn't disagree, I believed that we needed guys for all three fixtures and that maybe Stuart's best days at international level were behind him. I joked and said that he would be considered but that I concerned myself with the fact that were he not in the first-choice starting team, that he and the likes of Ally McCoist would perhaps be disposed to think they were on a holiday jaunt. It was said in light-hearted fashion and accepted in that way. Imagine, though, my surprise, when after the squad was announced Stuart indicated that he was very disappointed in me because I had said that if he were not selected he would be partying all the time. I knew from previous experience that Stuart could enjoy himself, but one thing I also knew was that he would train very hard and that, when the chips were down, he was the kind of man to have in your side. My value judgement, made with complete candour, was that we would be better with the midfield players I had included in the squad, guys like Craig Burley, John Collins, Billy McKinlay, Darren Jackson, Paul Lambert and Scot Gemmill.

I have already alluded to the omission of Ally McCoist. This was confirmed when my colleague, Alex Miller, and I went to Amsterdam to see Utrecht play Ajax in the famous Amsterdam Stadium. I had phoned the coach of Utrecht several times to ask about the form of Scott Booth. On every occasion, I was assured that Scott was playing brilliantly and was completely fit. Alex and I saw this for ourselves during our visit to the game against Ajax when he helped his side to a convincing away victory. So it was Booth in, McCoist out; Billy McKinlay in, Stuart McCall out. I think these were the main controversial issues surrounding the selection which, otherwise, was fairly predictable.

We were soon ready to embark on our transatlantic flight for our preparatory matches in North America. This trip, as is often the case, was a perfect opportunity for the press to obtain some controversial copy. Imagine my astonishment one morning when, on arriving for breakfast, I was intercepted by Andy Goram who was holding a large brown paper envelope. Andy asked me to read the contents of the envelope which he said would explain everything. I did not, at the time, anticipate the bombshell which was to be contained in the envelope and, in leisurely and relaxed fashion, took time to have my usual, anything-but-healthy, cooked breakfast! On completing my meal, I opened the envelope and read a letter from Andy which indicated that for personal reasons he had to return home to Scotland urgently. I should have known there was something afoot because I saw his good friend, Jim Fox from Largs, and one or two other pals of Andy in the Hotel bar the previous evening. At the time, when I shook hands with Jim, I thought he was over to watch our matches to give his mate some support. But then thoughts came flooding into my mind and I realised that Andy really did have personal problems back home and that his departure was inevitable.

I took the lift to the room he was sharing with Gordon Durie to find his bags already packed and I spoke to him in an attempt to dissuade him. I knew, deep down, that I was wasting my time because of the manner in which the luggage had been packed and placed at the door for his slick getaway. Frankly, I was a bit disappointed later when Andy said that I had made no attempt to dissuade him from leaving. It was very apparent that his mind was thoroughly made up and this, I am sure, was confirmed by his later newspaper revelations. Indeed, some time later I met with Andy and his delightful partner Miriam (who now is his wife), and his agent, Kenny

Moyes, to discuss his willingness to return to international action. The four of us had a most pleasant lunch in Hamilton when Andy, Kenny and Miriam all wished to put the record straight. Much of the conversation, naturally, was confidential, but I can confirm that it was an extremely positive meeting and one I really appreciated.

In passing, I should say, that I am delighted to see that Andy had his new set of Frank McAvennie-type teeth in time for his wedding in Ayr in July 2001. It was apparently a splendid affair in the Brig O' Doon Hotel, one of several salubrious establishments owned by Bill Costley, former Chairman and still Director of Kilmarnock.

For a time, the Andy Goram episode overshadowed our preparations in New Jersey. We were in a superb hotel with first-class training facilities at Pingry School, the venue used by the Italian National Team during the 1994 World Cup. Every possible facility was put at our disposal, including access to the local golf club where we used the excellent clubs kindly supplied by the Scottish firm of John Letters.

I was a little disadvantaged on this occasion because our Video Technician, Brian Hendry, was not on the trip with us. This meant that I was responsible for my own editing of material which necessitated trips down to the Giants Stadium to use the magnificent equipment belonging to the Metrostars. Charlie Stillitano, General Manager of the club, couldn't have been kinder, but I must admit that I envied the superb filming and editing suite which the MLS coach had.

There were occasions, in the afternoons, when the players and staff managed to get off for a game of golf while I, usually with my trusty colleague, Alex Miller, was involved in producing video material to show to the players at team meetings. We did manage, also, to arrange a closed-door practice match against the Metrostars in which we used the players who were not likely to be selected from the start of the friendly matches against Columbia and the USA. Guys like Neil Sullivan, Matt Elliott, Jackie MacNamara, Scot Gemmill,

Simon Donnelly and Scott Booth were among those who were pleased to get this semi-competitive workout. As always, when we went to a major tournament, we take aspiring young professionals with us to help make up sides and assist generally in the organisation of laying out training, laundry and so on. On this occasion, we had young Mark Burchill and Kieran McAnespie, then with St Johnstone, and currently at Fulham. In fact, young Kieran scored a fine goal in his debut for Scotland in this 'bounce game'.

During this trip, we did have some discussions involving the player pool representatives and the President of the SFA, Mr McGinn, regarding the contractual arrangement with our main sponsor, Scottish Gas. But, fortunately, there was no eventual hassle as common sense prevailed, as it usually does among the Scottish international players.

The game against Columbia, played at the Giants Stadium, New Jersey, was a thrilling affair for a friendly match. Vivid in our memory was the previous match against Columbia some two years earlier when a horrendous tackle on Craig Burley could have resulted in a broken leg. We were a bit wary about a repetition, but were assured by the Columbian officials and team coach that, although they were desperately anxious to please the large South American support in New Jersey, the game would be played in a sporting manner. This, in fact, was the case and it resulted in an exciting 2–2 draw. The highlight was a magnificent goal from John Collins with his right foot from 20 yards, and our major disappointment was the soft penalty conceded by Christian Dailly which allowed the Columbians an easy opening goal which, in my opinion, they didn't fully deserve.

Whilst our fitness regime was progressing well, and relatively few injuries were sustained, there was still a worry that we hadn't won in our last three matches. The media lads were quick to point out that a 0–1 against Denmark, 1–1 at home with Finland and another 2–2 draw with Columbia was hardly looking like the best preparation for the opening match against Brazil in the World Cup. As usual, the pressure was on. This time, we had to beat an accomplished USA side on home territory in what was likely to be a white-hot temperature.

The game in Washington DC was unique in my vast experience of international football. The heat was quite unbearable. I'm told it reached 108 during the match and this was apparent because everything was played at walking pace. Even the substitutes on the bench sat with towels over their heads to protect themselves from the intense heat of the sun and some even went to the dressing room to get cold water on the towel.

We heard an interesting piece of news prior to the match – Claudio Reyna, then of Wolfsburg in Germany and now with Rangers, the American playmaker, had withdrawn through injury. In spite of this, it was very apparent that the Americans had a fine side.

It was an entertaining game, with our team having the usual tremendous expatriate support and although no goals were scored there was no lack of entertainment. In fact, we had the chance of the match when Kevin Gallacher outstripped the entire US defence only to fail with just their keeper to beat.

There was no time to linger in Washington, nor was there the opportunity to give the lads a night out because we were flying home quickly to allow a few days' break before we left for the big event in France.

We had tried, during our spell in the US, to mix work with pleasure. This was our deliberate attempt to foster team spirit and to ensure that there were no real cliques in the squad. In addition to the training, which Alex Miller and I always tried to make interesting and competitive, we had golf outings, visits to various restaurants to change the scenery and one or two free nights for the lads. Unlike our previous visit to New York, there was no possibility of going to see Rod Stewart at Madison Square Gardens. Indeed, on the one occasion when we did allow the lads freedom in New York, several made their way back to our hotel without waiting on the team coach, which was scheduled to depart at 1.00am. I am touching wood when I say that we haven't had problems with our players because they knew the ground rules. I have a phrase which I use when talking to coaches on the various courses we conduct – 'The standards you set are the standards you get'. I am aware, as a manager, you will always be let down but your job is to minimise the risk and postpone the inevitable. I cannot think of any manager, even the most illustrious, who hasn't been let down by a player or players. However, the effectiveness of the backroom staff in this regard cannot be over-estimated. We had Stewart MacMillan, for example, who had an excellent rapport with the players and as well as engaging them in fun activities and enjoying tremendous humour with him, they knew that he would stand absolutely no nonsense whatsoever. At all times, the lads heeded my usual warning – 'Don't think that three lagers make you invisible!'

One example of our common sense approach occurred in May 2000, when, after a long arduous season, we had to play a friendly match in Dublin against the Republic of Ireland. Naturally, the players were anxious for a night out in that 'fair city'. As usual, I decreed that they must go as a group and be under staff supervision at all times. Whilst some of the players remained in the hotel and were fresh for the morning flight home, Stewart MacMillan, or 'Omar' as the lads call him, took a group of a dozen or so into the city where they had a thoroughly enjoyable time and returned to the hotel, as a group, without anything newsworthy taking place!

The use of a charter aircraft after matches in Europe is obviously beneficial in this regard because I recall in my day as a player many years ago we travelled by schedule flights and it meant that we had to stay overnight in European cities prior to our return to Scotland. This provided one or two of the what I would call 'harum scarum' guys the opportunity to break curfew and sneak out. Having learned most of the dodges over the years, I think I was in a good position to recognise any potential misdemeanour! Fortunately, we have been spared that but I am very conscious of the fact that it would have been foolish to be complacent.

During my time with Scotland, I have noted that both the English and Irish teams have had some unfortunate media coverage. After a fine performance in Prague against the Czech Republic, Sammy McIlroy found that some players had been detained for questioning by police while the main party flew home.

England, too, had their troubles in Hong Kong prior to Euro '96 and on the Cathay Pacific flight home. The FA's David Davies, a master of diplomacy, repeated the phrase 'collective responsibility' to help lessen the embarrassment which could have resulted. Still the press made quite a thing of it and, as we were returning home from Miami a few days later, I warned the players of the foolishness of any indiscretion and that absolutely no alcohol was to be consumed on the flight to London. On arrival at Heathrow, I have never seen a larger media corps awaiting the appearance of our team. It seemed that every TV camera in England had been positioned to film our arrival.

Walking through Customs with Ally McCoist, he was heard to say on seeing the voracious journalist pack, 'I can see the headlines tomorrow – SCOTS IN SOBER SENSATION!'

On our return from the USA, we had to ensure that all players were fit as a confirmed squad was required for the FIFA World Cup squad list. We had contacted Jonathan Gould, the Celtic goalkeeper, to come out to replace Andy Goram and he responded with predictable alacrity and enthusiasm. Gouldie is a good squad member in that he is always bright and full of humour, not unlike his father, I may say. Dad, Bobby, is a good pal for whom I have a great deal of time, having spoken to him at length and having worked on various TV football assignments with him.

There is a good camaraderie amongst international managers, but it was even stronger when we had Bobby in Wales, Bryan Hamilton in Northern Ireland, Glenn Hoddle or

Kevin Keegan with England and Mick McCarthy with the Republic. We met, informally, on several occasions and the banter was always first-class. Now only Mick remains from the original group but I did get on very well with Mark Hughes and Sammy McIlroy, although I did not have any dealings with Sven Goran Eriksson. I do, however, know his colleague, Tord Grip, very well as he was Assistant Manager of Sweden when we were in the same qualifying group for the World Cup for France '98. I hope Tord will forgive me for reminding him that Austria and Scotland qualified from the group!

All was ready for the take-off to fly to Marseille and we left a busy Glasgow Airport to a good send-off from players' relatives, friends and other travellers. There was no flash formal farewell such as Ally MacLeod agreed to prior to Argentina. I like Ally a great deal and think that he was unfairly vilified after the Argentinean World Cup but, one thing is certain, he managed to unite the country in an unbelievable manner in 1978. I'm afraid that my style is not too similar, but I do wish I had a bit more of the Ally MacLeod charisma. Our departure was dignified and cautiously optimistic.

21

The Ultimate — the World Cup '98

THINGS SETTLED DOWN a bit in a the few days preceding our departure from Glasgow and it was noticeable that, to match the large majority of people in the country, the goodwill from the media had improved. There were still one or two, predictably, prophesying doom and warning about a thumping defeat against Brazil. However, I was still, up until the last minute, studying video of our first opponents in an attempt to be totally conversant with everything they could possibly produce. I think everyone in the game would appreciate that, even although you know the opposition thoroughly, if they are better than you it is still very difficult to compete. I knew that every one of us would have to be on his best form and there would require to be one or two Brazilians slightly below par if we were to have a chance of victory.

Anyway, our departure from Glasgow was, as I have said, well, but modestly, effected. The Valrugues Hotel, St. Remy, staff were out to greet us on arrival and their kindness and diligence remained throughout our pleasant stay. At the request

of the players and through our physio, Pip Yeates, we had
organised Techno-gym apparatus to be installed to enable our
players to maintain their individual fitness programmes. We
had a games' room including snooker, billiards, video games
and facilities for the lads who liked to watch movies on a large
screen and in comfortable seats. Unlike teams from some
countries, who are quite happy to share a large hotel with
normal holidaymakers and business people, we generally
prefer to have exclusive use of the hotel. This was a costly
exercise because the restaurant was well known locally for
excellent cuisine and, consequently, the Scottish Football
Association had to compensate the proprietor for loss of
revenue. It was in the best interests of team preparation,
though to have the hotel to ourselves and to have exclusive use
of all the facilities, the impressive swimming pool included.

In conversation with Bo Johansson the Danish manager, he
indicated an opposite philosophy. He said that he preferred his
players to be in a normal environment, one shared by other
hotel users. Most teams exclude wives, families and partners
from the training headquarters and have separate facilities for
the media. We are no exception. Our compromise was to invite
nominated family and friends to the hotel the day after the
match where they, too, were afforded all the hotel facilities.
This worked very well for us except, of course, when we
travelled to Paris to play the opening match against Brazil. On
that occasion the guests were invited into the stadium to meet
with the players after the match before our charter aircraft took
us back to the base camp in St. Remy. Inevitably someone will
gatecrash such a gathering but the gentleman who often does
so, is a most welcome intruder. He is a Travel Club member,
Andrew Gibson, who is always clad in tartan from head to toe
and who is the essence of courtesy and support to all the
players. The fact that he is an Income Tax Officer is
coincidental and is nothing to do with the fact that we turn a
blind eye to his various intrusions!

Above: Chairman Willie Dunn congratulates me on winning the Second Division Championship in May 1978.

Below: With Clyde FC captain, Brian Ahern, at the launch of British Oxygen Company sponsorship in 1980.

A very familiar face. Congratulating Alex Ferguson after Aberdeen beat Clyde 2-0 in the Scottish Cup. My excellent colleague Rab Thorburn is also in the photograph.

Above: The Scotland Youth Team, World Cup Runners Up in 1989.

Below: The boys relax by chucking me in the pool at Italia '90. In the picture are Alex McLeish, Craig Levein, Dave McPherson, Gordon Durie and Mo Johnston.

Above: Ally McCoist wears the Greek strip after scoring the only goal at Hampden in 1995.

Below: Scottish team training (*left to right*) Ian Ferguson, Paul McStay, Craig Brown, Gary McAllister, John Collins and John Robertson.

Above: Goal scorers Colin Calderwood and John Collins with me at the airport upon our return from San Marino in April 1995.

Below: Back-room staff celebrate World Cup qualification and Dr Stewart Hillis becoming a professor, in 1997.

The launch of the SFA National Schools' Pack at Rugby Park, Kilmarnock.

bove: I won Manager of the Month on several occasions. Here I am
ith the trophy in 1995.

elow: Prime Minister Blair meets the boys in Paris, prior to our
pening match in the 1998 World Cup.

A very proud moment for me, at Buckingham Palace with my CBE in October 1999.

Our press conferences were not held in the hotel. They were, in fact, in the local village hall which had been decorated by the town's school children prior to our arrival. St. Remy is famous for artists and it was easily seen because the offspring of some of the most creative artists in France lived locally and produced superb works of art for the village hall. Later on our visit we were invited by the Mayor to the Town Hall where the local youngsters again excelled. This time they did Scottish country dancing and the school choir of youngsters sang Flower of Scotland and other Scottish songs. The welcome in this most delightful part of France could not have been better.

Our training pitch was only a short distance from the hotel, five minutes by bus, and it was, quite naturally, used extensively. At most training sessions the small stand holding maybe 1500 people was full but when we requested privacy the locals respected this and we were allowed to do some workout activities in private. We did have visitors to our training, people like Bobby Gould the then Welsh Manager and Davie Moyes, Manager of Preston North End, who has a voracious thirst for knowledge about football. Davie was a welcome spectator at many of our training sessions. He would have seen a great deal of good-natured banter amongst the players and some really hard work. My experience is that players relish being challenged, and being asked to go through the pain barrier at the appropriate time. Our lads were no exception to this and I must say that their response was always extremely wholehearted.

I believe that preparation dispels pressure because it builds confidence. We were particularly interested in defending corners and free kicks, although the horrendous goal which we lost in the first four minutes against Brazil would tend to refute that. It was most unusual for us to lose a goal from a set piece in this way and I am pleased to say that, not only in the World Cup Finals but in most qualifying matches, we were seldom caught out from set-piece situations. Our wall was usually well organised with the participants identified in advance and we disbelieve in a synchronised jump. The Dutch, in Euro '96, knew this and tried to drive the ball below the wall but I always feel, in spite of a goal that Liverpool lost in the UEFA Cup last season, that a ball driven below the wall should be a save.

We do spend a great deal of time on the offensive side of things and take throw-ins and corners repeatedly in training to ensure that there is a slick operation in the match context. I am pleased to say that with Messrs. Collins and McAllister around things were superbly executed. On this occasion, Gary McAllister being injured, he was invited along to join the group to lend his experience to the cause but, unfortunately, was not on the field to produce the superb delivery for which he is renowned. Therefore, John Collins was our key man in the free-kick situation and we were desperately unlucky in the opening match when our well executed 'Mess Up' free-kick nearly resulted in success. Our corner kick preparation, too, almost had the desired effect. This all came from patience and diligence on the training ground so there were occasions when Alex Miller and I took a select group of players to an unscheduled session on the pitch for free-kick, corner kick and throw-in practice. There were no complaints from the lads because they knew what was at stake.

After several days of preparation in St. Remy we flew, the night before our opening match, to Paris and booked in at our hotel in Chantilly. This was an ideal location some 45 minutes from the Stade De France, the impressive venue for the opening fixture. On our way to Chantilly we made a detour to the match venue for our training session on the pitch. We arrived early to see some preparation for the opening ceremony which promised to be most impressive. Unfortunately, we would not be able to see the action because we would be inside preparing for the match. The training session went well and the lads were pleased with the playing surface and the overall environment. Not long after our return to the hotel we could see a massive security presence. Armed guards on the roof of the hotel, a helicopter above and police strategically placed along the streets. This was in anticipation of the arrival of the Prime Minister, Tony Blair, who had requested permission to meet the team to offer his best wishes for success.

I introduced him one by one to the players and I found his knowledge of individuals, and of the game in general, to be impressive. We presented him with a Scotland jersey for each of his children and I could tell that he was genuinely delighted. The Prime Minister was received by our Vice-President Mr John McBeth in the absence of Mr Jack McGinn, our President, who was at an official function in Paris. This thoughtful gesture by the PM was much appreciated by the players. I've got to say that many Scottish MPs including the late First Minister, Donald Dewar, did send messages of goodwill and Mr Dewar, whose recent death was mourned by people of all parties in Scotland, came to visit us at a training session prior to our departure at the Pollok Junior Football Ground in Glasgow. Another keen football man, Alex Salmond, then leader of the Scottish National Party, was at pains to express his good wishes to the squad. It was apparent to me that football transcends politics and that members of all parties, particularly in Scotland, are happy to align themselves with the National Teams in every sport, particularly the national sport of football.

The team selection for the opening match was, I think, fairly predictable and I did break from tradition and give it, privately, to the Scottish daily paper journalists the day before the match. I felt that Mr Zagallo, the Brazilian coach, knew all that was to be known about Scotland and in giving him the personnel I would not disclose too much about the way in which we proposed to play.

I hadn't mentioned the fact that our Captain, Colin Hendry, had been approached by a kilt manufacturer, Kinloch Anderson, who asked if we would be interested wearing the kilt to the opening fixture against Brazil. For this the donor was very happy to make a contribution to the player pool and to provide all members of the squad with traditional Scottish dress, free of charge. I always wanted each player's appearance to reflect pride and patriotism. The lads were thrilled at the prospect and I do believe that we were by far the most impressive team to arrive for a match in the entire tournament. Oh that our play in the games had matched our dress sense!

Proudly wearing the kilt our players arrived at the Stade De France and promptly made the customary walk out onto the pitch to look at the environment. The response from the Tartan Army was quite unbelievable. So pleased were they to see the players wearing the national dress that they cheered and cheered and I wondered if they would have any voice left for the actual match not due to start for at least another 90 minutes. Our players, also, went over to acknowledge the enthusiastic response from the Brazilian fans who seemed equally intrigued at the dress sense of our squad. Although the kilt would not win any match I felt it would raise out standard of appearance above every team. Dr Martin Luther King once said, 'Your self-image should not come from the job you do but from how well you do your job.' We had a real job in hand and I was determined that we would do it well.

With the opening ceremony in place we were advised well in advance that we would not be able to warm up on the pitch but would require to use the rubber surfaced indoor area. This proved to be an acceptable, although less favoured warm up environment but, as I kept reinforcing to the lads, it was the same for both teams. It was interesting, too, that in the final against France the Brazilian team did not come out to warm up on the pitch. My contention was that they felt they had a very good warm up prior to the opening match against Scotland and that they would repeat the same procedure for the final. After all they did score against us in 4 minutes!

Some of the lads have superstitions prior to matches. I confess that I don't have any such quirks but I did have a feeling of glow inside as the team which I helped to prepare, left the dressing room to go out to represent our country. After the traditional handshakes all round it was apparent that the lads were more nervous than usual. One, in particular, the experienced Colin Calderwood, actually turned the wrong way when he left the dressing room door and walked in the opposite direction from the pitch. This was merely due to the fact that the player was psyching himself in his usual way by slapping his own face and shouting loudly. It was good to see the Brazilians hand-in-hand and the thought crossed my mind that if I tried to suggest that to Scottish players I wonder what the response would be? This ritual started in the time of Carlos Alberta Parreira, the manager who won the World Cup for Brazil in 1994 when, after a defeat against Bolivia, he was trying to ensure that in the return game his side was ready for the battle and together as one. Without instruction, quite spontaneously, they held hands entering the pitch and won the game 6-0. Carlos told me that they have done the same ever since with, of course, a great deal of success.

I would never envy anyone out in the stadium prior to a match when I had the privilege of being with the team in the dressing room but on this occasion I would love to have been in two places at the same time. My indefatigable Secretary, Andrea Anderson, repeatedly tells me, and has reminded me when typing the copy for this chapter, that the atmosphere was absolutely fantastic. The Scotland fans lustily sang the stirring French National Anthem as well as our own. Each spectator held up the piece of card placed under every seat to form huge national flags and the pageantry and noise revealed that the biggest football event in the world was about to commence.

I have mentioned the opening goal several times but,

thereafter, we settled reasonably well and managed to claw our way back into the match. We were the recipients of a rather soft penalty award but the Spanish referee Jose Garcia Aranda, was in no doubt and when John Collins equalised from the spot many people thought a shock result was possible. One thing was certain, the Tartan Army was delighted. Second half was equally favourable for us but we were caught by a diagonal ball into the path of Marcel Cafu whose goal attempt was unluckily parried by Jim Leighton on to Tom Boyd's chest from where it rebounded agonisingly into our net. The 2-1 scoreline I think flattered Brazil but we had given a creditable performance in a game which many people described as the best World Cup opener for many years.

Our post match meeting with our families and friends was abbreviated somewhat because of the call to return to the team coach for transfer to the airport and back to St. Remy.

Disappointed but not disgraced was the overall feeling and a huge crowd turned out to witness our warm down training session the following morning. Press reports were relatively favourable so we looked with optimism to the forthcoming challenge in Bordeaux against the Norwegian team, expertly organised by Egil Olsen. I had watched his 4-5-1 formation in operation several times and felt that we were in with a real chance of gaining maximum points as long as we didn't lose our concentration. Two obdurate teams took the field for this match. Not a player on either side could spell the word 'yield'.

I thought our performance was excellent and although Havard Flo put Norway ahead we were always the better side and should have managed to record a convincing victory. As it was, an excellent long through ball into my favourite inside right position from David Weir enabled Craig Burley to streak through between Stig Inge Bjornebye and Ronny Johnsen to lob an excellent equaliser for us. In spite of considerable pressure thereafter we couldn't get the elusive equaliser so it was all down to the final game against Morocco. Although we were again missing the excellent service usually provided by

Brian Hendry, our multimedia expert, time passed quickly because of the keen anticipation for the final match. Everyone seemed to be very upbeat about our prospects against Morocco but I had seen them in the past playing at home in Casablanca and had watched numerous videos. I knew they would be formidable opponents. A country of 35 million people, more than seven times the size of Scotland, the African champions, and still some correspondents were predicting that it would be easy for Scotland! It was difficult for me to try to temper the euphoria which was beginning to surround the camp. News had filtered back from home via relatives and friends that everyone expected us to have a comfortable victory in this final match. That the game was to be played in St. Etienne was an advantage to us because we had been there for the friendly match against France 9 months earlier.

I think the least said about the game the better. It was my 44th game since my appointment in November 1993 and only once before had we lost 3 goals, in a friendly against The Netherlands in Utrecht in May 1994. Our defensive record had been superb so it was a genuine shock to me to lose three goals, especially in the manner in which they were conceded. All of them could have been averted and, of course, Craig Burley's ordering off for a reckless tackle symptomatic of the frustration felt by all of us, meant that we had a mountain to climb during the second half. The prophetic words of warning from Hugh Dallas, Scotland's top referee, were ringing in my ears. Hugh had visited our squad prior to our departure for France to brief us on the new, and very stringent, guidelines regarding the type of tackle we just had witnessed.

The dressing room was like a morgue after the game because we knew we had let ourselves and, more importantly, our fans down badly. It is difficult for a manager to know what to say on occasions like this, but I tried to be as positive as possible and insisted that the players held their heads high when they left the stadium and for the remainder of our sojurn in France. This they did admirably.

It was a bit disconcerting, though, as our coach left the Hotel Valrugues, to see some members of the media with photographers waiting to go straight into the hotel as we departed. My experience told me their agenda so I jumped off the bus and asked the hotel manager to discourage journalists from coming in to photgraph the pool, the lavish buffet in the restaurant and the very comfortable bedrooms. I predicted a picture story showing the opulence of the hotel in three pictures on one side of the page with a heading something like WE GAVE THEM THIS and on the other side of the page, the three goals scored by Morocco with a heading AND THIS IS THE RESULT. I know I was correct because the hotel manager telephoned me later to say that he had indeed had a request which would have tied in accurately with my prediction.

Since France '98 a great number of fans have written to me, spoken to me and thanked me for the experience in France which they thoroughly enjoyed. The critics have been few and far between unless, that is, they refuse to be seen or heard … and this is not my experience of disgruntled patrons. Following our exit from the competition I was invited by BBC Radio 5 Live to join their commentary team for the remainder of the tournament. This I did with great enthusiasm because it was a way of getting me back to see the remainder of the World Cup and to improve my knowledge of the game. I think in management and leadership circles they call it 'personal development'. For me to do it at the behest of the BBC was, I think, good value for the SFA because I saw many other national managers, either eliminated ones from the tournament or those who didn't qualify, as interested spectators representing their respective countries.

It was a pleasure for me to work with such gifted commentators as Mike Ingham, Alan Green, Ron Jones, and John Murray. I also was reunited with my summarising colleague, Jimmy Armfield OBE, doyen of the radio, and a man for whom I have enormous admiration and respect. Not only has he had his club side, Leeds United, in the final of the European Cup, he has a magnificent playing record for England. He always tells me to remind our Goalkeeping Coach, Alan Hodgkinson, of Alan's game for England against Scotland when Tommy Ring of Clyde scored against him in all of 50 seconds. Needless to say, Hodgie is never too pleased when I recount Jimmy's description of the soft goal which the Clyde left-winger scored. But he is still a superb Goalkeeping Coach!

I travelled the length and breadth of France on BBC business and was privileged to see many superb matches. It was an honour for me to be asked to be one of the summarisers in the semi-final and final matches, but it was back to earth with a bump after the streamlined, favoured treatment as coach with a competing country to queue for a taxi with Ron Jones in Montpellier and to join the Brazil fans on public transport in Marseille. Everyone whom I met on the media side of business was full of praise for Scotland's performance, particularly our opening match against Brazil. But that was small consolation.

I did see David Beckham being ordered off in the game against Argentina and felt that it was a very harsh decision. My position with the SFA precludes me from saying anything which is in any way critical of a manager, player or referee. Although I have strong opinions sometimes it is necessary, and I think quite rightly, for me to retain a discreet and diplomatic silence. My colleagues on Radio 5 Live appreciate this and allow me to make praiseworthy comments while they, without fear of recrimination, can be a great deal more outspoken.

It was carnival time after the final as we drove back to Paris in the cavalcade of cars with horns hooting and flags waving. As I sat with my radio colleagues enjoying a meal at 4.00am, and a nice glass or two of red wine, I thought of the slightly nervous Aimé Jacquet on 12 November the year before when I spoke to him prior to our friendly match in St Etienne. In spite of fierce criticism and many reservations from his own countrymen, he stuck to his guns and emerged triumphant. I was delighted for him, as I was four years earlier for Carlos Alberto Parreira. It's amazing how sometimes the best coaches are not the most popular. However, Aimé became a hero overnight and I am delighted to say he remained so in the eyes of the cognoscenti of French football. His successor, Roger Lemerre, was to be no slouch either. We all found that out a couple of years later.

It was back to the coaching courses at Largs for the remainder of the summer when, yet again, I had to apologise to my colleagues for my intermittent presence. As always, my doughty Football Development Department staff guys, Frank Coulston, Ross Mathie, Jim Sinclair and Jim Fleeting did their usual outstanding job.

The Americans have a phrase "Good job coach", (pronounced "Good Jaw-b!!) when you visit their country to conduct a clinic. Last summer, in May 2001, I did a course in Texas for Butch Lauffer, one or our UEFA Pro-Licence coaches. It was a stimulating experience in Amarillo where the enthusiasm of the group was without question. I am happy to say that I did hear the occasional, "Good job coach." Maybe that's why I like to go to the States, when invited, to conduct whatever type of session they request, but the best "jobs" in coach education circles are done by the guys of the SFA, now including our new Head of Children's Development, Tommy Wilson.

22

Another Qualifying Campaign

THE SUMMER PASSED quickly, as usual, and it was no time at all before I had to select a squad for the first match of the European Championship qualifying campaign. At the dates' meeting in Prague we had managed to obtain our customary opening away fixture, this time in Vilnius against Lithuania. One or two players were doubtful through injury even this early in the season.

I had gone to see a match at Rugby Park in which Kilmarnock were playing Hearts. Ally McCoist, a new Kilmarnock signing, whom I had eliminated from the World Cup selection, scored three great goals in this fixture. It was obvious that I had to bring him back because we were not exactly over-endowed with goal-scoring forwards.

The hoped-for McCoist-inspired performance did not materialise in Vilnius which one of the lads described, rather unkindly, as the 'Backside of the world'. McCoist's reply was cutting as usual, 'And you must just be passing through it then!' Our Ally's never stuck for a response

The performance was moderate but the banter, as usual,

was superb. We did get the opportunity, though, to blood one or two younger players, particularly Barry Ferguson, Callum Davidson and Neil McCann, and the fans, in spite of seeing no goals, enjoyed themselves in yet another attractive European city.

If we were to win our Group, the three home games to follow had to yield at least seven, if not nine, points. Estonia at Tynecastle Stadium in Edinburgh proved to be an inordinately difficult task. Those who fault us for being 2–1 down at home midway through the second half have a case, but when recent Estonia performances are considered it must be realised that they provide tricky opposition. It was as recently as March this year, 2001, when they led Holland with six minutes remaining, only to lose three goals in the dying moments. Billy Dodds came off the bench to our rescue against Estonia who, rather unluckily I thought, had Marko Kristal sent off.

The Scottish media were extremely critical of our players and one newspaper photographed a number of conscientious international players, and really good lads, and wrote across their faces FLOP FLOP FLOP FLOP FLOP. The criticism was extremely cutting at times with no one escaping censure. Some of the cruellest criticism was directed at our goalkeeper, Jim Leighton, whom some people thought was responsible for the Estonian goals. Always one to highlight the positive, I emphasised the couple of saves which Jim had made which kept us in the game, but this did not detract from the vitriol.

Nevertheless, it was a complete shock to me the next day when we arrived at Aberdeen for the match against the Faroe Islands for Jim to meet me and tell me that he was retiring from international football. I tried to dissuade him but he had made up his mind. I knew that he was very close to my colleague, his Hibs manager, Alex Miller. It was pretty obvious then for me to ask Alex to work on Jim and see what he could do to help him to reconsider. However, I think that Jim, his wife Linda and family had decided that enough was enough and he returned the next morning to meet with me in the car park outside the New Marcliffe Hotel where we were staying. I had a chat with him there and shook hands and wished him well, only to find a newspaper report the next day saying that we had a stand-up fight in the car park. Again, the journalist responsible was man enough to apologise, but some people still believed the erroneous story and therefore the damage had been done.

With Neil Sullivan in goal, we won the match against the Faroe Islands more comfortably than the 2–1 scoreline suggests, so we were set up for the spring encounter, the vital match, against the Czech Republic at Celtic Park.

We lost 2–1, the better side winning, and I was left with the impression that there could be few more accomplished teams in Europe than the Czech Republic. They were inspired by Pavel Nedved, the Lazio midfield player, and had great strength and ability throughout the side. This game was overshadowed by one of the most unfortunate incidents which I have come across in all my years watching international football. For a group of people, whom I'd rather not call Scottish fans, to boo our Captain Gary McAllister, was, I thought, despicable. I have subsequently found out from one of our Development Officers seated near the culprits, that in his opinion they were not Scotland supporters at all, but wearing club colours. Aware that things were escalating out of control every time Gary went near the play, I decided, reluctantly, to replace him for the good of the team. This was not on account of inferior play, because I did not have that feeling at the time. Subsequent scrutiny of the match reveals that Gary had played well but had made a couple of mistakes, one when he was attempting a difficult through pass. It is relatively easy for players to keep themselves right by making simple square and back passes. This is not Gary McAllister's philosophy. He always tries to make a penetrating pass and, of course, there is a consequent risk. To discourage him from that could be to the detriment of the team. The loss of the match, and the loss of Gary who, not surprisingly, decided to retire from international football, was a double blow to Scotland and to me.

I have known Gary McAllister since my days at Motherwell when he was a young member of Fir Park Boys' Club. He was always a committed, enthusiastic and reliable player who just lives for the game of football. I had detected, in some television interviews in particular, that Gary was having to defend his selection more and more as he got older. I, too, when each team was picked, had to justify Gary and one or two of the more experienced players. I always did so by referring to other countries, such as France, and listed the number of their players who were 30 or over – and they were World Champions. Sadly, though, Gary stuck to his decision and although he did make a casual remark in an interview that if I were stuck he would come back to help, I asked him point-blank in Porto (when I was watching Liverpool play the Portuguese side in a UEFA Cup), if he would return, and his answer was that he wished to stick to his original decision. Even the wonderful finale which he had to season 2000–01 in which his club, Liverpool, won three cups, didn't change his mind about international football. I hope that those who booed this great player, and fine gentleman, feel thoroughly ashamed of themselves.

It is always difficult for the Scotland manager to obtain the generous and willing release of players for friendly international matches so it was not surprising when one or two key players called off prior to our difficult game in Bremen on 28 April 1999. As usual, it was a great trip in the company of our congenial and highly efficient backroom staff, and our group of committed players. In the couple of days prior to the game, we met the Riverdance entourage of over 100 performers and staff who were staying in the same hotel. Some of us managed to see part of their performance in the adjacent hall the night before our match and it was reciprocated when a number of the dance troop came to watch us have a light training session in the nearby public park the following morning. I remember the fun involved in the head tennis matches amongst our players while Alex Miller and I extracted groups and individuals for set-piece practice.

The game was a resounding success for us, particularly in a tactical sense. Whereas normally we instruct our strikers to be the first line of defence by defending wide, on this occasion we advised Billy Dodds and Don Hutchison to stay central and to pick up Lothar Matthaus and Jens Jeremies, the two key opposition players. The Germans were astonished to find a sweeper and a deep-lying central midfield player tightly marked and, frankly, could make nothing of it because their usual strategy was to play out from the back via Matthaus. Don Hutchison scored a fine goal for us after great play from Paul Lambert and Callum Davidson, to give us a 1–0 victory against all the odds. Our usual vast support was ecstatic and remained singing for about an hour after the match. We were proud of our performance and of the result because Germany were at full strength and don't play friendly matches.

I was privileged to have as guests at the match Lothar Meurer and his wife Ushi who run the organisation called UEFT, the Union of European Football Trainers. Lothar is a gentleman respected throughout Europe as an experienced coach and now as organiser of this very strong coaches' association. I am privileged to be second Vice-President of UEFT but, whoever is in charge, the organisation is dependent on the industry and nous of General Secretary Lothar Meurer and Ushi, who excels in her administrative role. Ushi knows my liking for ice-cream so wherever we go in Europe for a meeting or a convention, ice-cream is invariably high on the catering agenda.

Toftir? Where is that? This is a quiz question which would baffle many football aficionados. But after a few years on the European circuit more and more people are becoming familiar with this unique football outpost, the former ground of the Faroe Islands.

The Faroes are managed by Allan Simonsen, ex-Danish

international and European Footballer of the Year, and who displayed his mercurial skills for Charlton Athletic some time ago. The visit there is unique because the landing strip is short and your aircraft lands on one island, you live on another island and you play on yet another island. However, I understand that a new stadium has been build in Torshaven, the main town, thus obviating the hour-and-a-quarter journey by coach from the team hotel to the original Toftir Stadium.

Many countries who had very basic stadia are now upgrading their facilities, another significant example being Estonia. We had to play in the windswept Toftir Stadium and, again, it was a disappointing performance against opponents who are well organised by Allan, but should be beatable by a squad of full-time professionals. We went a goal ahead when Allan Johnston scored from a tight angle but there was drama just before the interval when the assistant referee, Nelly Viennot from France, saw our centre-half, Matt Elliott, lift his hands to Todi Jonsson. It was a foolish act, a kind of open-palm slap, but when you lift your hands in football you know the consequences. Naturally, I was very displeased with Matt because, not only was he destined to miss the second half and leave us short-handed, he was out of the next, very important, game in Prague against the Czech Republic who had ariel prowess which would have required Matt's considerable presence. When the Faroes equalised in injury time, the afternoon of misery was complete. As usual, there were calls for me to ban Matt from playing again for Scotland, but I knew that his indiscretion was out of character and that in fact he is anything but a dirty player, certainly not one who would normally strike an opponent. He received a five-game ban from UEFA and, when it was over, I telephoned him to advise him that I was not including him in the selection for the play-off matches against England as I felt that our central defensive cover was more than adequate at the time. I remember now that the call was on Guy Fawkes' Night, because Matt was in charge of a bonfire with his children in his back garden while speaking with me on the phone. Luckily, there were no fireworks between Matt and me and our relationship remained friendly.

Although I had one match temporarily in charge of the team against Italy in Rome in October 1993, the Faroes game was my fiftieth since my official appointment. Players reaching this target, receive official acknowledgement and thereafter enter the Hall of Fame. Each player in this category receives a gold medal and a framed painting from the SFA, a copy of which is displayed in the Hall of Fame. This did not happen to previous managers Jock Stein and Andy Roxburgh, but my good friend, Warren Mersereau, formerly of Umbro and Adidas, acknowledged my predecessor Andy's achievement and commissioned the SFA's chosen artist to produce a painting for Andy. I know how pleased Andy was with this wonderful gesture and I, too, was surprised and delighted when Warren presented me with a similar gift to mark this milestone in my managerial career. They say the camera doesn't lie but, unfortunately, neither does the artist. Whilst I was really pleased with the quality of the large painting in my SFA blazer, I've got to admit that I constitute no rival to Brad Pitt.

We were now half way through the qualifying group having played five matches and it looked as though, unless we could produce a miracle in Prague, we were destined to be competing for the second qualifying place. We had our usual tremendous support in the attractive Czech Republic capital. Maybe the fact that the game was played in June was appealing to many of our fans who stayed for a week's holiday in the city. One such fan was Bev Mayer of the Perthshire Tartan Army, now a veteran of 13 overseas trips. She described Prague as both 'brilliant' and 'fantastic' – 'mainly because folk just wheeled their trolleys of drink straight from the supermarket to the square where thousands of us were drinking surrounded by the most beautiful architecture!' Whatever the reason, the support was unbelievable. We set about our work in our usual businesslike manner and coped admirably in the opening spell. It came as a surprise, really, when we went into a two-goal lead, particularly as we were somewhat depleted, not only because of the suspension of Matt Elliott, but an injury to Colin Hendry had kept him out of the action as well. When you add the fact that Gary McAllister was no longer with us and that John Collins was injured, you will appreciate that there wasn't as much experience as usual in the Scottish line-up. If the first hour was a delight which made our fans delirious, the last half-hour was like a horror movie.

The Czech coach Jozef Chovanec, with nothing to lose, threw on the giant Jan Koller in sixty-fifth minute, as substitute. Tomas Repka, the former Fiorentina centre back now with West Ham, scored with a glancing header from a dubiously conceded corner; Pavel Kuka scored a fine equaliser; and substitute Koller headed the winner with only minutes remaining. It seemed like daylight robbery after our accomplished performance for most of the match but I must give credit to the Czech Republic, where I have many friends. One in particular, Dr Zdenek Sivek, who is Technical Director there, is a good ally who regularly invites me to contribute on the Czech Pro-Licence coaching courses. My visits to Prague are a real pleasure because of the kindness of this perfect gentleman. Mind you, I don't think I'd have been invited back had we managed to knock his team off the top perch of our qualifying group.

It was always a delight for me to get away with the national team, especially in the double header context when we had more time with the players and an opportunity to get to know individuals and to foster team spirit. There were also huge media demands, particularly in the two games in four days context, because the travelling journalists have copy to produce and are always on the lookout for snippets to fulfil their, in many cases, burdensome commitment. Clearly, I was more than happy to co-operate, as everyone knows, when there were genuine attempts to fill the back, sports pages with material.

However, no one could have predicated the bombshell which I received just under a month later when I found myself on the front pages.

I could not possibly in my wildest dreams have envisaged that anyone who knew me, however slightly, could possibly have gone along with the headlines which appeared on consecutive weeks in the Sunday newspapers, branding me a bigot and a traitor. Fortunately, my solicitor, Rod McKenzie, of Harper MacLeod in Glasgow, was quickly into action to make positive and unequivocal denials. The vast number of football colleagues, and people outside the game, who spontaneously responded with offers of assistance, was quite remarkable. Many players, managers and people from business and education with whom I had contact over the years phoned to offer their services as witnesses if required. A perfect example was Billy McNeill who, the next day in his newspaper column, wrote, 'If Brown's a bigot I'm a ballerina.' Such support was invaluable and reassuring and although I think I have written to and thanked hundreds of people who expressed their support, if I have missed anyone, please be assured that I am most grateful.

Throughout all this, I received tremendous support from my loyal colleague Alex Miller and his wife Ann. Fortunately, I had kept Alex advised of the circumstances many months prior to the article so he was extremely supportive, and this meant a great deal to me. So, too, were my employers, particularly our President Jack McGinn and Vice-President John McBeth. I think it was a happy coincidence that I had worked for almost ten years for Mr McBeth's club, Clyde, and he knew instantly that the allegations were completely without foundation. With all the legal ramifications, it took until February of 2001, almost 20 months later, before the issue was settled and a full apology printed in the offending publication.

I could have done without that distraction but I was completely assured that my innocence would be confirmed.

During the summer of 2000 I had another dose of

'personal development' as I was invited to do some commentary and summarising on the Copa America for Sky TV. This necessitated trips to the studio in London where, once again, I worked with superb commentators like Martin Tyler and Alan Parry. Summarising with me was Bobby Gould, whose company is always a pleasure to enjoy.

This championship invariably throws up some new South American stars but, as usual, Brazil was still the dominant force. They were not so convincing the following year, when Producer Jonty Whitehead again teamed me up with Ian Crocker, Bobby Gould, Chris Waddell, Tony Cottee and the consummate professional presenter Paul Dempsey.

In September it was back to qualifying business again with a tricky away double-header in Bosnia and Estonia. Our first match was in Sarajevo where we saw examples of the atrocities which had taken place recently that country. The graveyard on a hillside overlooking the stadium was a timely reminder of what had been happening in recent months in the trouble-torn country. Sights like that remind us all that no matter how important football may seem, some people are faced by real-life disaster on a daily basis.

There was a huge military presence in the city and in nearby Kosovo. I was asked if a small group of the soldiers, representing the thousands who had come to support us, could meet with the players during a training sessions at the stadium. I readily agreed. I think it is good for players, whom many people consider to be molly-coddled, to be made aware of what is happening amongst less fortunate people. A footballer's world, particularly that of a highly paid international, is undoubtedly a favoured environment. Whilst I in no way begrudge the guys anything, I am always at pains to make them aware of people who are not so privileged. It was for this reason when we visited Chile with our Under 20 team in 1987, that I took our players on a bus trip to observe some of the far from salubrious areas of Antofagasta. To see the nature of the homes there, and the lack of sanitation, was a salutary experience for our young players. Similarly, in Sarajevo, without becoming too melodramatic, it was salutary to remind ourselves of the benefits which we enjoy living in Scotland and being involved in the great game of football.

The pitch was heavy and far from perfect, the environment a bit hostile, but our performance was superb. We scored two good goals, the winner a blistering left-foot shot from Billy Dodds, and we looked thoroughly composed throughout the match. Bosnia, however, gave warning that they would be difficult opponents the next month in the return game at Ibrox because they appeared to be lightning fast on the counter-attack.

No sooner had we obtained three points, than we were off to the testing environment of our old friends from Estonia. It's on flights – and you will appreciate that I make many – that I take the chance to do some reading. There is not much opportunity for this is in the rest of my busy life schedule. On this trip I was lucky to read a cracking paperback and was pleased to see the author among the press corps on the trip. The book in question was called *Penthouse and Pavement* and I took time to have a word with the writer, Bill Leckie, to compliment him on his work. Bill's a bit like myself, in that he is a champion of the underdog and likes to encourage the lesser teams. Maybe that's why he is a Scotland fan? Seriously, though, having worked so long with Clyde FC, I, like Bill, appreciate and know that all clubs have a part to play in the overall structure of football in Scotland. His description of a week's training at Dunfermline, under the direction of Bert Paton and Dick Campbell, was an absolutely hilarious interlude in an absorbing read.

There were comments coming from Estonia about what they were going to do to Scotland and how they fancied themselves to finish above us in the Group table. I usually take with a pinch of salt comments from opposing coaches but I do know that there was a confidence about the Estonians after their visit to Tynecastle, when they considered themselves unlucky to lose. We were the better side in a dreary 0–0 draw, so we were still comfortably on course for the runner up spot in the Group.

Once in Tallinn I spoke with Brian O'Neil whom I knew to have a game on the Friday night for his club side in Germany, Wolfsburg. I indicated to Brian that we would not be using him among our 18 players to strip for the match and that if, to help him in his preparation for the Friday fixture, he wished to go straight back to Germany, he would be free to do so. I assumed that this was the thoughtful action of a manager with a caring interest in his players and Brian thought likewise. Imagine our astonishment to read a column which said O'NEILL WALKS OUT ON SCOTLAND. I know that Brian's father was incensed and the player, too, was very upset at the erroneous allegation. Since I'm used to such inaccuracy in the interest of a sensational story, I simply shrugged my shoulders, but felt that there was no need for this kind of false reporting.

The final two matches in the Group were successfully negotiated; a double-header at home where we beat Bosnia Herzegovina 1–0 at Ibrox and Lithuania 3–0 at Hampden. Unusually, the last game in the Group was a formality because we had already qualified for the play-off, our opponents still be determined. The Lithuania game gave me the opportunity to experiment with two new strikers, Gary McSwegan and Mark Burchill. Both did well, Gary scoring a good goal but, unfortunately, Mark hit the post with a penalty kick. It is safe to say that I have not had a great deal of luck with penalties in my spell with the Scotland national teams.

23

CBE —
Can't Beat England

I'VE HAD MANY honours in my time with, and before, the SFA, including numerous Manager of the Month awards and League Championship medals with Dundee and Clyde. But one of my proudest moments was when Scottish Disability Sport asked me to be their first ever Patron. I think this was recognition for my colleagues in the Football Development Department of the SFA – Jim Fleeting, our Head of Community Programme in particular – because of their superb work with disabled footballers. We have no fewer than 37 coaches working in the community. Some are Community Coaches attached to senior professional clubs and others are Development Officers working regionally throughout the country. These lads, some are former international players like Davie Provan (ex-Rangers) and Neil Simpson (ex-Aberdeen), have a wide-ranging remit from grass-roots development for boys and girls to the production of regional development squads of the best possible youngsters. Their multifarious duties include anti-drugs advice, sponsored by Alistair Ramsay and his Scotland Against Drugs team and the provision of opportunity for disabled footballers of both sexes and all ages. I think it was because of this input from our Community Scheme and from Tommy Wilson who supervises the disabled footballers' programme that I was asked to be Patron of Scottish Disability Sport.

I am always reminded of a humorous incident when we had a group of disabled youngsters at the National Sports Centre, Inverclyde, Largs. Richard Brickley from the Glenrothes Institute in Fife, in charge of the group, asked if our coaches would play against the disabled group. This would be motivational for his young footballers. I picked a team comprising Jimmy Bone, Alex Smith, Walter Smith, Tommy Craig, Frank Coulston and most serious selection error, Archie Knox! In no time at all, the disabled team were running rings round us and a limbless young lad from Castlemilk had scored three goals inside the first five minutes. Each time he scored, he propelled his chair over to Archie and said, 'How did you like that, you big useless B?' Archie pointed at him and said, 'I will do you, son.' Many people laughed at this threat but I knew that Archie meant it!

A few minutes later, the young lad was going down the side of the hall dribbling brilliantly, knocking the ball with the front of his chair, and Archie came across the diagonal at speed. By half-way across, Archie had lost complete control. But just as the young fellow was about to play the ball across the goal, Archie whacked him and the two chairs got mangled up together. The young lad fell out the chair to one side and Archie also spilled from his. To be fair to Archie, he helped us lift the young lad back into the chair when further words were exchanged.

Immediately afterwards Archie came past me struggling to move his chair along and asked me to substitute him because his arms were hanging off. 'My arms are knackered.' The young lad overheard this and he came spinning along towards me at great speed, smiled and said, 'No wonder his arms are knackered; I put his brake on when he fell!' That story always sticks with me when I think fondly of our disabled footballers.

Talking of honours, it was around the month of October 1999 that I received a letter which astounded me. It was to the effect that I was being considered for inclusion in the Queen's Honours List and would I accept the title Commander of the British Empire? Naturally, I was quite delighted to hear of this and promptly replied that I would happily accept. At the end of the month, I was invited to Buckingham Palace to receive the CBE.

Coinciding with the award was a course conducted at Wembley by the FA Technical Department's Howard Wilkinson and Robin Russell. It was under the auspices of the UEFT, the Union of European Football Trainers to which I have previously referred. Howard and Robin had a magnificently varied course in prospect for coaches, not only from Europe but from all over the world, quite a number coming from South America. I attended with my colleagues Frank Coulston and Jim Sinclair. Also staying at our hotel, the Wembley Hilton, at that time was David Findlay, our Head of the International Department at the SFA because he was Venue Director at the Arsenal Champions' League match on the Wednesday evening.

I escaped from the course in my formal outfit to go to meet my son, John and daughter Val, who were accompanying me to the Palace. Unfortunately, my older son, Hugh, had an important business appointment and couldn't be there. Somewhat embarrassed, I sneaked out of the hotel and was soon in the comfortable company of Johan, John and Val. We taxied to the Palace and, hearing the Scottish accents and seeing John in the kilt the taxi driver was obviously a little confused. Just as I was paying the fare at the Palace gates, he said, 'Have a good day Sir Alex.'

There were two journalists with notebooks standing waiting for a word when I disembarked and said to the driver, 'I think you've got it wrong.' Whereupon the driver remarked, 'Oh sorry, Alex's the one with the blotchy face!' Imagine my embarrassment the next day when I was quoted as the one who had made the remark. I tried to phone Alex to explain but I knew that, in any case, he wouldn't bother too much about that kind of thing.

This was confirmed some time later when we met at the funeral of Jimmy Steel, the real legend who was the masseur of Celtic and Scotland for all those years. Steelie always used to say that his funeral would be all-ticket and that there would be no complimentaries. This was indeed the case when almost everyone in the Scottish football world attended his funeral at Daldowie Crematorium in Glasgow. Sir Alex gave a most eloquent eulogy about Steelie tempering the serious stuff with a degree of humour. It's not often you see smiles at a funeral but everyone knew that that's what Jimmy Steel would have wanted and there was laughter, particularly when Alex referred to two of his favourite stories, the Czechoslovakian coach and Big Tam the Tipster.

Talking of fun at a funeral, I attended one such gathering not so many months ago, that of my good friend Gordon Brown the famous British Lions rugby player. At his funeral in Troon, everyone was encouraged to come wearing club colours. It certainly was a service with a difference, conducted brilliantly by the Reverend Howard Haslett, the ex-rugby referee and former chaplain of Edinburgh Academy.

I had the pleasure of knowing Gordon for many years and speaking with him occasionally. He always brought the house down and it was a good idea to be on the same bill as Gordon because the clients were guaranteed a great night. For many years, I admired his wonderful outgoing personality and latterly his tremendous courage. I was privileged on several occasions to join with the Brown family, father Jock and brother Peter in particular. I recall doing 'An Evening with the Broons' at the Bowling Club in Troon where Peter, Gordon and I were speaking guests and their father, the great Jock Brown, former Clyde FC goalkeeper, was guest of honour. In addition, Peter and Gordon played against my brother Jock and me at golf. The last occasion was a year ago at Muirfield where, unfortunately for us, the rugby Broons won, but I put it down to Peter's local knowledge as he is a former captain and committee member of the famous Muirfield Links.

Two functions were held for Gordon when it became apparent that his bone marrow cancer was terminal. One was a lunch in Glasgow which was a spectacular occasion with the greats of the sporting world in attendance to honour Gordon and his charming wife Linda. The other event was in London attended by the greats of the rugby world – and I mean world, because they came from South Africa, Australia and New Zealand, as well as the local heros from the UK, such as Andy Irvine, Ken Scotland, Ian McLaughlin, Willie John McBride, Cliff Morgan, Jim Telfer, JPR Williams, Sandy Carmichael and Ian McGeechan. Gordon told a story from a Lions tour of his immediate opponent in the line out, whom he christened Cyclops. This was because he had a glass eye which was lost during the game, and found again. When he put it back in place, there was still grass sticking out from the eye socket. Gordon's description of the sight was a classic. I was delighted when, recently, Peter asked me to consult with Jock and continue the foursome with Gordon's place being taken by his other brother, George.

Whenever I feel upset as a result of a poor Scotland performance, or the rare indifferent result, I think of how fortunate I am in relation to the late, great Gordon Brown. I was with him at a speaking engagement in England the day after his illness was diagnosed. His courage, then, was immense and he was determined not to give in to the dreaded disease. Alas, eventually, after all medical intervention possible, he had to succumb, as all of us will some day, to the inevitable. I only hope that, when the time comes, I will be viewed favourably in the eyes of the Lord.

Reverend John Boyers, Chaplain of Manchester United FC, is a man who is attempting to encourage sports chaplaincy among football clubs. I have had several meetings with John, and have heard him speak, and I do wish him every success in his laudable objective. Indeed, I was present when Sir Alex Ferguson launched the scheme in Paisley, Scotland, a couple of years ago but, because John Boyers has been busy south of the border, things have not quite taken off as yet. There is an initiative for later in 2001, when John proposes to relaunch his scheme. I have been asked to contribute, and will be honoured to do so.

There are many Christians in our sport, but perhaps the most well known in Scottish football is Brian Irvine, the former Falkirk and Aberdeen centre-half. I had the privilege of working with Brian when I gave him several of his international caps and found him to be a tremendous ambassador as a Christian in sport. He overcame a career-threatening, debilitating illness and, I'm glad to see, is prolonging his career in Dingwall with Ross County FC.

And it was while on my way to Buckingham Palace that these thoughts came into my mind!

Not surprisingly, everything was extremely well organised and Her Majesty was in exceptional form, managing to make appropriate comments to each of the 115 recipients of various awards. She had a word with me about the forthcoming play-off matches against England, which revealed that she was extremely well advised and I even suspected that she had something like a mini-earpiece in her ear to receive information about each recipient as he or she approached. Otherwise, her memory and knowledge must be incredible.

No sooner had I received the CBE award than, whenever I was being introduced, it was invariably Craig Brown CBE and, depending whether or not I was in Scotland or England, the chairman would say 'Can Beat England' or 'Can't Beat England'!

The more accurate one was soon to be discovered in our play-off matches for a place in the Euro 2000 Finals in Belgium and Holland. The hype surrounding the opening game was so intense that my whole world became a football match against England. Trying to keep things in perspective was difficult because of the incessant demands from the media wishing to fill every radio and TV programme, newspaper and magazine with information. Journalists even came from abroad to interview me about the match which had captured the imagination of the whole of Europe.

In circumstances like this, there is inevitably a ticket problem. Tickets for football matches are one of my pet hates but I know that a clamour for tickets represents great interest in the match. I learned many, many years ago as a young player at Ibrox how people can be totally thoughtless when requesting tickets. To give folk the benefit of the doubt, I do think that there is a perception that the players and management get unlimited supplies of free tickets. Nothing could be further from the truth. I have always said throughout my playing and managerial career that someone has to pay to get in and that not everything can be complimentary. I witnessed, and suffered from, abuse of ticket requests as a young player. When I was with Rangers while we were consistently progressing in Europe, my pals would ask for tickets, seemingly thinking I got them for nothing and, not wishing to let them down, I would be massively out of pocket after each match. Even today, people ask for tickets and the phenomenon is that if the money is not received prior to the match, it is often very difficult to obtain payment if it happened to be a poor game. Very few of the requests are accompanied by a cheque or a stamped-addressed envelope and hardly anyone puts the price of the postage together with the payment. Please don't gain the impression that I begrudge my friends anything because I don't, but there are so many others, termed in Scotland – 'hangers on' – who appear out of the blue whenever there is a ticket shortage.

My job was to make representation to the International Committee, now superceded by the Executive Committee, to obtain the best possible arrangement for players and staff. I've got to admit that our officials have always been extremely co-operative because I consistently emphasise the fact that the most important people to be satisfied are the players. I don't think any of our players involved in the games at Hampden and Wembley would have had any cause for complaint because each received a generous allocation. The other danger is, of course, leaving tickets at a collection point because the football spivs are notorious for chancing their arm by coming and asking for tickets in the name of a prominent player. For example, a well-known player must have at least half a dozen fathers because of the number of requests for tickets in the name of, for example, Mr McAllister. I always urge the players to dispose of them well in advance where possible, or to put a code name on the envelope.

With the first game at Hampden, I decided to retain our normal home match routine. Our preparatory hotel was the Marine Highland in Troon and our training venue Somerset Park, Ayr, the ground of Ayr United FC, where Davie Harkness keeps the pitch in tip-top condition.

When there is a match of importance, maybe it's my imagination but there invariably is a vital club match, either domestically or in Europe, immediately prior to, or after, the international fixture. On this occasion, it was a Rangers v Celtic match at Ibrox which preceded the game against England. I always go with my fingers crossed to these fixtures hoping that all our players will emerge unscathed. If there was one player whom I didn't wish to be injured in such a fixture it was Paul Lambert because of his tremendous European experience, composure in a pressure situation and terrific natural ability. And who was the one to suffer a severe facial injury in the match? Paul Lambert! So we knew we had to operate without our key man in midfield, our anchor player in our 3-5-2 system.

Another major worry was the fitness of Captain Colin Hendry. Colin hadn't played for many weeks because of a leg injury, so I visited Ibrox and spoke with assistant manager, Bert Van Lingen, and Dr Gerd Goudswaard. I was anxious that

Colin take part in a reserve fixture on the Monday evening prior to the England match where Rangers Under-21 team was playing at Livingston. The doctor said that if Colin played in that match he would take no responsibility for the outcome because he had estimated that the recovery period for that particular type of injury was 4 weeks without competitive action and the 4 weeks would not have elapsed until the Wednesday. Dr Goudswaard said that if Colin completed the treatment period without match action, then it was up to our medical team and me whether or not he was fit to play.

So it was mixed news on the injury front prior to the vital play-off matches against the Auld Enemy. Paul Lambert was definitely ruled out but there was at least an even chance that Colin Hendry would be able to take part. Having complied with the advice of the Rangers' doctor regarding Colin's non-participation in the Under-21 fixture in the Monday evening, we put him through stiff training sessions in a controlled environment. Unknown to Colin, I had asked members of the backroom staff to watch him at times when he didn't think he was being observed. Every response I got both from the player and from my medical colleagues was heartening and, when we played a full practice match on the Thursday morning to shape up our team for the match on Saturday, Colin came through unscathed.

It's safe to say that Colin Hendry, unimaginatively called 'Braveheart', (but it is an apt description) was desperate to play himself, not only because it was a game against England but because it was also against his former Blackburn colleague, Alan Shearer. Colin confided in me that he felt he knew how to deal with Alan and was extremely confident of coming out on top in that particular man to man contest. I had other worries, particularly regarding the pace and elusiveness of Michael Owen, but I was reassured that Alan Shearer would be capably handled. This proved to be the case, although Colin was given a yellow card for a 'heavy slap' from behind early in the match. Thereafter, however, he drew on all his experience to ensure that he did not offend for a second time.

Adhering to my old adage about killing the chief, I asked Paul Ritchie to do a close attention job on David Beckham. This Paul did effectively; suffice to say that I've seen Mr Beckham play many more significant games for his country. Unfortunately, the man whom we didn't cater for adequately in that depressing first half was Paul Scholes who scored two tremendous goals to give England a terrific start in the match. We were flat-footed when he scored the first and equally slip-shod in our marking when he headed his second goal.

0–2 down at half-time called for stringent action from a proactive coach. Had there not been a second leg to follow I most certainly would have gone for all or nothing by changing the team, possibly by bringing on an attacking player in preference to a midfielder or defender. I was always, and am always, confident about scoring in away fixtures and I was sure that we could do so at Wembley. The important thing was not to go to the second leg with England having an unassailable lead. To lose another would have been disastrous, so I elected not to introduce Neil McCann, for example, at the interval, but to try to stabilise defensively and to ensure that Scholes made no more unmatched runs from midfield. We did ease our way back into the game but failed to score to please our long-suffering, tolerant fans. At the end of the day, we lost a match which we needn't have lost and we gave ourselves a mountain to climb in the midweek fixture at Wembley.

There could be no complaint about the environment, the pitch or the support. Nothing but our own carelessness could be pinpointed as the reason for our defeat. I'm told that the England players enjoyed the playing surface at Hampden and were very impressed with the players' accommodation in the stadium. The dressing rooms are spacious and well appointed, with a large television monitor for the coach to replay action at half-time and at the end of the match if he so desires. The medical facilities in the sports injury clinic are superb, including a large hydrotherapy pool and, most importantly from the players' point of view, the indoor warm-up area with artificial grass is ideal. Not even the biggest clubs in Europe, nor the most high profile players, had any complaint when the European Champions League Final was played at Hampden in May 2002.

I gave the players the night off following the match and asked them to report to our team base at Troon late on the Sunday afternoon for a light session back at Somerset Park, Ayr. I returned to the hotel on the Saturday evening to look over video footage of the match and to check the injury situation with our medical people. I was pleased to hear that there were no additional injuries, but obviously disappointed to know that Kevin Gallacher, who had received a yellow card, was out of the second leg because of suspension.

The Sunday afternoon was wholly occupied by the media in our hotel. I spent almost three hours responding to questions from television, radio and the written media. My philosophy is that, after a defeat, there is no case for disappearing, hiding or being anything other than fully co-operative. My instinct was to lock myself away with the videos of the match and of other recent England games, but my responsibility was to shoulder the blame and accept the criticism. As always, after a defeat, there are calls for the manager's head. This was unfortunately the case between double-header matches when Kevin Keegan resigned. I respect Kevin greatly and know that he must have had his own reasons, but the thought of resigning never crossed my mind because I am a fighter and, particularly in adversity, gain strength to do what I think is right.

There was one particularly resourceful, but hurtful, piece of journalism and it came from Sky TV's Pete Barraclough. He asked me if I would be prepared to come into the town of Troon to give him a different environment for the interview. I declined and said that it would create a precedent and that he would have to interview me during the time alotted in the hotel venue seated in front of the sponsors' backdrop. It is only fair to sponsors to give them maximum coverage and one of the ways of doing so which has become very apparent is that when managers and/or players are being interviewed, they sit in front of the appropriately labelled board. I felt that this was my duty and declined to go into the town.

It's not often that I get the opportunity to see the result of my interviews on the news in the evening because we invariably have a 6.30pm squad meeting. However, on this occasion I saw Pete Barraclough introduce his piece from a street in Troon, then cut to some match action, then to me in the hotel and eventually he finished his piece back in the street by saying, 'And if Scotland don't do an awful lot better at Wembley on Wednesday it will be the end of the road for Craig.' At this juncture, the camera left his head-and-shoulder shot, and panned up the wall of the building to the street name which was Craigend Road. I can only say that I was glad I did not accept his invitation to find a different environment for the interview.

Players, as always, when they get a ball at their feet and are back in among their colleagues, forget about the disappointment of the past and renewed hope and vigour comes into their minds. Those who did play in the match against England had a light warm-down and the others, to their great credit, put in a very sound, thorough training session.

The Monday morning saw us have a bright, lively session at Ayr and a not-too-critical post-mortem of Saturday's proceedings at Hampden. Even although the food in our hotel was excellent, we always try to change the environment by taking the players out to a local restaurant. When in the Glasgow area, we go to the Italian restaurant, Il Castillo where Marco was extremely attentive, and when on the Ayrshire coast we used to go to Pierino's in Ayr where Piero and Luisa Vannucci produce wonderful food in a restaurant where the ambience is delightful. We had our 'carbohydrate loading' as it is called, by enjoying a pasta evening, and were ready to fly to London to our base at St Albans the next day. As Alex

Ferguson had advised me during Euro '96, it is important to get the feel of the Wembley turf before you play there, so we were pleased to have a training session en route and to confirm the excellent condition of the playing surface. I had known this because of the recent UEFT course which was held there and had seen some fine practical demonstrations on the pitch.

On the morning of the match, we did a session at the new Arsenal training ground adjacent to the M25. This is a magnificent complex with every possible facility but, as usual, when conducting a coaching session, there is invariably someone cutting grass, an aeroplane flying overhead or cars speeding past on a motorway. The only minor debit factor I could possibly envisage concerning this superb facility would be the noise of the traffic making it difficult to communicate with players if, as in our case, a pitch near the road was being used. Further from the noise of the traffic, Arséne Wenger and Pat Rice were working with the Arsenal group minus, of course, Tony Adams, Martin Keown and David Seaman, who would normally be working under the expert guidance of goalkeeping coach, Scotsman Bob Wilson. But Mr Seaman was with the England squad at Bisham Abbey, as we were to find to our cost later that evening!

The players know I didn't ever allow tracksuit bottoms to be worn in training but this was one morning when I had just a little sympathy with them. It was bitterly cold, and we were, at times, relatively inactive while we refined our set-piece arrangements. On the way back to our team coach, I had a word with Bob Wilson and Pat Rice, but Mr Wenger was at the far side of the pitch and, unfortunately, I didn't have the opportunity to express my thanks to him personally for the use of the excellent facility.

Kevin Keegan had announced his team in advance, which is something I never do, and this knowledge helped us with our team selection. Usually Alex Miller and I would produce, separately, our ideas for each match. It's amazing how seldom we differed. On this occasion, we were completely in concert when we knew that Sol Campbell would be playing at right back. We both thought that we should try to isolate a one-on-one situation using the speed and trickery of Neil McCann on the left. Also, the introduction of Gareth Southgate for Martin Keown prompted us to play Don Hutchison as our mainline striker where we felt that his physical presence would be important. This would have been less of an issue against the tougher presence of Martin Keown. Our idea was to keep Don away from the imposing figure of Tony Adams, particularly in the air, and leave Adams to contend with the bustling, energetic Billy Dodds. Our main objective was ball retention – keep possession and try to frustrate the opposition on their home territory. With midfield players like Barry Ferguson, Paul Lambert and John Collins, I knew it was well within our capability to control the midfield area.

Most players go to bed on the afternoon of a match and I know that from years of working with him, Andy Roxburgh did the same. I normally take the opportunity to catch up with some work, mainly correspondence, at this quiet time, but I took the unusual step of trying to steal a couple of hours' sleep because it was to be a late kick-off thus making it a long day, the end of a demanding, but thoroughly enjoyable, ten days with the squad. Although I had asked for no interuptions, somehow several calls got through to me all expressing their good wishes for the evening encounter. Believe it or not, there were still people contacting me to look for the most elusive tickets I have ever known for a football match!

In this context I've got to thank the SFA for ensuring that, as I have said, the players and staff got a good allocation but my gratitude is also due to one of the sponsors, Nationwide, who helped me to obtain one or two additional tickets. This was because I had travelled to London a couple of weeks earlier to be with the England coach, Kevin Keegan, at a joint press conference inspired by Nationwide and the English FA. When I was being thanked for taking the trouble to travel from Glasgow for the conference, I was asked if there was anything they could do for me. The response was easy, the same as I had heard from dozens of people in the last month: 'Any spare tickets?' I am one of the managers who do not, in any way, complain about the intrusion of sponsors. Indeed, as I have written elsewhere, I feel that sponsors are very necessary to support the modern game and to assist with the massive financial implications involved, especially, in top-flight football. Our own main sponsors, Scottish Gas, were always well represented by Hamish McPherson and Clare Welsh, ably supported by David Brown representing The Sports Business. Fila, too, our kit manufacturers, look after us extremely well, with Dominic Munnelly and John Thompson taking an avid interest in our equipment requirements. I know there is often criticism, I think a bit unjustified, of the seats which sponsors get for matches. In view of the amount of financial support they give to the game, I feel that they are due favourable consideration, but not to the detriment of the 'real' fans who, at their own expense, follow their team through thick and thin. Anyway, I was grateful for the extra few tickets which I received because as is well known, it is anticipated that the manager has an unlimited supply!

The afternoon passed quickly – a mixture of sleep and phone calls meant that I had little time to worry about the prospect of travelling away from home with a two-goal deficit. Everyone had been well warned that to lose an early goal could be disastrous and I don't think the players could possibly have been more emphatically briefed for any game. A fairly recent and excellent idea of the International Committee is to invite staff colleagues, who otherwise wouldn't be involved with the team, to join the squad on selected away trips. This is appreciated by the staff and, on this occasion, it was the turn of Liz Robertson, one of the four secretaries we have in the Football Development Department. I have already referred to Andrea Anderson, but she is joined in her diligent toil by Siobhan Boyd, Amanda Rudden and Liz Robertson. Liz, the longest-serving of the quartet, was very excited at the prospect of being in the official party but this did not stop her – as I was walking along the side of the team bus in the dark (literally, but I hope not metaphorically) to climb on to the coach for the trip to Wembley – from coming along in the glare of a large floodlit TV camera and giving me a kiss to wish me good luck. You could imagine my embarrassment when dozens of people at home asked, 'Who was the girl who kissed you beside the bus?' The kiss apart, Liz confirmed that it was a wonderful experience for her being at the away match, and travelling with the squad. This thoughtful and sensitive idea is undoubtedly a morale booster for Association staff.

As usual, thousands of fans were in the stadium in advance of the team and many Scottish supporters turned up at the entrance to welcome their team on arrival. Wembley is a fairly unique venue with both team coaches being able to be driven into the narrow alleyway right by the doors of the dressing rooms. For the large squads involved in modern international football the dressing rooms are somewhat cramped so it important to ask the players not involved to remain outside to give maximum space to the participants.

The FA kindly provide two gentlemen in the dressing room area to cater for all the needs of the team, particularly in the form of liquid refreshment. There is invariably great banter amongst our lads and not uncommonly, Ian Durrant started to berate the two Englishmen in the Scottish dressing room. To say he gave them a hard time is putting it mildly! This undoubtedly helped to relieve the tension and Durranty had everyone in stitches with his attack on the representatives of the opposition.

We were fortunate to have one of the world's best referees in charge of the match, so when I bumped into Mr Collina from Italy, who speaks perfect English and whom I had met at the World Cup, I passed the time of day with him and joked that he was allowed to move outside the centre circle in the course of the match. Referees usually smile when I give them that piece of advice which I stole from a remark I overheard around 40 years ago from the late Jim Baxter, directed at Tom 'Tiny' Wharton. One thing everyone does know about Pierluigi Collina is that he is extremely fit and will always be up with the play.

As was our intention, we took the game by the scruff of the neck and some of our possession play was a treat. After 39 minutes we scored an excellent goal when Neil McCann's perfect delivery was met by Don Hutchison who outjumped the entire English defence to head a fine goal. Unfortunately, in spite of valiant efforts in the second half, we couldn't score the equaliser which would have sent the game into extra time. We had a number of chances but none better than Christian Dailly's header from a well-worked corner kick, which was brilliantly saved by David Seaman. Yes, the same Seaman who had prevented Gary McAllister's penalty from hitting the net in our previous meeting with England at Wembley. The game ended in an anticlimax for Scotland and I was quick to congratulate Kevin Keegan, for whom the victory meant so much.

On leaving the pitch, feeling very disconsolate, a large arm in an England shirt was hooked round my neck. When I turned round there was Tony Adams, the England Captain, saying to me that I should be proud of my players because they were magnificent. I thought this was a tremendous gesture from Tony, a player whom I have admired over the years. My respect for him increased, if that were possible, a thousand-fold when he took the time and trouble from his celebrations to acknowledge the contribution of the Scottish team. Thanks, Tony, and very best wishes for your future, which I suspect will end up in management.

There was to be no Scottish team in the Euro 2000 Championships in Holland and Belgium. After the wonderful experience I had had in 1992 in Sweden and in 1996 in England, this was a big disappointment. The thought of a major tournament without Scotland's involvement, particularly as it was relatively close to our shores, gave me withdrawal symptoms. I thought enviously of the coaches who would be involved in the competition and sympathised with Mick McCarthy, the Republic of Ireland coach, who had also been eliminated at the play-off stage.

24

Changes on and off the Field

PRIOR TO THE matches against England, my colleague Alex Miller had indicated that, because of his new role with Gerard Houllier at Liverpool FC, he would have to resign from his position with me with the national team. I fully understood Alex's reasons for this because, when international and Under-21 matches were being played, his remit was to look at potential Liverpool signings, most of whom were operating at this high level of involvement. Although I had known for some time of Alex's intention, we kept it quiet from the players and staff, all of whom respected Alex greatly, none more so than I did. Alex's dedication, loyalty and game appreciation were second to none and I knew he would be an extremely difficult man to replace. Alex's wife Ann, along with his sons Graeme and Greg, were great Scotland fans and attended every game. The fact that we managed to finish on a high with a victory against England at Wembley was some consolation to the Miller family, to whom I will always be indebted.

Another departure from the SFA was that of Chief Executive, Jim Farry. A fair bit of controversy surrounded his demise, but it is not for me to become involved in the politics of the situation. It would be true to say that I had slight differences with Jim over the years, but nothing insurmountable. I felt sorry for his lovely family, Elaine, and their two children Ewen and Alyson, because it could not have been pleasant to see all the newspaper coverage, initially over the speculation and, thereafter, confirmation of his departure. I did say that we disagreed on occasion, exchanging forthright memos, but for the most part Jim was a good colleague, and always supportive in public. Any disagreement which we had was behind closed doors and, to my knowledge, he did not bear a grudge.

One such occasion arose many years ago when I was in charge of the Under-21 team. At that time, nothing had been formalised among the four home countries regarding the eligibility of players for international matches. According to FIFA, if a player had a British passport he was eligible to play for any of the home countries. It was in February 1993 that an agreement was made which stated that a player could only play for the country in which he was born or in which one of his natural parents or grandparents was born. In the event of a player fulfilling more than one of the criteria, he had his choice of country.

Before this rule had been put in place, I selected Matt Jackson, then of Everton, to play for the Scottish Under-21 team. In conversation with Jimmy Gabriel, then a coach at Everton, he told me that he had a fine defender whose mother was from Scotland. I was very grateful for this information and, having watched Matt in action, I decided he would be an acquisition for our Under-21 team.

The day before I announced the squad, I telephoned Joe Royle at Everton to confirm his availability and eligibility. Joe asked me to wait a minute while he went out to confirm matters on the training pitch with Jimmy Gabriel and came back to tell me that Jimmy said he had spoken to the player and that everything was in order. Naturally, when Matt Jackson was selected, the press boys phoned him for comment and asked him where his mother was born. He confirmed that she had been born in England and, I think from memory, did admit that it was his grandmother who was Scottish. Since, at that time, we did not go down the grandparent route, it was not surprising that when the media found out about this error, we were all over the television, radio and newspapers. Quite understandably, our Chief Executive was far from pleased and informed me in no uncertain terms. I pointed out what had happened, and said that I was unintentionally let down by the communication at Everton, but this was to no avail. I was in the dog house! It was as a result of this incident that the administration of our Association is so punctilious about eligibility checks with players.

This was proved when, once again, some years later, George Burley telephoned me to advise me that he had a striker who could be eligible for Scotland. His name was David Johnson and he had been banging in the goals for George's team. I asked that he check his availability before I agreed to come down to watch him in action. Unaware of the home nation's agreement, Ipswich Town FC and David's agent, Phil Graham, made contact with FIFA who confirmed that he was entirely eligible. This was on the basis of his British passport but, quite understandably, FIFA did not take into consideration the internal arrangement in Britain. I accepted the situation and went to watch David in action. Having confirmed for myself that he was very much worth a game for us, I met with him and his wife after the match. And when I went to his home, I saw a most delightful sight. At the match, a great number of the Ipswich fans had been wearing the replica number 9 jersey with the name 'JOHNSON' emblazoned above the number. Once back at his house, his three-year-old daughter also was wearing a replica strip with number 9 on the back. Above the number was written the word 'DAD'. Delightful!

In an attempt to be kind and welcoming to the Johnsons, I arranged for them to come to Scotland the following week to experience the atmosphere and to see Rangers play in a Champions' League match. The Johnsons were flying into Prestwick, with Phil Graham, and I arranged to pick them up, take them to their hotel and, thereafter, transport them to Ibrox where Campbell Ogilvie had kindly agreed to provide tickets. All this was done quietly and unobtrusively but I received an incessant number of requests from the media asking what was happening. To avoid having to sneak David in and out of Ibrox and to prevent him being pursued and pestered, I arranged for a press call on his arrival at the airport. Naturally, I was displeased when I was accused later of presenting David Johnson to the media. I was merely trying to help, as I always do, the reporters in their duties. He received a very fine welcome at Ibrox, both in the vicinity of the ground and during the match. Numerous fans came up to him wishing him all the best and expressing the belief that he would enjoy playing for Scotland.

All the while, our administration in the International Department of the SFA had been in contact with David for the necessary documentation to confirm his eligibility. It transpired that there was a problem because his natural mother had apparently been born in England. I can assure any doubter that this took some time to determine, but it was well in advance of my next squad announcement. When we found out that he was eligible, therefore, only for Jamaica or England, I had to inform David and drop all interest. This was a case of my attempt to assist the media backfiring on me because I was heavily criticised. I did feel aggrieved because I was genuinely trying to help a number of people get worthwhile copy, while I felt the SFA administration, through the previous insistence of Jim Farry, should have been praised for thoroughness.

Our next match was scheduled for March against the World Champions, France, a reciprocal arrangement following our visit to St Etienne in November 1997. We plunged again into the deep end following our disappointment in the play-off matches against England because, after France, we had two very difficult away friendlies, one against Holland in Arnhem and the other a visit to Dublin to take on the Republic of Ireland.

In January 2000, I was invited by BBC Radio 5 Live to join their commentary team for the Club World Championship in Brazil. This was an opportunity not to be missed because to go to the centre of football excellence, and to be able to scrutinise the development programme in Brazil, as well as being involved in summarising matches involving some of the top clubs in the world, was a terrific opportunity. There was a great deal of controversy surrounding Manchester United's involvement in this tournament because it coincided with their withdrawal from the FA Cup back home in England. I, for one, was pleased they had undertaken the commitment in the Club Championship of the World, because it enabled me to be in Rio for a fortnight summarising with Mike Ingham and Alan Green. We had wonderful weather and were privileged to be in a fine hotel overlooking the Copacabana Beach. Some distance south in Sao Paulo, Ron Jones and Mick McCarthy were less fortunate because they were unlucky with the wet, sultry weather while we were basking in blazing Brazilian sunshine.

It was good to meet up with Alex Ferguson after all these years and to marvel at how he handled his players, staff and, more particularly, the media. I felt that, after his rather harsh ordering off in the opening match against Necaxa, from Mexico, there appeared to be a bit of a witch-hunt against David Beckham. He was appearing on the front page as well as the back pages of some papers back home. His reliability, stability and appropriateness for, not only playing for England but as a potential captain, were called into question. It was obvious the day after the match that Alex was going to have a grilling on the Beckham incident, so after he had answered the first question by saying that David had been ordered off and he and the club accepted that, a journalist tried to push him a little further. Alex's response was, 'You all have your own agenda about David Beckham. I will be saying no more about him, nor will David be making any comment either. End of story.' Later, I watched with admiration as Steve McClaren, now Middlesbrough manager, handled the players at training and also noted the work ethic which was reinforced when Jimmy Ryan took the players who were not involved in the matches for a stiff training session immediately after the final whistle.

Since Howard Wilkinson, my equivalent in the Football Development Department in England, was in Rio working for FIFA undertaking their technical study of the competition, I made fairly regular contact with him in an attempt to liaise with regard to observation of training methods and soccer camps. Also working for Walter Gagg, Technical Director of FIFA, was Jean Paul Brigard, a former Swiss international, who is on the coaching staff of FIFA. We took the opportunity to visit, for example, the Zico Soccer School, an hour's drive from Rio.

The facility was first-class, with a large number of small pitches appropriately fenced to accommodate 4-a-side, right up to 9-a-side matches. Significantly, there was only one full-size pitch and, during our visit, it was never in use. It was reassuring to see the work taking place in small-sided game formats, but Howard and I agreed that we saw nothing which was new. Indeed, it appeared quite expensive for the youngsters to be coached there and our opinion of what went on was that it was certainly no better than back home in England and Scotland. Because of my visit to Brazil, I didn't make the trip to Hong Kong which, occasionally at this time of the year I have undertaken.

25 January each year, we celebrate Burns' Supper in Scotland and, since I am a Burns enthusiast, I am often asked to speak on such occasions. I missed out on the year 2000, but in 2001, I returned to visit my friends in Hong Kong and to propose the Immortal Memory at the Hong Kong Football Club Burns' Supper. Over there, the expatriate contingent invariably gives a right royal welcome to visitors from back

home and I am always flattered by the kindness and attention which I receive on such occasions. Hong Kong FC Chairman, Alastair MacLeod, and his wife Debbie, are charming hosts and it is always a pleasure to meet up with Walter Gerrard and Derek Currie, two Scots who became very famous in the Far East because of their football prowess for many years with Hong Kong Rangers. Walter, a former Berwick Rangers centre-half, became known in Hong Kong as 'The Water Buffalo' and gave years of sterling service for his club. Equally, Derek Currie, a fleet-footed tricky winger, was the Hong Kong equivalent of George Best – on the football field, he emphasises!

Walter and Derek, with their wives Barbara and Stella, couldn't be kinder to me when I visit their adopted city and it is amazing when travelling with them how often they are recognised in a population of over eight million people. A visit to the horse racing is a must in Hong Kong and with Derek the chief racing reporter and tipster for the South China Post it is useful to get some insight into what is happening behind the scenes. On one occasion, I met with Philip Robinson and Kevin Darley, two well-known jockeys from the UK, but predictably they were reluctant to offer betting advice. Derek was never so slow but I'm afraid that I did lose, let's say just a few, Hong Kong dollars during my visits to the races.

There is a unique group of men in Hong Kong who meet regularly under the auspices of the Hong Kong Hamilton Accies Supporters' Club. Yes, this really is the name of the club and it is headed by Roger Perrin, a fervent Hamilton Accies fan who is supported in his enthusiasm for the Accies by Dr Frank Lynch. They always have a gentleman's lunch in honour of the Accies when I am there and it is never a teetotal affair. Manager of the Hong Kong Football Club premises is Tony Sealy, who played for a number of teams in England, particularly Tottenham Hotspur. Tony is an accomplished coach who worked with me when I did some coaching sessions for the youngsters in the city. My other contact there is a local gentleman, Ken Ng. Ken is currently Vice-President of the Hong Kong Football Association and previously owned the club, Instant Dict. He recently had one of our staff coaches, Billy Kirkwood, as his Team Manager, until Billy returned home to work as assistant to Mark Hateley at Hull City. He is now assistant manager of St Johnstone FC in Scotland but he, too, has fond memories of his time in Hong Kong.

The months of February and March each year are devoted to preparation for the coach education programme which traditionally runs throughout the spring and summer. In addition there are numerous grass-roots courses and regional development work which is being undertaken by our Community Scheme coaches. My job is to support the various initiatives undertaken by the members of my department and this I try to do to the best of my ability and availability.

Scotland is one of the few countries in Europe to have dedicated awards for coaching youngsters. Tommy Wilson, the former St Mirren Cup winning full-back runs our Children's Licence Diploma Course and Jim Sinclair, a proud winner of three League Championship medals with three different clubs in Scotland, (Queen's Park, Clyde and Hamilton Accies) is in charge of our Youth Licence Programme. We feel it is appropriate that coaches train for the area in which they will operate and that the adult A and B Courses are not specific enough for dealing with younger children.

My attention, obviously, is often distracted because of forthcoming international commitments. My mind was turning towards a team selection for the friendly in March against the worthy World Champions from France. I mentioned earlier an ineligible player, David Johnson, and there was another later when Mark McGhee, successful manager of Millwall, telephoned me to advise me that he thought that Neil Harris, his prolific scorer, had Scottish connections and that he may be worth a look. So I travelled south to watch a Millwall home match against Bournemouth, whose player/coach was Peter Grant, a former Scotland, Celtic and Norwich City midfield player. Whilst Neil Harris did enough in the game to merit a further look, I was hugely impressed by the performance and attitude of AC Bournemouth. In fact, I commented afterwards that it was like watching eleven, or rather ten, outfield Peter Grants. Later that summer, at the coaching course at Inverclyde, Largs I had the opportunity to congratulate Peter and to confirm that he was an excellent A-Licence candidate. Peter is one of the most enthusiastic and likeable players around, and was quick to support me when the incorrect front-page newspaper allegations appeared. In fact, I recall that Peter was my first ever Under-21 team captain in the game against Germany at Ibrox in the autumn of 1986.

Although my researches in Scotland and in England for eligible players sometimes happened to draw blanks there were other successes. But, predictably, they receive less publicity. Guys like Neil Sullivan, Jonathan Gould, Matt Elliott and Don Hutchison were all controversial inclusions when first selected but Don, having headed the winning goal against England at Wembley is now a special national hero!

I am not making excuses, but it was not a full-strength Scottish side which lost to France 0–2. With the exception of Zinedine Zidane, the French had all their stars on display and I did agree with Roger Lemerre before the match that he could strip all 20 players and use 7 substitutes. As long as we were in agreement, the referee saw no objection. This was eminently sensible. I felt that we did very well in the first half, but I received a blow walking in at the interval when Paul Ritchie advised me that he had a stomach strain. I immediately replaced him by Steven Pressley whom I asked to play in the unfamiliar role of left-centre-back in our back three. He took a little time to settle and, during this spell, Sylvain Wiltord scored a fine goal for the visitors. We changed things immediately afterwards to a back four with Steven moving to right-back where he was more comfortable, but we were hit a body blow in the final minute when Thierry Henry scored again for France.

Next we had to play the first of our away friendlies in the magnificent enclosed Vitesse Arnhem Stadium in Holland. Again, some of our players were leg weary at the end of a long demanding season but as usual they dipped into their reserves of energy for Scotland and produced a determined show against the highly talented men from The Netherlands. The Dutch were warming up for the European Championships and were trying new strikers Jimmy Floyd Hasselbaink and Roy MaKaay with Patrick Kluivert on the bench. Frank Rijkaard, a perfect gentleman whom I had met previously on a course in Barcelona where he conducted a fine session with the Barcelona youth team, had at his disposal a wealth of talent. I always find it straightforward to play against the Dutch tactically, even although it involves changing from our normal three-man defence to a back four. I feel that when their wide players and central striker are carefully marked, it allows you a free player at the back. I always tightly mark the man who plays in the hole just off the front, usually Dennis Bergkamp, and Paul Lambert did this job with his usual efficiency. With Edwin Van Der Sar, their goalkeeper, arguably the best distributor of a ball from his position in Europe, our strikers had to be co-ordinated in their defensive duties.

It's all very well to organise our team defensively against them but, frankly, our problem is scoring against Holland! On the last two occasions we have played against them they haven't managed to score – in Euro '96 in Birmingham and in this match in Arnhem – but we, too, have struggled to break the deadlock. However, in this match we had the best chance of all when a great cross from Neil McCann found Don Hutchison. It looked like Wembley all over again, but this time Don's great header hit the woodwork. The 0–0 scoreline, away from home with a depleted squad, against the team which was to fail in the forthcoming European Championships only because of their inability to score with penalty kicks (how I sympathise with Frank Rijkaard), was no disgrace.

Still there were doubters, and it was unfortunate when our

new Chief Executive, David Taylor, was reported to have been quoted as saying that our team was 'boring'. I believe David when he says he was misrepresented, but it did provide quite a bit of journalistic mileage and, having failed to score in our last two matches albeit against top class opposition, it was difficult for me to find any form of redress.

As the number of games played by the top players in the season moved into the fifties and sixties, increased by our play-off matches against England, I asked the lads for one final big effort in our friendly match in Dublin against the Republic of Ireland. Both sides were under strength because of injuries and, although the Irish had Robbie Keane up front to partner Niall Quinn, they were missing the other Keane, Roy, in midfield. Nevertheless, a healthy crowd of 30,213 turned out for this friendly match, not surprising in view of the wonderful success which Mick McCarthy has had since taking over from the legendary Jack Charlton. It was good to see Packie Bonner, another local hero, on the bench as Goalkeeping Coach and to renew acquaintance with Brian Kerr, whose success with the Republic youth teams has been nothing short of phenomenal. There is a great reciprocal respect amongst coaches and it is no secret that I have the highest regard for the achievements of Mick, particularly as he had to slot into the job after Big Jack.

We lost an early goal, a free-kick which was deflected from Craig Burley's outstretched leg past the stranded Neil Sullivan. Thereafter, we played reasonably well and although it was disappointing to hear some boos for Rangers' Neil McCann, everything was played in good spirit. A piece of individual brilliance from Don Hutchison laid on our winner for Barry Ferguson, his first goal for his country. The first had been scored by Don himself, so we earned a 2-1 victory which I genuinely thought flattered us a little. But it was reassuring to get back on the victory trail and to score a couple of goals into the bargain.

I have delayed mentioning my new colleague. I prefer to call him that, rather than 'assistant' – Archie Knox. Archie was a wonderful acquisition to our squad, a specialist in his role. He has been a manager in his own right at Forfar Athletic and Dundee, but has teamed up with Sir Alex Ferguson at Aberdeen and Manchester United and with Walter Smith at Rangers and Everton. Archie, whom I'm sure would make a great manager if he wished, does the back-up job to perfection. Not only is he a fine trainer of footballers, he has a tremendous sense of humour which is infectious and is a vital ingredient towards the development of squad harmony or, as the psychologists call it, group dynamics.

When training at Landsdowne Road for this match, there was the large scoreboard still showing the previous week's result of an Ireland v Scotland rugby international. I can't remember exactly, but I think the board showed something like Ireland 12, Scotland 15. On arrival at the stadium, Archie saw this and said, 'Who said Scotland can't score? Someone should bring David Taylor over here to look at this scoreboard!'. We played a training match on the pitch the morning before the match, and I have to admit that no goals were scored. Again Archie said, 'David's right, it's just as well he didn't see this training session.'

Archie had joined as my choice, when Alex Miller resigned. I have known Archie since I crossed swords with him when he was at Forfar Athletic. In fact, he was the cause of one of my appearances before the SFA Disciplinary Committee because after he abused (that's euphemism for 'kicked') one of my Clyde players, Sean Sweeney, in a game at Forfar I ran on to the pitch during play wearing my club blazer to confront Archie. Before I knew it, I was almost in the centre circle when the referee, Jim Renton of Cowdenbeath, now a good friend, called me over, booked me and asked a police officer to escort me to the stand. I was hardly proud of my actions but Archie had provoked me to the point of irrational behaviour.

Archie was with us on the staff in Mexico and I knew him then but, most importantly, I had worked with him for years on the staff at the SFA coaching courses at Largs. That he was the man for the job was even confirmed by a pal, Alex McLeish, the Hibs manager who left a message on my voicemail when Archie's appointment was announced saying that he felt it was a brilliant piece of business on my part. I have absolutely no regrets and I hope Archie feels likewise.

Anyway, in his third game with me we did manage to score and we did manage to record a victory. No goals against France and Holland was hardly disastrous, but it would have been easy to acquire a pessimistic outlook. It is well known, though, that that is not my style.

I said that I suffered withdrawal symptoms because, having been to five major tournaments on the staff with Scotland, and several at youth and Under-21 level, it was not pleasant to look from the outside at the countries competing in the Euro 2000 Championship. Fortunately, though, I had an interest because again I was invited by Radio 5 Live to be a co-commentator on, I think, 19 matches, including the final and semi-final. In addition, Paul Newman, Sports Editor of the Independent newspaper, asked me if I would write some copy every three days or so. I found both roles very interesting and most worthwhile in my endeavour to keep abreast of the tactical developments in the game.

In addition to trying to extend my own knowledge, we also had a group from the SFA delegated to analyse training and matches as part of their UEFA Pro-Licence Award. The second group in Scotland was under the direction of my colleague in the Football Development Department, Frank Coulston, the coaches were in pairs and delegated to report on the strategy and tactics of selected matches. The group included men like Jim Duffy (Dundee), Jimmy Nicholl and John Ritchie (Dunfermline Athletic), Sandy Clark, Billy Kirkwood (St Johnstone), Davie Moyes (Everton), Steve Kean (Fulham), Tom Hendrie, Maurice Malpas (Dundee United), Ernie Merrick (Australia), Willie McStay (Celtic), Peter Houston (Hearts), Jim Griffin, Tommy Moeller Neilsen

(Denmark) and Butch Lauffer (USA). We also had superb contacts to assist in the task, men like Andy Roxburgh, Gerard Houllier, Roy Hodgson, Berti Vogts and Josef Venglos, who were members of the UEFA Technical Study Group. It's fair to say that, sometimes, more can be learned when not with your own team. I was in a position to visit many matches and talk with coaches from other countries, both participating and, like ourselves, on the fringe of things. For example, I had the opportunity to sit beside Morten Olsen and Michael Laudrup, the new Danish management team who would be taking over from Bo Johanssen, at the match involving Denmark and the Czech Republic. Our own 5 Live commentary team apart, the media hotels in which I was staying had people like Terry Venables, Alan Hansen, Ron Atkinson and Gary Lineker in residence, so the topic of conversation invariably centred around football.

My principal interest, of course, was to look at one of the host countries, Belgium, our forthcoming opponents in the World Cup qualifying group. I genuinely felt that they were extremely unlucky not to qualify from their group. A couple of goalkeeping errors proved extremely costly, with the one in their final group match against Turkey being catastrophic.

There were Scotsmen involved, and I was privileged to meet up with most of them. Men like David Will, Vice-President of FIFA, who gave a superb address prior to the tournament regarding refereeing matters; Ernie Walker, Chairman of the Stadia Committee; Andy Roxburgh, of course; Brian Hendry, our multimedia expert working then for UEFA; Hugh Dallas, our top referee; and David Findlay of the SFA who was Venue Director of Charleroi where England had to play important matches. A large contingent of the Scottish media was out in force, and some of our Anglos – Paddy Barclay, Hugh McIlvanney and Phil Shaw, whom I regard as an honorary Scot. It was a footballing Who's Who.

What intrigued me most about the European Championships was that the two countries which, in my opinion, had the best team spirit competed in the final. I'm not suggesting that they didn't also have the best players, but I watched, with great interest, the group dynamics in every team. For example, in their match against Belgium on 14 June, the Italian coach, Dino Zoff, made a controversial selection decision, leaving out Allesandro Del Piero and replacing him by Francesco Totti. When Italy's first goal was scored early in the match, it was a glancing header by Totti. Who was first to jump punching the air from the Italian bench? Yes, Allesandro Del Piero. This, to me, was very revealing, as was the manner in which the Italian team linked arms over each other's shoulders during penalty-kick deciders. There clearly was excellent harmony and camaraderie in that camp.

The same could be said for the French, the world's most highly-talented squad, who looked every inch like a club side in perfect harmony. It's always my philosophy to look at attitudes and body language of players, particularly when substituted, so, for me, this Championship was a revealing study.

On the debit side, there were instances like the Kerimoglu Tuguy substitution. His coach, correctly in my opinion, sent him home after a blatant display of petulance. The Portuguese attitude when Abel Xavier handled the ball on the line to concede a penalty kick against France was completely indisciplined and told me much about the character of their squad.

25

No Korea/Japan?

I HAVE ALLUDED TO the importance of the dates' meeting involving the countries competing in each World Cup qualifying group. For the first time in many years, we had been drawn in a five team group meaning that we would have to play eight matches. This should have made things much more straightforward, but our delegation was in for quite a shock.

Bryan Gunn, the Scotland goalkeeper in my first match in temporary charge of the team against Italy in September 1993, is now the Commercial Manager of Norwich City FC. He had invited me to propose the Immortal Memory toast at the combined Burns' Supper of his Football Club and the Norfolk Caledonian Society. The venue was the impressive restaurant at the Carrow Road football ground.

I was delighted to accept, particularly because I knew the management team of Bruce Rioch and Bryan Hamilton very well and therefore would be assured of a fine welcome. Everything was comfortably in place for me to make my evening trip to Norwich, and return the following morning using the direct Edinburgh to Norwich flight route. However, when the timing of the dates' meeting involving the five countries was established, it happened to be the morning immediately following the Burns' Supper in Norwich. I telephoned Bryan Gunn to explain my problem and to apologise for the fact that I'd be unable to attend because, quite obviously, my work had to come first.

Bryan expressed his disappointment and reluctantly accepted what I had to say. Imagine my surprise, though, when an hour later he telephoned me with the offer that, if I kept my commitment to speak, Delia Smith's private plane would fly me the next morning to Brussels. Naturally, I was a bit surprised but Bryan was insistent, so I accepted his kind offer.

The Burns' Supper was a most convivial affair, during which we enjoyed a spectacular entrance of the haggis. With the playing pitch in darkness, a spotlight was the focussed on the centre circle. Just prior to the start of proceedings, we saw a kilted gentleman with bagpipes followed by another also in the kilt wearing a chef's hat. Following the piper was Bryan Gunn himself proudly carrying the haggis from the centre circle in dramatic fashion into the stand and up to the restaurant area. It was a novel way of piping in the haggis but one appreciated by the entire company.

My great privilege throughout the evening was to sit beside Delia Smith, Director and major shareholder of the club, and her husband Michael. I found them to be extremely charming hosts who could not have been kinder to me.

The following morning, Delia's driver picked me up and ran me to the airport where I was transported in style in her magnificent private plane to Brussels. We departed at 7.00am and at 7.50am I was in a taxi to the King Baudouin Stadium in Brussels, the home of the Belgian Football Federation. I am pleased to say that I arrived well in advance of my colleagues, President Jack McGinn, and Chief Executive, David Taylor.

The surprise I had was that, in spite of there being only eight matches for each team to arrange, it became quite awkward, mainly because of the obstinacy of the delegates from San Marino. What astonished me was that the country likely to gain least points was the most difficult when it came to agreeing match dates. Some countries have different motives at such meetings and, in San Marino's case, it was to have a fixture schedule geared to obtain maximum income from attendances and TV revenue. With our large travelling support we were a prime target for their most favoured date. They had to build an extra temporary stand for the famous Tartan Army and this would not be ready in the early part of the campaign. Anyway, after a somewhat fraught day we were not displeased with the schedule, particularly as we like to begin away from home, against potential major rivals. At that point, I identified Croatia and Belgium as our principal competitors, the latter being a well organised, functional outfit under the direction of Robert Waseige, whereas Croatia had undoubted flair with the vastly experienced Miroslav Blazevic in charge.

I loved my work with the national team, especially since the response from the players was so enthusiastic. At school, I learned that enthusiasm is a word derived from the Greek, meaning 'to be inspired by God'. I've always associated it with success. Everyone has enthusiasm for something at some time in his life, and sporting history confirms that people who maintain it long enough achieve their goals. At the start of this campaign I had great enthusiasm for the task in hand – qualification for the World Cup in Japan/Korea in 2002.

I referred to the co-operation from the players and I can think of numerous examples where narrow victories would have been narrow defeats had the practice from the training ground and information from team meetings not been adhered to. A perfect example was in our previous visit to Riga when John Collins opened the scoring with a well rehearsed free-kick. I suspected that our opening game away from home against Latvia would be equally tricky and that we would have to be extremely vigilant. A home friendly match against Finland had been arranged by Latvia and I went to see a fine performance from the home team coached by Englishman Gary Johnson. With Finland in England's group, I was surprised no one from the England camp was at the match, but he would have learned little in any case because Finland played poorly and Latvia signalled a warning to me that they would be no pushover in Riga on 2nd September.

The opening game of the previous campaign had been in Lithuania; this time we had to travel to the neighbouring Latvia. Having competed against the Latvians in an earlier campaign, I was very familiar with the situation in Riga but delighted to see that they had moved to the newly-built stadium. It had a unique surface, a composition of artificial and natural grass which, when we arrived, was extremely dry causing the ball to be much more lively than usual.

As well as the new stadium, they had a new manager, Gary Johnson. Gary had come from being the Youth Coach at Watford and was highly recommended as the man to change the fortunes of a country which, in view of the relative success of club side Skonto Riga, could be considered an awkward opening fixture.

I had been to see the victory over Finland and, as usual when in Latvia, was very warmly received by the General Secretary, Janis Mezeckis. It was no secret that Latvia, under new management, fancied themselves against us and, for them, a large crowd of 9,200 turned up in the Skonto Stadium.

Our team was as near full strength as I could get, with the exception of the injured Paul Lambert. I decided to spring a surprise and play Matt Elliott up front along with Billy Dodds. This was because Don Hutchison was required in midfield to compensate for the absence of Paul. After every international I have a post mortem, usually on my own, but often with my colleague Archie Knox, and/or with some well-informed coaching colleagues. Exchanges are frank and I've got to say that, on the whole, on very few occasions do I think that things could have been done differently. As everyone knows, the hindsight 11 is the easiest one to select and it is simple and straightforward to make substitutions after a match. On this occasion, I must admit that my instructions could be considered to have been wrong.

I'm not, however, admitting that Matt Elliott's role up front was a mistake; rather I must confess to faulty instructions to the back three defenders. I knew that at any given time in the game, one of the Latvian strikers would drop off to supplement their midfield. I therefore instructed David Weir and Christian Dailly not to be sucked in out of the defensive structure, thus allowing the lively Latvian strikers Marian Pahars and Andrejs Stolcers to go into midfield unchallenged. I felt that they were trying to pull us out of position at the back in an attempt to exploit the space vacated. Because we had Neil McCann available, we were playing a 3-4-3 formation. When a Latvian striker dropped into midfield, it gave them an extra player and for spells in the first half their ball retention in that area was very good. Barry Ferguson and Don Hutchison, our central midfield pair, were being outnumbered but at no time did the home team manage to get in behind us. As a result of the midfield stranglehold which Latvia maintained, the service to Matt Elliott was non-existent. I had hoped that Neil McCann could be successful against Yury Laizens, the right-back opposition, but it did not work out that way.

Half-time changes were urgently needed. Many things flooded into my mind, but I remembered the words of Bobby Robson: 'A coach must be proactive!' We made significant changes at the interval, including returning Matt Elliott to a central defensive position, replacing Callum Davidson with Colin Cameron, and bringing on Gary Naysmith for David Weir who was suffering from an ankle injury. Tactically, too, I instructed Neil McCann to go up front to form the twin striking partnership with Billy Dodds. But the most significant piece of advice was that if either Latvian striker dropped off, he had to be pursued and carefully challenged by his marker. In this vital second half, we were well on top but it was not until minutes from the end that a fine bit of play by Don

Hutchison enabled Neil McCann to score the winning goal. To run the clock down I put on Gary Holt for Billy Dodds, and we survived the testing 90 minutes to depart with three vital qualification points. I felt sorry for Latvia, and Gary Johnson in particular, but I'm afraid that sentiment shouldn't come into highly competitive football matches. We departed confident that our next match in San Marino a month later would yield another three points.

The second fixture in the double-header, following the game with San Marino, was a visit to Croatia. This meant that I had to take a larger-than-normal squad of players for two away matches. Aware of the danger of injury and possible suspension, we left Scotland with 22 players. An interesting addition was Paul Dickov, the Manchester City striker, who had been doing well at Maine Road and who had been in my mind when we went to the play-off match at Wembley, but a telephone call to Willie Donnachie, the coach at City, confirmed that he was unfit.

As we were waiting for luggage at Rimini Airport it became apparent to me that the journalists were gathering in small groups and seemed to be fairly animated about something which, at the time, I was unaware of. It didn't take long for the reason for the huddles to transpire. In our previous match in Latvia, goalkeeper Jim Leighton had been invited by Radio 5 to do summary work for them and, when I was aware that he had time on his hands during the day I asked him if he would like to work with the young goalkeepers in our Under-21 squad. Alex Smith, Maurice Malpas and Goalkeeping Coach, Jim Stewart, welcomed Jim's help in the training of the young goalkeepers. He was popular with the players and I'm sure they benefited from his experience. Consequently, when I was selecting the squads for the matches in San Marino and Croatia, I was aware that since San Marino had no Under-21 team, our young players would have an excellent opportunity for additional training and what the psychologists call 'bonding'. This made me think that, because of the fine contribution made by Jim on the previous trip, he would be a useful addition to our backroom staff. After clearing his inclusion, on a one off basis, with his manager Ebbe Skovdahl, I contacted Jim and he was, again, happy to co-operate.

The fact that he had, in the eyes of some people, walked out on Scotland after the game against Estonia at Tynecastle in October 1998, meant that quite a number of the journalists thought he should be banned for ever from becoming involved with his country. I'd explained earlier my feelings about his premature retirement and I certainly was in no mood to hold that against him when I felt that his expertise could be of assistance to our keepers. However, the sight of Jim Leighton in his Scotland blazer and flannels did cause quite a stir and I was called upon to justify his inclusion.

But that was the tip of the iceberg. Jim was also bringing out his autobiography. He confirmed that the serialisation by a Sunday newspaper would not involve anything to do with the national team while we were involved in qualifying matches. His appearance with the group was the catalyst, I think, for the paper concerned to rescind that agreement with Jim. The editor sent me a fax and 'apologised', but it became common knowledge that the serialisation would imply criticism of Goalkeeping Coach, Alan Hodgkinson, and me. I was unconcerned because the truth is the truth and I knew that my dealings with Jim had always been very much upfront and, in fact, I considered myself to be hugely supportive of him. Although Jim reassured me that there was nothing critical about me in the text, I felt that, all things considered, it was better to ask Jim to step down from his duties with the Under-21 squad and work, if he so wished, for BBC Radio 5 Live. Our Chief Executive, David Taylor, and I spoke with Jim and explained the situation. He was fully understanding and accepted the fact that it would be wise for him to dissociate himself from the coaching role which had been offered to him.

When I returned from Croatia, I received a letter from Jim Leighton which I hope he won't mind me quoting. He started by saying, 'I don't know how to begin to apologise to you about last week ...' He went on to say, 'I feel responsible for loading the bullets for the media ... I sincerely apologise for any embarrassment caused to you.' There is no doubt that it must have taken a lot of courage to write such an honest letter. I totally accepted Jim's apology and bear absolutely no grudge against him.

Things settled down within 48 hours and we were soon ready for the match at the Stadio Olimpico, Serravalle. As predicted, San Marino had, for them, a huge crowd of 4,377 in attendance and we had Kevin Gallacher as Captain to acknowledge his fiftieth appearance for Scotland.

As is often the case against San Marino, it was an awkward match. I felt that our play was of a high standard but, as has happened in the past, we couldn't score the vital opening goal. Injuries to Christian Dailly, who received a horrendous facial knock requiring numerous stitches, and to Neil McCann's ankle in the first half, didn't help matters.

My decision to play Matt Elliott up front had received quite a bit of criticism in the previous match in Latvia but, early in the second half, I moved Matt forward in this game when there was more of a supply of ammunition for the strikers. It was much to our relief that, in 71 minutes, Matt headed the opening goal and, a couple of minutes later, Don Hutchison made things secure with a fine second goal. Amazingly, it was reported that Matt Elliott should have been moved up front earlier. This was quite surprising as the decision to play him as a striker in the previous match had been roundly criticised.

We were not at full strength because of a long-term injury to Paul Lambert; Barry Ferguson was also unfit, and Craig Burley was recovering from a leg knock. Craig had phoned me to indicate that he hoped to be able to join us for the match the following Wednesday in Zagreb and, with an injury list from the San Marino match, I was very pleased to receive the call from the Burley mobile phone. Substitutes Allan Johnston and

Paul Dickov had certainly staked a claim for inclusion from the start in Croatia and I was determined to bring back the experience of Tom Boyd for this testing encounter.

We remained overnight in Rimini before flying the next day, somewhat depleted, to Zagreb. Christian Dailly, Neil McCann and Jackie McNamara all had to return to their clubs suffering from injuries. To compensate, Craig Burley joined the group.

It's always important to know what's happening in the opposing camp, so as soon as I arrived in our hotel in Zagreb I heard that Croatia had arranged a friendly match against a club side on the outskirts of the city. Archie Knox and I decided to ask for transport to watch this match and, since we met Executive Travel Club Member and loyal supporter, John Murray, in the hotel foyer, we invited him to fill the unused seat in our vehicle. It was an interesting experience for the three of us, because we saw a full strength Croatian side play conscientiously on a shocking pitch against a moderate club side. The player who interested me most was Igor Biscan because my former colleague, Alex Miller, had told me that he had signed for Liverpool in a £7 million deal just prior to the international. When I looked at the players in the Croatian team, I realised that there was a great deal of experience in their squad and that they would be extremely difficult opponents. Names like Jarni, Stimac, Simic, Prosinecki, Balaban, the Kovac brothers and, of course, Alen Boksic, the Middlesbrough striker, who at that time was reputed to be the highest-paid player in the Premiership. These were our opponents. When you add that they had the wily old fox, Miroslav Blasovic in charge, it must be agreed that it became a daunting prospect, particularly with Dailly, McCann and MacNamara unavailable after San Marino, Billy Dodds returning home and Paul Lambert and Barry Ferguson at home still recovering from injury.

While we were training at the stadium the day before the match, I had a joke or two with Tommy Boyd who was telling me about the difficulties Celtic had when they came to play a European tie a couple of years previously against Croatia Zagreb. It was hardly very reassuring to hear that Celtic were really put through the mill in this same stadium.

It became apparent while we were resident in the city that our large travelling support, who had been so enthusiastic and noisy in San Marino, had made their way, very resourcefully, to Zagreb. My son John and his usual Prestwick Tartan Army comrades Steven Pollock and Colin Ross made the trip round the Adriatic Coast via Venice (stopping long enough for a cornetto) and Slovenia. On arrival, John and Colin were giving 'Pollock Travel' some serious stick about his planning of the 12-hour, very uncomfortable train journey. In reply, Steven could only respond that 'It was only half an inch on my old school atlas!'

The good humour and spirit of adventure with which the troops of the Tartan Army go about their travels will never cease to amaze me and fill me with national pride.

As has often been the case recently, our striking positions were the main areas of contention in the team. Billy Dodds had informed me, some months in advance of the fixture, that his wife was expecting a baby and I had agreed that, if he would come to San Marino and the baby was due while we were in Croatia, it would be OK for him to return home. So, in addition to the players who were injured and unavailable, Billy took a flight back to Scotland leaving us a little depleted up front. This prompted me to try the Gallacher/Hutchison partnership which I knew would provide plenty of energy and no little craft. I introduced Allan Johnston from the start and was happy with our central midfield involving Craig Burley and Colin Cameron.

Croatia started at breakneck speed and it looked as though the writing was on the wall when Boksic confirmed why he is so highly rated with a magnificent goal after only fifteen minutes. Eight minutes later, we got one back after some tenacious and skilful play by Colin Cameron. He released the ball into the path of Kevin Gallacher who made no mistake from a well-timed run into the box to meet Colin's inch-perfect pass. Although Robert Prosineski hit the post, we had great chances to score the winner but, unfortunately, Colin Hendry headed wide from a good position and, after a flowing move, Don Hutchison's 16-yard shot went narrowly past.

I've got to hold my hand up and admit that I was in trouble in this match. I always pride myself on Scotland's good disciplinary record which has helped to get, in the past, an additional club into the UEFA Cup. On this occasion, there were some very dubious decisions in my opinion from the standside linesman, and the fourth official was extremely officious. Many overlook the ruling that only one coach can stand to give instructions, but this gentleman was insistent that either Archie Knox or I stood, not both of us. This meant that I was on my feet in front of Archie and I still contend that I was sent to the stand by referee Gilles Veissiere from France because Archie Knox is a superb ventriloquist! One thing is certain – at no time did I use foul language to any official. I did complain, as did Archie, about some of the decisions, and I think I was identified as the sole culprit because I was the one who was on his feet when some of the comments were heard by the official. It is true that we did complain about the decisions but we did so without either abuse or malice. After one tackle in which I thought that our substitute Paul Dickov was badly scythed from behind and the offender, Stimac, received neither a yellow card nor a warning, I protested and this was the end for me. I was dismissed to the stand where, standing at the side of the press area in the company of David Findlay and Dr John MacLean, I had an excellent view of the final half-hour of the match.

It's interesting to note the points that people make to you after a game. I was asked why I had substituted our substitute! The truth is that I had put Paul Dickov on for Allan Johnston at the interval and, in an attempt to run down the clock, he had been replaced a minute from time. This came about because Dr

John MacLean was dashing up and down to the dug-out with advice to Archie and the message to Archie was to take off the 'further away' striker towards the end of the match. It just so happened, at the time of the substitution, Paul Dickov was further away than the other striker, Kevin Gallacher. Paul has known me for years and was aware that this was no reflection whatsoever on the excellent effort which he had produced during his spell in action in the second half. One point in Croatia was a satisfactory conclusion to the match, but of more importance, was the fact that Croatia had dropped two home points against one of their major rivals, Scotland.

I referred earlier to my search for players eligible to play for Scotland. I think we have unearthed another star in the making, Dominic Matteo, although his credentials could hardly be in question because he was born in Dumfries. He was first brought to my attention many years ago by Paul Dalglish, Kenny's son, who was his pal in the early days at Liverpool. I'd assumed, after hearing that he had been around some England youth squads, that he was committed south of the border. I was delighted, though, when my more recent researches revealed that he still was eligible to play for Scotland because he hadn't turned out in a competitive match for England. As Dominic was athletic, powerful and naturally left-sided, he was of great interest to me, and his expensive transfer from Liverpool to Leeds heightened his profile because he went straight into a Leeds side which was doing extremely well in domestic fixtures and in the Champions' League.

Our friendly with Australia on 15 November was an ideal opportunity to introduce Dominic to the Scottish scene. The unfortunate aspect about his home début was that he had played two difficult away matches earlier in the week, one in the San Siro Stadium where he had headed the winner against AC Milan, and the other on the Sunday against Chelsea at Stamford Bridge. It was a bit much to ask him to play three games in a week but I was so determined to make him feel wanted, and to see him in action, that I selected him for the friendly match against the improving antipodeans. It was asking a great deal of him to run the left side on his own after such an arduous week, but he did well and reaffirmed that he will be a very valuable acquisition to our squad. For smaller footballing nations like ours, versatility is important and the fact that Dominic can play in several positions will, I am sure, be useful to us in the future. We have already seen the use of Tom Boyd, Christian Dailly and Craig Burley, in particular, in a variety of roles. Nations with bigger populations usually find themselves able to recruit specialists for each position but we have more juggling to do because of our lack of resources.

The attendance for a friendly match was exceptionally good, 30,985, but our performance was mediocre. I did experiment a little and, in a competitive situation, would more than likely have replaced Dominic Matteo who was exhausted in the last half-hour. I didn't want to do so in a friendly international and in his first game as it would hardly have been motivational for him. In addition, I played Billy Dodds for 90 minutes because he hadn't been featuring for Rangers and I wanted to give him a full match. The experimentation continued at the back where regulars Matt Elliott and Colin Hendry remained on the bench at the start.

The Australians were very much up for this match and scored a fine early goal through Emerton, the Feyenoord winger. Even although we brought on four substitutes – Matt Elliott, Colin Hendry, Neil McCann and Paul Dickov – we failed to stamp any authority on the match and Zdrilic completed the scoring with a softly-conceded goal from our point of view, a looping header which floated over Jonathan Gould into our net. Whilst we like to win all matches, friendlies included, it was not the end of the world because we were still in a good position in our qualifying group.

One brighter aspect of the evening was the small ceremony which took place prior to the kick-off. Our first batch of successful UEFA Pro-Licence coaches received their certificates from SFA President, Mr Jack McGinn. These coaches included Roy Aitken, Eric Black, Jimmy Bone, Tommy Burns, Dick Campbell, Jim Clark, Neale Cooper, Tommy Craig, Jim Fallon, Jim Fleeting, Archie Knox, Murdo MacLeod, Ross Mathie, Gerry McCabe, Kenny McDowall, Alex McLeish, Iain Munro, Donald Park, Jocky Scott, Jim Sinclair, Alex Smith, Walter Smith, Billy Stark, Paul Sturrock, Bobby Williamson and Andy Watson. Invited guests included three men who were very influential at the inception of coaching courses in Scotland – Roy Small, former SFA Youth Team coach from the Scottish School of Physical Education; John Hagart, former assistant manager of Rangers and manager of Hearts and Falkirk who assisted Ally McLeod in Argentina in 1978; and Bobby Seith, former Burnley and Dundee player whose contribution to our courses was publicly praised in Sir Alex Ferguson's autobiography. I felt it appropriate to acknowledge the superb contribution made over the years by these classy colleagues and they were joined, at the last minute, by Robert Waseige, my Belgian counterpart, who had come over to do a spying mission on us. Although I visited only briefly prior to the match, it was obvious that whenever coaches get together the atmosphere is most convivial.

I was disappointed to hear soon after this that the Belgian coach, Robert Waseige, had been admitted to hospital for heart surgery. He's always been a perfect gentleman in my company, so I was quick to send him sincere 'get well' greetings. He did indeed get well, well enough to mastermind a tremendous 10–1 victory over San Marino at the end of February. With goal difference a significant factor in our group, it was a wonderful result for one of our major rivals.

The Champions' League had resumed and I was still doing some commentary work for the ONgoals programme, a superb show dreamt up by Jim 'Jippo' Ramsay, in the company of the effervescent Harry Redknapp. The former West Ham manager was never stuck for words and I found his company engaging as well as informative with regard to what was happening in the English Premiership. His encyclopaedic knowledge of the players, particularly Scottish players south of the border, was of great interest and help to me. When he transferred Rio Ferdinand for £17 million, he was very complimentary about the replacement, one of our players, Christian Dailly.

There were many more than usual charity and fundraising events at this time of the year and, as well as Tartan Army functions, I seemed to find myself all over the place. I went to Banff to give a talk to the Highland Coaches' Association, and a couple of days later was a spectator at the Inverness Caledonian Thistle v Kilmarnock Scottish Cup Tie, followed by attendance at the Highland Tartan Army Annual Dinner. The response from every supporters' group when I visit has been most reassuring and it is comforting to know that the real fans have great goodwill towards, and appreciate the efforts of, our national team.

Interspersed amongst these visits were one or two speaking engagements which I undertake only if there is a personal contact involved or if it is a charitable event which I feel merits support. Such examples include the Strathcarron Hospice function on 26 February and a fundraising event for MacMillan Nurses the following evening in Dumbarton.

On my way to watch Christian Dailly play against Arsenal at Highbury on the Saturday, I spoke at a function for a good friend, Stephan Brearley, whose appearance, rather unkindly, has given him the nickname of 'the flying pig' as goalkeeper for Huddersfield Amateur FC. Then Stenhousemuir FC had a fundraising dinner in Grangemouth and the following week I was off to continue my football education in Portugal to see Porto v Liverpool and to have a chat with Gerard Houllier and Gary McAllister. I was also pleased to get the opportunity to renew acquaintance with Peter Shreeves and Terry Yorath, the management team at Sheffield Wednesday, at their Player of the Year function.

It was becoming time for me to finalise the squad for the

forthcoming double-header against Belgium and San Marino, so I made the trip to Leicester to have a look at Matt Elliott and Callum Davidson in action. It couldn't have been a worse day for the home side who were beaten by a team from a lower league, Wycombe Wanderers, but our two lads did well enough to ensure their selection.

Every game played by Scotland was the most important in my managerial career. This was the case according to sports' journalists. If we were playing an allegedly 'weaker' team, it is important because it would be a real disgrace to lose to one of the minnows and if it was a major competitor it is still 'the most important match in Brown's managerial career'.

Frankly, it would have been hard to refute the importance of the forthcoming home match with Belgium, particularly because everywhere I went in the weeks preceeding the game it was the main topic of conversation. Whether it was a visit to Laurencehill Academy in Alloa, then the Alloa Athletic FC Annual Dinner, Oatlands Nursery School for Red Nose Day or the Kilmarnock v Celtic League Cup Final, everywhere the goodwill was overwhelming.

A week before the match, we had an interesting visitor to our Technical Association and UEFA Pro-Licence Course. Jacques Crevoisier, who had won the European Youth Championship with France and who was employed with UEFA, but now Liverpool FC, came to provide an excellent lecture and demonstration at the Garscube grounds of Glasgow University. We are always on the lookout for coaches who will contribute to, and help, our development here in Scotland and Jacques certainly came into that category. In the afternoon I watched Celtic, on their way to the treble in Scotland, beat Kilmarnock in his company and that of my colleague, Frank Coulston.

With no major injury worries on this occasion, the squad selected was larger than usual and when we met on the Tuesday prior to our Saturday fixture, a group of the players willingly co-operated in a 'Give Racism the Red Card' initiative. Ged Grebby, who runs this organisation, had come to Hampden to launch a new video condemning racism in football. Key members of our squad – Neil Sullivan, Johnathan Gould, Matt Elliott, Colin Hendry and Barry Ferguson – willingly came to join 200 or so youngsters and other players, such as John O'Neil of Hibernian, Rangers' recent signing from Wimbledon, Marcus Gayle, Tony Higgins of the Scottish Professional Footballers' Association and SFA Security Adviser, Willie McDougall. My distinct feeling is that well-publicised events such as this have helped to reduce, and almost eliminate, racism in Scottish and English football. I don't mind repeating the compliment which I regularly give to international players. When requested to give of their time to support worthwhile causes, they are always quick to respond.

Particularly with games of such importance, I find that the time passes very quickly indeed. Our training was efficiently conducted at Ayr United FC and the players were in extremely good heart. We decided to use Tom Boyd on a wide-right midfield position and give Dominic Matteo his competitive début on the left. Billy Dodds had been in and out of the Rangers team, mainly out, during the weeks prior to the match but with Billy what you see is what you get and I have always been delighted to get what Billy can give! That is, 100 per cent endeavour and a real scoring threat.

I couldn't believe it! As is always the case, I travelled with Archie Knox and Alan Hodgkinson to see the Under-21 fixture the night before our game. On the way to East End Park, Dunfermline, I was repeatedly interrupted by telephone calls asking me to confirm a story that I had allowed the players' wives and partners into the hotel that afternoon, on the day prior to the match. There was absolutely no truth in this allegation, which even included the fact that I was insisting that the players be available at 6.00pm for a team talk. At that time, we were driving on our way to the Under-21 fixture. It didn't look too good the next day when the irresistible pun was used about Scotland 'scoring'. Apparently, the arrival of one player's wife and mother-in-law, that of Steven Pressley, to collect tickets for the match, was the catalyst for this totally inaccurate story. It is sometimes hard for anyone to appreciate the number of interruptions which I receive from the media in order to verify a story. Like the major club managers, though, I have found that it is often more expedient for the journalist to run the story and then get a further day's copy from the denial! Since I try to make it a habit to return all calls out of courtesy, this can be extremely time-consuming. We do have an efficient Communications Department with press officers, Andy Mitchell and Catherine Smith, conscientious and diligent, but they know, and I know, that most of the sports journalists want to hear it from the horse's mouth. I remember asking Alex Miller to deputise for me after eight consecutive days at a press conference in St Remy at the World Cup. When Alex appeared at the press centre he was asked, 'Where is he?' When Alex explained that I was having a day off from the press commitments, he was told that I had no right to have a day off!

But whatever our efforts achieved behind the scenes, this did not prevent the players from being in full focus for the important game against Belgium. In spite of some reports indicating that we weren't so hot at home, I had to remind people that in the previous three campaigns we had played 15 qualifying group matches and lost only one, by the single goal to the Czech Republic. Defeats at home to England, France and Australia had been highlighted by the press, when I felt that the accent should have been on the positive. I suppose, though, that that was my job, but often when I quote facts I am accused of referring to statistics. Statistics are facts, though, and not opinions.

When you are in the public eye you expect to be a target, and I must admit it has taken me a long time to realise the extent of recognition which I receive. I feel it's a waste of time and energy hurling back every brickbat that someone directs at me. I've always tried to consider my critics' side whenever they have voiced their disapproval. If I recognise some validity in their comments, I do whatever I can to rectify the problem. But if I feel the criticism is unwarranted, I generally ignore it. This obviously leaves me open to additional attacks but I still feel it is the best way to handle the situation. As I say to the players, let no-one mistake kindness for softness! Anyway, in the context of adverse criticism, I always remember the Chinese proverb:

If everyone thinks well of you
It surely would be wise
To examine each facet of your life
And weed out compromise

Bluntly, you shouldn't try to please everyone!

The next day we drove to Hampden in positive mood. I kept saying to the players that it's their talent which determines what they can do. Their intrinsic motivation determines how much they are willing to do and their attitude determines how well they do it. I don't believe in great passionate speeches, although I think all our players know I am passionate about them and the team in general. Of course, I want them psyched up, but I'd rather have a steely determination than a reckless, uncontrolled assault. Everything must be positive at the kick-off. If it was ours, the ball had to be played forward and we rehearse such kick-off moves. If we are defending the kick-off, I insisted that the opposition should get no more than three passes before they were challenged and our mental attitude started immediately with pressing the ball.

Our start against Belgium was as desired. It was impressive. Our insistence on penetrating teams in our own inside-right position, between their right-footed left-centre-back and left-footed left-back was never more clearly demonstrated than when Craig Burley crossed for Billy Dodds to score our opening goal in the first minute. We continued to dominate and when Colin Hendry's powerful header was making for the net, full-back Eric Deflandre stopped the ball on the Belgian goal-line with his arm. A penalty was the obvious outcome, but I felt that an ordering off was slightly controversial. I seem to be out on a limb here, but my understanding is that if by handling the ball the player prevents a goal from being scored, it should be a sending off. In this case, had Deflandre not handled the ball, it would have hit him on the chest and no goal would have been scored. However, in conversation with top referees, I'm told I am wrong. Not for the first time, I may add!

We did well for the remainder of the half against a resolute ten-man Belgian side. At the interval, I warned the players about complacency and about the danger of playing a depleted side. I even illustrated the fact that, the previous weekend when Chris Sutton was ordered off against Kilmarnock, Celtic scored two goals with ten men against Killie's eleven. No team could have been more emphatically advised at half-time. Still, I didn't, for one minute, expect that Belgium could come back because we were playing extremely well and our ball retention was first-class.

Throughout the second half, I still thought that we were playing well but our defending became deeper and deeper. With nothing to lose, the Belgian coach, Robert Waseige, put on two big fellows, Bob Peeters at the interval and Daniel Van Buyten after 57 minutes. Just before his arrival, we missed a chance when a wonderful flowing attacking move resulted in Barry Ferguson having only the goalkeeper to beat from 12 yards out. His shot was saved but he must be given credit for being in a superb position.

I must admit that I sat calmly in the stand at Hampden during the second half, never too worried about the eventual outcome. FIFA had given me a one-game ban because of my sending-off in Croatia and this meant that I was sitting a few rows from the front in a very good viewing area of the stadium. Communication to Archie in the dug-out was easy, either by using one of the substitute players or one of my additional staff colleagues. There was no need for any walkie-talkie type contact because this would have been more bother than it was worth when signals, or even a loud shout, would suffice!

Even when Marc Wilmots scored for Belgium after 57 minutes, I still had the feeling that we were in a comfortable position with each player playing his part. Normally, I would try to waste time using substitutes but Archie and I agreed that we felt that every player was playing well and it would be foolish to disturb a settled side and formation. It's true that I normally 'run the clock down', and try deliberately to break up the play when we are ahead towards the end of a match. On reflection, it's easy to say that I should have used more than one substitute, Kevin Gallacher, but had I done so, and then lost an equalising goal, there would have been self-recrimination for upsetting the apple cart. Don't imagine for a minute that all these thoughts didn't go through my head, as they have done on numerous occasions in big matches before.

When Daniel Van Buyten scored in injury time to equalise for Belgium, the vast majority of spectators in the stadium felt as I did, that it was like a defeat. Having been in a seemingly unassailable position, with the opposition reduced to ten men, it should have been an automatic three points for Scotland. All credit to my Belgian counterpart Robert Waseige for his inspired substitutions and for ensuring that his players played like men possessed. I could not point the finger at any individual in our side because, having had time to analyse the match on video, we did perform exceptionally well throughout but conceded ground towards the end and lost two bad goals.

Not unexpectedly, I was blamed for the result. It is seldom a case of simply giving the opposition credit for having some excellent players and producing a fine performance. I was accused of blaming the very efficient Hampden ballboys when I pointed out that the actual playing time in the match was around 64 minutes, whereas normally this is between 56 and 60 minutes. I did say that our ballboys were very honest, but at no time did I 'blame' them for that. My suggestion was that, being reduced to ten men, gave, as often is the case, the depleted side extra energy and incentive. This was distorted into blaming the referee for ordering off Eric Deflandre. The blunt truth is that it was a drawn game between two evenly matched teams and, given the advantage we deservedly obtained at the outset, we should never have conceded two points.

Next to feature in this double-header was the game against San Marino, again at our national stadium. With a draw against Belgium feeling like a defeat, there was a bit of picking up to do but, as soon as the training session started on Sunday, I knew that this would not be too difficult. The goal avalanche by Belgium, when they scored ten against San Marino, had been set as a target, but I knew that this was quite unrealistic. It was to be Colin Hendry's fifty-first cap for the country he had served so well over the past seven years.

The comfortable victory, the good play and the three points were all completely overshadowed by one distasteful incident towards the end. Colin Hendry, who had scored two quite magnificent goals in the twenty-first and thirty-second minute, came up for a corner kick in the dying seconds. Everyone knows that 'blocking' is part and parcel of the game at the top level these days, but manhandling is universally deplored. Indeed, FIFA had recently issued a directive to referees regarding shirt-pulling and the holding of opponents. Each time Colin had gone forward he was not only being blocked but being manhandled forcefully. It happened yet again when substitute Nicola Albani ran all the way from the half-way line to defend the corner by holding Colin's jersey. This resulted in Colin trying to free himself rather aggressively. Everyone, including Colin himself, now appreciates that what he did was wrong. But I maintained that there were mitigating circumstances.

I was accused of 'defending the indefensible'. This was a rather harsh description of my reaction. Everyone knows that no manager should make adverse public criticism of any player or member of staff. And don't forget, I was wheeled in to a press conference immediately after a match without having had the benefit of seeing television pictures. My immediate, and stated, reaction was that I expressed great surprise that Colin Hendry would have resorted to such an action. Here was a man with a virtually unblemished record who was being vilified. There had been quite a bit of play-acting from the San Marino team throughout the match so it was difficult to establish, certainly without close-up TV evidence, whether or not it was a genuine injury. I had my doubts at the time, but careful scrutiny of the pictures revealed that Albani had received a blow, but not before he had himself tugged at, and punched, Colin. Medical confidentiality has prevented, even now, an accurate record of extent of the injury but I understand that the player, after spending the night in hospital at the insistence of his team doctor, did manage to go sightseeing the following day in a car provided by the SFA.

I have always felt that there is an anti-hero syndrome in Scotland. When Sandy Lyle won the Open, it was stated that the top Americans didn't turn up that year. Paul Lawrie didn't win the Open, Van de Velde lost it! Here was Colin Hendry, scoring two great goals in his fifty-first appearance for Scotland and, the entire focus was on his provoked indiscretion. It was even suggested to me that there was something in his mind because he didn't celebrate his goals as one would have expected. What was disturbing him, and I knew this prior to the match, was that his wife Denise, and youngsters Rheagan, Kyle, Callum and Niamh, had been robbed in the holiday villa in Portugal which they were sharing with Colin's in-laws. He had received a call during the night to inform him of this and, clearly, was very upset and was questioning whether or not he should be with his family or captaining his country.

During the team meeting prior to the match, I had emphasised to the players that it would be better to take a matter-of fact-approach every time they scored rather than make a great play of choreographed pyrotechnics. When you don't overdo the histrionics, it indicates to everyone that you are expecting, and are used to, success. I didn't want them to waste time and energy celebrating, particularly when we were trying to score as many goals as possible. I always emphasise to the players that they should never taunt their opponents, nor should they let anyone know they are rattled in adversity. The fact that Colin didn't over-react when he scored was a combination, I feel, of responding to instructions and having the family predicament in his mind. This frustration spilled over into the match, particularly the unfortunate incident at the end. Neither the referee nor the FIFA observer reported adversely about the situation. They had the same view as I did. However, television evidence, and the fact that the incident was highlighted by the media, drew FIFA's attention to it and Colin was banned for six matches. I contributed to the letter of appeal and got Brian Hendry to submit television evidence, not only of the Colin incident but of other things which happened during the match. Advice was sought from Heather Barton, the SFA Lawyer, and eventually our Chief Executive, David Taylor, joined Colin's agency representative, John Colquhoun, in a trip to Zurich to present the appeal. The convincing argument produced by David and John resulted in the savage six-game ban being halved. This was more appropriate but it did mean that Colin was destined to miss out on the remaining group matches.

We next played a friendly against Poland in Bydgoszcz. For this match, in the last week in April, we were seriously handicapped because of the vast number of players who, for one reason or another, were unavailable. There was also the controversy of the Chief Executive of the Scottish Premier League, Roger Mitchell, referring to some 'meaningless', (in his opinion) international fixtures. Referring, I think, to matches played by Australia against very weak opposition which they were winning by a barrowload of goals he is reputed to have used the term 'diddy' internationals. I was asked to respond to this but I felt that, although Roger did not take too kindly to us having an international fixture at that time, he did not intend to include Scotland's game in the 'diddy' category. What did annoy me, however, was the fact that a match scheduled between St Mirren and Dundee United was on the Monday prior to our two friendlies in Poland, an Under-21 match on the Tuesday and the full team game on the Wednesday. By arranging this Premier League fixture, it meant that our Under-21 coaching staff, Alex Smith and Maurice Malpas would be unavailable, because they would be required at the League match. In addition, I had hoped to be able to include Charlie Miller in the national team and, had he not been suspended, he would have been required for the vital league fixture. As it happened, Charlie was suspended and, consequently, was able to come with us to make his international début.

In the movie, A Bronx Tale, a father, played by Robert De Niro, tells his son, 'The saddest thing in the world is wasted talent.' I had hoped that, by including Charlie Miller, and a former Dundee United player Andy McLaren, reformed from alcoholism, that I was acknowledging that there was an opportunity for them because, undoubtedly, both were talented players who had lost their way a bit.

Charlie's manager now is Alex Smith. How I admire Alex, a man of real substance! He was asked to play arguably the most important match of the season away from home against St Mirren with his best player, Charlie Miller, suspended and one or two other key men injured. He also was missing out on further experience with the Under-21s. Although Alex actually lost the game to St Mirren, he went on to finish above them in the league and produce a remarkable overall recovery. For this he should be given maximum credit.

Andy McLaren of Kilmarnock is another interesting case. When he was a teenager and youth player he was in the squad which got to the final of the World Youth Championships against Saudi Arabia at Hampden in June 1989 before over 53,000 spectators. Andy progressed well, and not long afterwards he was in our Under-21 squad and appeared to be a player of great potential. However, as they say, 'he lost his way' and ended up being released by Reading.

Such was his alcohol-related behaviour, he could have no complaint. However, after a period of counselling and, I'm sure, some personal soul searching, he got himself going again and I credit Bobby Williamson, the Kilmarnock manager, for giving him another chance. Andy grasped the opportunity with both hands and has played exceptionally well since going to Rugby Park. When it became likely that Andy was going to get his first senior cap against Poland, joker Ally McCoist phoned and quipped, 'If Andy gets a cap, take my picture down from the Hall of Fame!' It's not possible for Ally McCoist to be disparaging, only jocular, so I had no reason to believe that he wished anything other than success for his new team-mate.

Charlie Miller is another of the hugely talented players in Scotland who have not always realised their full potential. Fortunately, there is time yet for Charlie to, as they say in Scotland, 'screw the nut'. As a young Rangers player he was a prodigy, going into the first team along with players like Brian Laudrup and Paul Gascoigne to hold his own at age 17. Whether it was the pressure of the adulation of the vast Rangers following or not, I don't know, but Charlie was eventually picked up by Graham Taylor at Watford. I'm not sure if it's true or false, but I heard the story that, since the Watford players were required to launder their own training gear and bring it with them each day, Charlie's laundry just happened to be next door to a bookmaker's and a pub! The net result – rejection from the English First Division club.

Charlie's return to Scotland was at the shrewd instigation of Alex Smith who had gone to manage Dundee United when the club was in the depths of despair. Alex can certainly get the best out of players so it was no surprise really when Charlie started to display the promise which he had shown all those years ago as a youngster at Ibrox. He was suddenly available because of his suspension, and his form was such that I included him for the friendly match against Poland. Deliberately omitted were Dominic Matteo, who was concluding an important and arduous first season for Leeds; Colin Hendry whose suspension would make him ineligible for the forthcoming qualifying matches; Paul Lambert, who was still struggling with a leg knock; Barry Ferguson; Matt Elliott; Don Hutchison; Paul Dickov; Craig Burley, also injured; and Kevin Gallacher, whom I left out to have a look at younger strikers, Kenny Miller and Scott Booth.

It became obvious when we arrived at the Hilton Hotel in East Kilbride on the Sunday evening that I was badly in need of reinforcements. I had brought in Scott Booth, who was in good form in Holland, and had added Stevie Crawford because of his excellence at Dunfermline Athletic. When Archie Knox and I did a final head count we realised that we would need to supplement the squad still further. I have a mental, and written, list of all possible international candidates. Careful scrutiny of this, and consultation with Archie and Pip Yeates, the Dunfermline physio, prompted me to try to make contact with Barry Nicholson, the young ex-Rangers full-back or midfield player, doing so well at Dunfermline. I was assured that Stevie Crawford would have his number as they were personally friendly. I asked Stevie where I could find Barry and he kindly gave me his number. At least, Stevie thought it was his number! When I phoned Barry he seemed surprised that he was being invited to join the squad, but I reassured him that his manager Jimmy Calderwood had given authority. The voice at the other end of the line said, 'But Jimmy Calderwood is not my manager.' I quickly realised that I was telephoning Barry Wilson, the ex-Ross County winger who had been transferred to Livingston FC. I confirmed this with Stevie Crawford who quickly got me Barry's correct phone number and telephoned Barry Wilson for me to enable us both to apologise.

Anyway, Barry Nicholson did come and we played him from the start in the wide-right position. He performed without any hint of inferiority complex and was one of our better players on the night. To give some indication of the changes from normal, here is the team which lined up against Group 5 leaders, Poland: Sullivan – Boyd, Dailly, and Davidson – Nicholson, C Miller, Rae, Cameron, O'Neil – Dodds and Booth.

To spread the workload, and to be respectful of the wishes of various club managers, I made a rash (I hope not a hash) of substitutions: David Weir for Callum Davidson; Scot Gemmill for John O'Neil; Steve Caldwell for Charlie Miller; Stevie Crawford for Billy Dodds; Andy McLaren for Colin Cameron; and Kenny Miller for Scott Booth. Some of these changes were enforced, but most of them were deliberate.

As I indicated, we were stretched to the limit and this meant that I had to speak to Bobby Williamson and Jim Sinclair, who were in charge of the Under-21 side, for the use of Stephen Caldwell. The Newcastle United youngster came into midfield in the second half and did a fine marking job on the Polish main aerial threat Radoslov Kaluzny, who had come on at the interval for Jacek Zielinski. Unfortunately, Kaluzny had scored with a glancing header before we introduced Steve to mark him, but for the remainder of the second half he was very well policed. Scott Booth took great delight in firing our penalty kick into the roof of the net after a bit of gamesmanship by the then Feyenoord goalkeeper, Jerzy Dudek, now signed by Liverpool. We had another couple of great chances to score the winner but, bearing in mind that we had an experimental team in action, an away draw against Poland was far from unsatisfactory. It meant that we were now unbeaten in our last nine away matches, and when consideration is taken of some of the difficult venues, I think it was a very good achievement. The problem was then to ensure that we made it ten when we got to Brussels on 5 September for the vital World Cup qualifying match against Belgium.

The vital group qualification process was interrupted as usual, during the summer close season break. Whilst my colleagues in the SFA Football Development Department once more bore the burden of our extensive coach education programme, I made my customary contribution to each course; I also took the opportunity to see our remaining opponents in action. I saw Bosko Balaban score a fine goal in Riga to give Croatia a fortunate 1-0 victory in an uninspiring fixture.

In August I had declined the opportunity of a friendly match because a look at the fixture list identified important Champions' League commitments for Glasgow's two big clubs. To obtain the willing release of players right in the middles of Celtic v Ajax and Rangers v Fenerbache was not a prospect I relished. With no match of our own, Archie Knox and I went to Dublin to see the Republic of Ireland play a low-key friendly against our forthcoming opponents Croatia. We had the pleasure of sitting beside Mick McCarthy's wife and daughter at the match, and also the pleasure of confirming why Mick's excellent side was top of its qualifying group. The 2-2 draw flattered Croatia who seemed to be playing in leisurely fashion merely to fulfil the fixture. We knew it would be different in 3 weeks' time in Glasgow.

Having been pleased with the players I brought in for the friendly on 25th April against Poland, there was a temptation to include many in the squad for the important double-header against Croatia and Belgium. I decided, wisely I'm sure, that this was an assignment for experienced guys, but I did invite Barry Nicholsen and Steve Crawford of Dunfermline, along with Scott Booth of Twente Enchede who had performed well in our creditable 1-1 draw in Poland.

Since the start of the season I had watched our players carefully, especially those whom I thought would be in contention for the remaining qualifying games. This took me to Holland to see Scott Booth play well as the lone mainline striker for his club. With youngsters Mark Burchill and Kenny Miller not featuring regularly for their club sides and with

Billy Dodds confined at best to the Rangers' bench, it looked as though my visit to Enchede would be worthwhile. Kevin Gallacher, too, our goalscorer in Zagreb, was to be unfit for the return fixture. To say that we had a striking problem was an understatement.

Furthermore, the Gary McAllister issue reared its head once more. It was reported that I had tried, again through my friend and former colleague Alex Miller, who works at Liverpool FC, to entice Gary back. I had said to Alex in passing that if he found himself talking to Gary he might ask him about a return to the international scene. Indeed, I phoned Gary myself but he reaffirmed his intention to stick to his original decision. Even after I watched him play so well in Monaco in Liverpool's victory over Bayern Munich I spoke to him, but once more he declined in the nicest possible way.

So, no Gary McAllister, no John Collins and no Barry Ferguson (out through injury) meant that our midfield of recent years would have to be reconstructed. Tom Boyd, too, was to be unfit for the Croatia match. Because of the availability of Neil McCann we decided to play a very positive 3-4-3 formation with Neil wide left and Don Hutchison and Scott Booth up front. This was exactly the strategy used in our success against England at Wembley yet some observers were critical. 'Brown got it all wrong' was a typical headline. The fact of the matter was that my counterpart, the Croatian coach, decided that his back three could cope with our front three without much reinforcement. A minor adjustment which brought his wide right midfield player, Vugrinec, back slightly was his only response, when most coaches would have brought about a four man defence against our front three.

After 25 minutes, which Archie and I felt was adequate time for the strategy to have a decent trial, we changed to the normal Scottish house-style of 3-5-2. Still, though, we failed to score and recorded another draw against a fine side which had finished third in the previous World Cup.

So it was off to Brussels with the biggest ever travelling

support, of around 13,000, Scotland has had for a qualification match. Injury doubts over two key players, the existing elimination of Barry Ferguson, Callum Davidson and Kevin Gallagher and suspensions to Colin Hendry and Neil McCann meant that our normal constraints were in place. The injured players concerned were Dominic Matteo and Paul Lambert suffering from ankle and blister trouble respectively. By his own impressive standards Paul had a poor game against Croatia and was criticised. But had those who were complaining seen the raw, tender foot ailments that he suffered there is no way they could possibly have been critical. Here was a player, our Captain, who, rather than come off, played through the pain barrier for his country. How many others would have done the same? How many would have used the blister excuse? I hope that the spirit of Scotland is such that everyone would have done likewise, but I have experienced instances, mainly many years in the past, when players would have 'copped out' at the slightest available opportunity especially against difficult opponents. But this is not Paul's style.

Anyway Paul returned after excellent treatment from our medical staff to have a great game in Brussels. Unfortunately too few of his colleagues could say the same. As a result we lost this vital match with the inevitable recriminations. One was that our team was too old, yet comparison with the very experienced Belgian squad would have revealed similar ages. Young players who had been part of our famous Wembley victory were unavailable through injury or suspension – Barry Ferguson, Callum Davidson (injured), Neil McCann (suspended) and Mark Burchill was not getting match practice. So, as usual, we had to patch up a team from a defeated squad.

The blunt truth is that, not for the want of effort, we did not play well. We lost for the first time in 10 away matches, and for the first time in the qualifying campaign. A palpable penalty claim ignored by the inexperienced replacement referee, Manuel Mejuto Gonzalez from Spain could have cost us a play-off place, but it would be churlish to complain when it was we, ourselves, who dissipated a two goal lead at home against the Belgians.

I still feel that something could have been salvaged in Brussels, but our World Cup aspirations were severely dented in the match at Hampden.

Calls for my head were anticipated and certainly not unexpected. Indeed, I had been 'threatened' with the sack by members of the media prior to the match. Although we could at least get to the play-off stage again, I had decided in my own mind that this campaign was to be my last in charge of the National Team of Scotland. I had hoped that this would have been at the end of a successful stint in Japan so my announcement was necessarily unduly premature. The media people wanted me to make a declaration at the post-match press conference but I insisted that I would be sadly lacking in courtesy were I to fail to discuss the situation with my employers in the first instance and offer to complete the remaining months of my contract. After over 15 years working for good employers it was the least the Executive Committee, and more especially, the President, deserved.

There was unavoidable delay in meeting with Mr McGinn because he had a lengthy meeting already scheduled for the following day after the match and the following day I was off to a UFA Course for Coach Educators, co-incidentally to be held in Zagreb.

One paper couldn't resist what everyone described as a 'dig' or 'cheap shot' by erroneously describing my attendance at the course as if I were to be coaching the Croatians. The pathetic line (meant to be funny?) was that now Croatia would fail too. Fortunately this type of reporting is water off a duck's back to me, but it rather comes across as, at best, desperation for any story or, at worst, irresponsibility.

In Zagreb the course was, as usual, very informative but everything was overshadowed by the news of the horrendous events in America where terrorists had hijacked four aircrafts with subsequent disastrous consequences. Football was put firmly into perspective. Just as Sir Alex Ferguson wrote in his autobiography in the context of his sister-in-law's death from cancer, there are more important things in life than football. This is very true, but when football has been one's life and is one's all-consuming hobby it is sometimes difficult to reconcile the really important matters in life with absorption in the world's most popular sport.

Although there was an air of depression surrounding the course it was good to be in the company of many European football luminaries such as Roger Lemerre (France), Michael Laudrup (Denmark), Rinus Michels (Netherlands), Berti Vogts (Germany), Howard Wilkinson (England), Allan Simonsen (Faroe Islands), Josef Venglos (Slovakia), Lars Arnesson (Sweden), Erich Rutemoller (Germany), Dr. Zdenek Sivek (Czech Republic), Frans Masson and Michel Sablon (Belgium), Gerhard Hitzel (Austria), Paul Phillipp (Luxembourg), Roy Miller (Northern Ireland), Jimmy McDermott (Republic of Ireland), Jean-Paul Brigger (FIFA), Andreas Morisbak (Norway), Mariano Moreno (Spain) and Guido Vantaggiato (Italy), all under the superb direction of Andy Roxburgh, Head of the UEFA Football Development. All colleagues were stunned by the tragic world news but managed to concentrate on the matter in hand – the continuing development of coach education in Europe where, as I've stated already, Scotland marks high in European terms. Of the 51 countries in UEFA only 13 have been granted full recognition to offer the full Pro-Licence Course. So far Scotland has 42 qualified coaches with England now embarking with 12 candidates on their first course, admittedly a resourceful one using the most modern technology available such as the internet and conferencing facilities. There is general acceptance of the need for better coaching provision in England because it was pointed out that none of the young England team which defeated Germany is coached by an English manager at club level. Also, since Howard

Wilkinson's success, no Englishman has managed a team to win the Premiership. Our pride and delight is, of course, that Sir Alex, one of the 'Largs mafia' is the doyen of English, European and World coaching!

Although I have to hold my hand and admit culpability, in spite of mitigating circumstances, for failure to qualify for Japan/Korea 2002, I am proud of our coach education structure in Scotland which, along with improved facilities, will give us a better chance of future success.

26

People, Places and Post Mortems

EVERYONE ASKS ME about Richard Gough and why I never picked him for Scotland. In as dignified a way as possible I shall now discuss the situation. Things have been said by many people concerned except me. There have been statements, biased reports and all kinds of speculative assertions. One of the first things I was asked, and certainly the 'big issue' when I was first appointed as manager of Scotland, was whether or not I would pick Richard after he had refused to play international football for Andy Roxburgh. There were suggestions that loyalty to Andy would stop me from recalling him. Yes, I was loyal to Andy, and I am still loyal to him, but what had happened between him and Richard had little bearing whatsoever on my decision to leave him out of my plans.

Having been a part of the regime that Richard very publicly disowned, I was in the privileged position of having seen the international set-up at close quarters over a number of years. I decided that I must look to the future and that it would not be in the interests of the Scotland team and of my style of management to recall Richard to the side.

Richard had certainly carved a very fine image with the media and the fans and I am aware of his playing performances with Dundee United, with Tottenham and with Rangers, as well as the impression he made during his short playing spell in Kansas City and on his return to England to play at Everton. However, taking all things into consideration, I made the decision not to select him.

My decision did not please Rangers fans, nor certain members of the media, but my thinking was based solely on what I felt was the right choice for Scotland. That was my job, after all. I think the results have vindicated my decision because we have emerged with an excellent defensive trio drawn from four or five very good players.

We used Colin Hendry, for instance, who has been immense in the heart of the defence, and also Colin Calderwood, who has performed extremely well. I believe that Alan McLaren was destined to become a star and quite likely a future Scotland captain, but he has been sidelined by a knee injury that has finished his career. Tommy Boyd has been first class when called upon to play in that area, and the recent emergence of Christian Dailly, Brian O'Neil and Paul Ritchie and Matt Elliot has proved that there is no problem with the Scotland defensive set-up.

I was questioned about Richard Gough fairly non-stop since I was appointed. One of the questions I received came in the form of a letter from a Rangers supporter. I responded, thinking that my reply would be read out to the supporter's friends and fellow Rangers supporters. I did not expect to see it reproduced in a newspaper. I replied factually to the letter without giving any opinion, and simply pointed out the record of Scotland under Andy Roxburgh – both with Gough in the side, and without him. The writer had told me that Gough was indispensable to Rangers and to Scotland. Gough's record with Rangers was, as I emphasised, nothing to do with me. The Scotland record without him spoke for itself.

I would not want to appear to be knocking members of the

media at every given opportunity. On the whole they do a fine job and I know the difficulties they face, having been in their position myself for a time. However, I always wished that they would show a little less favouritism and not get everyone involved in discussing players who have not been selected rather than featuring those who have. There are many players like Tom Boyd who has made 38 consecutive appearances. Players like Tom give everything for their country and yet hardly get a mention, while pages are devoted to players bemoaning the fact that they have not been picked. I was drawn into the conversation and the next day all kinds of quotes and counter-quotes were being flung about, making it appear that the players and the management were at each other's throats, which was rarely the case. I often have cause to kick myself for allowing myself to respond to questions about players who have not been selected rather than championing those who have.

There is very little I can add to what I have already said about the Gough situation.

One well-known Scottish journalist, Jim Rodger – sadly no longer with us – actually met me solely to ask whether I was going to pick Gough or not.

We arranged to meet in the Marriott Hotel in Glasgow, and when I got there Jim was sitting with a cup of tea. I never did see him drink anything stronger. I sat down with him and he said quietly: 'Son, I've known you a long time and you've got a major problem. Your problem is concerning the captain of Rangers.'

Jim highlighted the issue much more than I had – once I have taken a decision I put it behind me and do not become introspective about it. In preparation for our meeting he had written a list of six pluses and six minuses concerning the selection of Richard Gough.

'Take this and have a good look at it, son, and then make up your own mind. It is a very important decision and, whatever you decide, you know I will fully support you. If you need any advice, come to me!'

I still have that piece of paper, and it raised some interesting points about Richard's following among the Rangers supporters and his friends in the press – as well as posing the key question about who could be left out to accommodate him. Those were the plus points, I think. On the minus side, Jim pointed out that the player himself had taken the decision not to play again for his country. It was his firm choice.

That there were six points in both columns was interesting in itself because, to select someone to play for your team, you need to have a weightier argument more in favour than against.

I would not want anyone to get the false impression that I selected a team on the advice of journalists, cab drivers or anyone else. I was obviously not entirely alone in my opinion and, at the end of the day, my view as manager was the one that matters. I am no philosopher, but when you start to get on a little bit in years, you realise that there is no point in worrying about decisions you have made – or indeed games that you have lost. You do your best and there is point in being a martyr to anxiety afterwards. I can assure everyone that I have never lost a moment's sleep over any decision that I've made or a defeat that I've suffered. I would stand or fall by what happened when it happened. I would like to say, though, that while I did not seek advice from Jim Rodger – or Scoop, as he was affectionately known – I have been well advised from time to time by him and other members of the press, and I like to think that I always have a listening ear.

To conclude the Richard Gough affair, earlier in 1998 I attended a Rangers game and found myself sitting in front of Richard. He warmly congratulated me on our qualifying for the World Cup. There was no hint of bitterness or resentment. He assured me that his good wishes were genuine, but I had no need of such assurance – I could see that they were heartfelt.

Earlier this year I again met Richard in the 'Il Castillo' restaurant when he was having a meal with his in-laws.

Pleasant greetings were exchanged much to the surprise of some of the customers. Richard Gough is not the only player who has not been in the frame for a while. I expected loyalty and respect from players, not because of who I am but because of the position I hold in the country they were representing.

David Robertson surprised me when we were waiting for our luggage at the airport carousel after returning from Greece and our European Championship qualifier. Tommy Craig was there as well and will, I know, confirm everything that was said.

I spoke to David and asked him to be patient and said that his turn would come. He had been capped three times but was not, at that stage, a regular in the side. He was only 26 and had a good few years ahead of him. I had taken him to Greece in the squad but had not used him in the game. I reminded him that Andy Goram had remained patient for years before he became first-choice goalkeeper for Scotland. My words were designed to encourage him, but he responded by telling me that he did not really want to be travelling anywhere if he was not going to be in the team.

'Are you really saying that I have to pre-select the team for your benefit?' I asked. David just looked at me and nodded his head. I took the decision there and then that, if he was going to attach conditions to his selection, I was not interested. I know there are many players who would crawl over broken glass to play for their country, and I did not appreciate David's rather negative approach. I'm afraid that situation did not change until David had to retire early through injury. Other players have served us well in that department. I have mentioned Tommy Boyd, but what about Tosh McKinlay? I remember that he left the building site of his new home to travel all the way to the Faroe Islands just to sit on the bench. He never took part in the actual game but he was thrilled to bits at being a part of the Scotland set-up. That is the sort of attitude we wanted in the Scotland camp.

More recently we have had the case of Duncan Ferguson.

Duncan announced that he did not want to play for his country. I have known Duncan for years, and have had him under my management as a youth player right through to senior international level. I even had to send him home from an Under-21 squad once, but I put that down to the impetuosity of youth. If Duncan Ferguson or anyone else decides that he does not want to play for Scotland, I respect this decision. He has made his choice and life goes on without him. After the initial announcement you would think it would become old news, and yet I still got reporters asking me about Duncan Ferguson's situation in my plans for Scotland.

I do not feel the need to dwell on players who do not want to play. My attention was on the players who did want to wear their country's shirt. I believed that we had an excellent squad of players, with guys who really want to play for their country. If I felt that there were those who were just cap-collectors, or have doubts about why they were there, I have to consider seriously their position and, in some cases, eliminate then altogether from my plans. We always had a happy squad of players who really wanted to be there and give of their best for the privilege of playing for their country. Those who have eliminated themselves must live with their actions and decisions.

Ally McCoist is one of the greatest servants ever to pull on a Scotland jersey. He is so popular with everyone, even people who do not like football. He has been a great goalscorer, one of those players you wish could go on for ever because you never get tired of seeing him. He has won award after award for his scoring feats.

Alistair has become more than a top footballer, though – he is a superstar. Who else could get on stage at a Wet, Wet, Wet concert and almost steal the show? His success on A Question of Sport led to him getting his own chat show with Fred McAuley on BBC Scotland, and he is destined to continue being a star long after he has hung up his boots.

McCoist is one of those players that you just love to have

around. In the dressing room he was always full of life and a lot of fun. He played terrible jokes on people but was just as enthusiastic when the joke was turned on him. Never trust him if he is quiet, because you can guarantee he is plotting something, and you could well be his next victim. He is also very quick-witted and never short of a smart reply.

Early in the 1997/98 season, Walter Smith had a go at him for putting on weight. Walter told him that he didn't care how many goals he had scored for Rangers, if he didn't lose weight he would not be considered. He was really angry and was laying into the whole team after an indifferent performance, saving his most scathing attack until the end, when he blasted McCoist. Walter stormed out and slammed the door, but not before he heard McCoist say, 'Where the hell does he think he's going to get a Biafran to score him thirty goals a season?'

Another McCoist story involves the time that Rangers were playing Ajax in a Champions League away match. He was unfit and did not make the journey. Instead he was invited to be one of the commentary team for the television coverage. That morning he was in the treatment room at Ibrox with three of the Rangers apprentices. They were surprised to see him there, having expected him to travel with the team even if he was not playing.

'I'm going to be seeing the game at the television studio,' Ally told them. 'I'm an expert and I'll be giving my opinions. If you look in tonight you'll see me on the screen.'

One of the lads asked him what he would say.

'That depends on the match,' said Ally, who then decided to have a bit of fun with these young lads. 'Why? What do you want me to say?'

They laughed, but Ally pressed them and told them to pick something for him to say, and then go to the pub to watch the TV and make a few pounds by betting on him coming out with those words. The lads decided to take him up on it, and one of them, seeing a pools coupon in the room, said, 'There's one for you, Ally – say the word "coupon".'

'That's not really about football,' protested Ally, but the lad insisted. A second one looked at the diagram of a human body on the wall and told McCoist he must use the word 'tibia'. Not to be outdone, the third one picked the word 'piriformis', which is a muscle around the backside.

Ally squirmed a little, but the lads jibed that he had boasted he could say anything on television so he decided to do his best, but insisted that the boy write 'piriformis' down on a piece of paper which he tore from the Daily Record – or the Daily Ranger, as he likes to call it.

Later, in the studio, the presenter, Dougie Donnelly, asked him how he thought the game would go.

'Well, this is going "tibia" difficult game for Rangers, but if we win it will be a real "coupon"-buster,' said Ally, delighted that he had already managed to squeeze in two of his designated words. The third word was a real struggle, however. Eventually, about halfway through the first half, Rangers were two goals down, Paul Gascoigne had been ordered off, and there was an air of depression around the studio. He was asked for a comment and Ally as usual had the perfect response, 'This is the worst Rangers "piriformis" I've seen all season!'

The McCoist stories and pranks go on and on. The well-known referee Brian McGinlay was caught for what Ally described as having too little blood in his alcohol stream. He had been stopped by the police while driving, and the story made the Evening Times headlines the night before he was due to referee a Rangers' game.

When he turned up at Ibrox he was expecting to have his leg pulled, but no one mentioned the incident. Neither of his assistant referees said anything, and Brian was beginning to think that nobody had seen the newspaper. He went down to the Rangers dressing room to check their boots. (Just to digress a moment, I think that checking the boots is one of the most futile exercises that referees undertake. I remember that at Motherwell we had a player called Harry Hood, who boasted that in the fourteen years of his senior career he had never had his boots inspected. Like many players he was superstitious about his boots being touched by the referee, and he went to extraordinary lengths to avoid it. He would hide them, hide himself, tell the referee he'd already seen them, anything to avoid the inspection.) Anyway, after Brian had looked at a couple of pairs of boots, Ally McCoist piped up and said, 'You had a long walk today, big man, eh?'

That was when the referee realised that his transgressions were indeed common knowledge. If he needed confirmation, it came five minutes after the start of the game. He gave off-side against Mark Hateley, who voiced his disapproval at the decision. McCoist ran over and said, 'Mark, you're wasting your time with him. If he cannae see a big white car with a blue light on top of it, how can he tell if you're off-side?' That is typical of Alistair. There are many tales about him, nearly all true. Ally McCoist is a tremendous player and a great character.

The Shanklys are among the best-known names in British football. Bob Shankly eventually became general manager at Stirling Albion. This is a comparatively new role in football. David Pleat has that position at Tottenham, Billy McNeill was at Hibs and my brother, Jock, was in a similar capacity at Celtic, but it was Stirling Albion who created the role some years ago. In the late seventies, Bob was the man for Stirling.

The team manager was a young guy by the name of Alex Smith, who will be the first to admit that he learned more in his short time with Shankly than in the rest of his career to date. One very good story that Alex told me about his time at Stirling was to do with fitness. The old school of managers like Bill Shankly and his colleagues at Liverpool, Reuben Bennett, Joe Fagan, Bob Paisley and the rest, hated players to be unfit or injured. When they were injured, the players would very often be snubbed, ignored until they were fit again.

Bob Shankly was no different, as I found out during my

time with him. He would take it very badly if a player could not be considered for selection. You would be frightened to tell the manager if you were hurt, let alone venture into the treatment room.

There was a guy called Rab Duffin, a very good inside forward who played for Stirling. He had been out for some time with a shoulder injury, and during one particular evening training session at Annfield, Stirling's ground before they moved to their plush new stadium, there were a number of players participating. Bob Shankly saw Rab Duffin pressing himself against a wall. The player was embarrassed at the general manager seeing him not training with the other players but having his own work-out. Bob grunted something, which was his way if he came across a player not training to the full because of a fitness problem.

'I'm doing exercises, boss,' Rab said, not wishing to appear to be taking it easy. Shankly replied with another grunt of apparent disapproval. Rab tried his best and continued, 'In fact, I feel like Christ.' This was a reference to his exercise, in which his arms and legs were outstretched against the wall.

Shankly's response was both quick and clear. 'Well, son, you might feel like Christ, you might even look like Christ – but Christ was back with us in three days ... you've been out for six weeks!'

That was Alex Smith's favourite Shankly story and I hope I haven't ruined it for him.

One of my own favourites is the time when there was a problem with mice at Dundee. Mouse-traps proved to be useless so Lawrie Smith, our physio, was sent to get a cat. Sure enough the cat took up residence and did a fine job devastating the Dundee mouse population. However, the cat was a bit lazy and used to love to curl up in the boot room where it was always warm.

One morning Alex Hamilton came in early, probably because he had not been home from the night before. He went to the boot room and there was the cat snoring across his boots. Very gently Alex put his toe under the cat and flicked it a little way into the air so that it landed safely on all four feet. He did not realise that Bob Shankly was standing in the doorway behind him.

'Hammy,' said Shankly, 'when you've done as much for this club as that cat, then you can put your boot behind him!' As you can see, the Shanklys' reputation for bluntness and wit is not without foundation.

Talking of Bob Shankly, he had a way of elevating his players to the opposition while keeping them humble within their own company. Just to give you an example, at the start of one of my seasons at Dundee we were having the usual team photograph taken and Bob was organising where everyone was to be in the photo. If you had not re-signed for the season than you could not be in the photo at all. Those that were in could tell how they stood in the manager's estimation by where he positioned them. If you were in the middle you knew that you were in good standing with the manager. I can remember Doug Houston and I were waiting and waiting while he gave thought to where he wanted everyone. Fortunately, we were among those placed early on. It was usually the young lads who were left until last, and Bob would have them positioned at the very ends of the rows with such encouraging words as, 'A pair of scissors'll get rid of you two.'

I learned a lot from Bill Shankly, even though I never played for him. I had copies of the Shankly Tapes, and I used to play them over and over again, listening to every pearl of wisdom that dropped from the great man's lips. I considered that he had everything that a manager should have, and I looked upon him as a wonderful source of management sense.

One of the things Bill Shankly said on those tapes was that the first time a manager walks into the ground and doesn't change into his training kit, the rot has begun to set in. I have always kept that in mind and, when I became a manager, I made sure that I lived by that little gem. I did it as team manager of Scotland. I didn't do anything until I had changed into training kit. Even though some of the training was started by a Philip Yeates warm-up and activities by Alex Miller, or by Archie Knox I was still there directing things.

I have not always seen eye to eye with referees, as I've already explained. I defy anyone in football to say that he has never had a cross word with a referee at some stage in his life. We all know that it is a waste of time because the referee always has the final word and the protection of the authorities – but we still lose our heads from time to time and say our piece.

One referee I fell out with was Donald McVicar from Stonehouse. This was during my days as manager of Clyde. He was a good referee and a very nice chap, and I now see him almost every day as he is in charge of referee development at the SFA. At this particular game I was getting angrier and angrier, and I think he soon realised that I was reaching boiling point because he took the heat out of the situation. At the end of the game, when I was complaining to him, he put his hand on my shoulder and calmly said, 'Craig, the tide goes out and the tide comes in.' It was one of the most pertinent phrases I have ever heard, especially from a referee who could so easily have exacerbated the situation instead of calming it down. I am not allowed to forget it!

John Spencer is one of the game's characters and has proved his worth at all levels. I think one of his favourite goals was one that he would not have scored if I had had the choice. It is a story against myself, but I'll tell it anyway.

We were playing Switzerland away from home in an Under-21 match and I had Spenny on the bench. I told him to prepare himself because we were losing our way a bit. John Watson, our physio, put him through his paces and then told me that he was ready to go. I was just about to send him on when the Swiss conceded a corner kick. I make it a practice not to put a substitute on at such a point – and especially since we had not been practising set pieces with Spenny – so the last thing I wanted was to send him into the game at that moment.

Also, with his lack of height, I did not see much point in taking off a player who might just get his head to the ball and replacing him with Spenny.

The referee took the decision for me and signalled for us to send Spenny on. We were all ready so I couldn't say that I had changed my mind. You can imagine what happened. The corner came over, a fiercely driven ball, straight into the area, and, of course, John Spencer's head was in just the right place at just the right time and he nodded the ball home brilliantly. He had heard me trying to avoid sending him on so, after the game, he delighted in telling everyone about the goal he was not supposed to have scored. I was very pleased that he did, though.

The John Spencer saga does not end there. I don't allow the players to wear baseball caps while on duty, but only if they must, in their own time. Spenny was one of those guys who liked to wear his baseball cap round the wrong way, but he didn't appreciate it when Alan Hodgkinson, our goalkeeping coach, started calling him Norman Wisdom. Personally, I would have thought it was a compliment, but Spenny didn't like it one bit.

When we were staying at Sanary on the Cote d'Azur for the Under-21 tournament in Toulon, we told the lads that if they did well we would take them to the disco in the neighbouring village of Bandol. We kept our word and took them in the team bus. They went into the disco while the backroom staff and I dined in a restaurant nearby. Dr John Maclean went to the disco with them to make sure things were all right. Suddenly, while we were eating, he burst into the restaurant and said, 'Come quickly, you've got to see this!'

We didn't know what to expect, but what we found was John Spencer breakdancing in the middle of the floor with about 1,500 youngsters clapping and cheering him on.

On another occasion we decided to take the Under-21 side to Aix-en-Provence to watch the England Under-21 side play a tournament game against the Russians. We went for a meal in an outdoor café after the game. It was beginning to get a little chilly, especially for the players, who were in their T-shirts. The French coach-driver was in the cafe with us, plying himself with rather more glasses of wine than I would have done had I been driving. He was in no hurry to finish his meal, but we thought we might just impart some sense of urgency by heading for the coach, which was parked some distance away across a park. Andy Roxburgh had flown over to watch one or two of the games and so it was Andy, Tommy Craig and I who took the lead and arrived at the coach first. When we got there we found that it was locked and there was no way we could get in.

We began to chat, and were vaguely aware of the arrival of John Spencer and Alex Rae, the first of the players. Within a moment they were inside the bus and Spenny was sitting in the driving seat. We were amazed because we had tried every possible door.

'How did you get in?' I asked, to which Spenny replied, 'Alex is from Dennistoun!'

Without wishing to cause any offence to residents of that area of Glasgow, there was no need for further explanation. A simple thing like a locked coach door was not going to keep Alex out in the cold. You could always guarantee that Spenny would never be too far from any mischief like that.

A word about Tommy Burns, who was a very fine player in his day, and also a gentleman and a singer. Yes, a singer! To give you some idea of what Tommy is like, I have to go back to two incidents in 1988, when we were playing against England at Wembley. We trained there, and it was the first time I had ever set foot on the pitch. I soon realised why it was so energy-sapping. You really have to put some force into your passing, so your legs are asked to use up much more energy than usual.

We were staying in an hotel in Windsor, and Andy used to like to organise some sort of entertainment for the players. We were having a singsong which had developed into a sort of talent contest. Ally McCoist was the star turn with his rap number – at least, he was until Tommy Burns burst into 'Mack the Knife'. He brought the house down and showed that he had great musical talent which he kept in hiding.

There was also another side of his character which was revealed when he was told to prepare to take the field in the game. He left the subs' bench and warmed up. As he waited to get into the game, he turned to Andy and me and said, 'Thank you for making my life's ambition become real.' I'm sure he had a tear in his eye. He had always wanted to play against England at Wembley.

Another moment to remember was before the 1992 European Championship in Sweden. We played in Denver in the Mile High Stadium. The conditions were very difficult, not only because of the heat but also because of the altitude. The air was very thin, and you could very easily get out of breath by just walking around, let alone running.

After the game we were due to fly to Toronto but, because of the lack of air in Denver, the weight on the aircraft was too great for the plane to take off. The captain asked if six people would volunteer to leave the plane. They would be able to travel on the very next flight and would also receive $300 in compensation. We could not split our party, although there were one or two people on the coaching staff who would have been quite keen to subsidise their salaries with the extra cash.

A well-known Scottish journalist, Doug Baillie, the former giant Airdrie, Rangers, Third Lanark and Falkirk player who is top football writer for the Sunday Post, immediately volunteered to leave the plane. He said, 'Now you'll only need two of us to get off!' It gave us all a laugh. In fact, five other media men also volunteered, and presumably they made the usual good use of the extra money, although they soon caught up with us in Toronto.

It was a bit worrying that, even with the lightened load, the aeroplane seemed to take a long time before it took off. I think it was the longest I have been on a runway. We seemed to be speeding along the tarmac for ever before we finally managed to get airborne.

Just for the record, that game in Denver was won by an excellent Pat Nevin goal in which he combined with his pal Brian McClair. I have often thought that their play together reflects the great friendship they have off the field. There is a sociological message there which underlines the need for players to have a good relationship if they are to work together during a game.

While we were in Canada some of the lads clubbed together and took a helicopter ride over Niagara Falls which, I understand, they enjoyed very much, considering it to be a memory that they will cherish all their lives. We also went as guests to see the Blue Jays baseball team in action at the famous Skydrome Stadium – and that was quite an experience too.

They say that travel broadens the mind and there is no doubt that it does, but incidents and events when you are travelling as a squad also cements relationships among players. When they have shared wonderful experiences, as they do, players often become pals for life.

I must mention Jim Farry, the former Chief Executive of the Scottish Football Association. He was often given a very bad press because of decisions he has to make that cannot possibly please everyone. I have seen and heard him being maligned by people who were not in possession of the full facts, so I think it is only fair to set some matters straight in connection with him.

His negotiating skills were quite incredible. He and Yule Craig, chairman of the International Committee, when given an indication of the fixtures we want, were very, very adept at the negotiating table, and I am sure their expertise before a ball is even kicked has undoubtedly helped us qualify for the various tournaments.

My philosophy has always been to play one of our major rivals away from home first, if at all possible. This means that if you win the game you are off to a flyer, if you draw you are still in contention and, if you lose, you can still redress the situation when you play at home. If you play at home against a rival early on and lose, it leaves you with a real mountain to climb.

A lot of countries think in terms of the finances generated by playing their stronger rivals and try to get a home game with them early on so that they can benefit from the bigger crowds. If their campaign proceeds well they will continue to get big crowds against lesser opposition, and if it fizzles out they have had the monetary icing on the cake anyway.

We have been a bit more positive than that. Our sole aim is to qualify, and the financial spin-offs are well down our list of priorities. If possible, I have asked our negotiators to leave us with a couple of home games at the end of our campaign, preferably against the weaker nations. Similarly if we have to play them, I try to get an away fixture or two during the summer against weaker opposition. Their pitches are usually in better condition than ours, and we are away from home at a time when home interest in football is taking a sabbatical in the wake of the stresses and emotions of a rigorous season. That formula started when Andy was in charge, and I reinforced it. It was usually the skills of Jim Farry which enable that ideal programme to become reality, and as I have written elsewhere, David Taylor has taken on that mantle.

One of my fondest fun memories goes back to the 1992 European Championship in Sweden. The support from the Scotland fans was just amazing, and we wanted to make a gesture to thank them. This was after we had played our first two games, and before the 3–0 victory over the CIS. We knew that many fans were staying in tents on a campsite so, after training, we decided to pay them a surprise visit.

We probably arrived at around midday. Many of them

were still asleep, but the word went round like wildfire and it was quite a sight to see hundreds of bleary-eyed Scots tumbling out of their tents in various stages of dress – and undress – to acknowledge the team. The visit was greatly appreciated by both the players and the supporters, and was a credit to its instigator, Andy Roxburgh.

During 1995 I was asked to give a talk to managers of oilfields in the North Sea. A professor at Robert Gordon's College in Aberdeen is one of our travel club members, and she approached me to ask if I would give a talk about motivation.

I would not for one minute suggest that I am the best motivator in the world, but I usually managed to get the team together and inject the right sort of spirit. I was being questioned on this, and I explained that the motivation must come from within. In the Scotland squad, for instance, the motivation required is different from that needed at club level because it is a much higher-profile platform. Most of all I liked to appeal to the fact that the players are Scottish and should take pride in wearing the shirt.

There are some who criticise the use of players who are not actually born in the country, especially since we are now down to the grandparent rule. That rule is the same for everyone, and I don't see why we should penalise ourselves and not use players with a Scottish heritage just because their place of birth was not within the boundaries of the country. I very often find that those players who have Scottish parents or grandparents are even more motivated to play for Scotland than those who are born in the country.

The criterion now is that if a player has a British passport, and a bloodline reaching back to a grandparent, he can play for whichever country picks him first. For instance, if a player is born in Cornwall with Welsh parents and a grandmother from Kilmarnock, he could play for any one of the three home countries. There is no question of rule-bending. That is the rule, just as it is the rule that it is permissible to head the ball back to your goalkeeper, but not to kick it back. Selecting players who fall within the rules is an excellent option.

Players like Stuart McCall, Neil Sullivan, Don Hutchinson and Matt Elliott are typical of those players from outside Scotland. Try telling them that they are not entitled to wear the Scotland jersey – but don't stand too close! Their passion for Scotland is as fervent as that of anyone with a Glasgow accent.

I was explaining this at the talk I gave to those oil managers and reminded them that money is no motivator. It can be a form of bait to get someone to take a job, but it will not motivate them once they have started the job. You don't find Scotland internationals talking in terms of money – it has no bearing on their motivation for being there.

The day after my talk one of the tabloids featured the headline 'I Failed – Says Brown!' It went on to suggest that I was saying that I had failed to motivate the players. The story alleged that I had said this while giving the talk. It was complete nonsense, of course, and I had video proof of exactly what I had said and in what context I'd said it. I was telephoned by the professor, who was absolutely distraught at the story, and asked if she could help redress the matter in any way.

Usually I treat such things with a pinch of salt, but I thought this story was out of order. I did contact the newspaper in question and later received an apology from the editor – although there was never a retraction printed in his newspaper. It just goes to show that even at private functions you have to be very careful that you are not misquoted.

In order to get to this function on the oil-rig, I had to fly by helicopter which I've done several times since. It was a very interesting experience to fly from Aberdeen to the Shetlands and then out to the rig. I travelled with a group of guys who were quite laid back about the whole thing because they had done the same journey many times, but for me it was a totally new experience. Before the final stage of the journey I was issued with a survival outfit, which is rather like a shell suit. I was also given a helmet and goggles as well as some instructions, and off we went in the helicopter.

While everyone else was either sleeping or reading, I couldn't help but look out of the windows. Those rig platforms look very small, very vulnerable and very, very rusty from above, and I was beginning to wonder if these were not some kind of mini-rig – until we landed at our chosen destination.

The platform did not look any less rusty when I stood on it with the wind howling and the waves crashing into the air. I wondered if all my insurances were up to date. Then I went inside and it was like entering a different world. I have seen five-star hotels that did not match up to this. I was barely inside when a Tannoy announcement said, 'Come to the cinema this evening at eight thirty to hear the Scotland manager, Craig Brown, talking about why he hasn't picked Richard Gough!' I nearly turned round and walked out again at that stage, and it did not get any better. I was still wearing my survival gear as two guys walked past me. Upon hearing the announcement, one said to the other, 'They should have sacked that b****** months ago!' They nodded to me as they went past, obviously not recognising me beneath all the gear. I did give them a second look in case they were executives of the SFA!

Later, in the cinema, they were sitting up near the front. I looked at them and said, 'Hi, I'm the b****** who should have been sacked months ago!' We had a good laugh about it and the evening went very well. It is experiences like that, though, which help you to keep your feet on the ground – so to speak!

I am not one of those people who likes to make himself readily available for after-dinner speaking. Some have made a second career out of it – but not me. I restrict my speeches to special occasions – charities, testimonials and events where there is personal contact. I know that there are many others in my position who are not given to be entertainers, and 'He wasn't very good' or 'I didn't think much of him' doesn't do your confidence much good. People tend not to take into consideration that you haven't asked to be there, much less to stand and talk when you have so many other commitments that you should be getting on with.

As well as after-dinner speaking and visiting oil rigs, I have often been invited to talk in prisons. I'm not sure if someone is trying to tell me something. I do enjoy these visits, because the men – and the women – inside those establishments really know their football. They glean every scrap of available information from their newspapers, radios and televisions, and they ask very significant questions. They also appreciate the fact that you have made the effort to go and see them. I know they are all in prison for a reason but, if one of my visits helps just one guy to want to stay out of trouble so that he can be free to go and watch football instead of getting it second-hand, then that has to be good enough, doesn't it?

I did mention visits to oil platforms which have been initiated by men like Jim Flockhart, Willie Watt and Keith Alexander. The people offshore are 'captives' too, and clearly appreciate a visit from the outside world. I usually have to emphasise a safety message and also give my views on teamwork and motivation.

As I said, most of my talks are for charitable purposes and I think it's the least I can do to give of my time for people who, unlike myself, have experienced great misfortune in their lives. One such example happened to my colleague, Joe Murray, who is in charge of our education programme for apprentice players. No one could think of a finer person than Joe, and to think that he and his wife Rosa and family should have the tragedy of their 15-year-old son, Johnny, falling to his death in a freak accident, is extremely harrowing. Therefore it was without hesitation that I responded to Joe's request to be present at the launch of a CD, 'So the Child', in memory of Johnny which is being sold to raise funds for TIME (Transplants in Mind) and to highlight the necessity for organ donor cards to be carried. The organs from Johnny's body have been used to save the lives of five others. In June of 2001, I was privileged to be allowed to say a few words, along with Sir Alex Ferguson and Alex McLeish at the Marie Curie Cancer Care fundraising dinner, organised by Alex's brother, Martin, whose wife, Sandra, sadly died from cancer a few years ago. As Alex rightly says in his book, 'It was another of those occasions when real heartbreak made me wonder why we take football so seriously.'

Then Alison Shaw had a dinner for melanoma, from which her daughter had died and, again, I was pleased to contribute at the top table along with the doyen of after-dinner speakers in Scotland, former prison governor Robbie Glen. Robbie is a great guy whose prison stories are a legend in Scotland. He talks about Barlinne as the biggest hotel in Glasgow with the highest occupancy rate, the greatest amount of repeat business, where everyone gets three meals a day and a roof under his feet! I marvel at Robbie's fund of stories and dynamic delivery, and know that I could never begin to compete. However, I do get considerable mileage from the introduction which I use. At a school in Kilmarnock, when launching a health fayre in the company of George Foulkes MP, the usual happened! The person who speaks first, on this occasion Mr Foulkes, invariably says all that I was intending to say. However, after fifteen minutes of extreme eloquence, he turned to me and said, 'Well boys and girls, we have a special guest here today. Does anyone know who this is?' A forest of hands went up and a young lad was nominated to answer. 'Well son, who is he?'

'The Scotland janitor!' I felt it was a compliment to be given the accolade of being identified as the most important person in any school, but was a bit disconcerted when Mr Foulkes said, 'Yes, son, but I think the janitor could have done a better job in the previous international than the manager!' A sense of humour is essential in my job!

We were staying in Connecticut, preparing for a summer game against the USA as part of our preparations for Euro 96. Rod Stewart was in concert at the famous Madison Square Garden in New York, and he contacted us to make arrangements to come and watch the game. We thought it might be a good idea to invite him to come and train with us, because it would be great for the team's morale.

Rod is a huge football fan and in particular follows Scotland – as indeed Scotland follows him and his career. He has a full-size football pitch alongside his house and runs his own team as well. He has been a close pal of Gordon Strachan for some years, and I remembered when we were in Los Angeles prior to the 1986 World Cup he had invited us to his house, and it was good to be able to repay his kind hospitality.

Rod arrived in a stretch limo and we had a huge problem with all the press, who were obviously keen to get their photos and stories. We asked the Scottish press in particular to take it easy. We wanted to train, he wanted to take part, and he was happy to pose for a few photos if we would then be allowed to get on with it. The press guys were very helpful and did their job professionally without causing too much hassle for us.

The popular image of Rod Stewart is one of arrogance, flamboyance and mild conceit. I found him to be a very humble and down-to-earth guy who called me Mr Brown, and Alex Mr Miller. He never presumed anything and asked, 'Is it all right if I warm up with you, Mr Brown?' He was a real gentleman and enjoyed his training session with us.

Rod was also kind enough to supply us with 32 tickets for his concert at Madison Square Garden so that we could all go. They were seats near the front, too. We had a few moans before we left the hotel because the coach was late arriving. I think we are spoiled by the treatment we receive from Douglas Park of Park's of Hamilton, who provide the coach for the national team. He is always conscious of our every need, including punctuality. Mick Reilly is our regular driver, and his Celtic tattoo gives you some idea of where his heart lies. If we travel anywhere near Ibrox, Ally McCoist suggests that if Mick has a couple of days to spare he should go and visit the Rangers trophy room. Mick is used to the ribbing and takes it all in his stride. He is an excellent driver who again takes very good care of us.

The American bus, however, was late, and we had to dash to the concert, cancelling a plan to get something to eat on the way. We arrived a few minutes late, and it was amazing to see the number of people who had been unable to get in. They were a complete cross-section of all ages, giving some idea of the universal popularity of Rod Stewart.

Hugh Allan, our physio, had taken along a Scotland shirt to give to Rod if there was an opportunity. He did not have to wait long. As soon as Rod knew we were there he summoned us up to the stage, which was in the centre of this huge venue. Hugh gave Rod the jersey, which he immediately put on, and then he went into a number which we clapped along to. I looked around the vast arena at the thousands of people singing, dancing and clapping along with Rod, and I thought, Hammy and the Hamsters were never quite like this!

Afterwards Rod had arranged some hospitality for us in his dressing room, where we chatted to him for some time and met his lovely family. He said that he'd try to see some of our World Cup qualifying matches, and indeed he did, along with his pal Ricky Simpson, who is also a great gentleman and has been very helpful to me on my European fact-finding missions.

The game that Rod was able to fit into his busy schedule was our penultimate World Cup match against Belarus at Aberdeen. It was scheduled for a Saturday, but the unthinkable happened and Princess Diana was killed in Paris.

There was a lot of controversy over whether or not the game should be postponed. Part of the delay was that no one knew when the funeral would be. I was interviewed by a TV crew on the Monday and could only say that, unless we heard anything to the contrary, the match would go ahead as planned.

During the day the funeral plans were announced, and that same evening I saw myself on television saying that the game was going ahead.

I was made to look a little callous. Right away I was phoned by Ally McCoist, who said that he had discussed the matter with his wife, Allison, and his mother, and he didn't feel that he could take part in the game if it was to be played on that day. Not long after I had finished talking to Ally, Colin Hendry phoned to say much the same thing. He was doubtful because of injury anyway, but he told me that he could not bring himself to play on that day.

The SFA were in touch with Belarus, but there were communication problems because their president, Yevgeniy Shuntov, could not speak English. He and his general secretary, Vadim Zhuk, were doing their best but, in the end, the conversation had to continue through the president's wife, who could speak English. They proved to be very helpful and the date was changed.

I had no say in the matter, but I was able to represent the players, who were pretty unanimous in their view. I think we were all relieved and happy at the change of arrangements and the game being put back 24 hours. We were all pretty devastated by the reason, though.

As for Rod Stewart, he attended that game, and contacts us regularly to keep in touch with events – a great guy and a great supporter of Scotland.

Sean Connery is another of the world's great superstars who avidly follows the fortunes of Scotland. He is a very busy guy, but he attends matches as often as possible and regularly telephones me for a chat and an update on team affairs. He knows what he is talking about, too, as I found out when we sat together at the Aberdeen v. Rangers Cup Final in May 2000. It is always good to be able to say to Andrea, Liz, Siobhan and Amanda, 'Oh, by the way, Sean Connery was asking after you!' Then I'd joke and say, 'He wants me to be the new 007!'

Andrea always responds with a quick Craigneuk one-liner, 'You're not even 003½!'

On a professional note, I was delighted 16 years ago when the SFA appointed me. I have been to many places all over the world and met many famous people, some of whom have since become good friends. I don't know what road I would have travelled down if I had not entered the football profession, but I did, and I often feel that I have had the best life in the world – and a wonderful, impossible job!

27

Resignation

WHILST I REDOUBLED my efforts in my new title as Director of Football Development, I was still conscious of the fact that there was one remaining qualifying game in the World Cup campaign. On 6 October we had our final fixture, against Latvia, at the National Stadium.

It had been pointed out to me that, depending on the result in Croatia between the host team there and Belgium, there was an outside possibility that, with a huge swing in goal difference, Scotland could still qualify. This, to me, was pie in the sky. At no time was I foolish enough to make such a statement to the Scottish media, who would have been quick to pick up on the fact that this 'idiot' still thinks we can qualify for Japan/Korea.

Meanwhile, there was much to be done in the coaching arena with our newly developed children's licence course, based at Largs. The Director of Children's Development, Tommy Wilson, has extremely resourceful teachers working with him. He is also helped in no small part by parents and those interested in the development of youngsters in the three-to eight-year-old age group.

It is felt that this is the stage at which children should concentrate on acquiring fundamental skills. These skills will remain with them throughout their future footballing careers. I think I should acknowledge Tommy's great contribution in introducing the small-sided game, 'Mini-kickers', along with the new development of 'Futsal'. It's these activities that has placed Scotland in the forefront of many footballing developments.

Whilst aware that I was intending to resign after the match against Latvia, I was still looking for players who could make a contribution, not only in the final match at Hampden, but in the following qualifying campaign for the Euro 2004 tournament in Portugal. I was very interested in Dougie Freedman of Crystal Palace. I noticed that in the Nationwide First Division Scoring Charts he was well to the fore. Consequently, I made a trip to see him in action, and was encouraged by his popularity amongst Palace fans.

My arrival at the match was not only welcomed by the club, because all clubs like their players to gain international recognition, but by the many fans who intercepted me on the way from the car park to the main stand. I was assured that Doug was the man!

I put him in to play against Latvia, and sure enough he did head a goal for us which, after Christian Dailly's error in the first half, helped to redeem matters and we scraped through with a narrow 2-1 victory. This match was in direct contrast to our previous home game against Latvia when over 50,000 watched the final match of the World Cup qualifying campaign for France '98 at Celtic Park. This one was a very low-key affair, but the loyal Scottish fans were still to the fore and, as usual, very supportive.

I had told the President, Mr Jack McGinn, Vice-President, Mr John McBeth and Chief Executive Mr David Taylor that I would inform the players immediately after the match of my intention to resign.

I did forewarn the SFA backroom staff at the Marine Highland Hotel in Troon, the night before, in a rather emotional meeting. I am not too good at the 'tears-for-souvenirs' moments, but it was extremely difficult having to tell ten magnificent colleagues that I was relinquishing my post. One or two of them, like Hugh Allan, who had been with the Scottish team from five previous World Cups, and Alan Hodgkinson, who had been extremely loyal to Andy Roxburgh and me, indicated their intention to follow suit relatively quickly. I tried to dissuade the staff from being blindly loyal and to think of themselves and encouraged them to remain, at least until they had identified who my successor would be. In anticipation of what was going to happen, I had my secretary, Amanda, have letters of thanks ready for each and every one of a tremendous team.

If it was difficult to tell the staff, it was even more emotional having to inform the players. I was glad we won the match because it enabled me to come straight to the point on our return to the dressing room at the final whistle. It was reported that there were tears shed but this is not true. I was conscious, though, that my voice did break a little when I thanked the lads for their efforts, and told them I was stepping down. The one pity was that there were so many changes in the team for that match and young players, with whom I hadn't really had time to build up a proper relationship, were the recipients of my valedictory words. Guys like Paul Gallacher, Scot Severin, Dougie Freedman, Gavin Rae and Barry Nicholson hadn't been around the team very long, yet they had to suffer my faltering words on my departure. It was at this point that I had wished that the stalwarts who had served me so well throughout my time in charge had been there, so that I could have thanked them both individually and collectively.

I would have dearly loved to have thanked people such as Jim Leighton, Andy Goram, Colin Hendry, Colin Calderwood, Tommy Boyd, John Collins, Stuart McCall,

Garry McAllister, Don Hutchinson, Billy Dodds, Gordon Durie, Kevin Gallacher, Ally McCoist, Paul McStay ... and the many others who have made my job, without question, the best in the world.

As it turned out, one or two of the more experienced guys were still there, players like David Weir, Neil Sullivan, Christian Dailly and Craig Burley. As captain, Craig gave a warm and supportive speech on behalf of the players, which to my pleasure was followed by spontaneous applause.

Thereafter it was incumbent upon me to address the media and avoid being intercepted on the way from the dugout for what they call a 'flash' interview by the television companies who, having paid for the match, have priority access to players and managers. On the way from the stadium to the dressing room, I had studiously refused to be involved in responses to questions about my future. It would have been unfair to the large contingent of media representatives, who should be advised together as a unit.

It was my practice throughout my time with the Scottish team, never to give preferential treatment to any group of media representatives or any particular individual. It has been normal, ever since the days of the late, great Jock Stein, that each media group be treated separately. However, I always found myself saying the same things to three or four different groups, time and again. I felt that it would be more appropriate to have just one, all-encompassing conference, but apparently this is unacceptable. Thankfully, this was to be the last occasion when I would have such an encumbrance!

I shouldn't complain really – throughout the years, I received a favourable treatment from the media, with one or two isolated exceptions.

One of the early questions, from a certain individual, when I announced my intention to step down, was, 'Don't you think you should have done this three years ago?' It took a great deal of self-control from retorting, 'Do I not think that *you* should have resigned five years ago because I've been subjected to exactly the same banal, uninsightful questions for the past five years?' I was aware that the conference was not only given local, but national and international coverage, particularly to the other countries in the group, so I would have let myself down by retaliating in such a naïve manner.

In my discussions with the President and Chief Executive, they did emphasise that they wished me to continue in my other capacity as Director of Football Development. I was grateful to them for their support and vowed that I would do the job now, completely wholeheartedly. I had been frustrated over the years at not being able to feel that I was 'hands-on' enough in our department. I had magnificent luck in the support of colleagues, Frank Coulston, Ross Mathie, Jim Fleeting, Jim Sinclair and Tommy Wilson, with excellent help on the girls/women's side from Vera Pauw, Sheila Begbie and Tony Gervaise. Because of the demands on my time as national team manager, I had become more and more only a spokesperson for the department, and much of the workload was admirably undertaken by the aforementioned superb colleagues.

As I looked ahead to the end of year, and the end of my second four-year spell as national team manager, I found that, as usual, there were many events that required my attendance. A day or two after the Latvian match, I was off to Bratislava for a UEFT conference where the President of that organisation, Josef Venglos (a perfect gentleman), entertained his guests lavishly and courteously in his impressive home overlooking the river Danube. It was a fine experience for Frank Coulston, Jim Sinclair and myself to visit Josef's home, and to see the memorabilia which he had acquired over many years of successful football management and coaching. The course, as usual, was very instructive and excellent from the perspective of meeting colleagues both at club and international level.

No sooner had I arrived home, than I was off to speak at a sponsors' dinner at Leicester City, where Dave Bassett had been appointed.

Dave, or 'Harry' as he is called, was at the top table to answer questions after I had given my speech. With the congenial Alan Birchinall as Chairman, the event was a great success. Dave was asked how he and Micky Adams would integrate as a management duo, since both had come from number-one posts at previous clubs. In a most forthright and eloquent manner, the new boss indicated that he would mastermind the formula for success and Micky would implement it on the training ground.

Another question related to the fact that many of the season ticket holders and executive members of the club felt that a number of high-earners were underachieving. Dave emphasised the fact that for twenty grand a week they would get themselves moving, or they would be moving out the door! This sounded logical, but as a club manager I do see the problem of moving on players on lucrative long-term contracts, who are not performing to standard. It is extremely difficult, as Dave and other managers have discovered, to entice players to move when they are on to a 'good thing'.

After Peter Taylor's departure, Dave was seen as the answer to help them retain Leicester's Premiership status and lead them to later glory. Unfortunately, it didn't work out for Dave and Micky Adams took over the reigns after a relatively unsuccessful few months.

Perhaps the most emotional and poignant invitations that I received were from the Tartan Army groups, as I have said. I visited ESTA (East of Scotland Tartan Army), WESTA (West of Scotland Tartan Army), The Parliamentary Tartan Army in Edinburgh, Lunnain Albannach (London Tartan Army) and the Highland Tartan Army. All were extremely welcoming and effusive in their gratitude for my attempts as Scotland manager. I advisedly use the word 'attempt' because I think that everyone knows that within the constraints of the resources available I did everything I could to give success to the Scottish nation.

There is no formula nor prescription for successful

football, but a point I always emphasised was that there had to be a strong team spirit in the group. I never had a Scottish team who were not totally committed to the national cause. This was appreciated by the fans, who awarded me a giant photograph, in which I was holding a replica of the World Cup. The inscription, rather embarrassingly, referred to me as Scotland's greatest ever manager. I did hang it on my office wall for a couple of days, but felt that it was a bit over the top and removed it from public gaze. I have many mementos from the loyal fans, which I confess I will treasure for the rest of my life.

Engagements I was always happy to undertake during my time as national manager were invariably to assist in fundraising for the development of youth football. Two such events were in Aberdeen at Dyce Boys' Club and at Albion Boys' Club.

Hugh Little, that fine gentleman and director of Aberdeen FC, invited me to an impressive function at Albion Boys' Club, where he is also an official. It was a fantastic night in the Granite City, with Hugh an eloquent and humorous Chairman, ably supported, I hope, by my speech referring to my time as national team manager.

In the adjacent room, Sandy Jones, Secretary of the Professional Golfers' Association, was speaking at another event attended by Aberdeen legends Willie Miller and Alex McLeish. I was privileged to split my time between the two functions and to have yet another thoroughly enjoyable evening in the Granite City.

The Parliamentary Tartan Army function took place in the Apex International Hotel in the Grassmarket in Edinburgh. Stephen Donnachie, the General Manager, another loyal Scotland fan, has always been the essence of courtesy and support to me and my colleagues in the world of football. The Apex Hotels are most efficiently run, and I have been privileged to be invited to a number of events at impressive Apex venues. Stephen could not be more helpful and co-operative when it comes to hosting people from the football world, and colleagues like Alex McLeish, Willie Miller, Andy Watson and Jim Jefferies have benefited from his kindness.

There is, in the west of Scotland, a drinking team that occasionally plays football! It is called Dukla Pumpherston Sawmill and Tannery FC. The man behind this motley crew is Chick Young, BBC Scotland sports commentator and presenter. This group does wonderful work for charity and at the same time ensures that each member, whether playing or not, enjoys himself. Consumption of alcohol is not only condoned, it is obligatory! The high-profile players involved include goalkeepers Alan Rough, Jim Stewart and Ally Hunter. A motley array of outfield players of all shapes and sizes try to perform in front of the now overweight keepers. People like Jimmy Bone, Gordon Smith, Andy Ritchie, Gerry Collins, Jim Leishman, Derek Johnstone, Frank Coulson, John Lambie ... and many others. The opposition have the greatest possible difficulty bending a ball around a defensive wall of Derek Johnstone, Andy Ritchie and Jim Leishman! I was invited as guest to the annual dinner which, as usual, was a marvellous event with Jack Charlton as the main speaker.

November was concluded with a visit to London to speak at the prestigious dinner of Middlesex Wanderers FC, in the company of Queen's Park members, Austin Reilly, Tom Barr, Malky Mackay and Peter Buchanan. This was a super event in the Café Royale.

During this period there was considerable speculation about me returning to club management. Whenever a job became vacant, my name was mentioned in despatches. It was embarrassing to me because I had mentioned to our President, Mr McGinn, and our Chief Executive that I was happy to continue in my role as Director of Football Development. I could not control the speculation, but on each occasion I emphasised that there had been no approach. I did have tentative enquiries from two clubs south of the border, both done through agents, although in one case I had a conversation with the Chairman concerned. The discussions got no further than an assertion that I was, at that time, not interested.

Another genuine offer came in the form of several telephone calls and a fax from a contact in Saudi Arabia. He enquired as to my availability to coach the Saudi Arabian team in the World Cup finals in Japan/Korea. This was, I admit, an intriguing prospect, but I was assured that if Saudi were to be successful in the Gulf Cup competition, which was due to take place in January, there would be no appointment made. The present incumbent, a native coach from Saudi, would be asked to continue in the post. With hindsight, I am glad that Saudi didn't come seeking my services because in the opening match of the World Cup they were on the receiving end of an 8-1 hammering from Germany.

Around this time, the Executive Committee and Chief Executive of the SFA were compiling a list of possible successors for national team manager. I was asked by Mr David Taylor, the Chief Executive, to sound out availability and obtain contact details of one or two coaches. One such coach was a man I knew reasonably well, Berti Vogts, working then in Kuwait. He confirmed his interest, and also advised me that the Saudi team had the most potential in that part of the world. Having communicated this information to our Chief Executive, I took no further part in anything to do with the appointment of my successor. Berti's agent Andy Gross, a Swiss lawyer, took over the dealings with the SFA, at the start of the year 2002. Mr David Taylor was accompanied by the Vice-President Mr John McBeth, on a visit to Kuwait to secure the services of Berti, and later his colleague Rainer Bonhof.

It is totally and completely wrong to think that I had any input into the selection of my successor. I merely, on request, provided contact details and made a few enquiries. I feel that it is only right that I should have been kept out of the proceedings in any case. My understanding was that my former colleague Andy Roxburgh, and friend, Sir Alex Ferguson, were spoken to in a consultancy capacity.

The month of December 2001 flew because of the many events that the festive season encourages. One significant engagement was to visit Fort William for the retirement dinner of Dr John McAskill, a highly talented medic with tremendous musical strings to his bow, who had been doctor to our Under-21 team. My colleagues Ross Mathie, Jim Stewart, Richard Simpson and I were proud to present Doctor John with a Scotland strip bearing the name 'McAskill'. He and his wife Christine were proud recipients of this and many other gifts from the local community and the world of football.

As national team boss, I had little opportunity, and could hardly justify the time, to attend games not involving the top echelons of English and Scottish football. Consequently, I seldom managed to see my former club, Clyde, in action. Now relieved of national responsibility it was a pleasure to accept director Gerry Dunn's invitation to a Clyde v Ayr United match at Broadwood Stadium, Cumbernauld. Gerry was kind enough to invite a Clyde hero of my time, Neilly Hood, to accompany me on to the pitch. Needless to say, we received a wonderful ovation, but I am not deluded into believing that it was entirely for the former manager! Neilly, with his enthusiastic and aggressive style, is a real Clyde FC legend.

Possibly my final ever appearance at the BBC's Sports Personality of the Year Award took place on the 9 December. In my capacity as Scotland manager, I was regularly invited to this prestigious event. I thoroughly enjoyed what I imagine will be my last visit to the awards, and was pleased to see Sir Alex Ferguson and the England national team receive well-merited awards.

Two days later, I was in Tesco's in Aberdeen signing copies of the original version of this autobiography. Since then, I've added this final part to the book, but it was most gratifying to see the number of people who came to have the book autographed and to thank me for my services to the Scottish team.

The year 2002 began with the football world of Scotland being made aware that the SFA authorities were closing in on my successor as national team manager. Four names were very much in the frame – Troussier, Scala, Vogts and Rioch. Journalists kept calling me and asking me for information and I was glad that I could, in all honesty, inform them that I had no knowledge of the state of any of the negotiations with any possible candidate.

Leaving these questions behind, I travelled to Slovenia to help conduct the UEFA pro-licence course which had been instigated in that country of just over 2 million people. It was awe-inspiring whilst staying in Ljubljana, Slovenia's capital, to hear how this small country had qualified for the European Championships in 2000 and the World Cup in 2002. Their coach, Katanec, the former Sampdoria and Stuttgart player, had done a marvellous job with limited resources. I have the utmost respect for the progress of the game in Slovenia. The fact that more than 150 coaches turned up in early January for this course is testament to the fact that they realised that the development of the game does not happen by accident. Coaching, which sometimes in Scotland is frowned upon by the uninitiated, is greatly respected and carries great importance in many of the countries where performances have been noticeably good in recent years. Slovenia comes into that category as do many of the former Russian states such as Latvia, Belarus, Estonia, Georgia, Lithuania, Moldova and the Ukraine, as well as Russia itself.

It wasn't long after I returned from my travels in Slovenia until I was off again to Philadelphia, USA, for the annual convention of the NSCAA (National Soccer Coach's Association of America). Several thousand soccer coaches converged on Philadelphia where Ami Jacquet, Jorgan Klinsman and Renus Michels were all leading exponents. I was also called upon to provide a practical demonstration and to contribute to lectures. The expansive array of demonstration stalls and the overall organisation of this event was extremely impressive. Of considerable help to me in regard to duplicating and distributing material and the organisation of my sessions was Christine Tipping, wife of Jeff Tipping, Director of Coaching Education at the NSCAA. My departure from Philadelphia was, I think, quite a significant event, because it is unlikely that I will return in a similar capacity, due to events that were to overtake me in the ensuing months.

While I was away, it become known that Berti Vogts had been identified as the new Scotland manager and approached by Messrs Taylor and McBeth. Meanwhile, I enjoyed a further visit to the USA in February to conduct some sessions for Mike Saif of World-Class Coaching in Kansas City.

It escaped my notice that it was 40 years since Dundee FC had won the Scottish League Championship and various supporters' clubs of the team were in the process of arranging reunion gatherings. One such event occurred in Edinburgh and another in April in Dundee. I was proud to join with my former colleagues of that team, at both those events, but everyone was conscious of two key players missing. Sadly, Alex Hamilton and Andy Penman had both died in the intervening years and consequently the full squad was unable to appear. Nevertheless, it was very gratifying to hear renowned expert commentator, Bob Crampsey, describe that historic team as the best club side he had seen in Scotland, even surpassing the Celtic team of 1967 – the famous Lisbon Lions.

I was able to watch my pal, Dick Campbell, see his team Brechin City consolidate their position at the top of the Third Division with a fine home local derby victory against Montrose FC, and thereafter attend the club function that evening.

The next day in my capacity as a supporter of Action for

Crippled Children, I read the lesson at Glasgow Cathedral at the charity's annual thanksgiving service. Despite the fact that I was no longer national team manager, I still found that I was called upon to represent the SFA at many events and to speak on their behalf.

Berti Vogts had been appointed and made a big impression, advised, I suspect, by the spin doctor I was never privileged to have, as he appeared suitably attired in a Tartan scarf for his press conference. His first game was a testing one in Paris against World Champions, France. In fairness, he had little time to pick his squad for that tricky fixture. However the appointment of Tommy Burns was reassuring for many, because Tommy had a grasp of the Scottish scene, and would be in an excellent position to advise his new colleague.

I was pleased to welcome Berti to our impressive offices at the national stadium, and to accompany him on one or two early visits. One such game was the Scottish Youth Cup Final in early April at Hamilton where Ayr United played Rangers Youths. Berti commented favourably on the standard of play at Under-18 level at this match and was consequently optimistic about the future of the Scottish game.

When Scotland's opening fixture under Berti took place on 27 April, I was not invited as Director of Football Development to accompany the party to Paris. This, I admit, was disappointing, but I did accept an invitation from the BBC to watch the game in the company of Dougie Donnelly and Gary McAllister in the Glasgow studio. Knowing that I would have the privileged position of being able to view the match on a large screen and, since many of the players I knew well, I was happy to accept.

Quite naturally, there was no way whatsoever that I would state, or even imply, criticism of a colleague coach or player, and I advised the BBC of this. Even with this constraint, they were happy for me to be a studio guest, and I know that, having heard the tape of my comments, I was totally supportive of everything Scottish, in spite of our heavy defeat.

It was therefore very disappointing the next day to be met by Chief Executive, Mr Taylor, who expressed surprise that was a studio guest and instructed me to decline in future. To say I was shocked by this comment from the Chief Executive was putting it mildly, because he should have known there was no way I would offer any criticism of the Scottish team or its management. Surely it would be better to have a supportive studio guest, rather than an alternative pundit who might have been hugely critical?

Berti, I am sure, knew this and he asked me to assist him by going to Germany to watch our future group opponents for Euro 2004 qualification, Germany, in action against Argentina. He made a further request that I watch the German Under-21 side play Russia the previous evening. I was happy to oblige. I flew to Germany where I saw a fiercely contested Under-21 fixture, followed by a comfortable victory by Argentina over the home team at Stuttgart. I knew then that England would have difficulty against the South Americans, and have nothing but praise for Sven Goran Eriksson's performance against them in the World Cup.

It was around this time that I received a phone call indicating that, since Preston North End had been seeking a new manager, following the departure of David Moyes to Everton, I was in contention for that post.

I had the privilege of meeting the Preston North End Chief Executive, Mr Tony Scholes and Chairman Mr Derek Shaw, who impressed me greatly. It was like dèjâ vu, this meeting. Some 26 years previously, I had been invited to a meeting at Shawfield Stadium, Glasgow, where I met with William P Dunn, Chairman of Clyde FC and a young Director/Secretary John McBeth. Such was the similarity in the feeling that I had, I felt that if invited to manage Preston it could be a similarly enjoyable job, working for decent and honourable people. I again met key officials of the Preston club, and was delighted to accept the challenge of maintaining the superb progress that David Moyes had made over the past five years.

The next day, I informed Mr David Taylor of the SFA, and he was pleased to allow me an early release in one month's time to assume full-time responsibility at Preston. I shall always be indebted to Mr Taylor for his understanding and for the pleasant email that he circulated to the staff thanking me for my contribution to the SFA and wishing me well at Preston.

I had been at the Hilton in Dundee for the Dundee FC reunion beforehand and was advised that Dundee were to be playing Preston North End in a pre-season friendly. Again, it felt like dèjâ vu because my first game as manager of Clyde FC in 1977 was a friendly against Preston North End managed then by the legendary Nobby Stiles. Coincidence?!

The infrastructure at 'Proud Preston' impressed me greatly, as did the information I received from knowledgeable people about the club. I was assured that it was an exceptionally well-run club, with a solid group of pro-players who had a good work ethic. It was therefore with keen anticipation and considerable pleasure that I accepted the appointment and eagerly looked forward to the start of pre-season training. In the intervening period, I had agreed to a coaching stint in Montreal, Canada, a visit to Wales for a further look at Germany for Berti Vogts and a summarising job at the World Cup for BBC Radio 5 Live.

These events came upon me very quickly indeed, and my last official piece of work for the SFA was to provide a report for Berti on the Wales victory over Germany on 14 May at Cardiff. The Welsh team, under Mark Hughes, played extremely well and impressed me greatly. Germany, on the other hand, didn't seem to have a great deal of appetite for this friendly fixture and it was surprising, I must admit, that they got to the final of the World Cup some weeks later.

My World Cup schedule with Radio 5 Live was to take me to the final match but, with my new appointment at Preston, I decided to return early to enable me to give full concentration to the job in hand. Consequently, I returned from Korea on 23 June ready to start training on 3 July with my new charges.

Whilst in Korea, I had asked Tony Scholes to make one signing in my absence. Typical of his efficiency was the fact that I departed requesting that he sign Ricardo Fuller, if the cost was not too exorbitant, and sure enough Tony ensured it was all smoothly arranged.

I had seen Ricardo play for Hearts the previous season on numerous occasions and thought he was a superb striker containing all the necessary attributes. His club, Tivoli Gardens in Jamaica, had to be approached through his agent, Phil Graham. This was done and, after one or two phone calls from Korea, and a chat with Ricardo on the long-distance phone line, I was overjoyed to hear that my new club had come to an arrangement to sign the Jamaican striker. My research is always comprehensive when asking a club to indulge in such expenditure, and I asked Craig Levein, manager of Hearts FC in Scotland, and his colleague Peter Houston, about the attitude of Ricardo, particularly to hard work and commitment in training sessions. His ability was there to be seen, but I feel that it is important to assess a player's work ethic prior to an expenditure of any magnitude. Messrs Levein and Houston were fulsome in their praise of Ricardo and this convinced me that he was the man to support the already excellent two strikers in place, David Healy and Richard Cresswell.

My work with Radio 5 Live was really enjoyable, because I was privileged to be in the company of some brilliant commentators and good guys. Whereas the 'big-hitters' like Mike Ingham and Alan Green were confined to the England matches in Japan with Terry Butcher as summariser, I operated exclusively in Korea in the company of people like Pat Nevin, a fellow summariser, and superb commentators such as John Murray, Jonathan Pearce, Ian Brown, Simon Brotherston, and efficient interview and link man, Alistair Yeomans. Although we were sent to some fairly remote places like Jeonju, it was an interesting and worthwhile experience seeing some of the top teams in the world in action. You can imagine my feelings in the opening match, France v Senegal, because I had been acutely involved in the corresponding fixture four years earlier in Paris when our Scottish team took on the then World Champions, Brazil. Unfortunately, at that time we failed to emulate the achievement of Senegal who caused a major upset in the stimulating opening match.

28

Proud Preston

On 23 June 2002, I flew from Seoul in Korea back to Scotland, knowing that the following day my new life was to begin. The anticipation of managing in England was such that I couldn't get in contact with my colleagues at Preston quickly enough.

The following day I was introduced to the entire staff of Preston North End by Chief Executive Tony Scholes. This is, I think, an unconventional but very welcome move, because usually the manager is introduced to the media and then to the staff. Tony brought the entire staff from the club together to introduce me as the new manager, although I must admit to being somewhat embarrassed. I was pleased that former interim manager Kelham O'Hanlon, coach Jimmy Lumsden and chief scout Clive Middlemass accepted my appointment and welcomed me appropriately. In addition, youth coaches Simon Davey and Julian Derby were there to make me feel very much at home.

The world of football is such that, no matter the nationality, there is an affinity and a real bond based on love of the game. It was apparent that these fellows were all genuine football enthusiasts and were prepared to welcome another of a similar disposition into their midst.

Within days of my arrival, I had been informed by David Moyes that he wished to take Jimmy Lumsden and Clive Middlemass with him to Everton along with physio 'Baz'. I admired Dave's honesty with me because he telephoned to indicate his intention and, within a couple of days, Jimmy came to me to advise me that he was accepting the Everton offer. Since I had known him for many years as a dedicated and a loyal coach, I was pleased for him and gave him my best wishes on his departure.

It was a great delight and relief that Clive Middlemass had elected to stay with Preston North End. Clive is an extremely knowledgeable guy, hugely respected throughout the game in the UK. His decision to remain at Preston was appreciated because he has been of immense value and support since my arrival at the club. Equally understanding, in spite of his disappointment at not being appointed, has been Kelham O'Hanlon, whom I was happy to accept as Assistant Manager.

The vacancy created by the departure of Jimmy Lumsden enabled me to bring a first-team coach to the club. As I was privileged to have an intimate knowledge of all available coaches, I had no hesitation in approaching former Motherwell manager Billy Davies to come to Deepdale. Billy had built up a deserved reputation as a very fine trainer of footballers and a man of tremendous energy and enthusiasm. I was pleased when he agreed to come to the club and I knew that he would make a huge contribution towards not only the fitness of the players, but the tactical and psychological aspects which are so necessary at top level. No manager can do the job alone.

I have a superb team of colleagues, not, I hasten to add, 'assistants'. I prefer to have everyone as a member of a team and no one feeling subordinate. It is a co-operative effort at

Preston and, although I ultimately carry the can for the success or failure of the club, the operation is a team effort in every sense of the word.

Another very impressive aspect of Preston North End FC is the playing surface at Deepdale Stadium. When I walked out of the players' tunnel for the first time and looked at the stadium, particularly at the three newly completed stands, it was certainly inspiring. But without doubt, in front of me was arguably the finest playing surface in the country. This has not happened by accident but as the result of 27 years of loving care by head groundsman Peter McCallion. Unfortunately, he retired at the end of September, but not before he had prepared the pitch for the current season's activities. His assistant, young Richard Eastam, has been well trained and hopefully will maintain the high standards set by his mentor.

I was conscious of the fact that I had asked the club to incur the expenditure of several hundred thousand pounds to acquire Ricardo Fuller and that I was interested in USA left-winger Eddie Lewis, who was with Fulham at the time. It is not in my nature to make unreasonable requests on my employers for financial support to improve the team. I would rather try to do so from within by encouraging a burgeoning youth policy. But, although the team was in good shape, I felt that an additional left-sided player would be of benefit along with the striker Ricardo Fuller.

It was, therefore, with the thought of adding to the squad that I did not totally discount the possibility of club captain and talisman Sean Gregan leaving for West Bromwich Albion who were reputed to be interested. Sean, I was led to believe, had been promised that, should an acceptable offer be made, he would be permitted to leave to achieve his ambition of playing in the Premiership. I spoke with Sean and suggested that he remain at Preston with the same target in mind, but he pointed out, correctly, that at the age of 28, he might be running out of time to realise this objective.

Knowing the valuation placed on international midfield

players, I was aware that anything less than £2 million would be a bit of an insult for a player of Sean's calibre, even though he was 28 years of age. It was therefore with that figure in mind that I reluctantly agreed to the sale of Sean if he really wanted to depart.

I assured him that any interest shown, whether acceptable or not, would be intimated to him, and I had to tell him that we had a couple of offers from West Bromwich which we rejected. Sean's attitude was exemplary in that he bore no grudge and he continued to train to his maximum capacity during the intervening period. In fact, when I played him in a pre-season game against Manchester City in Ryan Kidd's testimonial match in the central position of a defensive back three, he commented that he thoroughly enjoyed the role and that he was happy to remain at Preston should the West Bromwich offer not be increased. It was a case of brinkmanship, but eventually, just prior to the start of the season, an acceptable fee was negotiated with the buying club and Sean's departure, which I felt from the outset was inevitable, was completed.

A replacement had to be found and again I relied on the knowledge of Kelham and Clive who informed me that Marlon Broomes, currently playing at Burnley, would be an admirable defensive replacement. After watching him in action during the pre-season, we made him an offer and he arrived at the club to bolster our defensive options.

My conscience now was clear in that, even with the purchase of Ricardo Fuller and the acquisition of Marlon Broomes, there was still a substantial transfer profit for the club. I renewed my interest in Eddie Lewis and eventually, after attending a work permit tribunal, we managed to secure his services as well.

Following a series of pre-season friendly matches at Burscough, Bamber Bridge, Blackburn, Carlisle, Dunfermline, Dundee, Manchester City and Wigan, I had begun to acquire a good knowledge of the playing staff.

The Manchester City fixture on 30 July, a testimonial match for Ryan Kidd, who had been forced to retire early because of a back injury, enabled me to assess the capability of the squad. We looked to have a vibrant and youthful squad of players such as Eric Skora, Dickson Etuhu, Paul McKenna and Michael Keane, all ready for consistent first-team action, but still we possibly lacked an on-the-field midfield leader. It was for this reason that I was pleased that Mark Rankine was still around. Chris Lucketti was more than capable of assuming the mantle of club captain in the absence of Sean Gregan. We appointed Chris Lucketti because of his sincerity and commitment and I have no regrets at this decision.

Around the club I had massive support from everyone, but further disruption was to ensue because David Moyes knew the value of Mick Rathbone and invited him to be physio with him at Everton. The lure of the Premiership tempted Mick and he departed along with Jimmy Lumsden. After careful scrutiny of numerous applicants, we were pleased to enrol the services of Macclesfield Town FC physio, Andrew Balderston, who has come to the club and made a big impact because of his first-rate knowledge and acute medical judgement. He quickly gained the respect of the players and staff alike, and Mick's departure has been covered very smoothly because of the capability of his successor.

There are so many good people around the club whom I must mention. The kit-men are absolutely invaluable in terms of producing immaculate training and match gear, always laundered and clearly identifiable. Brian Hickman and Russ Rigby devote hours of work to the football club, real unsung heroes of Preston North End FC. I have always had the feeling that, when playing away from home, we should leave the visiting dressing room exactly as we found it. In this regard, Russ and Brian are absolutely superb in that the last thing they do after the players have showered and dressed is to sweep out the visiting dressing room and leave it in an immaculate state. Many clubs have commented on this and I give credit to these gentlemen for carrying out what was initially only a request from me, and not an instruction.

Obviously, in my short time at the club, I have not managed to make contact with everyone. However, those with whom I have dealt – such as Eddie Harrison and Janet Parr in the secretarial department, Denise the telephonist, Simon Beard our financial controller, our sponsors Newreg, directors Steve Jackson, David Taylor and Hugh Nash, the club shop staff, John Booth and his colleagues Ben Rhodes, Matt Morris, David Allen, Tony Mathews and Simone Freeman in the media department – have all been absolutely fantastic in making me feel at home and making Preston North End proud.

At the training ground we have a fine atmosphere and excellent catering arrangements operated by Alan and Babs McKenna. The players' culinary needs are catered for each day on arrival and departure from the training ground because in the kitchen are two dedicated supporters, who supply the best of everything – all that is required for hungry guys expending a great deal of energy on the practice pitch.

This provision is extended, whilst on the road, to the team coach, one of the finest in the country. Alan cooks meals for the players on the many long journeys which characterise English First Division football. John, the masseur, Davie the driver, and those whom I'm sure I have omitted, all make a valuable contribution to the efficiency of the club and I owe them all a heartfelt debt of gratitude.

The opening league match of the season was against Crystal Palace and was awaited with keen anticipation by the fervent and loyal supporters of Preston North End. Chief Executive Tony Scholes asked me if I would take a bow on the pitch prior to the match. I was somewhat hesitant for obvious reasons and felt that it may have been tempting fate a little. Unfortunately, my fears were not unfounded. From being reduced to ten players following a very soft ordering off of Erik Skora for an alleged second card offence, we did actually take the lead with a fine Ricardo Fuller goal. However, defensive lapses enabled Palace, whom I had thought to be the poorer side on the day, score two goals and set our season off to a disappointing start. All sorts of explanations were sought and I gather that in one of the local phone-in programmes, it was suggested that playing a 3-5-2 formation was a reason for defeat.

Having just watched a World Cup final competed by two teams using that formation and having seen Manchester City win the First Division last year with the same strategy, it seemed quite a ridiculous accusation.

It has always been my intention to be flexible and to have sufficient game awareness amongst my players to cope with any tactical situation. Particularly with the Scottish national team my preferred formation was 3-5-2, but that was because of my feeling that it was suited to playing against traditional 4-4-2, provided the work rate of the strikers was sufficient. Since we had hard-working front players in Richard Cresswell and Ricardo Fuller, I felt that we could begin defending from the front and make this system efficient. It most certainly has been in a number of games, particularly away from home, where, as I write, after nine league matches this season we are unbeaten. Indeed, our only defeat so far has been on the opening day of the season, although we have had too many draws since the ill-fated defeat on the 10 August.

I have already referred to the attitude of the squad and the work ethic that surrounds the club. This attitude is reinforced by the example given by the coaching staff of both youth and senior teams – Simon Davey, Julian Derby, Billy Davies, Clive Middlemass, Kelham O'Hanlon and hopefully the club manager – in terms of industry and commitment. It is these qualities which have brought this proud club from relative obscurity to a prominent position in the First Division in the past five years. There have been recent changes including the loss of the manager, the captain, the coach, the physio and the highly-respected Chief Executive, but it is my intention to ensure that the playing side of the entire operation remains efficient and successful.

Only time will tell if the objectives are achieved, but I can assure the fans that it will not be for the want of a sustained effort.

Postscript

LIKE ANY OTHER football fan, I've sat and watched in awe as the England team has exceeded all expectations in the Autumn of 2001. I'm often asked, if I could take one English player into the Scottish team who it would be. The answer is Michael Owen, no question. We have had a striking problem since the days of Ally McCoist and Mo Johnston, and although Gordon Durie and Kevin Gallacher did well for us in recent years, an inspirational young goal-scorer would have made a huge difference to our results.

The English football scene is changing in a number of ways that are bound to have a knock-on effect on the Scottish game. I've always thought it inevitable that Celtic and Rangers would break away from the Scottish Premier League. Being a patriotic man, I would of course much prefer them to remain, but I feel sure that the greater financial rewards in the south will dictate their natural desires.

The influx of foreign players into club football, particularly those of moderate quality, had undoubtedly hindered the progress of our young players. Too many coaches look for the quick-fix and use experience rather than provide experience for their younger players by phasing them into the top team as quickly as possible. I have nothing but admiration, however, for the foreigner in charge of England. He is doing extremely well, and everyone must admire the style and quality of Sven Goran Eriksson.

And finally, as I look back on my life, I must take my hat off to the wonderful boys who have made up the Scottish teams past and present, who have given their all and who have helped make my job, then, one of the best in the world. Thank you to you all.

Similar appreciation is due to everyone at Preston North End FC, players, officials and fans alike, for helping to ensure that I continue to be the most fortunate guy in the world.